The West Indian Generation
Remaking British Culture in London,
1945–1965

MIGRATIONS AND IDENTITIES

Series Editors
Kirsty Hooper, Eve Rosenhaft, Michael Sommer

This series offers a forum and aims to provide a stimulus for new research into experiences, discourses and representations of migration from across the arts and humanities. A core theme of the series is the variety of relationships between movement in space—the 'migration' of people, communities, ideas and objects—and mentalities ('identities' in the broadest sense). The series aims to address a broad scholarly audience, with critical and informed interventions into wider debates in contemporary culture as well as in the relevant disciplines. It will publish theoretical, empirical and practice-based studies by authors working within, across and between disciplines, geographical areas and time periods, in volumes that make the results of specialist research accessible to an informed but not discipline-specific audience. The series is open to proposals for both monographs and edited volumes.

The West Indian Generation

Remaking British Culture in London, 1945–1965

Amanda Bidnall

Liverpool University Press

First published 2017 by
Liverpool University Press
4 Cambridge Street
Liverpool
L69 7ZU

This paperback edition first published 2021

British Library Cataloguing-in-Publication data
A British Library CIP record is available

ISBN 978-1-78694-003-2 cased
ISBN 978-1-80034-868-4 paperback

Typeset by Carnegie Book Production, Lancaster

To my mother, Pat,
for teaching me to be an intellectual.

Contents

Figures

Acknowledgments

The research for this book was possible only with the support of the Social Sciences and Humanities Research Council of Canada and Boston College, so my first order of thanks must be to these outstanding institutions.

My gratitude to two individuals is most pressing: Peter Weiler, for his excellent judgment, rock-steady commitment to his students, and talent for reaching to the heart of every prickly argument; and Stephen Brooke, for showing me that historical research is a creative endeavor. I could not have wished for two worthier role models.

My small and brilliant graduate cohort at Boston College became my family away from home and contributed to the earliest discussions of this work: Katie Aliberti, Brooke Barbier, Mike Chapman, and Greg Walsh. Jill Bender, Bethany Kilcrease, Megan Hektner Myers, and Sarah Nytroe endured my frustrations and became inspirations as well as dear friends. Thanks to Jim Cronin for his humor and insight, and for demystifying the book-writing process. Kevin Kenny and Prasannan Parthasarathi questioned and critiqued my first tentative approaches to this subject, and I thank them for their direction.

I offer my heartfelt thanks to all of the archivists—and there were many—at the BBC Written Archives Centre, the British Library and its Sound Archive, the British Film Institute, the George Padmore Institute, the Hyman Kreitman Research Centre, the Institute of Race Relations, the London Metropolitan Archives, and the National Archives. Rebecca Dowson at the Simon Fraser University Library was also a generous guide to available resources in British Columbia. Every small victory in my research process was possible only because of the perception and unparalleled knowledge of these professionals.

Patrick Doyle, Rosemary Farrar, and their families graciously hosted me during my three cold, rainy research trips to London. It was a joy to share food and conversation with strangers-turned-friends; one day I hope I can return the favor.

Susan Pedersen and my fellow participants in the 2007 Mellon Seminar in Modern British History—Alan Allport, Laura Beers, Nellie Boucher, Andrew Kellett, Bethany Kilcrease, Danielle Kinsey, Marc Matera, Michal Shapira, Penny Sinanoglou, Angela Thompsell, Aaron Windel, and Kathryn Yeniyurt—critiqued an early chapter of this book and offered treasured fellowship. I have fantastic memories of a hot NYC summer spent almost exclusively in the company of British historians. I doubt I will ever have such a concentrated experience again.

At Simon Fraser University I received tremendous teaching experience, and I am particularly grateful to Mark Leier for his early reinforcement as I balanced manuscript writing with teaching. Laura Beers, Amy Bell, Winston James, and Anne Rush commented on conference papers drawn from this research, and their fresh insights were much appreciated.

Alejandra Bronfman accompanied me through the revision process chapter by chapter. She helped me greatly and was fantastic company to boot—my intellectual touchstone in the final stages of this process. I hope we will always find an excuse for dinner and wide-ranging conversations together. My old friends, academic peers, and fellow union picketers Julia Lalande and Eric Bednarski have taken their graduate education in non-traditional directions, and I follow their example with pride.

Thank you to my editors at LUP and Carnegie Book Production, Alison Welsby, Patrick Brereton, Rachel Adamson, and Alwyn Harrison for their help and patience. And a hearty acknowledgment, too, to my anonymous reader, who commented so carefully and insightfully on early drafts of this book and with whom I would doubtless enjoy having a coffee.

My family has offered me nothing but care and positive encouragement, and I don't know how someone could write a book (or indeed accomplish any great task) without that foundation—I am spoiled in that way. Jeremy, your quiet acceptance freed me to follow my own tortuous path with the knowledge that you would always be beside me. Much love and gratitude to you and my two daughters, Amy and Jill, who play expertly around (and sometimes on) the books and papers on the floor.

I have received reassurance, guidance, and constructive criticism from these corners and from many individuals whose names I lost and whose paths I haven't crossed again (like the film buff who offered me access to movies so obscure that even the archives didn't have them). They have added greatly to the strengths of this book but played no part in its weaknesses, which are mine alone.

Introduction

I did three talks at a peak listening time: 9:15 p.m. on Sundays, after the 9 o'clock news. The talks were based on West Indian history and its effect upon the culture. ... Studio 3A Broadcasting House rang with the birth pangs of a new nation. The 9:15 p.m. programmes were important and the whole nation respected them. Here was West Indian history and culture presented so that the scholastic deficiencies of the listeners went unnoticed. Trinidad was almost unknown. Jamaica and Barbados were known simply for Henry Morgan and rum. At that time it was almost theatrical suicide to say an artiste hailed from the West Indies. I was determined to let people know I came from Trinidad.[1]

This book is about a generation. My subjects are artists, a small and scattered collective, but they viewed themselves, and were viewed, as representatives of that generation. These men and women were unique; they came of age as British subjects in the Caribbean colonies, but as adults were domestic citizens of Britain. In both their careers and their creative work, they built bridges, between the so-called "metropole" and colony, certainly, but they also connect two eras that historians like to imagine as discrete: an era of empire, with its associations of British world power and enforced racial order, and a post-imperial era of decline, insularity, and identity crisis symbolized by the political emergence of a "Black Britain" at odds with mainstream (white) society.

That story has a neglected but vital prehistory: in the first two decades after the Second World War's end, an earlier coterie of artists fused a catholic array of concerns in their work, and found an echo in the British

---

1   Edric Connor, *Horizons: The Life and Times of Edric Connor* (Kingston and Miami: Ian Randle Publishers, 2007), 64. The talks in question took place in 1945.

cultural establishment. In doing so, they were less symbols of a racial divide or national angst than a driving force behind a postwar cultural revolution.

In 1986, Carolyn Steedman drew a "landscape" for her self-sufficient— and Tory—working-class mother, who was invisible in social histories of postwar Britain and the working class and thus implicitly viewed as an anachronism. In a similar spirit, this story draws a landscape for many of those first-generation Caribbean migrants who optimistically carved out a space of belonging in British culture in the years before the full effects of anti-immigration legislation made themselves felt.[2] And, far from being peripheral historical agents, these artists, like Steedman's mother, were at the center of the crucial transformations happening after 1945.

*

I argue here that West Indian artist-settlers, in the roughly twenty years after the end of the Second World War, worked *within* British cultural institutions and trends and used their position to espouse a positive vision of national belonging that was multiracial, anti-racist, and that emphasized Britain's historic connection to its West Indian colonies. Migrant actors, playwrights, fine artists, novelists, and musicians from British Caribbean colonies arrived in the "mother country" with a strong desire to make their mark on the English stage, radio, or television. They used, among other qualities, their colonial background to claim a unique position within mainstream cultural institutions. It was a vision that encompassed the country's burgeoning "New" Commonwealth population and was actively opposed to the metropolitan resurgence, in the 1950s and '60s, of what Bill Schwarz has identified as "colonial frontier" narratives of white embattlement and black threat.[3]

In the middle years of the century, these artists were not all simply relegated to the margins or forced underground into professional isolation. They enjoyed a measure of success and acceptance within the British cultural establishment—those mainstream media outlets and institutions that both reflected and shaped popular tastes and national cultural trends— that provided a public arena for the expression of their own artistic and political priorities. Sometimes, their cultural or political commitment clashed with the aims of British producers, directors, and other cultural agents, but they shared goals and priorities as well. Both, for instance, wanted to challenge the cultural *status quo* by addressing new social issues

---

2   Carolyn Steedman, *Landscape for a Good Woman: A Story of Two Lives* (London: Virago, 1986).

3   Bill Schwarz, "'The only white man in there': The Re-Racialisation of Britain, 1956–68," *Race and* Class 38 (1996): 65–78.

and representing contemporary British society in (what they viewed as) a more authentic way, often from the perspectives of previously marginalized voices. Such a mandate, in theory, complemented that of the artists under examination in this project.

As a result, West Indian artists in London both influenced and were influenced by the political and aesthetic agendas of these institutions. The creative work of these Caribbean migrants embraced, drew upon, and repositioned the influences of colonial history, national independence movements, race politics, class-consciousness, cosmopolitan and diasporic artistic trends, and the English literary/artistic canon—all of which gave voice to their own transnational experience.

These artists still, however, experienced an uphill battle, and this book investigates how their success could be limited or blocked in particular ways.[4] Ultimately, by the mid-1960s, many mainstream cultural agents, as well as the British public at large, clung to a conception of national identity that was white, insular, and detachable from the nation's rapidly disintegrating empire. An early opportunity for the cultivation of a positive idea of a "multicultural" Britain was thus foreclosed. But the work and achievements of this generation demonstrate the extent to which their own agendas were at one time intertwined with those of mainstream cultural purveyors at the heart of the empire. Near the end of the century British officialdom would attempt to recover, with mixed success, its progressive reimagining of British identity—what Anne Spry Rush has termed "imperial Britishness."[5]

This study uses under-explored archival and media sources to probe the relationship between West Indian British artists and mainstream cultural patrons in London between about 1945 and 1965. These years marked a watershed not only in the history of British culture, but also in the histories of colonial migration, decolonization, and "race." Such a history only makes sense if we look at these narratives together.

*

In the early postwar period, social scientists, the media, and the government developed over time a multifaceted intellectual framework of "race relations" to portray new Commonwealth settlement in England. As insightful

---

4   Leon Wainwright has astutely explored this question with regard to Frank Bowling and the history of British Pop. See "Varieties of Belatedness and Provincialism: Decolonization and British Pop," *Art History* 35 (April 2012): 442–61.

5   See Anne Spry Rush, "Imperial Identity in Colonial Minds: Harold Moody and the League of Coloured Peoples, 1931–50," *Twentieth Century British History* 13 (2002): 356–83. On more recent cultural recuperations of British imperial identity, see Eva Ulrike Pirker, *Narrative Projections of a Black British History* (London: Routledge, 2011), 8.

historians and cultural theorists have since argued, such a framework was fundamentally conflictual, characterizing these settlers *a priori* as outsiders and thus rendering impossible true assimilation or integration into the "host" society. In the meantime, entire scholarly fields have grown up with the project of deconstructing the pernicious and discriminatory effects of the race relations framework on the British state, national culture, and the children and grandchildren of these postwar settlers.

This work is the foundation of my own, but what it does not acknowledge is the continued influence of "race relations" theory on historical accounts of race in postwar Britain, namely its privileging of a narrative of conflict. Scholars of a wide range of political persuasions share this perspective; it intersects, for example, with the underlying assumption of postcolonial theory "that every postcolonial migrant has suffered displacement and loss and is now exiled from his or her original culture or home." Such historical subjects can seem, almost by definition, to be "less capable of dealing with the modern than the white/European subject."[6]

There is, of course, a very good reason for using a conflictual historical framework: racial conflict and discrimination *were* fundamental factors that shaped the experience of New Commonwealth settlers in Britain after 1945, in both the short and long term. Nonetheless, racial conflict was not always and everywhere the only definitive experience; "had it been so, many more would have made their way back" to their place of birth.[7] Hence the present study explores moments of consensus and creative commerce as well as conflict; bridges as well as barriers. And the individuals whose stories are told here were, as mentioned at the outset, great bridge-builders.

Adopting such an approach involves studying these men and women as agents of history instead of objects of history, and prioritizing their voices and actions, for they did talk—and sing, write, and act out—their experience. There are collections of oral histories and interviews conducted with that first postwar wave of West Indian migrants that crested in 1961 before the cut-off of the Commonwealth Immigrants Act the following year.[8]

---

6   Rasheed Araeen, "A New Beginning: Beyond Postcolonial Cultural Theory and Identity Politics," *Third Text* 50 (Spring 2000), 8.

7   Winston James, "The Black Experience in Twentieth-Century Britain," in Philip D. Morgan and Sean Hawkins, eds, *Black Experience and the Empire* The Oxford History of the British Empire Companion Series (Oxford: Oxford University Press, 2004), 379.

8   Trevor and Mike Phillips's *Windrush: The Irresistible Rise of Multi-Racial Britain* (London: HarperCollins, 1999) is a collection of oral history based on hundreds of interviews with postwar New Commonwealth migrants and their descendants. See also Learie Constantine, *Colour Bar* (London: Stanley Paul and Co., 1954); Claudia Jones, "The Caribbean Community in Britain," in Buzz Johnson, "*I Think of My Mother*": *Notes on the Life and Times of Claudia Jones* (London: Karia Press, 1985), 137–54.

But analytical histories that capture how West Indian settlers conceived of their position in the imperial metropolis are much more rare.[9] There is also excellent work in the field of cultural studies as pioneered by Stuart Hall and Paul Gilroy in the 1970s, which poses sophisticated critiques of British culture, race, and ethnicity. But as one cultural scholar has noted, "its circumscription to the realm of theory" has "further postponed the appearance of the lived everyday experience of ordinary black and brown people and their own perspectives on this experience, at the centre of the frame."[10]

This study does encompass cultural analysis, but it privileges its postwar West Indian subjects as makers of history, by looking at the question of British and imperial identity, decolonization, and colonial migration from their perspective. My particular focus is on a handful of artists who achieved prominence in London, and whose creative work, to a greater or lesser extent, weighed in on these issues. Their politics varied, but from their work as a whole—produced through an engagement with British patrons and organizations—emerges a vision of Britain that is multicultural, cosmopolitan, and honestly in touch with its own history. Most strikingly, their combined vision posits, sometimes even *assumes*, the existence of a British community that is optimistic and proactive in facing the dramatic social changes wrought in these years, including, but not limited to, the influx of Britons from the Commonwealth.

Transition and Possibility

Thus the early postwar years—the years covered by the present history—were, despite their reputation for conservatism relative to the post-'68 era, a period of transition in almost every respect. And, characteristically, the moment was colored by a feeling of radical possibility and, as time went on, growing fear for the future. The careers of the Caribbean settlers I examine here were influenced by both sentiments.

In arguing that the postwar spirits of both possibility and fear encompassed New Commonwealth migrants and the imperial question itself, I tread in the footsteps of historians like Joanna Bailkin, Wendy Webster, Bill Schwarz, and Anne Spry Rush, who seek to heal the breach between imperial and domestic (British) historical questions, even, or especially, at the level of culture and society.

---

9   See Wendy Webster, *Imagining Home: Gender, 'Race' and National Identity, 1945–64* (London: UCL Press, 1998); Bill Schwarz, "'Claudia Jones and the *West Indian Gazette*': Reflections of the Emergence of Post-Colonial Britain," *Twentieth Century British History* 14, no. 3 (2003): 264–85; Rush, "Imperial Identity in Colonial Minds."

10 Roxy Harris, "Black British, Brown British and British Cultural Studies," in Claire Alexander, ed., *Stuart Hall and "Race"* (London: Routledge, 2011), 50.

This is not simply an academic exercise for it uncovers distinctive historical subjects and poses new historical questions. (It even begins to answer some of them.) Stephen Howe has encouraged practitioners of "new" imperial history—not new anymore—to consider more patiently the evidence of domestic insularity and use it to question just why cultural "barriers" between the British metropole and colonial periphery were "erected and maintained."[11] My study takes Howe's advice to heart and argues that colonial West Indian artists are distinctive historical subjects because they expressed the cultural and historical connections between Britain and her increasingly embattled empire. Their attempts to draw these worlds together, coupled with the commitment of certain British cultural agents to produce and exhibit their work, reveal the influence of imperial education, perceived racial difference, and colonial identity on the priorities of both parties. However, the persistence, and indeed strengthening, of cultural barriers between colonial and British institutions and audiences in the 1950s and '60s demands historical interrogation. Why did metropolitan and colonial Caribbean cultural priorities mesh creatively in the early postwar years only to clash and shrivel a decade later?

Bill Schwarz has remarked that "in the intellectual *disorder* of decolonization entire systems of thought were breached."[12] Joanna Bailkin perhaps puts the matter more optimistically when she states, "The collapse of the formal empire constituted an intellectual opportunity as much as a practical crisis."[13] Either way, this historical moment provoked an optimistic drive among intellectuals, social scientists, politicians, and activists to remake the postwar world for the better, and took place in London and out through the British Empire. Participants in this project were white social scientists involved in the postwar study of race relations, such as Ruth Glass, Kenneth Little, Michael Banton, and Sheila Patterson, and liberal institutions such as the Institute of Race Relations and the London Council of Social Service, which helped coordinate community efforts at interracial cooperation and activism.[14]

---

11 Stephen Howe, "Internal Decolonization? British Politics since Thatcher as Post-Colonial Trauma," *Twentieth Century British History* 14, no. 3 (2003): 289, 298.

12 Bill Schwarz, "Unspeakable Histories: Diasporic Lives in Old England," in Peter Osborne and Stella Sandford, eds, *Philosophies of Race and Ethnicity* (London: Continuum, 2002), 81–82.

13 Jordanna Bailkin, *The Afterlife of Empire* (Berkeley: University of California Press, 2012), 9. For nationwide post-imperial activism, see Jodi Burkett, *Constructing Post-Imperial Britain: Britishness, "Race" and the Radical Left in the 1960s* (Houndmills: Palgrave Macmillan, 2013).

14 See, for example, Michael Banton, *The Coloured Quarter: Negro Emigrants to an English City* (London: Cape, 1955); Anthony H. Richmond, *White and Coloured: The Behaviour of British People towards Coloured Immigrants* (London: Jonathan Cape, 1959); Ruth Glass, *London's Newcomers: The West Indian Migrants*, University

The subjects of this study were a part of this *zeitgeist*. They possessed a faith, yet undimmed, that their work, in conjunction with the government and media, could educate the British public about the Anglo-colonial connection and foster a liberal view of race relations—one that embraced the Empire-Commonwealth, supported the efforts and individualism of non-white Britons, and welcomed the prospect of a multiracial, multicultural Britain.

The work and orientation of these artist-settlers fit not only with this intellectual spirit of renovation, but also with radical attempts to renovate British culture in order to portray society in a more authentic way. In this respect, much has been made of the dramatically increased visibility of the working class in postwar British culture, due in part to its new economic empowerment after the war. As consumers, the working class and, most strikingly, working-class youth, asserted their cultural preferences like never before, and they had a vested interested in changing the cultural *status quo*. The result, in popular lore, was "Swinging London" and the Beatles, but these were preceded by a new wave of literature, drama, and film—Kingsley Amis, John Osborne, and Lindsay Anderson perhaps most famously.

However, the working class alone did not wreak all of the cultural changes reflected in the media at this time; this was "a transformation in the opportunities and freedoms available both to the majority and to distinctive individuals and groups within the majority."[15] Working-class youth comprised one such group, but new ethnic and racial groups also began to demand and engineer new cultural opportunities. Their achievements came more slowly and less sensationally, but they too gained public attention in these years. The present study focuses on the expressions of Caribbean artist-settlers and their colleagues, rather than those of xenophobic whites. The frankness and openness that, Marwick argues, characterized the postwar cultural climate served West Indian artists too, to a degree, though most postwar histories have inadequately integrated them into their larger narratives of cultural change. Without a full survey of postwar black British cultural production that offers an historical perspective on the period,[16] we are left

College, London, Centre for Urban Studies, Report No. 1 (Cambridge: Harvard University Press, 1961); Kenneth Little, *Negroes in Britain: A Study of Racial Relations in English Society* (London: Kegan Paul, 1947); Sheila Patterson, *Dark Strangers: A Sociological Study of the Absorption of a Recent West Indian Migrant Group in Brixton, South London* (London: Tavistock, 1963); Anthony H. Richmond, *The Colour Problem: A Study of Racial Relations* (1955; Harmondsworth: Penguin Books, 1961 revised edition).

15 Arthur Marwick, "The 1960s: Was There a Cultural Revolution?" (London: Penguin, 1982), 18.

16 James Procter, General Introduction to Procter, ed., *Writing Black Britain 1948–1998: An Interdisciplinary Anthology* (Manchester and New York: Manchester University Press, 2000), 8–9.

with a picture of the colonial settler community that is defined by racial antagonism, in part because we have few cohesive historical discourses or narratives to add to it.

This period of optimistic, exploratory engagement, roughly from war's end to the mid-1960s, is one to which Britons today cannot return. The fate of the multicultural experiment, for many, was sealed in July 2005, when Islamic militants (some of them British-born) bombed the London public transport system. However, for mid-century Commonwealth migrants and their descendants, who continue to struggle with social and institutional discrimination and whose collective memory is populated by racial hostility and violence from strangers, neighbors, politicians, and the police, multiculturalism's potential may have evaporated even earlier. This sad history has eclipsed the early postwar optimism that characterized the settlers under investigation here and—to an extent—the mainstream agents with which they worked. It is therefore all the more important that their stories are recovered, for they begin to give an idea, not just of *why*, but *how* this multicultural potential dissolved.

Thus the story I tell here is not only one of possibility and optimistic visions of the future of Britain, but also a story of fear, reactionary conservatism, and ultimately the foreclosing of several of those visions—including the vision of an inclusive, historically aware, Commonwealth-oriented, and anti-racist Britain. For those living in the aftermath of Brexit, it is not an unfamiliar story. Marc Matera's characterization of decolonization as "a history of persistent inequalities of power and unrealized and now largely forgotten political possibilities" also describes the careers of the settler-artists that I describe below.[17] The political dimensions of this shift have been astutely deconstructed by the likes of Kathleen Paul and Randall Hansen, and more generally by historians of postwar British foreign policy who argue that for decades after the war ended, successive governments struggled (and failed) to balance their allegiance to the Empire/Commonwealth with interests in America and Europe.

Nonetheless, scholars must jettison the persistent belief that the Commonwealth, and the New Commonwealth in particular, was little more than a half-hearted diplomatic idea used to maintain strategic alliances where there was little substantial affinity. Indeed, one of the distinctive strengths of the Commonwealth idea was its non-political dimension— its cultural arm, whose roots were as deep as those of its strategic and economic dimensions.[18] This was, however, a mirror to wider imperial

---

17 Marc Matera, *Black London: The Imperial Metropolis and Decolonization in the Twentieth Century* (Oakland: University of California Press, 2015), 322.

18 See David W. McIntyre, "The Unofficial Commonwealth Relations Conferences, 1933–59: Precursors of the Tri-Sector Commonwealth," *Journal of Imperial and Commonwealth History* 36 (December 2008): 591–614.

trends and, as John Gallagher maintained decades ago, imperial coherence and optimism, while on the decline after the First World War, resurged during and immediately following the Second World War.[19] This global war helped make the Empire and Commonwealth, once again, a going concern and postwar liberal feeling imbued it with a revamped mission that emphasized partnership over domination. Thus, while the Commonwealth ideal ultimately metamorphosed into a loose, multilateral association of nations promoting opportunities in education, sport, and the arts, at mid-century it constituted one way to manage decolonization by preserving military, economic, and strategic links between Britain and its former dominions and colonies.[20]

On the cultural front, Wendy Webster has argued that the postwar British media were dominated by particular narratives of race and empire that influenced popular perceptions of both decolonization and New Commonwealth migration, and which shifted in the late 1950s from celebratory and inclusive representations of the British Empire to "siege narratives" that portrayed empire as a threat to Englishness. Webster's chronology and emphasis on transition in this period corresponds with my own.

But it is scholars of race and identity who have taken the lead in exploring the cultural dimensions of this discussion, and a large part of their work revolves around questions of representation and identity in the context of strained and increasingly hostile race relations in postwar Britain. Furthermore, much of it has been written within that same context; it is driven by a political, anti-racist imperative as well as a scholarly one.[21] Black British cultural criticism since the 1990s has documented how the black British aesthetic tradition (especially in cinema) has broken away from the "race relations" narrative of the early postwar period, which "marked

---

19 John Gallagher, "The Decline, Revival and Fall of the British Empire," in Gallagher, ed., *The Decline, Revival and Fall of the British Empire: The Ford Lectures and Other Essays* (Cambridge: Cambridge University Press, 1982), 73–153.

20 See John Darwin, *Britain and Decolonization: The Retreat from Empire in the Post-War World* (London: Macmillan, 1988), 146–54.

21 Stuart Hall, Chas Critcher, Tony Jefferson, John Clarke, and Brian Roberts, *Policing the Crisis: Mugging, the State, and Law and Order* (London: Macmillan, 1978); Paul Gilroy, *"There Ain't No Black in the Union Jack": The Cultural Politics of Race and Nation* (Chicago: University of Chicago Press, 1987); Houston A. Baker, Jr., Manthia Diawara, and Ruth H. Lindeborg, eds, *Black British Cultural Studies: A Reader* (Chicago: University of Chicago Press, 1996); Michael Eldridge, "The Rise and Fall of Black Britain," *Transition* 74 (1997), 32–43; Kwesi Owusu, ed., *Storms of the Heart: An Anthology of Black Arts & Culture* (London: Camden Press, 1988); Benjamin Bowling, "The Emergence of Violent Racism as a Public Issue in Britain, 1945–81," in Panikos Panayi, ed., *Racial Violence in Britain in the Nineteenth and Twentieth Centuries*, revised edition (London: Leicester University Press, 1996).

a time of stereotyping blackness in the mainstream media."[22] I argue here for a more nuanced evaluation of the postwar media in this respect, one that acknowledges how artists *negotiated* representation *within* such a framework—the extent to which writers, directors, and actors *played* with existing stereotypes in order to challenge them, often along anti-racist lines (however incomplete their attempts might appear today).[23]

While the contributions of cultural studies in this respect are invaluable, they have had several effects on the historical field, of which at least three ought to be noted in relation to the present study. Firstly, in the work of both cultural and postcolonial studies there has been a preoccupation with racism and marginalization as the basic framework through which to analyze the experience of non-white settlers and their descendants.[24] The result is an historical account of the black (and brown) minority that is largely separate from the dominant narrative of postwar British history and culture. A second and related effect has been the application of the scholarship around "black British" art and culture—usually from the 1970s through the 1990s—retroactively, implicitly assuming that colonial artists and citizens of the 1940s, 1950s, and early 1960s had the same oppositional, underground experience and consciousness as later generations. As Stuart Hall has noted in his periodizing survey of postwar diaspora artists in Britain, identity politics was not a focus, or even a concern, of artists prior to the later 1970s and '80s.[25] Thirdly, as Roxy Harris has recognized, despite the increasingly "penetrating and sophisticated" incorporation of race and ethnicity into cultural studies, they "further postponed the appearance of the lived everyday experience of ordinary black and brown people and their own perspectives on this experience, at the centre of the frame."[26]

The experiences of the artists, writers, and entertainers under examination here were certainly marred by mainstream indifference, prejudicial treatment, and, often, professional marginalization. Artists

---

22 Barbara Korte and Claudia Sternberg, *Bidding for the Mainstream? Black and Asian British Film since the 1990s* (Amsterdam and New York: Rodopi, 2004), 51.

23 Legendary critic Raymond Durgnat has begun to evaluate this practice in the "puritan" films of Basil Dearden and Michael Relph, but more needs to be done. See Raymond Durgnat, "Two 'Social Problem' Films: *Sapphire* and *Victim*," in Alan Burton, Tim O'Sullivan, and Paul Wells, eds, *Liberal Directions: Basil Dearden and Postwar British Film Culture* (Trowbridge: Flicks Books, 1997), 59–88.

24 See, for representative examples, Dilip Hiro, *Black British White British: A History of Race Relations in Britain*, revised edition (London: Grafton Books, 1991); A. Sivanandan, *A Different Hunger: Writings on Racism and Resistance* (London: Pluto Press, 1982); Winston James and Clive Harris, eds, *Inside Babylon: The Caribbean Diaspora in Britain* (London: Verso, 1993).

25 Stuart Hall, "Black Diaspora Artists in Britain: Three 'Moments' in Post-War History," *History Workshop Journal* 61 (2006): 1–24.

26 Harris, "Black British, Brown British," 50.

responded to these challenges by establishing what Pearl Connor called a "West Indian grapevine" and by creating projects cooperatively. But at mid-century, neither institutional exclusion nor the assertion of an opposi-tional "black British" identity had hardened into normative practice. By the 1970s, a forceful case could be mounted against Arts Council neglect of black and Asian dance or theater, but in the 1950s, "ethnic arts" in Britain had not even coalesced into a visible community that official grant-giving bodies could ignore.[27]

Until the second half of the 1960s, the relationship among black artists, and between black artists and the British establishment, was *laissez-faire*; the latter had not yet criminalized the black minority, and the artists themselves had not formulated a preeminent politics of black solidarity.[28] Instead, West Indian artists collaborated with white British individuals and institutions, receiving professional acclaim (as well as discouragement), and the result was a number of cultural productions that showed the potential of a British culture that was not merely white. Some scholars have noted the more liberal cast of mid-century productions with black imagery, but have written them off as marginal instances that had no effect on the evolution of institutional approaches to the representation of ethnic minorities in British media.[29] I propose instead to take such productions seriously and to question the unique historical conditions that allowed them to proliferate, however briefly. That there are few vibrant reminders of that early potential today only renders this context more intriguing.

As the first generation of the mass colonial migration of the postwar period, the subjects of this study set the mold for what would later be known as "black British" cultural production. British society and culture today are widely and officially acknowledged to be multiracial and multicultural in character. If, as historians, we are interested in beginnings and turning points, then this neglected first wave of artists deserves further examination. If, instead of assuming an impermeable barrier of prejudice separating white from non-white Britons, we examine West Indian artist-settlers as an integral part of the cultural landscape in the early postwar period, some surprising intersections between their aims and those of other British culture workers begin to appear. In many ways, their progressive cultural politics—foregrounding issues of colonial independence, Commonwealth

---

27 See Naseem Khan, *The Arts that Britain Ignores: The Arts of Ethnic Minorities in Britain* (London: Arts Council of Great Britain, Gulbenkian Foundation, and the Community Relations Commission, 1976); Kwesi Owusu, *The Struggle for Black Arts in Britain: What Can we Consider Better than Freedom* (London: Comedia, 1986). Owusu argues that in the 1970s, official British arts funding policy "ghettoized" "ethnic arts," where before it had simply ignored them.

28 See Procter, General Introduction to Procter, *Writing Black Britain*.

29 "Introduction," in Jim Pines, ed., *Black and White in Colour: Black People in British Television since 1936* (London: British Film Institute, 1992).

status, education, race, and color—complemented the aims of at least two intellectual and cultural groups in postwar Britain more generally: the liberal proponents of postwar social and political reconstruction, and the proponents of the cultural revolution happening around issues of class, generation, and (to a lesser extent) gender. These two intellectual and creative movements overlapped.

In stating that some West Indian artists were able to leverage the climate of cultural redefinition to forward their own inclusive vision of Britishness, I tread carefully. The dominant narrative of postwar race relations, at least in scholarly circles, is a staunchly conflictual one that emphasizes the marginalization of the new black and colonial communities and the persistence, indeed sharpening, of white racism. This was, at times, true for liberal social scientists and left-wing cultural agents as well as for the conservative mainstream.[30]

Meanwhile, the past few decades have witnessed the growth of accounts of black British art and culture, but again, these deal overwhelmingly with the post-1965 period, and suggest a fundamental separation between this world and the world of mainstream "white" culture. Kwesi Owusu's assertion that "administrators and mainstream artists were guilty not of *ignoring* black arts, but of *refusing* to accept them" is indicative of the conflictual framework within which many of these analyses have been written.[31]

Sadly, this perspective accurately conveys much about the overall dynamic of the postwar relationship between black artists and the mainstream cultural establishment, especially after the mid-1960s, but the field is ripe for a more nuanced exploration of the relationship between colonial artists and the mainstream, especially in the first postwar decades when this relationship was not always as bleak and oppositional as it would become by the 1970s.

In order to understand what made British institutions and producers more receptive to Caribbean artists in the immediate postwar years, it is instructive to revisit Webster's conception of the "people's empire," an influential but short-lived cultural narrative that emphasized "a wartime empire that pulled together across differences of race and ethnicity" and after 1945 was "revised to an egalitarian idea of 'equal partners.'"[32] This narrative of British identity eloquently justified a place in London's cultural community for the first generation of Caribbean migrants (many of whom had fought in the war). It encompassed efforts like Lord Kitchener's London

---

30 Chris Waters, "'Dark Strangers' in Our Midst: Discourses of Race and Nation in Britain, 1947–1963," *The Journal of British Studies* 36, no. 2 (April 1997): 207–38.

31 Owusu, *The Struggle for Black Arts in Britain*, 60.

32 Wendy Webster, *Englishness and Empire 1939–65* (Oxford: Oxford University Press, 2005), 7.

calypsos, Ronald Moody's stately woodcarvings, and Edric Connor's BBC talks on West Indian history and folklore (mentioned at the outset of this introduction). As the 1950s wore on, according to Webster, the narrative of the "people's empire" began to stand at odds with a narrative that "invoked a quiet, private, and domesticated identity, and showed empire as a threat to Englishness." This competing narrative meshes well with that identified by Waters and others, wherein colonial migrants of color were positioned as "dark strangers." For much of this early postwar period, however, the Caribbean artists examined below managed to find a place within the cultural mainstream.

This study avers that the art and entertainment that West Indian settlers produced, or helped produce, in the twenty years after 1945 was an integral part of the landmark changes sweeping through Britain. Among many other trends, this shift included the liberalization of the British Broadcasting Corporation ethos, the spread of television and the introduction of independent television companies, the popularity of urban jazz and swing music, the popularity of the "social problem" film in English cinema, working-class realist drama, and abstract expressionism and primitivism in mid-century fine art and sculpture. The following case studies demonstrate how West Indians like Edric and Pearl Connor, Ronald Moody, Cy Grant, Lord Kitchener, Earl Cameron, and the Reckord brothers (Barry and Lloyd), among others, were a part of these developments, proving that they were not merely "*recipients* of cultural imperialism," but "*participants* in the development of a *shared* imperial culture."[33]

Not only were they a part of these developments, but they crucially expanded and redefined them. West Indian artists achieved this by injecting a cultural politics of race, empire, and colonial identity into British culture. Although Britain was undergoing a kind of "internal decolonization" in this period, only they, and colonial settlers like them, expressed this process in imperial terms.[34] As Christian Høgsbjerg has argued (with C. L. R. James as his case study),

> "imperial British" culture was not just there to be claimed for reasons of status and "respectability" by colonial subjects, but was also open to be re-claimed and re-imagined in the colonial context by "modern" and progressive black and Asian intellectuals in more creative and egalitarian ways that few in Britain … could have ever envisaged happening themselves.[35]

33 Anne Spry Rush, *Bonds of Empire: West Indians and Britishness from Victoria to Decolonization* (London: Oxford, 2011), 8.

34 Schwarz, "Claudia Jones and the *West Indian Gazette*": 284–85.

35 Christian Høgsbjerg, "'We Lived According to the Tenets of Matthew Arnold':

Thus, if we include a "colonial" perspective in our view of postwar Britain, an integral place emerges for the work of Caribbean artists in the larger narrative of cultural history.

As historical subjects, the Caribbean artists who migrated to London near mid-century have much to teach postwar scholars. They were unique. First, their transatlantic, transnational character meshes the histories of British culture, empire, migration, and race relations. Second, because they emigrated in the lead-up to political independence in the West Indies, they were representatives of the only generation to live and work as both colonial subjects and British citizens. Their experience straddled the historical boundaries of both world war and decolonization. As a result, their personal experience and cultural work contained elements of both their Caribbean roots *and* their new life in urban Britain; their desire for colonial independence *and* their desire to maintain strong ties to the mother country; their pride in Caribbean history, art, and folklore *and* their rooted admiration for British literary and cultural canons. Operating on the cusp of decolonization and the birth of a more visibly multiracial Britain, the artists under consideration here performed the difficult work of assembling a British identity that would be viable in the decades to come. As Schwarz puts it, the West Indian settler of these years "became an important, if often reluctant, agent in imagining a future for Britain after colonialism."[36]

Like all creative work, the artifacts that I examine here reflect the political questions and convictions of their creators, and I am fundamentally concerned with these sensibilities—what I call the "cultural politics" of British West Indian (or perhaps West Indian British) artists in London. I use this phrase simply to describe how artists used their creative work to challenge conventional representations of British society, history, culture, and geography, and to create their own. The change these artists worked to provoke was about their own "alienation" from British society more than is was about physical, legal, or economic exploitation, though it intersected with, and was never wholly discrete from, these political struggles.[37] Importantly, this cultural politics existed and was articulated long before the so-called revolutions of 1968.

I also rather like Hall's less formal understanding of culture as "something which is deeply subjective and personal, and at the same moment, as a structure you live."[38] Indeed, the work of the artists featured in this story

---

Reflections on the 'Colonial Victorianism' of the Young C. L. R. James," *Twentieth Century British History* 24, no. 2 (2013): 205.

36   Schwarz, "Claudia Jones and the *West Indian Gazette*": 268.

37   Brian W. Alleyne, *Radicals against Race: Black Activism and Cultural Politics* (Oxford and New York: Berg, 2002), 4.

38   Stuart Hall, "The Formation of a Diasporic Intellectual: An interview with Stuart

was simultaneously a reflection of their own idiosyncratic interests and a response to social and professional conditions shared by West Indian artist-settlers of their generation. They all, for example, catered to Anglocentric cultural producers and/or a predominantly white audience. In addition, they all contended with a critical and media reception that viewed their work as "exotic" or positioned it within the narrative framework of "race relations."

This is not to suggest that, for instance, aesthetic and commercial considerations were not central to their work, but West Indian artists also used it to *educate* their audience, about themselves and their place in domestic British society. Their cultural work was political in that it engaged with, challenged, and reshaped narratives of belonging, at the "intersection between culture and politics."[39] Most pertinent to this study is that much of this cultural politics dealt with the experience of migration and grappled with ideas of British and West Indian (colonial) identity that were only partly defined by residence and citizenship. These artists' sometimes idealized vision of Britishness, for example, was also about public virtues espoused in the heyday of the empire, and most recently during the Second World War, in which millions of imperial subjects took part: duty to nation and empire, a fair government, society and the justice system, the protection of minorities, and a respect for and celebration of imperial ties. Far from being "pre-political," West Indian artists attempted to critically harness such values in their work, which, taken together, constitutes a drive for an anti-racist multiculturalism that nonetheless acknowledged a shared history and culture among *all* Britons.[40]

Each of my subjects, of course, approached their work with distinctive attitudes, concerns, and prejudices. Some, like Edric Connor, always entertained with an eye toward immediately improving conditions for fellow Commonwealth actors in Britain and the West Indies; others, like Barry Reckord, dramatized political issues of race and racism, but became disillusioned with the efforts of fellow Caribbean actors. Still others, like actor Earl Cameron, remained—apparently—personally uncommitted to political goals, while simultaneously appearing in some of the highest-profile "race relations" films of the period. What they all have in common is their identity as artists/performers *first and foremost*. This distinguishes them from most other subjects of colonial and British histories, whose lives were marked by progressive intellectual exploration and/or exceptional political activism. In Britain, the most prominent of these West Indians, up to the middle sixties, were C. L. R. James, George Padmore, Marcus

---

Hall by Kuan-Hsing Chen," in David Morley and Chen, eds, *Stuart Hall: Critical Dialogues in Cultural Studies* (London and New York: Routledge, 1996), 490.

39   Gilroy, *"There Ain't No Black in the Union Jack,"* 13.

40   For a brief discussion of the distinctive politics of this generation of settlers, see Procter, Introduction to Part One, Procter, *Writing Black Britain*, 15.

Garvey, and Harold Moody. They put their classical English educations to good use in their theorization of racial and economic inequality. Communist and Enlightenment thought suffused their writing, while political service, international activism, and charitable work characterized their public lives.

My focus on artists, many of whom worked within the mainstream, results in a less radical, more populist picture of migrant Caribbean cultural politics; one that perhaps better represents the political sensibilities of the mass of West Indian settlers in postwar Britain. Firstly, these artists for the most part did not engage deeply in party politics, either in Britain or the Caribbean, and were not closely connected to the Communist movement, like (for example) Claudia Jones was. Moreover, their approach to the politics of race must be viewed as distinct from that which had evolved by the later 1960s, under the positive influence of the American Black Power movement, and the negative influence of the Commonwealth Immigrants Act and the increasingly overt racism of British politicians, most infamously Enoch Powell. Finally, their ongoing struggle for commercial and critical success in London impacted how their cultural and racial politics found expression in their work. Very often, career considerations trumped political concerns—this was a matter of professional survival. Proactive individuals like Pearl Connor worked tirelessly to provide opportunities for the expatriate Caribbean community, but the focus in these years was much more on building a commercial base for artists and cultivating individual careers than on debating aspects of racial identity and white power.

Some of the figures and cultural productions did not achieve a high profile during their own life span: Ronald Moody toiled in his studio for decades but gained the reverence of the British art establishment largely posthumously; Barry Reckord has been all but forgotten in the annals of the English Stage Company at the Royal Court. Nonetheless, it is important to recover the work and careers of all these artists, I argue, for at least two reasons. First, their work is not marginal to the narratives of British art and culture writ large in the postwar period; these artists engaged with many of the same themes and concerns as their UK-born counterparts. In the 1950s and 1960s, a younger, less privileged, and less conservative cohort of artists and intellectuals rethought what it meant to be British, questioning once-hallowed preconceptions about class, propriety, and the nation's place in the world. The West Indian figures examined below were very much a part of this story. Even more important, when they incorporated explicitly "Caribbean" or "colonial" perspectives into their work, it only enhanced the sophistication and richness of the canon of "British" culture that resulted.

It is impossible to pinpoint exactly when this story changed—when the *laissez-faire* relationship between London's cultural establishment and non-white artists became mired in conflict over the mainstream invisibility of what became consciously "black" creative work, the professional marginalization of black artists, and the increasingly shrill and panicked representation of non-white minorities in the media. There are some landmark dates convenient for the purposes of periodization: the arrival of the *Windrush* in 1948 inaugurated a period of increased artistic visibility for many of my historical subjects (two of whom were on that very voyage), while racial violence (1958, 1959) and immigration restriction (1962, 1965) provoked urgent responses in West Indian creative work. Later phenomena, such as the Black Power movement's establishment in England, had their landmark moments as well. However, most of the cultural trends and effects that figure prominently in my study arose over time and cannot be dated with precision.

I have chosen my chronological frame of reference, 1945–65, first because the war's end was more central to migrants' artistic climate than the celebrated 1948 *Windrush* voyage. This study, then, is part of a new and growing body of work that seeks to transcend the "*Windrush*-as-origins" approach to black British history, connecting, for example, the pre- and postwar contexts of black intellectual and political activity.[41] Although I do not wish to frame the *Windrush* voyage as the primary watershed moment, I have kept my focus on the postwar period, simply because large-scale Caribbean migration and settlement is the most important backdrop to the work of the artists and writers under review here. Not only were many early migrants directly inspired by their wartime service in Britain, but also (as Webster's research makes clear) British war propaganda emphasized the togetherness of the imperial family, a campaign that ultimately created a domestic context favorable to the acceptance, and even welcome, of West Indian talent.

The second obvious boundaries to my study are the passage of the Commonwealth Immigrants Act and Caribbean decolonization, both of which began in 1962 (with Jamaica and Trinidad and Tobago the first to declare independence).[42] The Commonwealth Immigrants Act reversed the provision of 1948's British Nationality Act (BNA) and severely curbed non-white migration from Britain's colonies and former colonies by requiring all migrants (who were not immediate dependents and family members of those UK residents already holding British passports) to have employment vouchers certifying their possession of British employment or their special qualification for such employment.[43] In 1961, in antici- pation of the restrictions, colonial migration for the year spiked at about

---

41   Kennetta Hammond Perry, "Black Britain and the Politics of Race in the 20th Century," *History Compass* 12, no. 8 (2014): 651–63.

42   The smaller islands became independent over the next twenty-one years. The Cayman Islands, Turks and Caicos Islands, Anguilla and Bermuda remain British territories.

43   Students, armed forces personnel, and those able to prove that they could support themselves and their families without working were not subject to restricted entry.

136,000 people before falling off dramatically.[44] Migration from the British West Indies fell from a high of 66,300 in 1961 to under two thousand the following year.[45]

At the same time, decolonization ushered in a new ideological era in the Caribbean. The still-rigid class- and race-based hierarchy began to lose its stability with the advent of democracy on the independent islands. With it, the aspirational, middle-class West Indians most enthusiastic about absorbing British ways were replaced by others who felt little connection to Britain and who embraced newer symbols of "Caribbeanness" or "blackness."[46] In Britain, although the shift in West Indian sensibilities to a more politicized, and sometimes race-based, cultural solidarity was a gradual one, it was an incontrovertible force by the second half of the 1960s. (The formation of the dynamic Caribbean Artists' Movement (CAM), in 1966, stands as one useful marker of that shift.)

Finally, I focus on the period 1945–65 because, as indicated above, it encompassed the formative phase of Britain's so-called cultural revolution in literature, theater, and film, which focused on characters and themes that were youthful, rebellious, and issue-based. The role of West Indians in that creative revolution has been overlooked.

There are multiple limitations to this study. Much new work on black British history is oriented toward the transnational and the diasporic, a development that has rightly drawn attention to the cosmopolitan and international dimension of black activism and culture in Britain, especially among those who hailed from the "migration culture" of the Caribbean and often arrived in Britain by way of Latin America as well as the United States, western Europe and, later, Canada.[47] However, while the present study is transnational in the sense that it addresses the transatlantic movement of colonial subjects (and British citizens), it focuses primarily on the Anglo-Caribbean connection and West Indian settlers' articulations of British and Britannic identity, emerging as they did in the context of public debate about New Commonwealth migration. Like Anne Spry Rush, I am most concerned with how "West Indians participated in a complex process of cultural transition—a struggle to re-define Britishness and their relationship to it—not only as Caribbean

---

44 See Kathleen Paul, *Whitewashing Britain: Race and Empire in the Postwar Era* (Ithaca: Cornell University Press, 1997). Please note that this figure includes migrants from all over the Commonwealth, not just the West Indies.

45 See Randall Hansen, *Citizenship and Immigration in Post-War Britain: The Institutional Origins of a Multicultural Nation* (London: Oxford University Press, 2000), 265.

46 See Rush, *Bonds of Empire.*

47 Elizabeth Thomas-Hope, "Globalization and the Development of a Caribbean Migration Culture," in Philip W. Scher, ed., *Perspectives on the Caribbean: A Reader in Culture, History, and Representation* (Chichester: Blackwell, 2010), 247–55.

peoples but also as Britons."[48] In other words, this is not a history of the black diaspora but rather an historical exploration of the potential and limits of consensus between native Britons and Caribbean settlers.

The existence of adequate archival sources has determined the subjects of this study, but in general terms each chapter is devoted to different artists and institutions in a particular field of art or popular media. Besides this introduction, Chapter 1 provides a narrative, research-based overview of the experiences of those West Indian settlers in London during the 1940s, '50s, and '60s: their social and educational backgrounds in the Caribbean, their reasons for emigrating, their living and working conditions in London, and their strategies for coping in a new environment. In addition, the chapter explores the attitudes of British government, industry, and cultural institutions toward West Indian newcomers, and the nature of English colonial and racial prejudice in the early postwar period.

Chapter 2 looks at the BBC careers of Trinidadian singer Edric Connor, Trinidadian agent Pearl Connor, and Guyanese actor and singer Cy Grant as they struggled, in different ways, to use their commercial success to expand their professional roles on the radio and television. Although the BBC was an early and (relatively) consistent supporter of both Connor and Grant, its narrow conception of the place of (non-white) West Indian talent meant that it, almost unconsciously, limited the creative growth of these performers.

Chapter 3 moves from the official position of the BBC to the more informal culture of urban popular music. This world included not only jazz and swing, but also Trinidadian calypso, performed by Lord Kitchener, Lord Beginner, and Lord Invader, among several others. Their topical calypsos combined the Trinidadian musical form with English subject matter, thus demonstrating one way in which West Indian settler-artists laid claim to a more inclusive imperial culture.

The fourth chapter takes as its focus the career and work of Jamaican sculptor Ronald Moody, which took shape only after his migration to London to attend university. His sculpture, created in a non-Western mold but profoundly influenced by his European experience and education, embodies Moody's struggle to articulate his own kind of cultural politics, without resorting to the pervasive dichotomies of race or class.

The final two chapters explore what I have called the "race relations narrative" in mid-century British film and theater. The subject of non-white colonial migration, and its effects on the native white English home, was almost obsessively rehashed on stage and screen, most often through the "specter" of interracial romantic and sexual relationships. Cultural critics have highlighted the gendered, racialized, and class-biased contours of some of these narratives; what my study emphasizes is the role of West Indian writers and actors in constructing, influencing, and subverting these

---

48 Rush, *Bonds of Empire*.

narratives, which scholars have assumed to be purely (white) English in orientation. At the same time, these two chapters, like chapters 2, 3, and 4, look at the role of West Indian artists—in particular Earl Cameron and the Reckord brothers—in high-profile British operations like the Rank Organisation and the English Stage Company.

*

On my use of terms: to describe my subjects, I use the terms "West Indian" and "Caribbean" interchangeably, although the former traditionally refers only to the British colonies, while the latter encompasses the region as a whole. The former, which has fallen out of use, was widely used in the 1950s and '60s. In addition, this study speaks of "West Indian" artists as well as "Trinidadian" or "Antiguan" ones. Not only did complacent English observers often label entire communities West Indian—or even "Jamaican" in some instances—but new settlers, regardless of their island of origin, tended in London to connect with other West Indian migrants for practical, social, and even economic support. There were also political reasons for this, since the advent of West Indies Federation in 1958 was accompanied by a cultural and media celebration of a regional Caribbean or West Indian identity.[49] And while the Federation only lasted until 1962, the more communal moniker grew in use, at least in Britain. It is, perhaps, not too much of a stretch to argue that "West Indian" as a key identification is unique to a single generation—the generation under examination here. This is what George Lamming meant when he wrote that "most West Indians of my generation were born in England."[50]

Where possible, I employ geographic designators over those, like "black," that describe "race" or color. The vast majority of artists under examination here did not describe themselves as black, or at least not until later in the 1960s and '70s, when the term acquired significance as a "political signifier."[51] In addition, in the early postwar West Indies, society still noted gradations of skin tone, which often mirrored social status; my subjects, therefore, described themselves as "colored" instead of black. When referring to skin color—as distinct from nationality—I sometimes use the term "non-white," not only as an alternative to the highly politicized "black," but also because non-whiteness was in fact the most significant

---

49 The Federation encompassed all of the so-called British West Indies except for the mainland colonies of British Honduras (Belize) and British Guiana (Guyana); Bermuda and the Bahamas were never considered to be part of the West Indies.

50 George Lamming, "Journey to an Expectation," in *The Pleasures of Exile* (Ann Arbor: University of Michigan Press, 1992), 214.

51 Procter, General Introduction, Procter, *Writing Black Britain*, 5.

indicator of racial difference in postwar England.[52] As Lord Kitchener wryly noted in one of his London calypsos, "If you're not white you're considered black."[53]

Secondly, although my research concentrates on the arts in London, I have chosen to retain "British" as this study's primary national descriptor, instead of the more limited "English." Wendy Webster makes a logical case for using "English" when one is really talking about media and culture that are substantively English in origin and values, and her argument also applies to many of my media sources. However, I have chosen "British," both because my historical subjects preferred that term over the more insular "English" and because the conception of culture that I posit here includes the efforts of West Indian and other colonial and Commonwealth artists living in London.[54] Surely the inclusion of their vision calls for an imperialized definition of Britishness that extends beyond English borders.

Finally, this study speaks of West Indian "settlers" and "migrants" in London, not "immigrants." The term "immigrant" suggests that these newcomers were not British, when in fact the 1948 BNA decreed that they were: "Our colonial status condemned us fortunately to the rights of full citizenship."[55] The rules did not change until 1962, when the provisions of the first Commonwealth Immigrants Act came into effect. Furthermore, and importantly for the project here, the culture that West Indian migrants brought with them was not a wholly alien one; on the contrary, it was a culture profoundly shaped by the colonies' centuries-long connection to Britain.

---

52 I use the terms "black" and "black British" only in the context of the later postwar era, when they gained currency among Britons of Caribbean, African, and Asian descent. "Black British" is a politicized term partly intended to foster solidarity among Britain's different racial minority groups (just as the term "West Indian" aimed to unite those hailing from various Caribbean territories).

53 Aldwyn Roberts, "If You're Not White You're Black" (Melodisc 1260, recorded November 1953), *London is the Place for Me: Trinidadian Calypso in London, 1950–56* (Honest Jon's HJR CD2, 2002).

54 My rationale for the preference of "British" over "English" resembles Eddie Chambers's in *Black Artists in British Art: A History since the 1950s* (London and New York: I. B. Tauris, 2014), 3.

55 George Lamming, "Journey to an Expectation," 212.

Chapter 1

West Indies to London

This chapter stands a little apart from those that follow. It provides the historical context for the case studies that comprise the bulk of the study and a narrative of Caribbean migration and settlement in England from the late 1940s to the early 1960s. It provides a sense of how this experience influenced the profiles, professional strategies, and cultural politics of the artists and institutions I examine in subsequent chapters. The description below is not intended to be comprehensive; certainly, it cannot address the myriad individual experiences that make up the collective memory of today's Caribbean-descended Londoners. But it points to some of the attitudes, motivations, and challenges that many émigrés and London settlers shared. It also explores the beliefs and prejudices that informed the official and unofficial reactions of native English people to the arrival of West Indians in this period.

Many of the West Indians who migrated to London between 1945 and the early 1960s came with a feeling of imperial affinity to Great Britain and optimism about their prospects. They were perhaps the last generation of settlers that could be so described—they were certainly the last to migrate before the independence of Jamaica and Trinidad, not to mention numerous African colonies as well. However, their official and popular reception was decidedly ambivalent. Initially, the loudest official claims invested in the phenomenon of Caribbean migration the vibrancy of the new British Empire and Commonwealth, as well as the triumph of British liberalism, especially regarding race. But by the late 1950s, newsreels, parliamentary debate, and many members of the public regarded the arrival of West Indians with foreboding, if not outright opposition. Thus was West Indian optimism gradually—and reluctantly—replaced with disillusionment and alienation. The fortunes of the artists whom I examine in later chapters reflect this shift in attitude, to which the present chapter provides the social and political background.

Conditions of Emigration

Contemporary commentators, and historians, tend to cite the arrival of the *Empire Windrush* in June 1948, carrying 430 Caribbean migrants, as the definitive "moment" of the birth of a multiracial Britain. But this is misleading, not only because West Indians had been settling in Britain for centuries,[1] but also because the conditions that facilitated postwar migration predated the famed *Windrush* voyage by at least a few years. There were both "push" factors, conditions that potential migrants wanted to escape, and "pull" factors, benefits that émigrés expected to gain by settling in Great Britain.

Perhaps the most important "push" factor was the deteriorating economies of the British Caribbean islands, which were largely dependent on the production of raw materials and foodstuffs: sugar, cocoa, bananas, rice (in British Guiana), bauxite (in Guiana and Jamaica), and petroleum (in Trinidad). (At mid-century, tourism was not yet an industry of central importance in the West Indies.) The plantation system, in place since the seventeenth century, still served as the framework for much agricultural production, the primary alternative being small-scale, sometimes subsistence, agriculture. As a result, employment was scarce and poorly paid. Throughout much of the Caribbean, unemployment in the first half of the 1950s stood at between fifteen and twenty percent, and employment in the sugar industry (which dominated in Jamaica and Barbados, two of the most important producers of emigrants) was usually seasonal.[2] During the Second World War, in Trinidad especially, the presence of American military bases provided new sources of work and income, but this situation was not lasting.

Similarly, only a small minority of the population had a secondary education: in a 1961 survey of 364 newly arrived Caribbean migrants, for example, only nine had more than an elementary (grade six) education.[3] That said, there is evidence to suggest that primary education in the Caribbean, which operated along English lines, was in fact superior to basic schooling in England itself. Barbadian D'Arcy Holder, one of John Western's interviewees, described his primary education as "a *solid* base. I was surprised when I got here to find my education was better than some

---

1   As Peter Fryer has soundly demonstrated in *Staying Power: The History of Black People in Britain* (London and Sydney: Pluto Press, 1984).

2   S. K. Ruck, Douglas Manley, Ivo de Souza, Albert Hyndman, eds, *The West Indian Comes to England: A Report prepared for the Trustees of the London Parochial Charities by the Family Welfare Association* (London: Routledge and Kegan Paul, 1960), 14.

3   R. B. Davison, *West Indian Migrants: Social and Economic facts of Migration from the West Indies* (Oxford: Oxford University Press, 1962), 19.

of the English people I worked with!"[4] The islands' best and brightest young students gained scholarships that took them in a steady trickle to universities in London, Oxford, and Cambridge, but up until the last years of imperial rule, the most prestigious and lucrative posts in government, law, medicine, and education were dominated, if not monopolized, by white men. By the interwar period, however, especially in the larger Jamaica and Trinidad, there existed an educated and politically active "black petty bourgeoisie, especially teachers, clergymen, journalists, urban artisans, and middle farmers."[5] Nonetheless, as one Jamaican migrant said, "The Governor was white, those in authority were white, the judges were white. The only people who weren't white were police officers, who were black."[6]

In addition to economic and educational blocks to upward mobility, there were social barriers. The hierarchy established under slavery still persisted in unofficial ways. Caribbean society has been labeled a "pigmentocracy" because social advantage was so often correlated to lightness of skin tone. Historically, West Indians recognized minute racial gradations, distinguishing between, for example, a *quadroon* (a person with one fully "black" or African grandparent) and an *octoroon* (a person with one black great-grandparent). Social rules encouraged people to "marry light," and professional or economic opportunities tended to be awarded to lighter-skinned individuals. Stuart Hall, who was conspicuously "the blackest member of my family," recalled:

> I performed that role throughout [my childhood]. My friends at school, many of whom were from good middle-class homes, but blacker in colour than me, were not accepted at my home. My parents didn't think I was making the right kind of friends. They always encouraged me to mix with more middle-class, more higher-colour friends and I didn't.[7]

In regions containing significant indigenous, south Asian, or east Asian populations, the hierarchy could be even more complicated. Cy Grant, discussed at length in the next chapter, remarked that it "seemed strange" to be referred to as a black man in England, when he had been deemed "colored" at home in British Guiana: "My father was a West Indian, my mother was Anglo Asian. So we definitely had privileges over the people

---

4   John Western, *A Passage to England: Barbadian Londoners Speak of Home* (Minneapolis: University of Minnesota Press, 1992), 28.

5   Howard Johnson, "The British Caribbean from Demobilization to Constitutional Decolonization," in Judith M. Brown and Wm. Roger Louis, eds, *The Oxford History of the British Empire: The Twentieth Century* (Oxford: Oxford University Press, 1999), 603.

6   Vince Reid quoted in Phillips and Phillips, *Windrush*, 14.

7   Hall, "The Formation of a Diasporic Intellectual," 487.

of purely black descent."[8] Generally speaking, however, Caribbean society was divided into three classes: white, colored (or mixed-race), and black (of "pure" African descent). The first filled most high administrative and professional posts, while the last performed much of the physical and agricultural labor. Partly because of the rough correlation between skin color and class in the Caribbean at this time, migration to Britain promised not simply employment, but a more flexible path to social mobility.

For all these reasons, many West Indians yearning for greater opportunity felt stifled at home; some saw this inertia reflected in the pettiness and torpor of their own communities. The flipside of the pride of parents whose son earned an English scholarship was the jealousy that some felt toward their socially, educationally, or economically mobile peers. V. S. Naipaul has most famously and controversially written on this, for example in his 1962 commentary on traveling through the Caribbean islands where he grew up, "territories which, unimportant except to themselves, and faced with every sort of problem, were exhausting their energies in petty power squabbles and the maintaining of the petty prejudices of petty societies." Most damningly he remarked, "In Jamaica my diary entries grew shorter and shorter and then stopped altogether. There was nothing new to record."[9]

But others who migrated overseas also suggested an upbringing where personal ambition was thwarted and endangered. George Lamming's Barbados-set novel *In the Castle of My Skin* refers to the local villagers as "low-down nigger people" because "they couldn't bear to see one of their kind get along without feeling envy and hate."[10] This condition was not simply a matter of small-island gossip; as Elizabeth Thomas-Hope has explained, urbanization and the experience of two world wars in the twentieth century expanded educational and professional opportunities in the West Indies. However, "for all this class mobility and the broadening of the parameters of racial and cultural status with which class was associated, it was not accompanied by a corresponding increase in relative income levels of the upwardly mobile. The necessary economic base for sustaining such expectations simply did not exist."[11] The subjects of this study were just such ambitious individuals who actively craved broader educational, creative, and professional horizons, and who were perhaps more sensitive to the prejudices of their own communities. In this respect, it is worth noting that of all the major figures considered in this study, only the calypsonians, and perhaps Edric Connor, had experience in their creative field prior to

---

8   Cy Grant quoted in Phillips and Phillips, *Windrush*, 16.
9   V. S. Naipaul, *The Middle Passage: Impressions of Five Societies–British, French and Dutch–in the West Indies and South America* (London: Andre Deutsch, 1962), 230, 224.
10   George Lamming, *In the Castle of My Skin* (1953; New York: Macmillan, 1970), 20.
11   Thomas-Hope, "Globalization and the Development," 249.

British settlement. Most commented on the lack of artistic training and opportunity available in the Caribbean at the time, as we shall see.

As all these "push" factors attest, social status and opportunity in the Caribbean were not simply a matter of income, but were determined by several factors, the most important, as Anne Rush outlines, being color, education, occupation, religion, and culture. Color was perhaps the least flexible of these—white people were guaranteed superior status despite anything else—although, as in the case of Hall's family, it was at times randomly assigned. Education, on the other hand, although still inaccessible to many, was the most flexible "push" factor. Thomas-Hope credits it with "starting the process of breaking down the rigid association of class and colour" in the early decades of the century, and links it explicitly with other coveted symbols of respectability, including the use of standard English, good manners, and a cosmopolitan outlook. Education, in this way, was also linked to the culture of migration.[12]

Because of the historically limited opportunities for advancement, migration, often temporary but sometimes permanent, was (and remains) a common strategy for ambitious workers. In the twentieth century, the construction of the Panama Canal drew thousands of Caribbean laborers from islands large and small. North America, especially its urban centers like New York City, was a preferred migration destination, but in 1952 the McCarran-Walter Act severely curtailed Caribbean immigration to the United States by reducing the legal quota of immigrants from 2,500 per colony to only 100. This effectively redirected the flow of West Indian emigration from the United States to Great Britain:[13]

> It was in most people's blood in Barbados to travel, it's a small place, there was no opportunity for young people in my day. You got to get out, get off to America, everybody's dream. Only time anybody thought about England was a doctor or a lawyer. If it was the money, it was America. But America closed down, and England opened up. There was a mad rush. It was fashionable in those days.[14]

There was also a great deal of travel between the different regions of the Caribbean, especially from smaller islands to larger ones. The singer and actress Pearl Prescod, for instance, moved the short distance from her home in rural Tobago to Trinidad, before making the leap to London.[15] But many

---

12 Thomas-Hope, "Globalization and the Development," 249.

13 See Robert Pastor, "The Impact of U. S. Immigration Policy on Caribbean Emigration: Does it Matter?" in Barry B. Levine, ed., *The Caribbean Exodus* (New York: Praeger Publishers, 1987), 243–59.

14 Audley Simmons interviewed in Western, *A Passage to England*, 46.

15 See RCONT 1—Pearl Prescod. Artists File 1 (1954–62). WAC.

West Indians cast their sights beyond the Caribbean, and Great Britain, the center of the empire, was an attractive prospect.

Britain's prestige value in this respect was considerable. For over a century, it had been where the best young students went for post-secondary education, and many graduates returned home to lucrative and respected posts in governance, education, medicine, and law. The "best" primary and secondary West Indian schools were also British in style and structure, and most of their curriculum was also British (or, more precisely, English). Those lucky enough to attend these institutions learned English literature, history, law, and sport. C. L. R. James famously wrote about the imperial transmission of English values through the medium of cricket, of which he was an avid fan and critic, but in *Beyond a Boundary* we see so many other ways in which his world was shaped by English culture, not least his love for Thackeray's *Vanity Fair*: "of all the books that passed through that house this one became my Homer and my bible."[16] Once arrived in England, West Indian university students remained somewhat insulated by their education, "their relative comfort in Oxford or Cambridge" helping "to reinforce the illusion" of equality with their white, British-born peers.[17]

But Britain's cultural reach extended beyond the school system of the West Indian middle class. There were obvious indications of this: the widespread popularity of cricket, the elated reception the royal family received whenever their tours took them to the Caribbean (as evidenced by some of the Trinidadian calypsos examined in Chapter 3), the British-manufactured goods familiar to West Indian consumers. Lamming's villagers in *In the Castle of My Skin* "enjoyed the parades and the flags and the speeches. It made them feel a little more important than they were."[18] But more than these outward, mass expressions of enthusiasm and loyalty, many West Indians, whatever their opinion on the question of independence, nourished a particular reverence for British culture broadly defined. Barbadian settler Audley Simmons remembered, "We were brought up so English. When we got here [to London], I was amazed in the cinema at the end of the film, we were the only ones who stood still for the playing of 'God Save the Queen.' Everyone else was rushing for the exits!"[19] There was, too, a certain West Indian pride that such a culture was part of their own. Sam Selvon, who wrote extensively on the experience of young West Indian men in Britain, acknowledged that Britain's, and London's, prestige persisted even in the face of unemployment, cold winters, and colder treatment:

---

16 C. L. R. James, *Beyond a Boundary* (1963; London: Hutchinson and Co., 1969), 27.
17 George Lamming, "Journey to an Expectation," 218.
18 Lamming, *In the Castle of My Skin*, 74.
19 Audley Simmons interviewed in Western, *A Passage to England*, 28.

Oh what it is and where it is and why it is, no one knows, but to have said: "I walked on Waterloo Bridge," "I rendezvoused at Charing Cross," "Piccadilly Circus is my playground," to say these things, to have lived these things, to have lived in the great city of London, centre of the world.[20]

Just before he decided to pursue acting, Earl Cameron had an epiphany reminiscent of the one Selvon described:

When I got back to London [from a stint in India], I suddenly felt this urge. I suddenly realised I had fallen in love with London. When the train pulled in to Euston, my heart was beating fast. I thought, 'I love this place. I love London.' The thought of Bermuda disappeared.[21]

When the war broke out in 1939, many young West Indians, over ten thousand, volunteered for the British armed forces, the Royal Air Force in particular. Initially, they were refused entry on account of their race, but in 1941, when "things were getting pretty bad in England," the RAF opened its doors to West Indian volunteers. British Guiana's Cy Grant was among the first.[22] He became a navigator, but the majority were confined to less prestigious posts as ground crew.[23] For these thousands, and those recruited to work in allied services and at munitions factories in Britain, wartime provided the opportunity to travel overseas.

An unexpected by-product of the Second World War, then, was its effect on migration to Britain; it—not the sailing of the SS *Empire Windrush*—was the trigger of the postwar movement. Military service, very often in the RAF, brought many West Indian men out of the Caribbean to bases in England and Scotland. Whatever hardships they may have endured during their years in service, these men also formed attachments to people and places that ultimately drew them back to the "mother country," usually as civilians: "At the end of the war these men returned home to find a disappointing situation. Jobs were hard to find and the standard of living was much lower than that which they had enjoyed in Britain. There were no restrictions on their entry into Britain."[24] They had become cosmopolitan, an important point to remember about the artists under review here. For the most part, their frame of reference extended well beyond the British

---

20 Sam Selvon, *The Lonely Londoners* (1956; London: Longman, 1989), 121.

21 Earl Cameron in conversation with Dylan Cave, National Film Theatre, London, September 16, 2002. Interview originally published at http://www.bfi.org.uk and accessed July 12, 2010 but since removed.

22 Cy Grant interview in Phillips and Phillips, *Windrush*, 29.

23 For specific numbers of Caribbean recruits in various branches of the armed forces in these years, see James, "Black Experience in Twentieth-Century Britain," 366–67.

24 Davison, *West Indian Migrants*, 2.

Isles, to the Caribbean, North America, Europe, and Africa, because their lifetime travels took them there.

The war, as Wendy Webster argues, also affected native Britons' frame of reference, officially and in the media: "The 'people's war' marked a twentieth-century high point in inclusive imagery of Britishness," which encompassed imperial "partners" as newsreels "emphasized a devoted empire coming to Britain's aid at a time of national peril, demonstrating love and support for the motherland."[25] Military propaganda repeatedly celebrated the achievements of the Empire-Commonwealth as a whole, and, at least for a few years after the end of the war, this was not merely lip service. On the contrary, the British authorities continued to look to the colonies, and especially the dominions, to provide diplomatic and military support, raw materials, consumer markets, and—not least—continued international clout.

The British West Indies occupied a unique position in this matrix; although not nearly as valued, economically, culturally, or ethnically, as the "Old Commonwealth" dominions of Canada, Australia, and New Zealand, they possessed long-standing cultural ties that set them apart from African colonies (with the ambiguous exception of South Africa) and even India. A 1955 survey of colonial students in Britain, for instance, noted that

> whereas one-quarter of the Africans and of the students from the Asian and Mediterranean territories stated that ... they ... found difficulties [making friends with the English] because of a lack of common interests or contacts, only a small number of the West Indians thought that this was true of colonial students in general, and none of them considered it to be true of themselves. The views of the West Indians probably reflected the fact that, as a result of some centuries of association of the West Indian colonies with Britain, there is a very large measure of cultural identification.[26]

A contemporary joke reflected such official findings: an English family is hosting a young West Indian student in their home over the Christmas holiday. For the occasion, they go to great lengths to prepare for him an authentic English-style feast with all the trimmings. After the meal, the grateful guest says, "That was delicious. And it was so thoughtful of you to make me feel at home by preparing a traditional West Indian Christmas dinner."[27] For this reason, as Randall Hansen acknowledges, the Colonial Office initially fought against internal and external pressure to halt Caribbean migration in the 1950s. Its reasoning was that these migrants,

---

25 Webster, *Englishness and Empire*, 21, 23.

26 Political and Economic Planning Group, *Colonial Students in Britain* (London: PEP, June 1955), 88.

27 Source unknown.

like their counterparts in the dominions, "possessed the work ethic and cultural baggage requisite to integration in British society."[28] Initial news coverage of the *Windrush* settlers, as we will see below, also emphasized their connections to Britain, such as their history of RAF service, or their enthusiasm at arriving in the mother country.

The ideal of Commonwealth solidarity, under Britain's continued guidance, was a major inspiration for the passage of the BNA, which came into effect just a few months before the arrival of the *Windrush* and facilitated the creation of a permanent West Indian community in Britain. As Hansen reminds us, however, the near-simultaneity of these two events is largely coincidental, and related more to the availability of employment in postwar Britain.[29] The Act was a response to Canada's new, independent citizenship legislation, and was intended to ensure that citizens, of the "white" dominions in particular, retained the benefits of British subjecthood—free entry and citizenship in Britain.

In the process of reinforcing ties to the Old Commonwealth, the BNA also reified the rights of British subjecthood for citizens of the colonies (and ex-colonies, like India and Pakistan). The result was guaranteed ease of migration and settlement for the first wave of West Indians, a guarantee that made Britain an even more attractive destination. Many migrants came over with only their personal belongings, and five pounds to see them through until they found a job. Welfare state citizenship was automatic, and minimized the stresses associated with settlement and employment. Britain thus compared favorably to competing destinations, like the United States after 1952 and continental Europe.

Perhaps the most potent "pull" factor for potential migrants was the apparent plethora of jobs in Britain in the late 1940s and early 1950s. Although over the years, state-controlled companies like London Transport, British Rail, and the National Health Service actively recruited about four thousand Barbadians to work in Britain, the vast majority of migrants were attracted simply by the nation's promise of full employment; in fact, the real significance of the Barbadian scheme "lay in its potential to publicise the migration opportunity and thus to stimulate a movement of labour which lacked this degree of *formal* institutional organization."[30] Settlers' "expectation" of employment was one of the first qualities about which native Britons complained; it seemed to some observers that West Indians believed that the streets were paved with gold. As early as 1947, according to James, while on a Caribbean tour, the Welfare Officer of the Colonial Office tried to "dispel the idea that there were jobs to be had in England.

---

28 Hansen, *Citizenship and Immigration in Post-War Britain*, 18.
29 Ibid., 53–54.
30 Margaret Byron, *Post-War Caribbean Migration to Britain: The Unfinished Cycle* (Aldershot: Avebury, 1994), 78.

He informed incredulous governors and the local press that jobs seen advertised in the British newspapers were 'paper vacancies', not real jobs."[31] From a distance, the Colonial Office issued notices to be posted throughout the West Indies, cautioning naïve travelers about the difficulties of finding housing in Britain, the higher standards demanded from skilled labor, the need to carry adequate money for security, even the colder climate overseas. Despite such warnings, greater numbers of West Indian migrants arrived every year, and many were men and women who intended to bring over their children, spouses, and other relatives once they gained a foothold in the city. Thus they were not merely wooed by the advertisements of shipping lines and Caribbean travel agents; they were very often part of a pattern or cycle of migration that brought relatives and friends successively into its orbit. To attribute the movement to a single economic, cultural, or other factor "is to misunderstand the institutionalized nature of Caribbean migration behaviour."[32]

Background of the First Wave

Several of the artists I examine had some post-secondary education, and many were also from a middle-class background in the West Indies. These ambitious men and women disproportionately populated the earliest wave of postwar migrants, as well as the cadre of artists, writers, and performers who made a splash on the British scene. They also made up part of a small but significant group of settlers who had been coming to Britain from the Caribbean for decades—students. Although these people, many of whom relied on scholarships, were officially viewed as temporary residents, many in fact settled in Britain once they finished their schooling: Cy Grant trained first as a barrister, Ronald Moody as a dentist, Barry Reckord as a teacher and literary scholar. Perhaps this is unsurprising. Their middle-class education furnished them with a knowledge of, and respect for, British cultural traditions and institutions. But their middle-class backgrounds and English-style educations also gave them the skills to integrate themselves more readily into London's arts and entertainment world. Edric Connor had letters of introduction to the BBC, Cy Grant had an RAF officer's title, Barry Reckord had a Cambridge education, Ronald Moody a King's College education.

In many cases, these artists' middle-class education and social *milieux* also nurtured a measure of political awareness. By this I mean that they

---

31 James, "The Black Experience in Twentieth-Century Britain," 369.
32 Elizabeth M. Thomas-Hope, "Caribbean Diaspora, the Inheritance of Slavery: Migration from the Commonwealth Caribbean," in Colin Brock, ed., *The Caribbean in Europe: Aspects of the West Indian Experience in Britain, France and the Netherlands* (London: Frank Cass, 1986), 28–29.

understood the social, cultural, and economic consequences of Britain's imperial relationship, and they gained a critical understanding of the operation of racial inequality as something to be transcended. Moody is a fitting example of such an upbringing; his elder brother Harold became a prominent London doctor and founder of the League of Coloured Peoples. And while Ronald rejected his brother's politically charged path, he did so consciously, and for critical reasons. As a young woman, Pearl Nunez studied drama under Beryl McBernie, a woman who, unusually, emphasized Caribbean folklore and dance over European forms. This imbued the ambitious Nunez with a reverence for Caribbean performance that she later applied in London. Her future husband, Edric Connor, shared her consciousness—he arrived in London with a collection of unknown West Indian folk music that he wanted to expose to the world. In different ways, many of these early migrant-artists, whether they were students, professionals, or already artists, felt themselves to be ambassadors of their culture, of their race, of their colonial societies, and they acted accordingly. In his 1954 book *Colour Bar*, cricketer and Caribbean settler Learie Constantine noted this tendency among successful migrants, arguing that they become "obsessed with the desire to do something to help the less fortunate of their race, and to improve conditions for colored people and try to give them more equality in an unequal world."[33]

The darker side of this middle-class consciousness was a distaste for the actions and attitudes of poorer, less cultured migrants who, some felt, were responsible for giving the entire West Indian community in Britain a reputation for ignorance, bad manners, and bad behavior, for example by playing loud music into the night, smoking marijuana, and cavorting with low-lifes of every race and sex (the substance of such complaints is discussed below). Even the well-intentioned West Indian representatives of the Family Welfare Organization were at pains to distinguish between the cosmopolitan, skilled settler who integrated easily into London life, and those bumpkins who required further maintenance: "It is the ill equipped in education, the country dwellers who have no inkling of what the living conditions in London are like, who need constant help in solving their day-to-day problems."[34]

These middle-class artists' frequent appearances on the membership rolls of well-respected charitable and political associations, as well as at important local cultural events, reflect their desire (or perceived obligation) to represent the West Indian community positively. The rather posh British-Caribbean Association, for example, founded in 1959 and chaired jointly by two Members of Parliament, aimed to "encourage and stimulate all forms of mutual aid between the people of the West Indies (including British Guiana

33 Constantine, *Colour Bar*, 173.
34 Ruck et al., *The West Indian Comes to England*, 85.

and British Honduras) and the people of the United Kingdom." Council membership was divided between whites and West Indians, and cultural figures were prominent among the latter, and included Pearl Connor; writer Jan Carew; Kenneth Ablack, a BBC producer; and Theo Campbell, music scene doyen and owner of one of London's first black record shops.[35] These select individuals served on interracial committees like the British-Caribbean Association, explicitly taking the role of ambassadors of the community of West Indian migrants and settlers, and played a similar role at political and cultural events *within* that community. Carew, Connor, and Ablack, for instance, were also judges at London's 1960 Caribbean Carnival (still at this time helmed by Claudia Jones of the *West Indian Gazette*), along with novelists George Lamming and Sam Selvon and actress Nadia Cattouse.

But not all of this study's subjects were highly educated or from privileged backgrounds. Earl Cameron, perhaps the most famous West Indian film actor in this period, first came to England as a merchant seaman. He worked in London as a dishwasher and fell into professional acting by chance. Cameron refrained from overt political statements in his personal life and his performances, but he was one of the first to appear in films that addressed the issue of race relations in Britain. His portrayals, therefore, set the tone for future representations of West Indian settlers in the media.

By contrast, the calypso artists (or calypsonians) Egbert Moore, Aldwyn Roberts, and Rupert Grant (aka Lord Beginner, Lord Kitchener, and Lord Invader) were already established names in the Caribbean, and they carved a successful niche for themselves performing live music in London and throughout England. Kitchener eventually opened his own club in Manchester.[36] In Trinidad, calypso's home, the practice of calypso writing and singing was historically looked down upon by the island's middle class, due in part, no doubt, to its coarse subject matter; C. L. R. James remembers being forbidden as a child to visit the calypso tents during Carnival (see Chapter 3). But, by definition, calypso also engages with current events and hot-button social questions; although a far cry from the politically active, educated West Indian elite, Beginner, Kitchener, and Invader cultivated their own astute brand of cultural politics.

Whatever the educational and class backgrounds of Caribbean migrants, in the early postwar years the majority were young men. The proportion of women migrants did not surpass men until the early 1960s, as many joined male family members already settled with employment and lodgings.[37]

---

35 West Indian general correspondence, Clump #1, London Council of Social Service Correspondence file ACC/1888/116, London Metropolitan Archives (LMA).

36 Liner notes, *Klassic Kitchener Volume One*, Ice Records 931102, 1993, National Sound Archive (NSA), British Library, London.

37 James, "The Black Experience in Twentieth-Century Britain," 373.

However, Margaret Byron has debunked the notion that female migrants crossed the Atlantic merely as dependents of male relatives. Many made the decision to migrate on their own. As one Barbadian migrant recalled, "In those days, especially if you were a girl, you weren't expected to think for yourself. You had to be home at such and such a time: 'Where've you been?' 'Who've you been with?' all the time. I didn't even tell my mother I was going."[38] Others had husbands or sweethearts in Britain, but Byron stresses that regardless of their marital status, "women migrated primarily to work as opposed to moving as dependants, contrary to popular opinion."[39] Often they worked outside the home and earned wages for the first time in Britain, and sent remittances home to help support relatives—older parents and younger siblings, as well as young children.[40] According to Byron, postwar migration to Britain set a precedent, for it was the first Caribbean movement in which female migration was not seen as auxiliary to or dependent on the migration of men. Thus, these women were primarily motivated by a desire for social mobility and better employment or education—the same "pull" factors that motivated their male counterparts.

Indeed, although only a few women appear in this study, they all migrated on their own, explicitly for the purposes of educational or professional advancement. Claudia Jones, active communist and editor of London's *West Indian Gazette*, and Una Marson, BBC broadcaster, are already the subjects of scholarly studies, and both possessed considerable experience in their fields before they arrived in England.[41] Pearl Nunez first came to London in 1948 to study law at the University of London, although she was swept into the entertainment world as a result of her courtship with singer Edric Connor, whom she later married. Others, like Connor, migrated as promising students, including pianist Winifred Atwell, textile

---

38 Marie Pilgrim quoted in Western, *A Passage to England*, 46–47.

39 Margaret Byron, "Migration, Work and Gender: The case of Post-War Labour Migration from the Caribbean to Britain," in Mary Chamberlain, ed., *Caribbean Migration: Globalised Identities* (London and New York: Routledge, 1998), 220.

40 To give a partial sense of the migration of wealth from Britain to the Caribbean, in 1959 the *New Statesman* reported that the Jamaican General Post Office received £177,933 in postal money orders from Jamaican migrants in the United Kingdom in April 1956 and £244,375 in May 1957. See Yehudi A. Cohen, "Passage to Notting Hill," *New Statesman* (July 18, 1959), 72.

41 See Johnson, "I Think of My Mother"; Marika Sherwood with Donald Hinds, Colin Prescod, and the 1996 Claudia Jones Symposium, *Claudia Jones: A Life in Exile* (London: Lawrence & Wishart, 1999); Delia Jarrett-Macauley, *The Life of Una Marson, 1905–65* (Manchester University Press, 1998); Glyne Griffith, "'This is London Calling the West Indies': The BBC's *Caribbean Voices*," in Bill Schwarz, ed., *West Indian Intellectuals in Britain* (Manchester: Manchester University Press, 2003), 196–208.

designer Althea McNish, and singer Pearl Prescod. But all of these women possessed the ambition and wherewithal to strike out independently, a trait they shared with the men who figure prominently in my research. And in great measure they, too, expressed a subtle but razor-sharp politics through their cultural work.

Which brings us to the question of "identity," that horrible term that can contain so many meanings that it renders itself moot. Here I am writing of national and racial identity; migrants' sense of their history and roots. It should probably not surprise us that the evidence paints no coherent picture. Indeed, one of the projects of some of the artists featured in this study, even (or especially) after their settlement in Britain, was to articulate a stronger sense of a shared "West Indian" identity—the cultural counterpart, perhaps, to the political drive for West Indies Federation. But if it isn't possible to get a clear sense of what these national or racial identities *were* at mid-century, we can perhaps get a sense of what they *weren't*. Stuart Hall, for example, has remarked:

> When I was growing up in the 1940s and 1950s as a child in Kingston ... I never once heard a single person refer to themselves or to others as, in some way, or as having been at some time in the past, 'African'. It was only in the 1970s that this Afro-Caribbean identity became historically available to the great majority of Jamaican people, at home and abroad.[42]

Not only was an African identity off the radar; relatively few migrants of the 1940s and '50s would have even thought of themselves as "black"—even if their white British hosts did. Blackness referred to skin tone instead of an imagined community.

"Britishness" (or "Englishness"), on the other hand, seemed to operate as a kind default identification, simply because it was so-called British values and history that were taught and practiced in Caribbean education. Phillips and Phillips interviewee Vince Reid confessed, "I knew more about England than I did about Jamaica. I mean, I knew absolutely nothing about Jamaica." And Cy Grant, who appears in Chapter 2 of this book, remarked:

> I didn't have any strong sense of British identity. ... But it's the only identity I had, because people from the Caribbean are not from the Caribbean originally. ... And I didn't have any strong great feeling for Guyana. But at that time, you know one didn't confront issues of identity.[43]

---

42 Stuart Hall, "Cultural Identity and Diaspora," in Jonathan Rutherford, ed., *Identity: Community, Culture, Difference* (London: Lawrence & Wishart, 1990), 231.

43 Vince Reid and Cy Grant quoted in Phillips and Phillips, *Windrush*, 12–13.

One of John Western's Barbadian interviewees put it this way: "You must appreciate the Englishness of the Barbadian. That's why we can love the British despite the hassles. We are what we are." Many have commented on the fact that Caribbean history and culture were never taught in school.

Whether or not they espoused a neat and tidy personal politics, however, those West Indians who pursued a career in entertainment and the arts became the public face of their fellow settlers, the majority of whom filled much humbler posts as blue- and white-collar workers. Despite the considerable ambition, skills, and education of the earliest wave of migrants, they were, more often than not, funneled into low-status jobs as porters, drivers, and unskilled labor.

Living in London

The ambiguity with which British employers expressed their aversion to West Indian employees aptly reflects the posturing of the media, government, and much of the public at large toward the growth of the West Indian settler community. It has proved challenging for scholars to untangle the strands of feeling that comprised the ambivalent reaction of native Britons to non-white immigration from the colonies and ex-colonies in the 1950s and 1960s. At different moments, different threads of nationalistic and political ideology were employed to buttress the case for West Indian belonging to or exclusion from the cozy "British" community. I will look at a few of these threads in turn, to give a sense of the ideological or imaginative context of West Indian migration and settlement.

From war's end until the mid-1950s, London papers, newsreels, television coverage, and official publications showed Caribbean migration in a relatively positive light. In many cases, they portrayed settlers as simultaneously exotic and part of the "family." West Indians' skin color, accents, clothing, and cultural traditions distinguished them from the crowd, but the media consistently emphasized their loyalty to the Crown and feeling of kinship toward the "mother country."

Reception and Representations of West Indian Settlers
During these years, Britons were still basking in the comforting afterglow of military victory. The nature of this victory was such that it not only acknowledged the efforts of millions of colonial soldiers and civilians, but also validated the status of Great Britain as a benevolent imperial leader. As a result, the media usually positioned the arrival of the earliest waves of migrants in the context of their recent military service. Many were ex-RAF men, and they were often singled out for a newsreel profile or brief interview as they made their way off the boat. A now iconic newsreel documenting the arrival of the *Empire Windrush* in 1948 began by stating that of the five hundred "Jamaicans" on board, "Many are ex-servicemen who know

England. They served this country well."[44] Their participation in the war made explicit their imperial fidelity and fitness for the British citizenship they would gain upon arrival. These settlers were living products of the British experiment in liberal imperialism, and the media and government were keen to demonstrate the mutual benefits of colonial migration, as well as the magnanimity of native Britons in welcoming the new settlers: "Prodded by public opinion, the Colonial Office gives them a more cordial reception than was at first envisaged. Many are to be found jobs." The Pathé script implies here the active intervention of ordinary people in the official treatment of these "citizens of the British Empire."[45]

By the middle of the 1950s, representations had shifted, as West Indian migration became less of a novelty and members of the public—native and West Indian—began expressing complaints. Newsreels now betrayed a strained tone as they conceded the existence of racial tension and controversy over the place of migrants in the workforce and housing market. Migrants were no longer portrayed as the brightest and most ambitious of their communities, but primarily as those who wanted to escape poverty and unemployment. Meanwhile, the emphasis on Britain's liberal legacy, once so proud and confident, now served as a stern reminder of its responsibility toward unfortunates in the colonies:

> Already their coming has caused a national controversy, but one point must always be borne in mind: *whatever our feelings*, we cannot deny them entry, for all are British citizens and, as such, are entitled to the identical rights of any member of the Empire. ... [shot of disembarking West Indians, struggling against the harsh winds] A pathetic sight. Yet they ask no pity from us, only that we respect that all human beings are born free and equal in dignity and rights. Does the answer to these Britishers' problems lie in Britain, or in the West Indies? And yet perhaps if we dig deep enough, we may find the solution hidden within the conscience of us all.[46]

Media coverage like this continued to insist on the liberalism and humanity of Britain's official immigration policy, even as it rebranded West Indian migration as a "problem," and as policy reacted by dramatically curtailing the entry of non-white colonial people in 1962.

Operating in tension with the Commonwealth ideal, which at least allowed for the possibility of non-white colonial Britishness, was the

---

44 "Pathé Reporter Meets Bergman and Hitchcock," Pathé newsreel (June 24, 1948): http://britishpathe.com/record.php?id=27376; accessed September 28, 2009.

45 Ibid.

46 "Our Jamaican Problem," Pathé newsreel (January 17, 1955): http://britishpathe.com/record.php?id=38974; accessed September 20, 2009. Emphasis added.

"little England" mentality that, according to scholars like Chris Waters, assumed its modern form in the interwar period but was illuminated in the 1950s by social surveyors like Geoffrey Gorer and Sheila Patterson. They argued that English people shied away from black settlers, not from racial prejudice, but "due to an innate reserve and a proclivity to keep themselves to themselves."[47] This kinder, gentler xenophobia—kinder because it purportedly stemmed from an inborn trait instead of a belief in racial superiority, and gentler because it rarely manifested in the form of violent acts—provided the ideological framework for explaining the everyday behavior of many white Britons toward the new settlers, when the latter applied for jobs or lodging, or even walked down the street.

The famous Trinidadian cricketer Learie Constantine, who, in addition to his cricketing fame, worked as a liaison officer at the Ministry of Labour, echoed the sentiments of many of his countrymen when he wrote of Britain's unofficial color bar that manifested itself most often simply in whites' avoidance of black people:

> After practically twenty-five years' residence in England, where I have made innumerable white friends, I still think it would be just to say that almost the entire population of Britain really expect the coloured man to live in an inferior area devoted to coloured people, and not to have free and open choice of a living-place. Most British people would be quite unwilling for a black man to enter their homes, nor would they wish to work with one as a colleague, nor stand shoulder to shoulder with one at a factory bench. ... Hardly any Englishwomen and not more than a small proportion of Englishmen would sit at a restaurant table with a coloured man or woman, and inter-racial marriage is considered almost universally to be out of the question.[48]

The coldness of many white Britons toward West Indians, just another symptom of their innate "reserve," was aptly summed up in the poignant title of a local newspaper article: "Friendship Is Number One Problem For West Indians—More Than Housing."[49] Similarly, a 1955 survey of colonial students from across the globe reflected that "many students found the reserve of the English the greatest single obstacle to making friends with them."[50] It did not elaborate on possible explanations for such reticence.

---

47   Waters, "'Dark Strangers' in Our Midst," 223.
48   Constantine, *Colour Bar*, 67.
49   *Kensington News* (May 20, 1960), 10, ACC/1888/116, London Council of Social Service Correspondence File, LMA.
50   PEP, *Colonial Students in Britain*, 90.

Challenges of Settlement: Home

Both contemporary observers and historians have tended to highlight sensationalized stories of outright hostility toward non-whites—the noisy violence of the Notting Hill riots, or the quiet violence of window signs that read, "No coloured, no Irish, no dogs." It is easy enough to find evidence of extreme cultural and biological racism rearing its head in urban Britain, especially in the aftermath of Notting Hill, an event that demonstrated the reality and persistence of white violence against colonial migrants. (I will touch upon a few instances later in this chapter.)

More common, though, are recollections of inquiring at a lodging house only to get the polite response, "The room has just been let," or "I don't mind, but my other tenants or neighbours might object."[51] Similarly, it was not uncommon for a West Indian applicant to receive an encouraging response from a potential employer on the telephone, only to be rebuffed on some convenient pretext once they appeared in person. One Jamaican respondent for a sociological study, who had moved to London in the 1950s, lamented, "You phone up a place and they say experience is not essential and you go there and they say someone else just take it. Nice on the phone and then you go. It's terrible looking for a job, so I just stay in the one I have now. It happen so often, it make you sick."[52] West Indians complained that native Britons could be perfectly polite, even friendly, if you met them on the street, but very few would invite you into their home or social circle.

Some prospective landladies, employers, and white neighbors offered more direct explanations for their reluctance to engage colonial settlers, complaining that they were lazy, undisciplined, loitered on the street, had too many guests, or had dirty living habits. One person wrote to the *New Statesman*: "Do you know what Notting Hill is like since the advent of the West Indians? Have you asked the police of the crime increase— the brothels, marijuana parties, the basement clubs, the obscenities?"[53] Another resident's letter of complaint found its way into a Colonial Office file:

Can they be taught that if they wish to be respected and live in peace they <u>must</u> be considerate to their neighbours. They always shout across the street and bang car doors late at night, and on Monday last Jamaicans in our road had a party. We had our mid-day lunch in our back room which is farthest away from them to what sounded like the thump of an

51 Ruck et al., *The West Indian Comes to England*, 82.

52 Female respondent quoted in Nancy Foner, *Jamaica Farewell: Jamaican Migrants in London* (Berkeley and Los Angeles: University of California Press, 1978), 44–45.

53 R. Thompson, Letter to the Editor, *News Statesman* (May 16, 1959); Clump #2: Press Clippings, ACC/1888/116, West Indian press cuttings, 1959–60, LMA.

engine in our front room, but which in reality was their music coming from 4 speakers of, I believe, the stereophonic type.[54]

It may seem astonishing that a complaint of this type made its way to the Colonial Office, but it gives the lie to the official spin put on the Notting Hill (and Nottingham) riots at the time: that they were an anomaly, in no way symptomatic of widespread racism. The Colonial Office, at least, interpreted evidence like this resident's complaint in terms of race and colonial migration. The resident's language ("Can they be *taught*"), furthermore, indicates that ordinary citizens too felt such troubles to be an "official" problem to be dealt with.

In more general terms, the *New Statesman*, in a 1959 article entitled "Background to Trouble," also pointed to the exacerbating influence of cultural difference on tensions caused by overcrowding and poor living conditions in London's worst neighborhoods:

> People of one race and similar habits would have difficulty in living at peace in such an environment; but the difficulties are greatly increased when one group, the West Indians, have different habits from their neighbours. These West Indians like noise and play their juke-boxes late into the night. They like to wear gaudy colours. They are shrewd bargainers who insist on handling the fruit in the market before they will buy it. Almost more exasperating still, instead of being the downtrodden inferiors of whom their white readers used to read at school, they are assured, enterprising and in other ways superior to at least some of the English and Irish with whom they now find themselves living.[55]

The media tended to echo this article's emphasis on jealousy when describing the attitudes and motivations of hostile residents, especially youths. A 1959 report drawn up by the Metropolitan Police characterized the majority of migrants as "simple minded people, extremely naive, sadly mis-informed and ill-equipped to start a new life in this country," but singled out the pernicious effect of "a small minority which led an idle life and lived on the immoral earnings of white and coloured women. They attracted hostility ... by their flashy attire, arrogance and apparent affluence, and their boisterous home life, natural to them but alien to their white neighbours."[56] The same year, after Antiguan settler Kelso Cochrane

---

54 Letter, Mrs. May Jackson (August 6, 1959), CO 1031/2543, Public Record Office (PRO), National Archives, Kew.

55 J. P. W. Mallalieu, "Background to Trouble," *New Statesman* (July 11, 1959), 40; Clump #2: Press Clippings, ACC/1888/116, LMA.

56 Metropolitan Police Special Report on Racial Tension (May 28, 1959), 2–3; HO 325/9, PRO.

was murdered in what many believed to be a racially motivated attack, *The Times* echoed the position of the police when it remarked:

> Many of the complaints about the West Indians appear to arise out of jealousy. Either their cars or their houses are said to be bigger and better than those of their white neighbours. Another source of complaint is the allegation that the coloured people join together to buy houses and then try to force out the white tenants.[57]

The preferred public and media position denounced extremists like Mosley and his ilk, but found explanations for racial tension in the personal/cultural "habits" of West Indians. These habits were always overgeneralized and included noise-making, prostitution and crime, illegitimacy, and a certain flashiness of both style and disposition. Echoing the social surveys of the black community in this period, the media positioned themselves as fair-minded, so it was the classically "non-English" qualities of the migrants that they most often noted.

The housing woes of new settlers extended beyond the experience of personal prejudice from landlords and ladies. Most of the latter would not rent to West Indians (or Africans) at all. Those who did, often charged exorbitant rents. Settlers, usually confined to the poorest-paid occupations, crowded their families into the available accommodation. One Christian welfare worker commented at a 1956 conference:

> There have been terrible examples in Lambeth of overcrowding where it was often not even a case of one room for the family but sometimes shared beds. How was it possible to meet the need? Very few of the mothers had any desire, in spite of the difficult conditions here, to return or to send their children back to the West Indies. They were anxious that the children should have the opportunities they themselves did not have in the West Indies.[58]

From a very different perspective, photographer and music aficionado Val Wilmer remembered visiting a Jamaican trombonist's bedsit, where he shared a precious fruitcake sent to him by relatives at home:

> Like many of the places where Black people lived in Britain then, it seemed claustrophobic to me. The sturdy old-fashioned bed groaned under the weight of the covers and took up most of the room, making

---

57 "Race Tension Increased by Murder," *The Times* (May 19, 1959); Clump #2: Press Clippings, ACC/1888/116, LMA.

58 Miss M. Raynes (Southwark Diocesan Association) quoted in summary of LCSS conference report (June 28, 1956), summary, 9, West Indian general correspondence, ACC/1888/116, LMA.

freedom of movement difficult around it. A couple of wardrobes were piled high with suitcases and the inevitable brassbound trunk, effectively blocking out much of the light that came through the heavily-curtained window. ... I think it was in places like these that I began to understand, in an emotional rather than intellectual way, something of what it must mean to be separated from one's culture and homeland.[59]

Meanwhile, the widespread demand for council housing, and the long waiting lists that came with it, inflamed the ire of native whites who found themselves behind a West Indian family in the housing queue, especially if that family was deemed in special need of lodging. Because the new settlers became naturalized British citizens upon entry, the authorities assessed their applications for council houses on the same basis as any British family. Some, however, interpreted this approach as hindering the housing prospects—even the entitlement—of those born and bred in the British Isles. In 1955, according to Lambeth's mayor, there were about ten thousand people on the waiting list for housing, "and, naturally, a further Jamaican influx is not favorable."[60] Four years later, Gallup recorded that more than half of their survey (fifty-four percent) did not think that "coloured people from the Commonwealth should be admitted to council housing lists on the same condition as people born in Britain." The housing issue, according to the polls, was considerably more hotly contested than the competition for jobs (regarding which, almost half were in favor of equal opportunity).[61]

Even more insidious is the evidence suggesting that real estate agents employed exploitative and illegal (or quasi-legal) tactics to deter prospective West Indian tenants and buyers from settling in particular areas of London. A memo from the Welfare Sub-Committee of the British-Caribbean Association listed eleven varieties of corrupt practice, and warned that they only exacerbated ill feeling toward West Indian settlers by suggesting that overcrowding was a result of settler preference. Instead, the committee astutely suggested that

> if estate agents are in fact only suggesting property in certain areas and streets usually where there are West Indians living and usually in decaying districts they are in fact directing and to some extent controlling the pattern of settlement of West Indians. They are also encouraging the idea that West Indians reduce the value of property

---

59 Val Wilmer, *Mama Said There'd Be Days Like This: My Life in the Jazz World* (London: The Women's Press, 1989), 49.

60 "Our Jamaican Problem," Pathé newsreel.

61 Gallup poll on "Race Relations" (September 1958), in George H. Gallup, ed., *The Gallup International Public Opinion Polls: Great Britain, 1937–1975* (New York: Random House, 1976), 477–78.

in the neighbourhood (in practice we have considerable evidence of prices rising considerably). Thus the distribution is being controlled by <u>commercial</u> interests and not by enlightened social and political sections of society.[62]

The results of this investigation provide an inkling of the degree to which the hidden or invisible actions of commercial agents could have a visible impact on popular evaluations of West Indian character.

Challenges of Settlement: Work

Similarly, although the postwar wave of West Indian migration began during a period of full employment, by about the middle 1950s the competition for good jobs meant that whites often resented the incursion of colonial workers. They expressed these feelings loudest when a particular company hired multiple non-white workers, or when it appeared that colonials were beginning to "color" the ranks of a particular industry. When a Birmingham bus company hired an Indian man as a trainee conductor in 1955, white employees went on strike. While they argued that their actions were motivated by the fear that "extra workers would cut their own overtime earnings," and not by racial prejudice,[63] the trainee's non-whiteness was what made him such an obvious—and apparently objectionable—addition to the payroll. In the areas of both housing and employment, the origin, and especially skin color, of new settlers made *visible* their insertion into the machinery of British society. Such visibility made it easy for the media to position West Indians as a problem that needed resolving, instead of equally entitled members of the British polity.

In a similar fashion, employers complained that West Indians' skills were not up to the English standard (in blue-collar jobs), or that their accents were too difficult to understand (in white-collar jobs). In a 1965 memo, a BBC appointments executive complained that the majority of colored applicants for clerical positions were not "up to standard" because they found it "difficult to understand or make themselves understood on the telephone."[64] At a 1956 conference on the dubious theme of "Problems arising in London as a result of West Indian Migration to Great Britain," representatives of the city's various social service associations attempted to

---

62 Memorandum from the Welfare Sub-Committee of the British-Caribbean Association (October 31, 1960), ACC/1888/116, LMA. The fact that the committee found evidence of rising property values in areas populated by West Indians suggests the high demand for accommodation by West Indian settlers.

63 "News Flashes—West Bromwich Bus Strike," Pathé newsreel (March 3, 1955): available at http://britishpathe.com/record.php?id=39072; accessed September 20, 2009.

64 Memo, R. M. J. Gillott, Assistant Head of Appointments Department to L. G. Thirkell, Controller, Staff Training and Appointments (February 23, 1965), R49/1,095/1—Coloured People Employment in BBC; WAC.

hash out some of the challenges for West Indian settlers. Its summary, while acknowledging the reality of these challenges, too often chalked them up to cultural differences and West Indian ignorance of common British customs and attitudes concerning, among other things, the operation of trade unions:

> West Indians frequently fail to understand the place of Trade Unionism in this country. They fail to realise the discipline on which the strength of the Unions is based, and the high standards of skill which the unions demand from their membership. Hence the West Indian is often unaware of the desirability of joining a Union while, on the other hand, he may be refused membership of a craft union despite a degree of skill which seemed adequate in the West Indies. Thus, although the official policy of British trade Unions is opposed to racial discrimination, it may often appear to the migrant that race prejudice prevents him from getting a job (for which union membership is necessary) or from joining a union. This feeling had been stimulated by difficulties which had occurred with some unions: to some British workmen any foreigner represented a threat of unemployment.[65]

It is interesting that even the xenophobia of "British workmen" is here distinguished from what was labeled "irrational" race prejudice earlier in the document. Similarly, in the minutes of the conference, welfare liaison officer Ivo de Souza (himself a West Indian) noted:

> In many cases, immigrant workers had found it difficult to join [a union]. Sometimes the convenors were absent or the secretaries away sick and it was possible that the trade unions themselves were not anxious to accept the West Indians as union members. They might not want to accept the responsibility of taking sides if a conflict arose between coloured and white workers as to who should be retained in a job. It was very necessary that people in the West Indies should be told of the importance of joining unions.[66]

De Souza was very reticent here, conceding only the *possibility* of union anxiety at the prospect of colored membership, and concluding by placing the onus on West Indian workers. But his remark highlights the persistent and petty difficulties that West Indians faced when attempting to penetrate the unions. It also suggests that union officials, as well as employers and landladies, feared that "taking on" colored people would trigger conflict and hostility within the ranks.

---

65 Summary of LCSS conference report (June 28, 1956), summary, 3, West Indian general correspondence, ACC/1888/116, LMA.

66 Ibid.

Challenges of Settlement: Race Knowledge

Many of the challenges West Indian migrants faced, as we have seen, were a result of native British ignorance and misinformation or social and cultural prejudice about the perceived education, habits, and leisure pursuits of the new settlers. There was another dimension to this racism that was (pseudo-) scientific or biological in nature. It was at times the expression of these beliefs that were the most panicked and vitriolic, and although publicly eschewed by officialdom, there is evidence to suggest that both ordinary individuals and individuals in the media and government continued to be influenced by these beliefs, with tangible results.

In 1950 the United Nations Educational, Scientific, and Cultural Organization (UNESCO), still reeling from the horrors of the Second World War, and the Holocaust in particular, released its *Statement on Race*, which announced:

> The scientific material available to us at present does not justify the conclusion that inherited genetic differences are a major factor in producing the differences between the cultures and the cultural achievements of different peoples or groups. It does indicate, however, that the history of the cultural experience which each group has undergone is the major factor in explaining such differences. The one trait which above all others has been at a premium in the evolution of men's mental characters has been educability, plasticity.[67]

UNESCO's statement is a document representative of mid-century liberalism, particularly in its presentation of a social, versus biological, definition of race, and its emphasis on educability, which implies that racial difference is indoctrinated and subject to change. According to this logic, the negative social effects of racial difference—and racism—could be "educated" away. In fact, as Gavin Schaffer has remarked, the statement provoked a backlash from scientists, who felt it ignored an entire body of racial science.[68]

A look at the British media in the '50s and '60s makes it clear that UNESCO's insistence on a social definition of race was not fully absorbed. Alongside the mild-mannered friendship councils and "no colour bar" dances, there was vehement local opposition to migration and integration. By 1959, for instance, the White Defence League had set up shop in the Notting Hill Gate neighborhood, offering, as one representative put it, "a constitutional political outlet" for opponents of black migration, those who shared the League's fear of "mass interbreeding": "Insofar as we believe that the civilization and culture of our country is the product of our race, we

---

67 UNESCO's *Statement on Race*, quoted in Gavin Schaffer, *Racial Science and British Society, 1930–62* (Houndmills: Palgrave Macmillan, 2008), 122–23.

68 Schaffer, *Racial Science and British Society*, 123.

feel that if we have a mulatto population in the future, that must mean the downfall of the civilization and culture of our country which we hold so dear."[69] The League thus defined British culture—"civilization"—in crudely conceived biological terms.

But even this vitriol had its milder, but equally insidious, counterpart in the media's representation of mixed-race sexual relations. The *Sunday Times*, hardly an organ of cheap sensationalism, published a series in 1960 called "Breaking Down the Barriers: Coloured People in Britain," in which it discussed the "problem" of illegitimate children of such unions:

> These children of mixed race are in a worse plight than the wholly coloured ones. The white mother often refuses to keep her baby, who may be one of several bastards. She may have left the father in search of further adventures or the child may have been the result of a chance encounter. ... White parents are reluctant to adopt a child of mixed descent and suitable coloured families usually have enough children of their own to support. The problem of the illegitimate child of mixed race who is spurned by his parents is one of the most difficult in the present situation.[70]

In one short paragraph, the *Sunday Times* followed a rationale based on several dubious and pernicious assumptions, none of which it made explicit. First, the article implies that all (or the vast majority) of mixed-race children were borne by a white mother and black father. Second, it strongly suggests that these mothers were, as a rule, sexually promiscuous and irresponsible, engaging in "chance encounters" and giving birth to "several bastards." Third, it obliquely hints at the uncontrolled growth of non-white families when it states that they "usually have enough children of their own to support." This reason contrasted with the simpler "reluctance" of white couples to adopt mixed-race children, a position that is itself left unquestioned. The media viewed the "threat" of miscegenation, as this article suggests, as perhaps the most controversial consequence of black settlement.

There is also evidence that the British public at large shared this feeling. A 1959 Gallup poll on the subject of race relations, for instance, found that while seventy percent of respondents claimed that they would not move if "coloured people came to live next door," almost the same proportion (seventy-one percent) disapproved of "marriage between white and coloured

---

69 Mr. Jordan of the White Defence League, interviewed in "Racial Troubles in Notting Hill," Pathé news footage (1959): available at http://britishpathe.com/record.php?id=64317; accessed September 20, 2009.

70 "Breaking Down the Barriers: Coloured People in Britain—3," *Sunday Times* (June 5, 1960), 22; ACC/1888/116, LMA.

people."[71] Actress and singer Nadia Cattouse, for one, herself married to a white Englishman, wrote to BBC *Woman's Hour* on the "superstition and fear" surrounding mixed marriages (she was later interviewed on the subject). In her letter she recalled, first, that Britons have "for generations indulged in the custom and still do at home—and abroad, quite often without the benefit of a legal ceremony," but concluded by speculating that those involved in interracial unions "are perhaps persons blessed with a larger ration of character and commonsense than the average couple, for the obstacles they face—socially created ones—can be quite damaging to those of lesser qualities." Cattouse was one of the very few drawing a positive image of interracial unions at this time.[72]

Biological fears around race were not expressed only in rhetoric. While the most shameful—and unfashionable—aspects of this kind of racism were suppressed in official pronouncements, Schaffer has shown that they played a part in government debates and decisions about New Commonwealth migration. A Committee of Ministers report stated, "We clearly cannot undertake to absorb in such a densely populated island inhabited by a different racial strain all the coloured immigrants who may wish to come here."[73] That was in 1956, long before the government openly acknowledged any internal discussion about immigration restriction.

To say that non-white settlers in Britain were portrayed as a problem obscures the differences between the reactions of the British government, the mainstream media, and the general public, each of which possessed their own multiple convictions about the nature of the British community. Between the BNA of 1948—which granted automatic British citizenship to any subject of the British Empire and Commonwealth who migrated to Britain—and the first Commonwealth Immigrants Act of 1962—which reversed the provisions of the BNA and effectively restricted the entry of non-white subjects to a trickle—official opinion made what appeared to be a dramatic about-face but was actually a subtler shift accentuated by the diminished clout of particular groups within the government, notably the Colonial Office. Randall Hansen argues that it was not until the arrival of several hundred West Indian migrants on the *Windrush* that officials fully grasped the implications of the BNA—that it enabled mass migration from the New Commonwealth as well as the Old, and that it made migration more enticing to the former than the latter. At that point, there arose a growing divergence within the government between those (more or less)

---

71 Gallup poll on "Race Relations" (September 1958), *The Gallup International Public Opinion Polls*, 477–78. Among respondents aged sixteen to twenty years, only fifty-five percent disapproved of mixed-race marriages.

72 Letter, Nadia Lindup (Cattouse) to BBC *Woman's Hour*, received November 24, 1958, RCONT 1—Nadia Cattouse, Artists File 1, WAC.

73 Quoted in Schaffer, *Racial Science and British Society.*

uncomfortable with the implications of the uncontrolled migration of non-whites, and those stridently committed to the principle of imperial unity in the form of free movement and the New Commonwealth ideal. According to Hansen, the Colonial Office remained most committed to this ideal, a commitment manifested by its attempts to protect the citizenship rights of colonial settlers in Britain and to keep the gates open for West Indians, with whom it believed Britain shared important historic ties. The Cabinet, ministries, and Foreign Office, by contrast, grew increasingly impatient with free colonial migration as Britain's imperial role and international clout shrank. Kathleen Paul has usefully employed the oft-repeated trope of the imperial "family" to trace the government's preferential attitude toward different parts of Europe and the empire in this period; she argues that while official policy embraced all Old and New Commonwealth nations as part of the seemingly cozy British community, some nations were praised as "kith and kin" while others, especially those of India, Africa, and the Caribbean, were declared closer to adopted sons and daughters. The translation of such images into action meant that by the 1960s non-white colonials still under British imperial rule had more difficulty acquiring citizenship within Britain than settlers of Irish descent. By dint of their "race," the Irish were deemed closer brothers to the British, their declared political enemies.[74]

In the same study, Paul avers that much of what has been viewed as *popular* racial prejudice in fact originated in official propaganda along the lines discussed above. But although the government increasingly betrayed its anxiety over the issue of colonial migration, culminating in its passage of the Commonwealth Immigrants Act, its actions alone cannot account for the attitudes and actions of the general public, which ranged from indifference to curiosity, acceptance, and hostility.

It is impossible to accurately capture the popular response in Britain to Caribbean migration in these years, due largely to the inherent biases of available evidence. Media sources tend to be sensationalist, emphasizing controversy and conflict, prejudice and violence—for example, coverage of the immigration debate in and outside of Parliament, and the Notting Hill riots in 1958. The mainstream media also privileged majority perspectives, so that it dwelt on the Notting Hill riots but gave little exposure to the 1959 murder of Antiguan Kelso Cochrane, though this event served as an outraged rallying cry for the Caribbean community. Another vital historical source is the recorded memories of "ordinary" Britons. There is a growing collection of interviews and published histories of first- and second-generation Caribbean migrants,[75] but far fewer accounts of white

74   See Hansen, *Citizenship and Immigration in Post-War Britain*; Paul, *Whitewashing Britain*.

75   See, e.g., Phillips and Phillips, *Windrush*; Western, *A Passage to England*; Ethnic Communities Oral History Project, *The Motherland Calls: African Caribbean*

Britons' reactions to their Caribbean neighbors, unless their lives were particularly shaped by the new arrivals. (White British musicians, for example, fondly remembered the important influence of West Indian artists like the bandleader Ken "Snakehips" Johnson on the urban jazz scene.)[76] But evocative, nuanced accounts are rare. Nonetheless, it is possible to glean a range of impressions from interviews, memoirs, and heavily filtered sources like newspapers, newsreels, and popular surveys.

A prominent element of popular British attitudes toward migrants, especially in the 1940s and 1950s, was ignorance, an ignorance that could be staggering in light of Britain's centuries-long connection to the West Indies. Although Peter Fryer and others have examined the historic presence of black communities throughout Britain, dating back at least to the Elizabethan period, most white Britons viewed their nation and culture as "white" until sometime during the postwar period, when the bulk of Caribbean, South Asian, and African migration took place. Gradually, the media and government registered this demographic shift in the news, on television and film, and, belatedly, in official images and depictions of British life.

But just as West Indian settlers had migrated with erroneous ideas about the mother country—some were astonished to see white people sweeping the streets—white Britons' initial preconceptions of West Indians were often informed by everything *but* first-hand experience; a 1955 Gallup poll recorded that fifty-eight percent of respondents had never known "any coloured people." (Three years later, in the aftermath of the Notting Hill riots and their radicalizing effect on public opinion concerning race, that proportion was still fifty-one percent.)[77] As Kenneth Little noted at the time, Britain's long and storied relationship with African, Asian, and West Indian societies left an ambivalent imprint on the imperial center itself:

> This complicated background of overseas exploration, slave trading, colonial expansion, and scientific rationalization helps us to understand the ambivalent nature of modern racial attitudes in Britain. They are a mixture of apathy and toleration because a large number of British people have never had personal contact with a coloured person and have little interest in or concern with the colonies.[78]

Experiences (Hammersmith and Fulham Community History Series, No. 4/ECOHP, 1989); Notting Dale Urban Studies Centre, ed., *"Sorry No Vacancies": Life Stories of Senior Citizens from the Caribbean* (London: Notting Dale Urban Studies Centre, 1992); Tony Sewell, *Keep on Moving: The Windrush Legacy* (London: Voice Enterprises Ltd., 1998).

76 See "The History of Black British Jazz," NSA lecture series, B9245.

77 Gallup polls on "Race Relations" (April 1955 and September 1958), *The Gallup International Public Opinion Polls*, 349, 478.

78 Kenneth L. Little, *Race and Society* (1965; Paris: UNESCO, 1958), 44–45.

These lapses in knowledge at times verged on the fantastical, as when one settler, newly arrived in 1950, was approached by a boy who, acting on information supplied by his parents, wanted to see his tail.[79] A more common example of native ignorance was the belief that West Indians spoke a different language. Ros Howells, who settled in South London in 1951, described an interview for a local library job as "quite amazing because people were complimenting me on my English. Well, I'd never spoken any other language, and some of the people who were speaking to me were not, in my opinion anyway, speaking good English themselves."[80] Karen Sands-O'Connor, in her analysis of West Indian imagery in British children's books, notes that until the aftermath of the first Commonwealth Immigrants Act and the independence of Jamaica and Trinidad and Tobago in 1962, novels featuring West Indians were substantially similar to those of the prewar period—adventure tales occurring in a "nonspecific, largely empty" Caribbean setting. In them, West Indians "stayed in the West Indies, and their British counterparts eventually returned home (albeit usually with a substantial profit)." It was not until the 1970s that significant numbers of books appeared that realistically portrayed a multiracial Britain.[81]

White people's misinformation concerning specific details at times snowballed into sweeping Eurocentric assumptions about West Indian culture. A 1955 pamphlet by the British Council of Churches, designed to encourage local ministers to welcome West Indian settlers into their flocks, ends up by making ill-informed judgments based implicitly on the belief in the superiority of British history and traditions:

> Could you not invite one or two to spend an evening in your home? In doing so you have an opportunity to stimulate one of the main ventures in West Indian life, for you are asked to welcome people who are slowly creating a new race. Hitherto they have not known a sense of community such as we have developed here throughout the centuries. One indication of this lack of responsible citizenship is the strange and tragic absence of a well-knit family life.[82]

Later the guide explains the greater exuberance of some West Indian services by suggesting that "their constricted life, their limited educational and cultural opportunities have made for a more emotional development that has not had the advantages of being balanced by intellectual interests."

---

79 Lloyd Miller quoted in Phillips and Phillips, *Windrush*, 153.
80 Ros Howells quoted in Phillips and Phillips, *Windrush*, 152.
81 Karen Sands-O'Connor, *Soon Come Home to this Island: West Indians in British Children's Literature* (New York and London: Routledge, 2008), 93.
82 British Council of Churches, *Your Neighbour from the West Indies* (London: Wm. Carling and Co., 1955), 18–19.

It was the newer influence of trade unionism, "club activities," and party politics that brought "an increasing poise in their personal life."[83] Statements like these were not just examples of ignorance; they elided the importance and even the existence, of a positive sense of family, community, or Christian identity among Caribbean migrants.

That concerned individuals viewed popular ignorance as perhaps *the* major factor in discriminatory attitudes and actions is reflected in both white liberals' and West Indians' approach to the problem of prejudice in the early postwar period. More than anything else, these activists believed that social education would do away with pesky misconceptions and superstitions about the newcomers. In addition, it would spread awareness of the important cultural and historical connections between the two groups, thus providing a substantive rationale for the British citizenship of West Indian settlers.

Both white and West Indian officials and commentators voiced a belief in the power of education to ultimately do away with the color bar and popular prejudice. As early as 1944, the distinguished doctor and civil rights activist Harold Moody concluded that although Britons were "woefully ignorant" on "inter-racial questions," he was "quite convinced that a wise and effective method of education of the public will achieve results far beyond our dreams at the present moment."[84] More than fifteen years later, the 1960 report of the interracial Family Welfare Association was typical in its liberal "policy of education" to address the existing "lack of understanding" between settlers and native Britons; the new migrant "had to be taught how best to react to the social environment in which he was placed," because his reluctant hosts,

> unaccustomed to any large numbers of colonial in their midst, developed fears which had to be dispelled. Trade Unions, the Workers' Educational Association, Townswomen's Guilds, professional and lay bodies, were among the groups where courses of lectures or general discussions were inaugurated to help place the West Indian migration in proper perspective.

Fortunately, the authors noted, "the transition period has been marked by a notable absence of rancour" due to "the traditional friendliness of the British working class" and "the fact that West Indian migrants in general are eminently adaptable."[85] The report aptly characterized the sanguine faith of white and West Indian liberals in their ability to educate the populace into greater mutual tolerance.

---

83   Ibid., 24–25.
84   Harold A. Moody, *The Colour Bar* (London: New Mildmay Press, 1944), 26, 27.
85   Ruck et al., *The West Indian Comes to England*, 67–68.

The liberal faith in the basic fair-mindedness of white British citizens was so strong that the dominant interpretation of the violence and intimidation in Notting Hill in 1958 was that it was simply an aberration; a symptom of the prevailing controversy surrounding black migration, yes, but in essence a marginal action by rebellious delinquents who in no way represented the public at large. Pathé's newsreel coverage reported that the racial violence was a "new and ugly" phenomenon in Britain, and commented, "Opinions differ about Britain's racial problems, but the mentality which tries to solve them with coshes and broken railings has no place in the British way of life. This violence is evil, and the law and public opinion must stamp it out."[86] The suggestion here seems to be that it is not white hostility toward non-whites that is objectionable, but rather its violent, illegal expression. Consistent with the perspective that the riots were a marginal event, Pathé's year-end review summed up the violence: "Riots in London and other cities blotted the hitherto fine record of Britain in racial relations. Firm action by the authorities quickly stamped out the trouble."[87] On the official level, the Home Office summarized a speech of the Home Secretary, Rab Butler, supporting the Association of Chief Police Officers. In it, he

> stressed that this was entirely foreign to our long traditions and that it was wrong to exaggerate its significance. Such incidents threw into relief the essential normality of our society as a whole: law and order were taken for granted, and this was as it should be. ... Experience in areas where coloured and white population [*sic*] had settled down peacefully together showed that the good sense of the British people could overcome problems.

His faith in the "good sense of the British people" was presumably so steady that he advised police chiefs to continue maintaining law and order and "not to be led to experiments."[88] Such a comment suggests that the Home Secretary was reluctant to give incidents of racial hostility too much social or symbolic weight.

Notting Hill was among the first in a series of events that damaged, and ultimately destroyed, settlers' faith in the power of education and activism to overcome hostile attitudes toward them. After Notting Hill, explanations of racism that emphasized white ignorance began to lose ground to those that emphasized the presence of a "deep-seated prejudice"

---

86 "Shameful Episode," Pathé newsreel (August 4, 1958): available at http://britishpathe. com/record.php?id=35366; accessed September 20, 2009.

87 "Review of 1958," Pathé newsreel (December 29, 1958): available at http://britishpathe. com/record.php?id=35560; accessed September 20, 2009.

88 Home Office Press Notice, June 10, 1959, 2, ACC/1888/116, LMA. Emphasis in original.

among British whites. In his 1958 survey of race and society, Kenneth Little deduced that "the fact that racial discrimination exists in Britain without any backing from the law or the constitution means that colour prejudice has developed as part of the heritage of British society,"[89] and his observation would have resonated particularly in the post-Notting Hill era. The riots prompted concerned West Indians to establish Defence for Coloured People, a committee of representatives from twelve pertinent local organizations and helmed by Aloa Bashorun and "Stewart Hall" (likely the West Indian activist and intellectual Stuart Hall, who was a high school teacher in South London at the time and taught a handful of the students directly involved in the riots).[90] The group was designed to quickly communicate any danger or hostility to local residents, so that they might prepare and protect themselves. Bashorun told *The Times* that the West Indian community had "lost confidence in the present police protection," and that most local councils had "failed to speak out" against the violence and intimidation.[91] National Association for the Advancement of Colored People official Herbert Hill echoed these complaints in the *New Statesman*:

> I have been assured by the official and private agencies concerned with these matters that the worst is over. ... But I am not so sure. ... the Negro residents of North Kensington have an acute sense of alienation from the rest of the community. Sharply aware of the abuse and victimi-sation they suffer daily, and with the feeling that no one really cares, they have formed a good many local protective organisations. ... I was especially struck by the absence of any vigorous and sensitive mobili-sation of concern on the part of liberal-minded people about this most urgent contemporary problem.[92]

The confidence of West Indians was further shaken with Kelso Cochrane's murder the following year, especially since his assailants were never brought to justice. Hill singled out the abuse of police power as a major factor in West Indians' feelings of insecurity, and his comments were seconded by one reader who noted, "It is no earthly good complaining on an official level, the public conditioning to the infallible majesty of the 'law' is so complete that a dissenting voice can always be disregarded."[93] The outbreaks

---

89 Little, *Race and Society*, 42.

90 Helen Davis, *Understanding Stuart Hall* (London: Sage, 2004), 99.

91 "Defence Group for Coloured People," *The Times* (May 22, 1959), in ACC/1888/116, LMA.

92 Herbert Hill, "A Negro in Notting Hill," *New Statesman* (May 9, 1959), 635–36; ACC/1888/116, LMA.

93 Letter, C. A. Smythe to the Editor, *New Statesman*, May 16, 1959; ACC/1888/116, LMA.

of violence in 1958 and 1959 revealed the beginnings of a major cleavage between the perspectives of concerned West Indians and the so-called "white liberals" with whom they had allied themselves in the preceding decade.

Mainstream newspapers and television, regardless of their underlying take on the immigration debate, target audience, or erudition, usually placed stories on West Indian settlers in an established context of racial, and sometimes cultural, difference and the climate of ambivalence surrounding their migration to the metropolis. The same could be said for other British media (such as film) and those agents operating on behalf of local, regional, or national government. Even the most determinedly liberal institutions and individuals eventually took it for granted that the citizenship of West Indian Britons was somehow more ambiguous, less secure, than that of their white counterparts, even as they pronounced the "fitness" of the new arrivals for British society. In very few instances, beyond the rote operation of the national laws and agencies, did Caribbean settlers' right to belong go unquestioned and uncontested.

This shroud of controversy hung over the cultural pursuits and voluntary associations designed for the settler community, especially when they functioned on an interracial basis. And there were a great many of them, including numerous citizens' bureaux, welfare agencies, international clubs, and friendship councils, not to mention the interracial dances and picnics these organizations sponsored. Some of these, like the welfare agencies, were sponsored by the British government; others, like the advice bureaux, were sponsored by councils. Others were independent initiatives: the British-Caribbean Association was a voluntary organization founded in 1958 in response to Notting Hill. It counted both Conservative and Labour politicians as members, as well as white and West Indian celebrities, and its function was both social and political.[94] International clubs, on the other hand, had a more modest goal: to provide a place where young international settlers could socialize, develop a network of friends, and gain advice about lodgings, employment, and the like. The implicit purpose of the international clubs, of course, was to serve as a place for *respectable* socialization and entertainment, in contrast, one supposes, to the unrespectable entertainment of basement nightclubs or the street.

But even the most leisured activities attracted media attention on account of their political significance, and socially prominent white liberals, as well as local politicians, attached themselves to such events, usually going on the record with a starchy statement celebrating the mutual society of Britain's sons and daughters, while a newsreel camera or reporter zoomed in on a respectably dressed black man and white woman dancing

---

94 British Caribbean Association website, http://www.britishcaribbeanassociation.org. uk/1.html; accessed September 24, 2015.

together. In retrospect, the frequency with which an interracial dance was staged as the first line of attack in the war against racial prejudice is almost embarrassing. The Borough of Lambeth held a "No Colour Bar" dance in 1955 that can best be described as unspontaneous. Exactly half the guests were West Indian, and half English; the music was evenly split as well. Nonetheless, a Pathé newsreel painted a livelier sentimental gloss on the wooden event: "East had met West on common ground, and had found a lot in common. And few were wallflowers for very long. The rhythm of the mambo was doing its bit toward racial unity."[95] In addition to its Christmas balls and "Summer Outings" to the country, the rather posh British-Caribbean Association held a cabaret-style "West Indian Evening" of dancing, again at Lambeth Town Hall, in 1960,[96] while a newly founded interracial club held an "inaugural social" at the South Kilburn Club the previous year, "designed to bring people of all races together socially."[97] This was by no means a new development; in December 1954 the 77 Cultural and Social Club, Bayswater, held what one attendee described as a "gigantic annual coloured children's party" in Leicester Square: "Some very clever coloured child artistes danced and sang."[98] In London alone, there were twenty-four such clubs and associations devoted to racial integration in 1959.[99]

These numbers may be misleading; although some of these organizations managed to gain a foothold in their communities, like the British-Caribbean Association, with over seven hundred members and branches in London, Birmingham, Nottingham, and Liverpool, many clubs of this sort struggled to survive. When they did survive, it seemed to have more to do with local contingency than anything else. *The West Indian Comes to England*, a report produced by the Family Welfare Association, concluded that while middle-class settlers were most eager to join the local Lodge or Friendly Society as a marker of status, most were reluctant to leave their homes to play dominoes or cards at their local club:

> The membership of social clubs fluctuates to such an extent that it is always doubtful whether it is worthwhile to continue. … In particular the Saturday night dance is something to which they look forward.

95 "Lambeth—'No Colour Bar' Dance," Pathé newsreel (February 17, 1955): available at http://britishpathe.com/record.php?id=39034; accessed September 20, 2009.

96 Flyer advertising a "West Indian Evening," British-Caribbean Association, October 22, 1960; ACC/1888/116, LMA.

97 "Good Start for Inter-Racial Club," newspaper unknown (June 5, 1959); ACC/1888/116, LMA.

98 Letter, Marjory Fox-Pitt, of Racial Unity to Alan Lennox-Boyd, Secretary of State for the Colonies, December 21, 1954; CO 1028/32, PRO.

99 List of West Indian clubs and associations in English cities, September 16, 1959; CO 1031/2545, National Archives, Kew.

Apart from this, during the winter months visits to the cinema and meeting friends for parties are generally the extent of their social activity.[100]

The Colonial Office concurred. Its 1954 report on "Conditions of Jamaicans in the United Kingdom" stated that these settlers "do not take kindly to Club life—in Church Halls, or to special efforts of that nature, made on their behalf. Their recreations are the public dance hall and the cinema. They do not drink heavily, but frequent certain public houses mainly for social reasons."[101]

The Welfare Association, however, overlooked those activities and meeting places more organically and spontaneously cultivated by the settlers themselves. Val Wilmer, a young white photographer and jazz scene regular from the early 1960s, worked for a time in the offices of the short-lived magazine *Tropic*, edited by Edward Scobie (who later wrote a history of the black presence in Britain). She possessed a good knowledge of London's cultural geography and referred to the office as an "unofficial cultural centre" for Africans and Caribbeans:

> Just as other settlers would beat a path through Theo Campbell's Brixton record shop in order to talk to Claudia Jones at the *West Indian Gazette* offices upstairs, so they would drop into the *Tropic* office with their problems and news or just to pass the time. The Golden Gloves Hairdressing Salon next door was one of the few Black barbershops in London, a centre where opinions were aired, gossip and information exchanged, and customers would often check to see who else was around before moving on. ... From insurance salesmen to writers, from boxers and tailors to night-club proprietors, a constant stream of ambitious individuals passed through that battered old shop-door. And along with them came ordinary women and men with a hundred and one problems. My help was enlisted to fill in forms and I would try to direct queries about housing and legal matters to the appropriate agency.[102]

This account suggests that the offices of *Tropic*, in conjunction with the nearby salon, served not only as a meeting place and commercial center, but as a kind of informal citizens' advice bureau. One wonders how many settlers turned to such haunts over the official bureaux monitored by local government.

---

100 Ruck et al., *The West Indian Comes to England*, 117.

101 Interim report on Conditions of Jamaicans in the United Kingdom, January 8, 1954, 8; CO 1028/36, PRO.

102 Wilmer, *Mama Said There'd Be Days Like This*, 48.

In a similar way, a few struggling, cash-strapped, often short-lived newspapers and magazines, like *Tropic*, offered an alternative to the mainstream British media's view of the West Indian community in Britain. They tended to express the perspective of the settlers themselves, and often positioned local events in a larger context that included the West Indies, other European colonies and ex-colonies, and the United States, where Jim Crowism became a negative standard by which to measure race relations in Britain. At the same time, the *West Indian Gazette*, *West Indies Observer*, and *Magnet News* were community papers, reporting on local Carnival efforts, beauty contests, and events around town. Local merchants advertised Caribbean and Asian foods and cheap passages back "home" in the pages of these papers.

Although in practice the citizenship status of West Indians in Britain was never felt to be quite secure, their racial status certainly was. Unlike in many parts of the West Indies, no "pigmentocracy" held sway in the mother country. Regardless of the lightness of one's skin, or one's economic class, being "colored" at all meant that you were treated as "black" by the rest of the "white" population; as Lord Kitchener sang in a memorable calypso, "You can never get away from the fact / If you're not white you're considered black."[103] (Compare this to the allegiances of a nineteenth-century Trinidadian calypso by the "coloured" calypsonian Hannibal, who sang, "I ain't black, I ain't white / If it comes to blows or fight / I'll kill the black to save the white.")[104]

Historians have long noted the presence in Britain of an almost binary racial code that by the 1970s allowed for, among other things, the invention of an extremely broad, but fragile, "black British" identity that applied to Britons of Afro-Caribbean, Indo-Caribbean, African, Middle Eastern, Asian, and South Asian descent. For West Indian settlers in the 1940s, '50s, and early '60s, however, the shift to a binary racial system, however informal, was significant because it shook up class distinctions as well. Nancy Foner, in her sociological survey of Jamaicans in England, concluded that class distinctions had become much less important to her survey group, in part because they were often judged on the basis of skin color; other distinctions were less important. As one interviewee put it, "Once you are black you are down and you are just down. Whether you is in good position or not these white people don't rate you."[105] Some of her respondents, however, acknowledged the benefit of the flattening of class differences within the migrant community, namely, the reduction of

103 Aldwyn Roberts, "If You're Not White You're Black."

104 Quoted in Bridget Brereton, *Race Relations in Colonial Trinidad, 1870–1900* (Cambridge: Cambridge University Press, 1979), 104.

105 Foner, *Jamaica Farewell*, 133–34.

professional and educational snobbery. One man, a successful engineer and community leader in London, remarked:

> I was very class-minded indeed [in Jamaica]. Back home, nobody in the locality was good enough for me. If I traveled, it had to be by car, never by truck. If I had a drink, it was with appropriate friends in the private room of a good bar. All this was wrong and I'm not proud of it now.[106]

In a similar vein, a part-time cleaner said:

> In Jamaica, nurses and teachers they walk different, move different, dress different, talk different, people look up to them. They are up there. But here you see the teacher and they are just the same. Here the factory worker and the teacher they are just the same. ... In Jamaica, if you not in a big job, you couldn't buy the same things.[107]

As this woman noted, whatever economic hardships West Indians experienced, they shared a closer standard of living in London than they had in the Caribbean, despite a degree of professional difference. Consequently, education and training carried less status.

In fact, a great many West Indian settlers, celebrities or otherwise, went on record to express their support of Great Britain and the empire and declared their determination to work their way up in British society without any special treatment from their new neighbors or from government. Bill Strachan, an ex-RAF man working in a Council Office, told Pathé reporters:

> I can assure trade unionists that there'll be no problem of them undercutting trade unionists, and I can assure them that they will help in the cultural life in this country. And every attempt on their part is at social integration, and being completely happy and cooperative with the British people. We don't want any special privileges, or anything more than any other British worker has in this country.[108]

As will be demonstrated below, West Indian artists and culture workers were also at pains to convey the community's willingness to integrate peacefully into urban British society. The high-profile racial violence of 1958 and 1959 came as a frightening wake-up call to observers both black and white; but although representatives of the West Indian community scrambled to raise awareness of the dangers of complacency regarding racial discrimination, the reaction of the British media and government suggested

---

106 Ibid., 151.
107 Ibid., 210.
108 "Our Jamaican Problem," Pathé newsreel.

that these incidents were aberrations that did not reflect the feelings of British officialdom or the general public. Despite such blasé reassurances, the Conservatives passed the first Commonwealth Immigrants Bill in 1961, which came into legal force the following year.

West Indians already settled in Britain firmly opposed the new legislation. On the campaign for immigration restriction, the *West Indian Gazette* questioned:

> is not the government in negotiation to join a European Common Market which will *"flood England with Germans and other Europeans"*, to the disquiet of many people in England and the Commonwealth? Does this not prove beyond a doubt that what this campaign to restrict immigration is all about is not immigration *in general*; but *coloured* immigration *in particular?*[109]

Two months later, when the bill was formally introduced, *Gazette* editor Claudia Jones had run out of patience: "The gauntlet is down. The Tory-gloved hands which held it palmed a Colour-Bar Bill to restrict immigration of coloured citizens. … It is to the shame of our Commonwealth—to the shame of England that such a measure was even introduced!"[110] The less radical *West Indies Observer* similarly viewed the Commonwealth Immigrants Act as a betrayal of imperial ties, conjuring memories of the colonies' valiant participation in the war, and accusing MP Cyril Osborne, an opponent of non-white migration, of being "determined to break up the Commonwealth."[111]

The disillusionment of West Indian Britons was complete when, in 1965, a Labour government strengthened the 1962 Act and reduced the number of employment vouchers available to prospective migrants. The Labour Party, which for more than a decade had seemed the natural choice for West Indian settlers, had, with its tiny parliamentary majority, folded under pressure from right-leaning MPs and those vocal sections of the public opposed to non-white immigration. By 1965, the debate about immigration had shifted from a discourse sensitive to Britain's long history of imperial connection and the role of the colonies in its military and economic success, to one focused squarely on the domestic race issue, which finally exploded into open conflict and nakedly racist political speechmaking.

With such official and unofficial scrutiny surrounding the state of race relations in London, it is no wonder that the Caribbean-Britons examined in the chapters to follow nourished politicized ideals as part of their developing

---

109 "The New Arguments against Migration Restriction," *West Indian Gazette* (September 1961), 7. Emphasis in original.

110 Claudia Jones, "Butler's Colour-Bar Bill Mocks Commonwealth," *West Indian Gazette* (November 1961), 1.

111 "Knight of the Immigrants Bill," *West Indies Observer* (November 24, 1962), 4.

artistic identities. Their work responded to the events and debates recounted in this narrative introduction, but in original ways. It offered meditations on the nature of British identity, the contradictory relationship between London and the West Indies, and the place of imperial and racial politics in artistic and commercial creation.

Chapter 2

West Indian Interventions at the BBC[1]

In 1955, Pearl Prescod, an obscure hairdresser and amateur singer, caught the ear of a few influential people in Trinidad. They immediately wrote to the Secretary of the West India Committee in London, hoping to secure her employment so she could pursue a classical music education in England. Not only did the secretary get her a job as a switchboard operator in his own office, but he also arranged for her to audition at the BBC— all on the strength of a personal recommendation.[2] Prescod was from Tobago, considered a rural backwater by many West Indians (and especially Trinidadians), but she procured a string of BBC contracts over the years and went on to a stage career. The BBC's reach, it seemed, extended to every nook and cranny of the empire.

As the most extensive and influential purveyor of British culture, the British Broadcasting Corporation attracted a steady stream of artists and entertainers arriving from the West Indies after 1945. In fact, the BBC was often their first stop in London for several reasons, not least of which was its international renown, based on its commitment to educating, informing, and uplifting listeners, and later viewers, throughout the Queen's realm. In the context of the Second World War, it forged a common culture to bind the empire together in the face of foreign aggression.[3] As one Jamaican settler remembered:

---

1   Some of the research from this chapter appears in Amanda M. Bidnall, "West Indian Interventions at the Heart of the Cultural Establishment: Edric Connor, Pearl Connor, and the BBC," *Twentieth Century British History* 24, no. 1 (2013): 84–109.

2   Correspondence between A. E. V. Barton and Josephine Douglas, Producer, Light Entertainment, September 2, 1955 and September 7, 1955, TVART 1—Pearl Prescod. TV Artists File I (1954–62); WAC.

3   See Gerard Mansell, *Let Truth Be Told: 50 Years of BBC External Broadcasting* (London: Weidenfeld and Nicolson, 1982).

even up to people like my grandmother who would listen to the radio at six o'clock every evening in the West Indies, World Service, and whatever was said there had to be gospel, you know. You couldn't argue that with everybody, couldn't say, "Well, that was wrong." It was said by the BBC and it was from England, therefore it was right and you had to agree to it and support it.[4]

Despite these connections, however, relations between West Indian artists and the Corporation were not always smooth. Artists found themselves circumscribed by producers who had a narrow conception of their role on domestic BBC broadcasts. As a result, their efforts to break out of the BBC's mold consisted of alternative and increasingly politicized articulations of what it meant to be both West Indian and British.

This chapter shows how three artist-settlers—Edric Connor, Pearl Connor, and Cy Grant—benefited tremendously from BBC patronage, but in turn brought their own interventions into British culture: a commitment to educate audiences about the substantive affinities between Britain and the empire, and to forge an historically informed, racially inclusive definition of British citizenship. Their work was a direct response to Caribbean migration, and the increasingly tense public debate about citizenship and immigration that led to the passage of the first Commonwealth Immigrants Bill in 1961. Their success highlights that postwar moment when the BBC was open to a progressive vision of a British culture of the future.[5] It was not until the 1960s were well underway that their cultural and show business priorities diverged from those of the Corporation, as these artists' cultural and professional goals became more ambitious, and the BBC implicitly fell back on a set of conservative assumptions about British culture in the face of intensifying public debates about race relations and immigration. By viewing West Indian performers as suitable for only a limited range of broadcast material, BBC producers and administrators sometimes inadvertently stifled the most promising careers. The result, by the middle of the decade, was a hardening of the disillusionment so characteristic of later generations of "Black British" artists.

---

4   Arthur Curling quoted in Philips and Phillips, *Windrush*, 12.
5   This chapter examines only the BBC work of these subjects, although they also appeared in many television programs, films, and theatre events beyond the Corporation.

Caribbean Artists and BBC Policy

It was not only the Corporation's status as a truly national cultural institution that made it attractive to West Indian writers and entertainers. First, unlike many other venues in London, the BBC welcomed West Indian talent as part of its extended imperial and Commonwealth network; several artists already had experience working with the BBC in the West Indies on its General Overseas Service. Poets and novelists who would later become famous in England submitted short stories and verse to *Caribbean Voices* before gaining employment on the program as readers. More often, singers and actors who had made a mark on their home islands arrived in London armed with letters of introduction to the BBC, like Pearl Prescod above.

Second, the BBC had the capacity to absorb far more West Indian talent—a specialized commodity at the time—than any other single company. Besides the external services which always provided regular jobs for West Indians (particularly the West Indies and West Africa Services), in 1945 there were three domestic stations: the Light Programme, the Home Service, and the Third Programme. Each of these possessed its own identity, but broadcast in a range of genres including Talks, Variety, and Drama. Television viewership was also skyrocketing, and until 1955 the BBC had no competition in this medium. The Television Drama Department alone was producing 120 plays a year in 1955, and by 1960 this number had risen to 350.[6] Thus it was in constant need of both fresh faces and fresh ideas, and West Indian writers and performers were eager to help satisfy that demand at an institution that was comparatively open to their contributions.

Third, a foot in the Corporation's door often resulted in multiple contracts; the BBC prided itself on its commitment to emerging talent and the development of individual artists. This was partly a conscious ethical tradition, and partly a luxury afforded by its monopoly on radio and (until 1955) television broadcasting. As Eric Maschwitz, Head of Television Light Entertainment, rather defensively boasted, "The BBC works for its artists, develops their potentiality, builds them and, once built, does its best to maintain them; they are never immediately 'expendable' at the whim of men who are only interested in ratings and the maintenance of advertising revenue."[7] For aspiring West Indians artists, such commitment was invaluable, because non-white entertainers were so often employed on the basis of color, and then never considered for other parts, regardless of the quality of their performance. The BBC, as Peter Kalliney has noted,

---

6   From Asa Briggs, *The History of Broadcasting in the United Kingdom, Volume V: Competition* (London: Oxford University Press, 1995), 194.

7   Eric Maschwitz quoted in Briggs, *The History of Broadcasting*, 197.

discussing writers of the Black Atlantic, was seen as an institution relatively "exempt from the systems of racial and political hierarchy operative elsewhere."[8]

Most importantly, however, the BBC's Reithian commitment to "educate, inform, and entertain" suited the artistic aims of West Indians working in London.[9] Many of the ideas submitted by artists like Jan Carew, Edric Connor, George Lamming, and Errol John, whether of a dramatic, variety, or documentary nature, were concerned to illuminate aspects of West Indian culture for an English audience. (As the next chapter will discuss, even the fun-loving calypso could teach about race relations or aspects of London life.) When, for instance, Talks producer John Bridges recruited George Lamming to advise him on a program about West Indian migrants:

> After a very few days of working with him I was of the opinion that he had such a thorough grip of the West Indian immigrant situation and also a good many strong personal views that the programme would be a very much better one if I left him to write the entire script and confined myself to studio and actuality production.[10]

Lamming's experience was not unique; V. S. Naipaul and actress Nadia Cattouse, for example, did many jobs for both the domestic and colonial Schools Programmes. As late as 1965, the BBC's Director-General, Sir Hugh Greene, explained at a meeting on the subject of "Programmes for Immigrants" that the BBC had two central tasks: "One was to decide how the BBC should make West Indians feel at home in the United Kingdom, and the other was to educate public opinion, both in general and in the particular communities in which West Indians lived."[11] Greene was giving voice to the Reithian commitment as it applied to the issue of Caribbean migration.

The BBC was also committed to reflecting British society in all its diversity, to "retain its care 'for the nation as a whole, including minorities' and for 'the standards and style of behaviour of civilised people.'"[12] (Of course, until recent years, when scholars wrote about the BBC's programming

---

8   Peter J. Kalliney, *Commonwealth of Letters: British Literary Culture and the Emergence of Postcolonial Aesthetics* (Oxford: Oxford University Press, 2013), 6.

9   John Reith was the first Director-General of the British Broadcasting Corporation in 1927, and his commitment to use radio, and later television, as a fundamentally educative tool shaped the BBC's official ethos throughout the twentieth century.

10 Memo, John Bridges to E. Kilham Roberts, Administrative Officer, Talks, March 19, 1957, RCONT 1—George Lamming, Talks File I(b) (1953–57); WAC.

11 Minutes for BBC meeting on "Programmes for Immigrants," July 13, 1965, T16/562, TV Policy—Programme Policy: Immigration (1965–67); WAC.

12 Briggs, *The History of Broadcasting*, 143. Briggs is quoting here from the BBC's Board of Management *Minutes* from 1957.

for "minorities" at mid-century, they were referring to "chess, gardening, and archaeology,"[13] not ethnic viewership.) Nevertheless, the creation of three separate radio frequencies after the war was an attempt to give the great majority of listeners more of what they wanted to hear while still producing experimental work and providing for those with particular interests.[14] This commitment boded well for West Indian writers and actors, who, largely excluded from mainstream drama, drifted toward productions with more challenging or alternative subject matter. On the BBC, this could be anything from documentary surveys of Jamaican politics and industry, to adaptations of Creole folklore, to race relations dramas set in London. In fact, the exposure of West Indian talent taught radio listeners and television viewers about Britain's changing ethnic and cultural profile, a practice that in theory worked to ameliorate race relations. As Jack Williams has noted with regard to the postwar period, "In general, white broadcasters have subscribed to a liberal-humanist view of race relations. They have wanted to reduce ethnic prejudices and to promote ethnic understanding."[15] At mid-century, this liberalism encouraged the involvement of colonial artists in BBC programming.

Finally, it should be noted that West Indian entertainers had more in common with the BBC than might be supposed given the latter's reputation for a "conservative and élitist cultural perspective" that resulted in the recruitment of "most of its own staff from the educated middle class."[16] With a few exceptions, those who worked closely with the BBC in these early years of postwar migration were from colonial middle-class backgrounds. They possessed an English education, and often had university training in their professions from British institutions. (Edric Connor, for example, originally trained as an engineer, and Cy Grant was a certified barrister.) Of the Colonial Service branch of the BBC, Anne Rush has written, "Middle-class West Indians and native Britons in the Colonial Service department, as well as those who listened to its broadcasts, shared a vision of an inclusive British Commonwealth, developed and sustained by a culture based on respectability."[17] West Indian artist-settlers in London drew upon the same "shared vision." Perhaps most importantly, they had a thorough knowledge of classic English art and literature. Judging from much of their correspondence in the BBC archives, their artistic perspectives and style

---

13 Asa Briggs, *The BBC: The First Fifty Years* (London: Oxford University Press, 1985), 310.

14 See Briggs, *The History of Broadcasting*. For a more general summary of the BBC's ethos, see Andrew Crisell, *An Introductory History of British Broadcasting*, second edition (1997; London: Routledge, 2002), 28–35.

15 Jack Williams, *Entertaining the Nation: A Social History of British Television* (Phoenix Mill: Sutton Publishing, 2004), 162.

16 Crisell, *An Introductory History of British Broadcasting*, 44.

17 Rush, *Bonds of Empire*, 174.

of communication fit well with those of the producers with whom they worked.

Despite the similarities between the values of the BBC and those of West Indian artists, BBC attitudes toward entertainers of color—never explicitly articulated—were very conservative and worked to relegate these performers to only a handful of roles. Exclusionary practices at the BBC were not perhaps as blatant or direct as those of other companies, but they were to an extent built into styles and traditions of programming for radio and television, patterns that confined West Indians—and all artists of color—to particular roles. Simon Cottle has pointed out that in the 1990s, within the Corporation, "the major difficulties and stumbling blocks confronting producers of ethnic minority programmes are thought to relate less to racism and more to the established working traditions, the social composition of the BBC, its institutional hierarchy and programme production conservatism."[18] Much the same could be said of the 1950s and 1960s.

It's worth pointing out that because these production values, programming patterns, and working styles were so "traditional," they often appear in the BBC files as a kind of common sense, an approach to broadcasting deemed entirely natural—and often beyond reproach. In fact, this deceptively neutral perspective obscured prejudices and double standards in the employment and representation of minorities, simply because BBC personnel truly believed that none existed.[19] As Scannell and Cardiff expressed so neatly, "Broadcasting mediates a seemingly unmediated reality, but the world that is organized in programme output is not a reflection, a mirror of a reality that exists elsewhere. It is a unique totality, a social whole constituted in the range of output, a universe that exists nowhere else."[20] The BBC "universe" had its own reality and set of assumptions that were hard to crack, and the West Indian artists I look at below were part of a larger shake-up that began in the late 1950s and caused a "clash between conflicting outlooks, attitudes and visions of the future" within the Corporation itself.[21]

In radio, the first challenge facing most West Indian artists at the BBC (in London) was penetrating the tripartite domestic broadcasting service. The General Overseas Service (which encompassed smaller departments like

---

18 S. Cottle and P. Ismond, *Television and Ethnic Minorities* quoted in Williams, *Entertaining the Nation*, 152.

19 I'd like to thank Sharika Thiranagama, Caroline Ritter, and Laura Beers for sharing their insights on this and other aspects of BBC practice in our panel at the North American Conference of British Studies, Portland, Oregon (November 10, 2013).

20 Paddy Scannell and David Cardiff, *A Social History of British Broadcasting, Volume One 1922–1939: Serving the Nation* (Oxford: Basil Blackwell, 1991), xi.

21 Madeleine Macmurraugh-Kavanagh, "The BBC and the Birth of *The Wednesday Play*, 1962–66: Institutional Containment versus 'Agitational Contemporaneity,'" in Janet Thumim, ed., *Small Screens, Big Ideas: Television in the 1950s* (London and New York: I. B. Tauris, 2002), 151.

the West Indies or Caribbean Service) was run quite separately from these, although there was a degree of program sharing. Many West Indian artists, whether writers, producers, actors, or singers, started their BBC career on the West Indies Service, being interviewed for their achievements on the islands, or reading poetry or prose (sometimes their own) on influential programs like *Caribbean Voices*, *West Indian Diary*, and *Calling the West Indies*. Actors Errol John and Nadia Cattouse, producers Una Marson and Kenneth Ablack, and writers George Lamming and V. S. Naipaul all got their BBC start on these shows. (The West Indies Service was extremely important to new artists and writers in the Caribbean, and though it is not the focus of this chapter, it has received some great historical attention.)[22] Even after proving their mettle in a variety of Overseas Service productions, however, it remained difficult to make the transition to the "home" services. For example, in the early 1950s *West Indian Diary* aired a succession of Shakespeare adaptations featuring almost wholly West Indian casts—*King Lear*, *As You Like It*, and *Macbeth*—but the idea of including any of the actors in productions for domestic transmission was never considered.[23]

Relative to other London media outlets, the BBC was an important sponsor of West Indian talent, especially writing, and producers did consider some of this writing for broadcast on the domestic services. Its conservative outlook at times rendered it out of touch with emerging trends in West Indian expression, however. This helps explain its tendency to reject the submissions of writers who quickly went on to literary or dramatic fame. Barry Reckord was consistently turned away, although his submissions *Della* and *King of the Blind Country* were successfully produced under different names[24] at the Royal Court Theatre, the latter to great success and critical acclaim. Of Errol John's *Moon on Rainbow Shawl*, one BBC television reader wrote, "It seems to me possibly too obscure in its language (merely because it is written in the simplified argot of the West Indian) and too indifferent to story telling to be a likely candidate for our schedule."[25] It was rejected, but later accepted—after it had won the prestigious *Observer* Drama Writer's Prize. In 1959, the Assistant Head of Drama for Radio rejected the play *The Lion and the Jewel*, stating that "there doesn't seem to be a market for it at the moment."[26] It was written by Nigerian and future Nobel Prize winner Wole Soyinka.

---

22 See, for example, Darrell Newton, *Paving the Empire Road* (Manchester: Manchester University Press, 2011); Griffith, "This is London Calling the West Indies."

23 Edric Connor was the first black person to appear in a Shakespeare production at Stratford-upon-Avon, as Gower (the Chorus) in *Pericles*.

24 Respectively, *Flesh to a Tiger* and *Skyvers*.

25 Television Drama Report, May 28, 1958; T48/344/1—Errol John, Drama Writer's File, Television (1953–79), WAC.

26 Letter, Donald McWhinnie to Lloyd Reckord, December 31, 1959; RCONT 1—Barry Reckord. Scriptwriter's File I (1955–62), WAC.

This is not to suggest that the flowering of West Indian literature completely passed the Corporation by; in one way or another, the BBC supported the early careers of writers such as V. S. Naipaul, George Lamming, and Jan Carew. But there were certainly moments when these writers' progressive analyses of colonialism, language, and identity were not fully appreciated by readers and producers.

Overall, and particularly in the case of domestic broadcasting, producers preferred conventional race relations dramas set in the heart of the empire. These usually featured innocent migrants who are quickly disillusioned by ignorant white racists, but later redeemed by supportive white liberals. As late as 1968, Errol John submitted three screenplays, set throughout the Caribbean, which producer Irene Shubik enjoyed very much but concluded that they "would be too exotic and romantic for Wednesday Play. If you do have any thought, however, about a story with an English setting: preferably, so far as I am concerned, one about West Indians in London, do please call me or send it in and let's talk."[27] Thus the BBC's desire to reflect British society in its programming could easily result in an insular preoccupation with the interests of the average (white) British listener or viewer.

The BBC had no explicit policy during these years on the employment of colonial artists or artists of color; in fact, senior administrators felt that to have such a policy would adulterate the Corporation's reputation for objectivity and even-handedness. As late as 1967 the Appointments Department declared that it had "no 'policy' with regard to recruitment of coloured people [in any capacity]. To have one would imply that they were treated differently from other applicants."[28] That same year, when a well-meaning friend of Huw Wheldon, BBC's Controller of Programmes, suggested that the Corporation might insert more black actors in everyday roles on television (as doctors, nurses, and policemen, for example) in an effort to "subliminally" improve British race relations, Wheldon wrote a chilly response. He began by asserting that "the BBC already does a good deal to counter racial discrimination," and concluded by surmising that such an approach would be impracticable because of the small number of black actors in London and because it would constitute discrimination against white actors. Most interestingly, he felt that taking such action would be damaging to the Corporation:

27 Letter, Irene Shubik to Errol John, February 16, 1968, T48/344/1—Errol John, WAC.
28 Memo, R. M. J. Gillott, Assistant Head of Appointments Department to L. G. Thirkell, Controller, Staff Training and Appointments, February 23, 1967, R49/1,095/1, Coloured People Employment in BBC, WAC. Gillott did, however, conclude his memo by stating his own tendency "to treat coloured applicants with extra courtesy as slight compensation for the discourtesy they meet with in some quarters."

To engage in this would be to abuse the BBC's special position and, once the policy became widely known, the results might be disastrous, not only in this particular field but on the BBC's standing as a whole. As you say yourself, "publicity would kill it", and the truth is if a policy of this sort were to be followed it would very soon become public knowledge.[29]

By and large, the question of BBC policy on the employment of artists or other workers of color was not an administrative priority until the mid- to late 1960s. (Two trailblazing meetings occurred on the subject of "Programmes for Immigrants" in July 1965, the second of which was exclusively concerned with West Indian migrants.) Prior to this, employment issues were resolved on a case-by-case basis, and most often in an effort to avoid complaints or controversy. Thus, when popular vocalist Adelaide Hall and her husband gained the "unfortunate impression that there is some colour bar so far as 'Starlight' [a variety show] is concerned," the program's producers made a conscious decision to give her an appearance.[30]

When it came to the question of programs' subject matter and treatment of racial themes, archival memoranda suggest that the BBC gave serious consideration to complaints—both internal and external—of discriminatory content on radio and television, even if its decisions on such matters seem hopelessly shortsighted today. Perhaps the war years had made BBC staffers particularly sensitive to questionable representations of black people in their broadcasts; in 1943 producers had received a general memo after the Colonial Office complained that an Entertainments National Service Association broadcast "was thought to be offensive to coloured people inasmuch as it held up a black man as a scare to white children." They were reminded "that there are a lot of coloured people in the country now— Africans, West Indians and Americans—and there is therefore particularly good reason to be careful not to say anything which might be interpreted as showing colour prejudice."[31]

This imperative was nonetheless interpreted through the Corporation's own, historically specific definition of prejudice. Kenneth Adam (then Director of Television), for instance, countered an internal 1962 complaint about the return of *The Black and White Minstrel Show* (which routinely featured white performers in blackface) with the following: "I yield to no-one in my detestation of apartheid and the Little Rock philosophy. But to suggest that to continue a perfectly honourable theatrical tradition of the British

29 Letter, Huw Wheldon, Controller of Programmes to Katherine Wadleigh, May 16, 1967, T16/562 TV Policy—Programme Policy: Immigration (1965–67), WAC.

30 Confidential memo, W. L. Streeton, Programme Contracts Director, to Cecil Madden, May 4, 1943, R34/306 Policy—Coloured People (1941–44), WAC.

31 Memo, Pat Hillyard to all producers, July 26, 1943, R34/306 Policy—Coloured People (1941–44), WAC.

music hall is a 'disgrace and an insult to coloured people everywhere' is, I submit, arrant nonsense." Five years later, amid the increasing din of complaints from the Campaign Against Racial Discrimination and other groups, he maintained that "introducing genuine negroes into the 'Black and White Minstrel Show' was … a quite unjustifiable breaking of the coon convention which has been our defence against the growing attacks upon the show."[32] Likewise, in 1950, still BBC Television's early days, there was some serious internal correspondence regarding a non-white singer's performance of love-themed songs to a white woman on the light entertainment program *Black Magic*. The Controller for Television, Norman Collins, wrote:

> There remains the question of good taste. Without question we should have avoided the coloured man's songs to the white girl. There have been a number of letters complaining about this point, even though some of the correspondents are badly confused by the lightness of some of the coloured artists. It is not too much to say that the production of "Black Magic" lowered the whole standard of the service.

He suggested that the BBC "terminate" the producer's "association with television."[33] Attitudes like those aroused by the *Black and White Minstrel Show* and *Black Magic* controversies served to segregate artists of color on the BBC even though this process was not systematic.

Although in theory the Corporation was relatively open to the employment and creative participation of West Indians and other colonials, in practice these artists were slotted into a limited range of roles on the home services. The race relations drama, which explored the impact of interracial romance and/or conflict on British families, was one of the handful of genres that regularly involved West Indian actors, writers, and advisors. Another was programs dealing specifically with West Indian culture or Commonwealth issues, including imperial epics where West Indians portrayed either noble or dangerous savages. The writer and actor Errol John appeared in a wide range of radio dramas in the mid-1950s, whose titles suggest their subjects: Conrad's *The Nigger of the Narcissus* (Home Service, 1955), Lamming's migration story *In the Castle of My Skin* (Third Programme, 1955), *King Solomon's Mines* (Light Programme miniseries, 1956), and *The Birth of Ghana* (European Service, 1957). And, due to their color, they were often cast in American drama or variety shows with "plantation" themes (even on color-blind radio, where they

---

32 Memos, Kenneth Adam to Barrie Thorne, September 11, 1962, and T. J. H. Sloan, October 15, 1967. T16/175/2 TV Policy—Race Relations, File 2 (1955–68), WAC.

33 Private staff memos, Norman Collins, Controller, Television to Patrick Hillyard, Head of Television, Light Entertainment, February 1 and 20, 1950, T16/175/1 TV Policy—Race Relations, File 1 (1950–54), WAC.

imitated southern accents the same as any white British actor). Finally, the genre that was the bread and butter for many young performers was that in which black performers were historically permitted to flourish: the singing, playing, and dancing of variety (or light) entertainment. As Pearl Connor observed of her own clients, "Light entertainment was one of the areas into which we broke into with our eyes closed ... We were able to work in clubs ... [it] was a very easy area for us and it was one that kept us going."[34] The careers of both Edric Connor and Cy Grant, discussed in detail below, began in this field.

The BBC's ambivalence about the proper place of West Indian performers on the domestic airwaves was perhaps due to the fact that its long-standing dedication to uplift audiences and cater to specialized interests was under pressure. The 1950s were formative years for television, not only because of the rapidly growing popularity of the medium, but also because the prospect—and, after the ITV's 1955 debut, the reality—of commercial competition forced the Corporation to balance "quality" programming with a greater consideration for television ratings.

ITV was on the offensive in the early decades of television competition. While it naturally had a mandate to cater to audience preferences in order to remain profitable, it had freedom to experiment and to encompass the different attitudes and priorities of the "Big Four" production companies whose work it programmed. In drama, for example, ATV was the most commercial, with an accent on classical revivals, while ABC took more risks with new writers, and "Granada, with their accent on social purpose, moved in the direction of plays with a message writ large—by such writers as Miller, Wilder and Osborne."[35] John Stevenson, who wrote for Granada television, characterized the mood in this period as "confident, optimistic and dynamic" and remarked that "it was much easier [at the time] to be bold and confident. ITV—as the sole commercial channel—still had a licence to print money."[36] Sydney Newman's tenure on *Armchair Theatre* between 1958 and 1962 meant contemporary British plays with an accent on social realism that catered to working-class and regional audiences, reliably every week.[37] (The BBC later wooed Newman away, and there he initiated *The Wednesday Play* in 1964.)

By the end of the 1950s it was debatable whether ITV or the BBC produced better drama; an American observer in 1961 came to the

34 Transcript, interview with Pearl Connor, June 25, 1997, 9704095/A, *Blackgrounds* oral history project on the experience of Black Theatre and Black Theatre Professionals, TMA.

35 Bernard Sendall, *Independent Television in Britain, Volume 1: Origin and Foundation, 1946–62* (London and Basingstoke: Macmillan, 1982), 346.

36 John Stevenson, "Experience of Life," in John Finch, ed., *Granada Television: The First Generation* (Manchester: Manchester University Press, 2003), 127.

37 Crisell, *An Introductory History of British Broadcasting*, 101.

conclusion that "there is little choice between the two, except for the BBC's greater emphasis on the classics."[38] But the Corporation was, in some ways, more at the mercy of its integrity. Before competition, it had made occasional concessions to public preference, for example with the creation of a tripartite radio service, evidence of an "attempt to respond to popular tastes and provide the listener with an element of choice without sacrificing the old Reithian seriousness of purpose."[39] Nevertheless, for these different reasons, BBC directors and producers in this period were especially torn between making less adventurous programs that reflected the attitudes of the greatest swath of the British public and making ones that challenged and educated the audience. As Grace Wyndham Goldie, Assistant Head of Talks between 1954 and 1965, wrote, "We, who were in the business, realised bitterly that if we [ignored audience ratings] we should rapidly become a small specialised channel which would not be supported by the mass public and would not therefore be entitled to a license fee paid by the public."[40]

It was televisual competition, combined with the debates surrounding the new wave of postwar drama and literature, that made questions of audience response most pressing by the end of the 1950s. Madeleine Macmurraugh-Kavanagh notes that there was "a sense of national schizo-phrenia during these years, potentially caused by Britain's ambiguous post-Imperial situation and exacerbated by widespread (relative) affluence pitched against anxieties focused on the direction in which society seemed to be moving."[41] As this condition expressed itself culturally, Macmurraugh-Kavanagh argues, there was a split within the BBC over how to deal it, and new public discussion of television's mass influence raised the stakes of this internal debate:

> Television drama suddenly appeared to have become a most urgent social tool since it had the means to saturate the nation's consciousness in a way that ... theatre and cinema could never achieve. Penetrating the security of the home, social television drama could reach the most complacent, reveal contemporary truths, dispel myths already accumulating around the affluent society and insist upon being seen and heard.[42]

Television embodied both the most fervent hopes and the deepest fears of British society, and in turn BBC decision-makers.

---

38 Burton Paulu, *British Broadcasting in Transition* (Minneapolis: University of Minnesota Press, 1961), 135.

39 Crisell, *An Introductory History of British Broadcasting*, 67.

40 Grace Wyndham Goldie quoted in Briggs, *The History of Broadcasting*, 17. Funding for domestic BBC broadcasting has always come largely from the license fees paid by British television owners.

41 Macmurraugh-Kavanagh, "The BBC and the Birth of *The Wednesday Play*," 150.

42 Ibid., 151–52.

The experiences of West Indian artists must be viewed in this context, especially since race was a touchstone of many popular hopes and fears in this period. No programming involving West Indian talent or themes of migration and race relations would have been produced without considerable forethought by producers—and, often, their superiors. In the aftermath of the "Black Magic" controversy alluded to above, BBC Controller Norman Collins suggested to the head of Light Entertainment that "Love songs between white and coloured artists must be very scrupulously considered … Such acts are not expressly forbidden, but are better avoided and must in all circumstances be personally approved by you."[43] That was in 1950, long before the public controversy over race and immigration reached its zenith.

The impact of BBC policy and practice on the West Indian artists it employed was variable but restrictive overall. While many Caribbean artists tried to negotiate new roles for themselves, or expand existing roles, others, grateful for employment in an environment of professionalism and mutual respect, simply accepted the *status quo*.

For the BBC's most famous and respected Caribbean artists, however, the Corporation's ambivalent stance on "colonial" talent meant that professional success was often coupled with a heightened sense of frustration and professional insecurity. Writer and erstwhile BBC collaborator George Lamming is one of the few to have recognized that, for better or worse,

> the BBC was a royal gateway to national recognition. In this respect it was a unique institution, endowed with immense cultural authority and trusted without reservations by all layers of the society. Within two years of his arrival Edric Connor had become a familiar name in the British music world. The speed with which this career took off allows us to see the complexities of race in operation in a context where it seems at once a veil of exclusion and a potential ticket of entry. In a sense, Connor had come armed with a certain kind of ticket … but it would never take him all the way.[44]

The cultural power wielded by the BBC had particular implications for Caribbean artists, who had so few avenues to professional success in London. The Corporation's relative willingness to hire and promote "coloured" artists, in a variety of capacities, was undoubtedly a boon to the West Indian artistic community. Its apparently open-door policy, however, made it that much more difficult when high-profile performers, like Connor and Cy Grant, hit the glass ceiling.

---

43 Private staff memos, Norman Collins, Controller, Television to Patrick Hillyard, Head of Television, Light Entertainment, February 1 and 20, 1950, T16/175/1 TV Policy—Race Relations, File 1 (1950–54), WAC.

44 George Lamming, "Foreword," in Connor, *Horizons*, x.

This conundrum had particular consequences for the West Indian artists under examination here because for the BBC and for many audience members they represented a minority interest. In 1965, Martin Esslin, then Head of Drama (Sound), articulated this feeling with specific regard to "coloured writers." While he declared himself in favor of promoting their efforts, he noted that, like "plays from Wales, Scotland and Northern Ireland,"

> such plays inevitably labour under a certain handicap from the point of view of listener reaction because there is always a small but significant percentage of listeners who feel it difficult to identify with characters however mildly foreign they may be, and of course another percentage who harbour prejudices against them. If we embark on such a policy we must do so knowing full well that in terms of reaction indices and perhaps figures the response will be slightly below average for plays of comparable quality. I myself am not worried about such figures, but there might well be a conflict between policy considerations based on our duty towards the Commonwealth and equally important considerations calling for the highest possible degree of listener a [sic] appreciation.[45]

When celebrated Trinidadian writer Sam Selvon, for example, submitted two stories to the radio Talks department in 1952, the producer enjoyed them both but rejected one: "It is beautifully told, but, frankly, the theme is a bit too uncomfortable and disturbing for a Morning Story on the Light Programme. As our audience is composed chiefly of housewives and hospital patients, the accent has to be on entertainment. A little sentiment and sadness, sometimes, yes. But bitterness, no."[46] The desire to appeal to the mainstream influenced decisions concerning style, subject matter, and casting. It is no surprise, therefore, that producers often praised the two West Indian entertainers most visible on the BBC in this period, Edric Connor and Cy Grant, for their smooth singing voices and gentle charm capable of wooing large audiences. This support disintegrated when they attempted to cultivate other artistic goals or aspects of their persona.

The above discussion of BBC programming and policy shows that the Corporation was a steadfast sponsor of West Indian artists in these years, and that the two shared a number of cultural priorities and goals. In practice, however, these writers and performers still had great difficulty transcending an institutional pattern that restricted them to a handful of "suitable" jobs. The next section, however, contains a selective overview

---

45 Memo, Martin Esslin to F. G. Gillard, Director of Sound Broadcasting, July 6, 1965; T16/562 TV Policy, Programme Policy: Immigration (1965–67), WAC.

46 Letter, Paul Stephenson, Talks producer to Sam Selvon, April 21, 1952. WAC RCONT1—Samuel Selvon, Talks File 1 (1950–62), WAC.

of some of the BBC television programs that dramatized the subject of Caribbean migration and settlement in Britain. It provides a sample of the type of serious material available to Caribbean writers and actors, and shows how the BBC projected its position on the issue of colonial settlement and race relations (described above) onto radio and television.

West Indian Drama at the BBC

West Indian artists performed in many capacities on BBC radio and television—in educational programming, cultural talks on the Overseas Service, and, perhaps most visibly, in the Variety genre, as singers and dancers. Edric Connor, for example, starred in a television broadcast of *Music Makers*, live from Alexandra Palace, as early as June 1946.[47] But it was in the 1950s that black artists began playing explicitly "West Indian" roles in dramas that commented, directly or indirectly, on migration and settlement in Britain or domestic race relations.

In the late 1940s and 1950s, the BBC was cautious in its presentation of West Indian entertainers and focused on light entertainment, but among its more adventurous early programming was Jan Carew's *The River Man*, inspired by Caribbean folklore, as a half-hour drama on the Home Service in 1957, with Errol John, Earl Cameron, Pearl Connor, and Andrew Salkey reading in pronounced dialect.[48] Having initially rejected it, the Third Programme dramatized Errol John's Trinidad-set *Small Island Moon* (based on his stage play *Moon on a Rainbow Shawl*) the following year, and while a few listeners felt it was too heavy to be entertaining—one viewer complained, "I found it appallingly realistic, but was not in the mood to be harrowed and could have done with a little more humour and happiness"— most applauded the BBC for broadcasting more unconventional subject matter.[49] These programs drew indirect connections to the contemporary situation in Britain, serving almost as narrative precursors to Caribbean migration, but such connections were only implicit.

The BBC was nevertheless the first broadcaster to tackle the subject of West Indian integration and white racism in its drama programs, and its approach demonstrates its belief that by educating audiences on the background and context of colonial migration, it could help eradicate the ignorance that bred white prejudice. We can see this in two of the most visible and ambitious BBC productions to offer direct comment on West

---

47 TVART1—Edric Connor, File 1 (1946–62), WAC. *Music Makers* was broadcast live on June 22, 1946.

48 Broadcast November 2, 1957. *The River Man* (1957), Radio Script, Microfiche, WAC.

49 WAC files on *Small Island Moon* (1958), Radio script, Microfiche; and R9/6/77— Audience Research Reports (Sound). Chronological Reports May 1958. LR/58/849, Week 22: "Small Island Moon."

Indian experience in Britain: the television "drama documentary" *A Man from the Sun*, which aired at 9 pm on November 8, 1956, and the radio "ballad opera" *My People and Your People*, broadcast at 7:30 pm on the Home Service, July 22, 1959. These programs featured well-known Caribbean actors, a few of whom appeared in both: Cy Grant, Nadia Cattouse, and Pauline Henriques. Both productions dealt with predominantly Caribbean characters, their arrival in London, and the particular challenges they faced, in particular white prejudice. But while both plays tended to be sanctimonious in tone, *A Man from the Sun* was more optimistic in its advocacy of a community-based solution to racial tensions. *My People and Your People*, produced partly in response to the Notting Hill riots, betrayed greater uncertainty about the race relations debate.

Jack Williams has called *A Man from the Sun* "the first play written for television about an ethnic minority in Britain."[50] And, indeed, the play is unique for the time in its loyalty to the perspective of its West Indian characters. It does not adhere to the "race relations narrative" outlined in later chapters, because it is not concerned with white domesticity or the prospect of miscegenation; the sexual politics of race are not at issue here. Instead, it tells the story of Cleve (Errol John), a young, uneducated, but honest and hardworking Jamaican who comes to England in hopes of bettering his situation. His cousin Alvin (Cy Grant) picks him up at the station, takes him in, and warns him about the prejudice he can expect in London with regard to housing and employment:

> Alvin: This fellow's right, Cleve. Maybe you think Englan's you' mother country, but over here you are a foreigner.
> Cleve: But Alvin man, we're all British citizens.
> Alvin: You're a British citizen in Jamaica, but here you're a coloured man.[51]

Also arriving at the station is the nineteen-year-old beauty pageant queen Ethlyn, whose brother in Birmingham does not show up to meet her. Both characters, over the course of the hour-long show, experience various trials and homesickness, but both, with the help of other Caribbean and African settlers, civic volunteers, and liberal whites, integrate themselves into the respectable expatriate community—Ethlyn marries a young Caribbean man from the local social club, while Cleve takes up reading and writing lessons to improve his employment prospects.

A Man from the Sun was far from the potboilers that sensationalized racial conflict in later years; as Carl Daniels put it, the film "conveys its

---

50 Williams, *Entertaining the Nation*, 155.
51 Camera script, scene 15, p. 21; FILMS 41/42—TV Drama Scripts, *A Man from the Sun* (1956), WAC.

message in the style of an instructional manual."[52] It was a drama with a documentary feel and educational purpose; according to BBC producer Irene Shubik, the drama documentary was a new genre of TV play, appearing for the first time only in mid-1955, and while the "drama" was meant to entertain, the "documentary" was based on thorough research, the use of some location shooting, and an explicit educational angle, such as "the plight of the unmarried mother, prostitution, strikes, handicapped children etc."[53] It was a form well-suited to *A Man from the Sun*, which had a clear social "problem"—West Indian migration—and pointed out for white viewers the dangers London presented to settlers as well as the good work performed by sympathetic whites and community services. This is illustrated in the characters of Cleve and Ethlyn, both of whom come within a hair's breadth of slipping into the urban underworld. Ethlyn, all alone at the train station, is unknowingly recruited into a prostitution ring until an eagle-eyed woman from the local church army rescues her. Later, the sociability of the interracial club gradually cures her loneliness and homesickness, culminating in a West Indian wedding replete with a calypso accompaniment courtesy of Cy Grant. Meanwhile, Cleve loses his job after a scuffle with a bigoted coworker, and is unwittingly lured into the drug trade. He dutifully shows his package to the liaison officer (played by Earl Cameron) at the social club and is steered away from the criminal life.

A Man from the Sun is thus, in many ways, a faithful exposition of the liberal—that is, community-oriented and educational—approach to the integration and accommodation of the West Indian population, and is easy to lampoon on this account. When, for instance, a recently arrived African reveals his class snobbery and budding nationalist feeling, Brent (Earl Cameron) and the English Miss Prior have the following instructional exchange:

> Miss Prior: It's a good job all your educated young men aren't like him.
> Brent: You mustn't judge us by a minority, you know.
> Miss Prior: And you mustn't judge us by the sort of people you'll meet
>   on the Housing Committee.[54]

The sententiousness in evidence in *A Man from the Sun* was not well received by all viewers at the time. The Audience Research Report drawn

52 Carl Daniels, "A Man from the Sun," BFI Screenonline; available at http://www. screenonline.org.uk/tv/id/475546/index.html; accessed June 17, 2010.

53 Irene Shubik, *Play for Today: The Evolution of Television Drama* (London: Davis Poynter, 1975), 37.

54 Camera script, scene 21, p. 37; FILMS 41/42—TV Drama Scripts, *A Man from the Sun* (1956), WAC.

up by the BBC noted that although overall response to the program was very good, one "Housewife (who frankly admitted that she was 'the kind of person who looks for a seat away from a coloured man') said: 'the knowledge of what is happening now in Brixton is enough to make me wonder if this was a realistic picture.'"[55] Moreover, some of the dialogue, aimed as it was at a domestic white audience, suggested a priggish disdain for what it viewed as un-English patterns of courtship. In the conversation below, the well-meaning Miss Prior betrays her discomfort with the fact that the genial Alvin is not legally married to the woman he lives with:

> Miss Prior: He's building up quite a family over here. He has his ... er ... wife with him already.
> Tobias: Oh, a lot of these fellows are sending for their wives.
> Miss Prior: I'm glad to hear it. It's much better for them than these unfortunate liaisons—they so often seem to pick the wrong type of white girl.[56]

This is a fascinating little exchange in the context of an ostensibly anti-racist teleplay. On the one hand, the writer (John Elliot), seemed keen to express no theoretical aversion to interracial relationships, since Miss Prior's remarks suggest that it is the white women, rather than the colored men, who are the problem in interracial "liaisons." On the other hand, the program clearly stresses the preferability of same-race unions, even if they are not legally binding. Elliot, through the voice of Miss Prior, expressed a vision of propriety that was almost impossibly narrow.

Despite its cloying tone, the program deserves historical recognition for at least two reasons. First, perhaps because it was released two years prior to the Notting Hill riots (and the more visible public anxiety that followed), the play is unique in its concentration on a (perceived) migrant experience. Although white racism figures largely in the challenges faced by several characters, it does not serve as the dramatic crux of the story. It is only one of a number of factors that shape the migrant experience. Instead, the play focuses on the development of a Caribbean and colonial *community* in London, punctuated only intermittently by white English players. Second, as Daniels has noted, unlike more recent "black" television drama, *A Man from the Sun* was centrally concerned with "social justice"; it "prescribed a community-wide approach to individual problems."[57] The same contrast could be drawn with most other race relations drama of the

---

55 VR/56/586—*A Man from the Sun*; R9/7/25, Audience Research Reports—Television, November/December 1956, WAC.

56 Camera script, scene 10, pp. 14–15; FILMS 41/42—TV Drama Scripts, *A Man from the Sun* (1956), WAC.

57 Daniels, "A Man from the Sun."

1950s and early 1960s, which presented racial hostility as a psychological issue most effectively resolved within the realm of the domestic.

But *A Man from the Sun* stressed the degree to which the community as a whole was responsible for the effective integration of colonial migrants. As one viewer remarked in a report for the BBC at the time, it encouraged white Britons "to revise their ideas about the coloured worker in this country 'who deserves more sympathy and understanding than he has met with hitherto. Obviously, his welfare is everybody's concern.'"[58] While it may seem like a liberal but rather bland statement, it is remarkable for its communal attitude toward New Commonwealth settlers. This viewer's sentiment would have seemed out of place if it had been expressed only five years later, when the government passed an immigration bill that implicitly blamed white racism on migrants and cut the (non-white) Commonwealth out of the fabric of British citizenship.

*

Three years later, the BBC adapted the West Indian migrant story for radio, this time producing a "ballad opera" set during the Notting Hill riots that had happened the year before. If it is possible, *My People and Your People* was both more sensationalist and more mawkish than *A Man from the Sun* and reflected the hardening of racial perceptions in the intervening years. Like other race relations dramas of its time, *My People and Your People* relied heavily on racial violence and interracial romance for its thematic structure, although again the BBC's concern to uplift audiences meant that there were strong liberal overtones. Cy Grant starred again, as Len, who moves from Jamaica to the Notting Hill neighborhood with his sister Kathy, who eventually falls in love with another migrant to the city, a young Scot. As a ballad opera, the production included several musical numbers (which perhaps dulled the impact of an issue as serious as racial violence), and Edric Connor served as the play's powerful narrator.

The production's overall effect, from a modern perspective, was to take an urgent political event like the Notting Hill riots and squeeze from it only the most anodyne lessons. Kathy's Scottish suitor, Ian, echoes the dominant Establishment assessment of the 1958 violence when he calls the rioters:

A lot of half-baked Fascists trying to get a bit of notice in the papers …! It's <u>not</u> a matter of colour at all. It's just that when a lot of strange people move into a district—all the <u>other</u> people have to start changing their ideas,—and they don't <u>like</u> that … The miners didn't

---

58 VR/56/586—*A Man from the Sun* Audience Research Report.

like having Italians work beside them in the mines—there wasn't any colour prejudice <u>there</u>![59]

Remarks like this deflected attention away from the institutional and historical reasons for endemic British racism and ignored the existence of widespread prejudice that operated in subtler, less sensational ways. Connor's folksy narrative conclusion reinforced this perspective and boiled the whole issue of British racial conflict to little more than parochial quibbling:

> [The] Mother Country ... had a real Arctic feeling, bad-bad-indifferent and even enemy hostile, sometimes ... No, and I guess <u>we</u> weren't all that easy to accept either—livin' different ways and doin' things sort of wrong—never havin' <u>lived</u> in a big, old time city before ... Some of us <u>were</u> no-good people, sure ... <u>Some</u> of us. ... But most of us were decent people like Kathy herself,—yes, and Len himself ... <u>He</u> was a good boy, if he'd taught himself not to be hurt so easy ...
>
> An' as for <u>your</u> people ... well, there were plenty bad ones there as well, like the kids who started it all that night—just for a fight, an' the devil at work in all of 'em. Those boys got what was comin' to them: they went to prison for it, and both sides were glad of that: As for the rest—they were mostly ashamed—the good an' decent ones ... And now the livin' is <u>quiet</u> again,—quiet an' friendly as it was before—<u>most</u> of the time, that is ...[60]

As naïve as this dialogue appears today, it garnered great approval from ordinary viewers, according to the BBC's report, which recorded much rapturous praise and only one or two remarks suggesting that "the colour bar is not entertainment" and "it was a pity to resurrect all the trouble at Notting Hill when it was all over and done with."[61] According to the report, a "Secretary" summed up the feelings of many when she wrote, "The comments on the disappointment of coloured people, coming to a mother country that has received so many coldly, almost had me in tears both of compassion for them and shame for the behaviour of some British people."[62]

Arguably, then, there was shift between the social aims of *A Man from the Sun* and those of *My People and Your People* three years earlier, probably because of the polarizing effects of Nottingham and Notting Hill. While

---

59 Radio script, scene 23, p. 46, *My People and Your People* (1959), WAC.

60 Ibid., scene 25, p. 50.

61 LR/59/1262 (Week 30)—"My People and Your People," R9/6/91—Audience Research Reports, Sound (July 1959), WAC.

62 Ibid.

the former taught viewers that the welfare of West Indian settlers was "everyone's concern," the latter elicited only tears of sympathy.

By the 1960s, perhaps in response to the more challenging (or at least sensationalist) fare offered in some British cinemas and theaters, the BBC became a little more daring in its choice of content. In 1963 it replaced its televised *Sunday Plays* with the *First Night* series of plays. Producer John Elliot wrote a promo for the *Radio Times* magazine emphasizing that the new series aimed to be "livelier and tougher" than the Sunday plays of the past.[63] Accordingly, BBC Drama producers viewed *First Night* as a suitable vehicle to expose the controversial race issue. Among its early plays for the series was John's Africa-set *Dawn*, about "an American negro sent to Africa to get a story about black nationalism. He meets Selena, an almost white coloured girl, whom he loved in the past."[64] Set amidst a backdrop of growing racial tension, *Dawn* was suitable for the *First Night* series because the medium allowed the BBC to "flag" it as a socially challenging drama about race.

Similarly, the "stark, explosive and contemporary" *Fable* (1965) made an impression for its dramatized reversal of English racism. The play was set in an imaginary England that has become a police state that practices apartheid—by a "coloured" minority over a white majority. It aimed to kill two topical birds with one stone; it was a rather crude lesson on the injustices of *both* South African apartheid and Britain's unofficial color bar. It did, however, give creative roles to West Indian actors like Cameron (in a small role), Thomas Baptiste, and Carmen Munroe. In addition, it implicitly suggests the ultimate impotence of white liberal protests in South Africa, and perhaps Britain as well. Perhaps as a result of its ambitious moral lesson, *Fable* received a widely mixed reaction from English viewers. While some "thought Fable an original, powerful and effective attack on race hatred," many others were disturbed, even frightened, by the story, which displayed an unusual level of violence. Some failed completely to grasp the play's larger meaning, like one woman who confessed, "It left me feeling angry and more in agreement with the colour bar then [sic] ever." Even sympathetic viewers felt that "it would have been much more convincing if it had not relied on violence but had shown the subtle indignities which exist in our country today."[65]

Fable's broadcast was deliberately pushed back by a week in order to prevent its influencing the outcome of polling day in the color-conscious

---

63 Memo, John Elliot, producer for the *First Night* series to Sydney Newman, Head of Drama Group, Television, August 28, 1963; T5/2, 081/1, First Night—General, WAC.

64 Revised *First Night* schedule (September 5, 1963), T5/2, 081/1, First Night—General, WAC.

65 Audience Research Report for *Fable*, February 12, 1965; T5/1349. Wednesday Play ("Fable"), WAC.

Leyton by-election. Behind the scenes, Kenneth Adam, Director of Television and Controller of Programmes, who was instrumental in the decision to postpone the broadcast, explained that it was "perfectly possible that a number, and it could even be a significant number of Leyton voters might indeed, in the mood of the moment, misunderstand this play, and taking it simply on face-value, vote <u>anti</u>-black as a result. I would not care to have that on my conscience."[66] Thus, whether intentional or not, *Fable* thus encouraged a kind of race panic among some viewers, putting it in line with the late colonial "siege narratives" that, as Wendy Webster argues, portrayed empire as a threat to cozy English domesticity.[67]

Although the above overview of dramatic programming about West Indian migrants and race relations is selective rather than comprehensive, there was in fact not much such programming produced. In 1952, at the request of the BBC administrative officers, a tally was made of programs concerning the "colour question" that had been aired on BBC radio that year; they numbered 31 in all, but only two or three of those listed dealt with the British situation (most concerned South African apartheid).[68] This, of course, was before the number of annual West Indian arrivals began exceeding 10,000. However, even twenty years later, in 1972, an independent consultant for the BBC found that in one week's viewing of all *three* British television channels (BBC1, BBC2, and ITV), only one West Indian appeared in a lead role in the dramas and films on offer.[69] While these randomly gleaned statistics are far from conclusive, they suggest at the very least that thoughtful dramatic pieces like *A Man from the Sun* and *My People and Your People* were exceptions to the rule of white Anglocentric broadcasting. (The number of radio talks and documentary, or news magazine-style television programs concerning the "colour question" did increase, especially after 1958.) They also suggest the difficulties faced by aspiring stars like Edric Connor and Cy Grant as they attempted to break out of their circumscribed roles, a topic to which this chapter will now turn.

---

66 Letter, Kenneth Adam, Director of Television and Controller of Programmes, to Sydney Newman, Head of Drama Group, Television, January 12, 1965; T5/1349, Wednesday Play ("Fable"), WAC.

67 See Webster, *Englishness and Empire*.

68 List of programs concerning the "colour question," March 12, 1953; R51/92 Talks, Coloured People, Files 1 and 2 (1943–54), WAC.

69 VR/72/56—"Non-Whites on British Television," 1971; R9/10/19 Audience Research, Special Reports Television, Chronological (1972), WAC.

"The Birth Pangs of a New Nation":
Edric Connor

Trinidadian Edric Connor began his career at the BBC in 1944, near the high watermark of that institution's enthusiasm for the cultural connection between Great Britain and her empire. It was a perfect fit; not only did Connor possess natural singing and dramatic abilities, but he was a trove of information on West Indian culture and history, including music and folklore. He was an immediate success at the Corporation, but when the afterglow of military victory had subsided and concerns about racial strife replaced the celebration of empire in the late 1950s, the BBC increasingly rebuffed Connor's efforts to create and broadcast more meaningful work.

Connor began working for the BBC only two weeks after he first arrived in London, via New York, in February 1944. An engineer by profession and education, Connor was also a trained singer, and his remarkable voice yielded immediate contracts with both the Home and General Overseas Services; producer Leslie Baily called him a "find" in an early BBC press statement.[70] In fact, it was producer Eric Fawcett who "discovered" Connor for the domestic audience after hearing one of his recordings for the West Indies Service. He helped launch Connor's career as a regular on the popular radio series *Serenade in Sepia*, which broadcast forty times on the Home Service throughout 1945. *Serenade* cemented his reputation among both listeners and BBC staff, and Connor enjoyed a long, fruitful, and diverse professional career, never concentrating on one television or radio series. All told, he did about five hundred broadcasts for the BBC over the course of twenty-three years. He suffered from a recurrent illness for much of this time, and died on October 16, 1968.[71]

This conventional biography conceals much about Edric Connor, in particular his creative passion, his lively interest in West Indian folklore, and his personal commitment to the promotion of West Indian culture and artists within England. Guyanese actor and singer Thomas Baptiste, Connor's contemporary, remarked, "He felt if he did anything which [didn't] really work out positively, it was a reflection on what he would call *his people*—black people; and I don't think anybody's got the right to carry that burden or responsibility on their shoulders."[72] It was this commitment to representing the Caribbean and black communities positively that informed so many of Connor's creative decisions at the BBC and ultimately directed the trajectory of his career. However, it also exposed the discrepancy between Connor's

---

70 Press statement, undated; RCONT 1—Edric Connor, Artist's File I (1944–49), WAC.

71 Memos, October 17, 1968 and April 24, 1970; RCONT 12—Edric Connor, Artist's File V (1968–72), WAC.

72 Thomas Baptiste, interview by Stephen Bourne, 1993; Stephen Bourne Interview Collection, NSA.

and the Corporation's commitment to the promotion of West Indian talent, leading to tensions in an otherwise tranquil professional relationship.

From the moment he stepped off the boat with ten years' worth of research on West Indian folk music packed in his luggage, Edric Connor had plans. Also packed in his luggage were letters of introduction to the BBC—Connor had already broadcast from Trinidad and lectured publicly on West Indian folklore. His goals in London never changed; he looked to fuse his natural talents as a performer and vocalist with his desire to promote the art and history of the West Indies. Connor's other ambition was to promote West Indian and other non-white talent in Britain, and he viewed his own success as a way to achieve this. At times his concern for other struggling artists caused him to overlook the demands of his own work, which, even given his success, was never guaranteed.

His relationship with the BBC was immediately fruitful because his desire to promote his colonial culture was shared by the London producers he met. Connor left his first meeting (with, among others, John Grenfell Williams and Una Marson) "feeling I was among friends." One of his earliest radio program appearances was in *Traveller's Tales*, for which he was able to use much of his research on West Indian folklore. This was a positive experience for Connor:

> The BBC provided the opportunities. I did all that was requested of me without compromising my conscience. ... And I brought what seemed an inexhaustible supply of material. I knew nothing at all about the machinery that ran the BBC and I didn't care to know. I worked hard. Made friends.[73]

Shortly after his arrival, Edric courted and married the young Pearl Nunez, who, upon entering the world of show business, began to join her husband in pushing for better opportunities for black and colonial entertainers in London. Of Edric's swift entry into the cultural mainstream, she has emphasized the receptive mood toward colonial people in the mid- to late 1940s, before the onset of large-scale migration:

> The British people knew that there was a [Caribbean] contribution [to the war effort], so there was a nice feeling. There wasn't overcrowding, there were not too many people around, and there was a good feeling about the war effort, so that he entered England on a better wave of interest, you know? And I think the BBC at that time were also interested in helping to promote and assist some of the third-world people and the Caribbean people to, you know, realize their dreams or whatever. So he came at a good time, when more doors were open. He didn't have to kick too hard,

---

73 Connor, *Horizons*, 62, 63.

like we did later. ... And I think he was appreciated; I think he gave a lot. And I think he got quite a lot out of it as well.[74]

Connor's history is thus one example of the convergence of metropolitan and colonial values in the immediate postwar period.

Connor revealed his altruism to staff at the BBC almost as soon as he began working with them. In July of 1945 the secretary for the African Service Director wrote to the Assistant Manager of "Variety" Booking:

> I spoke to Mr. Connor the other day and he told me that he was not anxious to make money out of broadcasts to his own people and would be prepared to do a "Calling West Africa" programme at his old rates. I feel, myself, that this generosity is to be definitely encouraged, but I think we might offer him a little above his original rates of pay.[75]

Connor's concern for "his own people" was apparently well known by those staff who worked with him. Later in 1945, when he refused to grant the BBC the transcription rights for *Serenade in Sepia* (a decision which actually lost him money), the Director of Overseas Programme Services wrote that he regretted his refusal, "because it seemed to me that these excellent programmes ... were calculated to do a service both to yourself as an artist and to the cause of your people which I know you have so much at heart."[76]

Connor's gestures did not simply demonstrate that his ethnic commitment outweighed his monetary ambitions (a position that must have thrilled the Booking Department). They also showed Connor's feeling of affinity for his black colleagues in London. When, in 1947, the question of reviving one of his radio programs arose, he opted for the one that would "afford employment to more musicians":

> Perhaps I can draw your attention to the fact that since this programme went off sound broadcasting in April, 1946, we have heard very little of the orchestrators, Max Saunders, Ralph Bruce, Jock Morgan and Dennis Moonan, who prepared our arrangements. Eugene Pini and His Orchestra have been doing some work, but I gather it has not been much and they have hinted it to me. Also my partner, Evelyn Dove, strikes me as being in want of regular work.[77]

---

74 Pearl Connor, interview by Stephen Bourne, 1993; Stephen Bourne Interview Collection, NSA.

75 Memo, Mary Treagold to Mr. Gilliott, July 30, 1945; RCONT 1—Edric Connor, Artist's File I, WAC.

76 Letter, Cyril Conner to Edric Connor, October 25, 1945; RCONT 1—Edric Connor, Artist's File I, WAC.

77 Letter, Connor to C. Lawson Dick, Home Service, Planning Department, May 3, 1947; RCONT 1—Edric Connor, Artist's File I, WAC.

This aggressive expression of his commitment might have surprised regular listeners to *Serenade*, had they been aware of it. Connor's correspondence with the BBC shows him to be a grateful, soft-spoken individual, as well as a devout Christian—one of his most well-loved numbers was his sung version of the Lord's Prayer—and his amiability won him a large and affectionate fan base. Petula Clark, who worked with Connor when she was a teenager, remarked that he was perhaps the first black person she "had ever seen": "And I think that's quite an important thing because I absolutely adored him, and that sort of first contact is very important."[78] Despite his naturally genial demeanor, his increasingly insistent efforts to integrate other migrant artists into his own programs, or to use his influence to expose them to BBC producers, did eventually complicate his relationships at the Corporation. In doing so, he denied himself the luxury of simply assuming the good intentions of BBC producers and directors.

By looking at Connor's career arc we can see that although he was consistent in his desire to forward the interests of other West Indian artists and promote West Indian culture, the BBC's interest in these issues waxed and then waned; by the turn of the 1960s, the Corporation valued Connor much the same way it had fifteen years earlier—as a singer of spirituals. In his early years at the BBC, Connor gained popularity on the radio show *Serenade in Sepia*, a program of "sweet music in the Negro style," singing spirituals, calypsos, and plantation tunes with his West African partner Evelyn Dove.[79] Their personal talents and charisma were great enough to land them on television as early as 1946. Performing live from Alexandra Palace, producer Eric Fawcett chose to present "them in vision very much as they appeared in the broadcast studios, without the use of extravagant settings."[80] After *Serenade* was discontinued in 1946, Connor maintained and even enhanced his singing success with the similarly conceived series *Plantation Echoes*. At the same time, he began acting in dramatic roles. A great many projects from this period were built around southern American music and themes, fashionable material for black entertainers in the 1940s. (Connor predictably had his share of singing "coon songs" and portraying Uncle Remus: "In dis worril, lots er folks is gotter suffer fer udder fokes sins.")[81]

The early 1950s, however, witnessed an opportune conjunction of Connor's interests and background with current trends when, starting

---

78 Petula Clark, interview by Stephen Bourne; Stephen Bourne Interview Collection, NSA.

79 *Music Makers* program calendar entry for June 22, *Radio Times*, Television Edition 91, no. 1185 (June 14, 1946); TVART 1—Edric Connor. File I (1946–62), WAC.

80 Undated newspaper clipping, July 1946; TVART 1—Edric Connor, File I (1946–62), WAC.

81 Memo, Freda Cann, Children's Hour, to Mrs. Hewitt, Variety Bookings, June 22, 1946; RCONT 1—Edric Connor Artist's File I (1944–49), WAC.

about 1950, his image became more overtly Caribbean in flavor as he capitalized on the emerging calypso craze (which will be discussed in greater detail in the next chapter). As early as 1946, he had appeared in recreations of Caribbean Carnival on the General Overseas Service, but he also performed on the Light Programme in six episodes of *Calypso Calling* in 1957. At about this time, too, Connor began pitching his own ideas to the BBC, tapping into his past research on West Indian folk music. Initially, he offered to do fifteen-minute talks on subjects like the origins of the calypso. (His offer was turned down by Variety, but only because two other departments had already jumped on the subject within the previous six months.)[82] His pitches became more imaginative over time. In 1954, Connor and writer Russell McKinnon submitted the following elaborate series pitch to Variety:

> I would like to suggest a half-hour series under some such general title as EDRIC CONNOR'S ENGLISH JOURNAL or EDRIC CONNOR'S OTHER ISLAND. The idea is that Edric makes a mythical journey each week to a different place in the British isles—either a different town, or a series of places famous in themselves, such as Hampton Court or Stonehenge—He is a West Indian immigrant who has read a lot about the Motherland and been taught about it in school in Trinidad—its history, customs, traditions etc.—and now wants to find out all about it for himself. He meets, on the boat coming over, say, a little English girl to whom he confides this ambition, and she offers to show him her—and his—mother country.
>
> So they go from place to place, on a pilgrimage of pleasure and song. For—and here, I think is the double 'twist'—the little girl discovers a song, an English song, in each place, and then Edric reproduces it in West Indian form. Finally he caps it with a proper West Indian song which the place evokes.
>
> ... I feel that Edric's considerable listening public would welcome a new series from him, and this is the sort of programme he himself wants.[83]

This pitch reveals much about how Connor wanted to represent himself (and the West Indian community) to the British listening public, and how he viewed the historical and cultural connection between the islands

---

82 Letter, Michael Standing, Head of Variety to Connor, March 2, 1950; RCONT 1—Edric Connor Artist's File 2 (1950–54), WAC.

83 Letter, Russell McKinnon to Gale Pedrick, Script Editor, Variety, June 8, 1954; RCONT 1—Edric Connor Artist's File 2 (1950–54), WAC. Although Pedrick expressed definite interest in the idea, there is no evidence in the files that it was ever developed for production.

and the mother country. His idea takes on heightened significance in the context of mounting white curiosity and anxiety over West Indian migration to England. Here, the migrant is no foreigner, but someone educated, articulate, embodied in the reassuring and familiar form of Edric Connor. The innocent English girl is not threatened by his presence, and she is not old enough to have imbibed prejudiced ideas about migrants. Finally, the whole structure of the show reinforces the pleasing picture of a kinder, gentler, imperial identity where cultural (in this case musical) cross-pollination demonstrates the shared history of England and her colonies. Connor is here positioning himself and other Commonwealth migrants within an image of emerging postcolonial Britain and shaping that image to include them as complementary and unique contributors.

Boosted by his positive experiences on BBC radio and television, and with years of success in variety and drama behind him, Connor tried to accelerate the penetration of West Indian subjects and talent into the world of the British, and international, media. Tensions sharpened considerably in the late 1950s. This was the result of Connor's attempt to broaden the scope of his creative activity and his establishment of the "Commonwealth and foreign" talent agency Edric Connor Limited, with his wife Pearl. These ventures competed for Connor's time and energy and caused him to focus less on the kind of singing and acting that had made him famous. At the same time, it seems clear that he and the BBC were diverging on issues of content and approach, for Connor more aggressively pursued the "West Indian" angle just as producers were losing interest in favor of a more British-oriented "race relations" slant.

As Connor grew more interested in developing his own ideas, and frustrated at the lack of employment for his fellow West Indian performers, he began to branch out independently, setting up his own film production company in 1959. The BBC was not supportive of these endeavors, although this was at least partly because his zeal to bring his ideas to fruition outstripped his experience as a producer and director. In April he submitted not only a pilot telefilm for the prospective series *Edric Connor Sings*, but also sample scripts for two other projects (including one titled *Calypso Story*), and a list of four film proposals planned for the future. His subjects were almost exclusively West Indian-themed: a story of the first Jamaican migrants to the UK, a dramatization of the Haitian Revolution, and a comedy entitled *Disputed Island* (there was no more information in the files, but this was likely about the Caribbean, or, conceivably, England). His central pitch for *Edric Connor Sings* was a musical variety show to be filmed on location throughout the West Indies and Africa, "strongly supported by local talent, with fresh and exciting ideas."[84]

---

84 Letter, Connor to Ronnie Waldman, Director, Film Department, Television, April 17, 1959; TVART 1—Edric Connor File I (1946–62), WAC.

From the tone of his correspondence, it was clear that Connor felt considerable confidence in the potential of his submissions to the BBC, and that he was anxious to begin filming in earnest. Although his chosen themes were certainly light entertainment, it was clear that Connor wanted to do more than entertain the English audience. Before Waldman had formally responded to the pitches, Antiguan Kelso Cochrane was murdered (on May 17) in the street by a gang of white youths, and Connor sent another, more serious appeal:

> In view of the recent happenings at Notting Hill and North Kensington over the past few weeks, I feel I must draw your attention to the urgent need for bringing a true picture of the people of the West Indies and their culture and ways of life to the British public.
>
> I would suggest that an indirect approach to this problem of human relations through the medium of film and television would do much to alleviate the grave tensions that now exist.
>
> ... I am organised and ready to roll but feel unable to do so without guarantees. I am appealing to you in this matter because I am sure you completely understand the implications.[85]

This letter demonstrates the degree to which Connor was aware of the representational power of his work, regardless of whether it was a race relations drama, Shakespeare, or a calypso. Scanell and Cardiff, writing about the history of British broadcasting, were aware of it too when they wrote:

> If the culture of radio depended on a shared public life brought into being by broadcasting itself, a central aspect of this process was that creation of a sense of participation in a corporate national life. The BBC fulfilled its mandate of service in the national interest by synthesizing a national culture from components that had begun to converge since the late nineteenth century. ... Radio, and later, television ... made the national real and tangible through a whole range of images and symbols, events and ceremonies, relayed to audiences direct and live.[86]

Connor understood, perhaps more clearly than others, the importance of cultural education in successfully fostering tolerant and open-minded relations between the wider white public and the West Indian community in Britain.

His pitches were rejected and internally dismissed as amateurish and lacking potential. Waldman called *Edric Connor Sings* "a very simple,

---

85 Letter, Connor to Cecil McGivern, Deputy Director, Television Broadcasting, May 19, 1959; TVART 1—Edric Connor File I (1946–62), WAC.
86 Scannell and Cardiff, *A Social History of British Broadcasting*, 277.

rather dull, rather muddled 15 minutes of mainly West Indian music and dancing which could and should have been done much better by us live in our own studios." The thinking behind his other ideas "is so confused that it is almost incomprehensible."[87] Deputy Director Cecil McGivern concurred but was sympathetic and respectful enough to send Connor a frank response (in addition to Waldman's form rejection) stating that they had "known one another for too many years now for me to be able to write you simply a polite and evasive reply."[88] McGivern's letter supports Pearl Connor's assessment of Edric's relationship with the Corporation: "Edric had many friends in the BBC, people who appreciated him as an artiste, but they never envisaged him as anything more."[89] Connor was disappointed and slightly offended by this outright rejection, without even the possibility of discussion, but he duly enrolled on the Corporation's Producer's Training Course. According to Connor's memoirs, which he wrote in 1964, two days before the course was to begin, the head of the school made him get the written approval of the Trinidad government before he could enroll. Then:

> Strange. At the end of the course he invited the students home for a drink. While I was talking to his wife he accused me of trying to seduce her. … If they can't get you on one charge, they try something else. When all else fails, they bring you in on a charge of Sex.[90]

Following his bizarre experience on the producer's course, Connor resubmitted his ideas to the Director of Television Broadcasting, Gerald Beadle, again to no avail; his training course instructor found him eager and charismatic, but "extremely emotional and not sufficiently clear-thinking to give practical realisation to his production ideas."[91] While Connor may have needed more experience in film production, and was perhaps too ambitious from the start, his frustration and confusion were in many ways understandable given his early successes with the Corporation and its previous interest in similar program themes.

But by the turn of the 1960s, BBC producers were little inclined to develop Connor as an actor or producer, or to delve more deeply into his particular passion for West Indian culture, at least on the Home Service. In 1962 he was turned down for two major roles in rapid succession, in *Green Pastures* and *A World Inside*. In the second case at least, Connor

---

87 Memo, Waldman to Cecil McGivern, April 29, 1959, TVART 1—Edric Connor File I (1946–62), WAC.

88 Letter, McGivern to Connor, May 25, 1959, TVART 1—Edric Connor File I (1946–62), WAC.

89 Pearl Connor interview in Pines, *Black and White in Colour*, 38.

90 Connor, *Horizons*, 118.

91 Memo, A. Miller Jones, Chief Instructor, Television to Eric Maschwitz, Head of Light Entertainment, January 26, 1960; TVART 1—Edric Connor File I (1946–62), WAC.

had received the distinct impression that he had already been accepted. In an internal memo to Holland Bennett, Eric Maschwitz wrote:

> I had a visit last week from Edric Connor. He seemed very distressed, being under the impression that there was some kind of prejudice against him here. ... I did my best to assure him that this kind of thing was always happening in connection with artists who had a run of bad luck. However, I pass it on to you for what it is worth.[92]

Regardless of whether or not, as Maschwitz suggested, these incidents (together with the Agency fiasco described in the next section) were unconnected misunderstandings, they certainly reveal growing friction between the two parties. (This is the only accusation of prejudice—of any kind—that appears in Edric Connor's files at the BBC.)[93]

Connor continued to work for the BBC on both television and radio but much less frequently. By the middle of the decade, he was scraping for appearances, asking for "any small mercies" in Light Entertainment and work "in Drama, Singing, Readings, or as a Disc Jockey" on the Overseas Service. When he reprised *Serenade in Sepia* for six programs in 1964, his thank-you note to the producer stated that the project "certainly came at a time when I needed the hand of a friend to lift me out of the morass into which I was sinking."[94] However, it is clear that by this time, the little work that Connor did continue to do for the BBC was just that—work, employment that did not accurately reflect his current creative objectives. *Serenade in Sepia's* brief return only highlighted the gulf that had gradually grown between Connor's vision for himself and other Commonwealth artists and that of the British Broadcasting Corporation. Connor stepped into his BBC career at a moment when it was enthusiastic about celebrating the nation's cultural and historical connection to the West Indies (and to the Commonwealth as a whole). But domestic events surrounding black migration to London helped set the two parties at cross-purposes; as Connor's desire to educate audiences about the West Indies grew more urgent, BBC producers grew reluctant to develop him beyond his traditional role as a "Negro" singer.

---

92 Memo, Eric Maschwitz, Special Duties, Programmes to Holland Bennett, Head of Artist Bookings, Television, October 15, 1962; TVART 1—Edric Connor File I (1946–62), WAC.

93 However, Patrick Newman, the Variety Booking Manager for Radio in 1954, did cynically suggest that his refusal to raise Connor's fee "is bound to make him flog the old hobby-horse of colour prejudice." Memo, Newman to Michael Standing, Head of Variety, Radio, January 11, 1954; RCONT 1—Edric Connor Artist's File II (1950–54), WAC.

94 Letters, Edric Connor to various BBC staff, August 10, 1964, April 24, 1965, August 4, 1965; RCONT 12—Edric Connor Artist's File IV (1963–67), WAC. The "morass" to which Connor refers was perhaps the fallout of his separation from his wife Pearl.

"The English Thing Just Suited Me": Pearl Connor and the Edric Connor Agency

In his drive to encourage other West Indian performers struggling in London, Edric Connor found a vigorous ally in his wife, Pearl Connor. Pearl took it upon herself to coordinate recently arrived artists from the West Indies and the Commonwealth, providing them with professional representation and (in some cases) training. Her correspondence with the BBC between 1956, when the Edric Connor Agency was founded, through the 1960s reveals how the Agency catered to the Corporation's perceived priorities when it came to West Indian and other artists of color. For the most part, these performers were considered for a narrow range of roles based on their skin color, or as exotic singers and dancers in light entertainment. Although most of her clients were considered unsuitable for "ordinary" roles, one of Pearl's major projects was to open up these opportunities for them as well as to push the BBC to produce more multicultural content in which Commonwealth artists could take part.

Pearl Nunez, born and raised like her husband in Trinidad, originally came to England to study law at London University. But her strong background in theater, as well as her energetic and entrepreneurial character, drew her back to the performing arts. She became instrumental in bringing together not just West Indians, but talented entertainers from throughout the Commonwealth who were assembled in London with few connections or qualifications that British institutions recognized. Marketing this talent to producers, theater directors, and club owners became the Edric Connor Agency's goal:

> Well the thing was that ... there was no representation ... people just had talent ... they were walking around London, in Baker Street or wherever else we could work and ... they didn't have any niche in which to fit ... [A]lthough people have trained in their own territory, whether Africa, Nigeria, whether Trinidad or wherever, their history, it wasn't a recognised history here, it wasn't a good CV note to put on your paper. You say, "I was trained in Trinidad in the Caribbean." "Who is that? Where is that?" So you had to explain. So we decided right, we'd take the bull by the horns and explain it all ... who they were, where they came from, their training, the fact that they knew Shakespeare and Dickens ... so they'd been educated ... they were able to cope with that kind of literature.[95]

---

95 Pearl Connor-Mogotsi, interview by David Johnson, June 25, 1997; Special Collections 9704095/A, *Blackgrounds* oral history project on the experience of Black Theatre and Black Theatre professionals, TMA.

Although the two co-founded the Agency, it was Pearl who carried out the lion's share of the day-to-day operations, as Edric was frequently filming away from home in the late 1950s and early 1960s. Her role increased even more after the marriage dissolved around 1964. As Pearl has remembered it, "Edric's name was the main attraction to these artistes, who all knew of him. I was still an unknown factor, the backroom girl."[96] In recent years, however, several artists and performers have emphasized Pearl Connor's pivotal role in galvanizing a professional Caribbean and Commonwealth arts community in Britain, pushing for the rights and acknowledgment of her clients, and taking care of fledgling colonial talent in London. George Lamming has written that this power couple

> created a partnership which had no parallel within the circles of Caribbean social and community life in London. The Connor residence became known as 'we going by Pearl and Edric': a self-evolving constituency of students, politicians, aspirants to political office, artists and the anonymous friend whom a friend had sent to seek assistance about jobs, accommodation, or advice about the best lawyer to consult.[97]

Pearl echoed Lamming: "[Edric] was very well known, so when people came off the boat, they migrated straight to us. We had a great reputation for looking after people."[98] And indeed, her name is scattered throughout the archival records: in letters of reprimand to the BBC, on cast lists at the Royal Court Theatre, as a cultural co-coordinator for London's distinguished British-Caribbean Association, on the judges' panel for London Carnival—even tucked into a 1955 newsreel about Princess Margaret's visit to the West Indian Students' Centre.[99] She worked tirelessly to procure Equity union membership for West Indian artists (who could never get forty weeks' work per year in the West End, "even if they were sweeping the stage"),[100] and she was a co-founder of the Negro Theatre Workshop in 1963. When talk of such a workshop began circulating as early as 1961, it was acknowledged that she was "the axis around which the whole concept of this movement revolves."[101]

Like Edric, Pearl also brought with her to England knowledge of, and pride in, Trinidadian folk culture, gained from her experience in the

---

96 Pearl Connor-Mogotsi, "My Life with Edric Connor," in Connor, *Horizons*, 151.

97 George Lamming, "Foreword," in Connor, *Horizons*, xiii.

98 Pearl Connor interview in Pines, *Black and White in Colour*, 39.

99 See, e.g., ACC/1888/116, London Council of Social Service Correspondence File, LMA; "Princess Opens Student Centre," Pathé newsreel (June 6, 1955): available at http://britishpathe.com/record.php?id=39394; accessed September 20, 2009.

100 Pearl Connor-Mogotsi, interview by David Johnson.

101 Ken Kelly, "W. I. Theatre: Cradle for Cultural Yearnings," *West Indian Gazette* (September 1961), supplement, 6.

Little Carib Theatre workshop under mentor Beryl McBernie. McBernie "was a dancer first but she was also a great folk poet herself and she brought all the information. She got us conscious of ourselves as nationals, because the Caribbean wasn't independent when I was a young girl."[102] In a way, Pearl Connor attempted to create the same sense of common identity in the international artists she later represented through the Edric Connor Agency. But her vision was wider, and embodied the multiracial Commonwealth ideal:

> We [Edric Connor Agency] had several Chinese, of course … because of the Caribbean set up from which I came, this multiracial society in Trinidad, we had Africans, Indians, Chinese, everybody … so I just slotted in … the English thing just suited me … all these Commonwealth people were flooding into London and had no representation.[103]

Pearl Connor's perspective here was an alternative to that of many involved in the British media. While the press discussed the infiltration of "white" English cities by non-white immigrants, she viewed London as vibrantly international and multiracial, like Trinidad, and her agency's approach reflected this.

However multicultural the Edric Connor Agency aimed to be, it catered to the needs and demands of mainstream companies and agents. To a certain extent, its promotional material presented clients the way casting directors often viewed them—in terms of color and, to a lesser extent, nationality. At least one official list classified artists by "type," under the headings Eastern Types, Negro Males, Negro Females, Coloured Females, Asiatic Types, Latin Types, and Continental Types.[104] Because at this time non-white actors and performers were usually hired as extras or bit players, it was their *look* that casting agents were most concerned about, not their specific country of origin or credentials. In this respect, Edric Connor Limited claimed to "specialize in finding coloured and foreign Artists of every nationality to meet the requirements of the most exacting producers."[105]

This does not mean that Pearl Connor, who managed the Agency, viewed her clients merely as racial types to be hired out as walk-ons. On the contrary, she worked tirelessly to seek out prominent roles for West Indian and other actors and to push for the creation of more such roles:

---

102 Pearl Connor interview in Pines, *Black and White in Colour*, 39.
103 Ibid.
104 Promotional letter, Pearl Connor, as Managing Director, Edric Connor Ltd. to Michael Barry, Drama Department, Television, April 17, 1959; TVART 1—Edric Connor File I (1946–62), WAC.
105 Letter, Pearl Connor, Edric Connor Ltd. to W. Worsley, Producer, Light Entertainment, Sound, December 9, 1957; RCONT 1—Edric Connor Artist's File III (1955–62), WAC.

We found that apart from waiting for an all-black play by a black writer … it was such a tough area, we went … to directors and producers and said, "Look, can't you get the doctor in this series to be a black fellow? Can't you use a black nurse? … So we worked very hard on that and we got it accepted eventually.[106]

Pearl Connor's ambitions for her artists were fierce enough to provoke and inconvenience others, even friends and colleagues. Playwright Barry Reckord humorously recounted a situation that arose during rehearsals for his play *Flesh to a Tiger* in 1957. When one of his central actors received an offer to star in the movie *Sapphire*, which was shortly to begin filming, Connor, also in *Tiger*'s cast, convinced him to take the higher-profile role even though it meant throwing the current stage production into chaos. According to Reckord, this incident simply reflected the desperate employment situation facing London's West Indian entertainers at the time.[107]

At bottom, it was the *professionalization* of minority entertainers that was Pearl Connor's, and the Agency's, central aim:

One of the problems we found early on with casting was that a lot of kids were being picked up at Baker Street station where they were hanging about, and they were being cast because of their behinds, or their eyes, or their faces, or how they walked, or what they did. It was a casting of extras, not necessarily of people who knew the job, or who understood the business, but people who were extremely cheap and who could provide padding for a scene. That was happening a lot and we wanted to break that system and to make production companies come to us for professional black people or Commonwealth people.[108]

This involved both the creation of positive propaganda for those artists who gained high-profile roles and performances as well as the cultural *education* of white audiences, who would perhaps come to view Commonwealth actors as more than African savages or migrant stereotypes. Edric Connor Limited worked on both fronts.

First, the agency seized upon every opportunity to publicize the achievements of its artists in British television, theater, and film. Their press releases routinely included long lists of current appearances by both individual clients and their talent roster as a whole. This practice

---

106 *Blackgrounds* interview with Pearl Connor-Mogotsi, June 25, 1997. In fact, Edric Connor Limited represented Joan Hooley, the first black actress to have a regular role on an English soap opera, playing a doctor in Associated Television's *Emergency Ward 10*.

107 Barry Reckord interview by David Johnson; Special Collections 9704091/A, *Blackgrounds* oral history project, TMA.

108 Pearl Connor interview in Pines, *Black and White in Colour*, 39.

served to promote artists, but its primary intention was to advertise their professional credentials, present them as artists who had gained British experience and could competently navigate the metropolitan entertainment world:

> [T]o get any kind of money and recognition was very tough … and that is where we were trying to build reputations, trying to get people recognised, recognition … because the minute you got it, we could talk, we could argue for you … so that's where Carmen Munroe, Johnny Sekka, and people like that came on the scene. They were people who got a chance to play an important part, got press reviews—you cut them out quickly, you blow them up … you transcribe them, you do whatever you could with them and send them round to let everybody know, "after all I am, you know, I can be recognised, I can perform, I am a professional."[109]

The second and more fundamental way to legitimize West Indian and other Commonwealth talent in Britain was of course to accelerate its acceptance in the eyes of white English producers and audiences. If the presence of West Indians in British society was naturalized, then the number and variety of roles in British programs would mushroom. The Connors were always aware of this, and the deepening of British-West Indian cultural connections was always at the heart of their agency's work, just as it was with Edric Connor himself. But Edric Connor Limited was particularly international in its outlook—it certainly reflected a concern with race relations in England, but also expressed its ethos in terms of the wider empire/Commonwealth and international cooperation. In 1962, the agency sent a long letter and memo to Eric Maschwitz, who had just stepped down as Head of Light Entertainment. In them, they presented an open-ended program proposal that would ensure a positive portrayal of the international community in England as well as the employment of Commonwealth artists. Like the Notting Hill violence a few years earlier, mounting anti-immigration sentiment, official and unofficial, informed the spirit of the proposal:

> In Britain today there are many talented Artistes from the West Indies, India, Ceylon, Pakistan and Malaya. The Immigration Bill regardless of its implications is here to stay. It is therefore important to use Television to minimize the problems the Immigration Bill will create by presenting a fortnightly programme on one of the Channels operated in Britain, featuring Coloured Artistes, Sportsmen, Politicians, Welfare Workers, Housewives, Children and a variety of people in all walks of life …
>
> These programmes would certainly interest stations in any part of

---

109 Ibid.

the Commonwealth or English speaking world, after being used for informative and educational purposes in Britain.[110]

The accompanying list of artists at their disposal was impressive, and included Edric Connor, Cy Grant, Shirley Bassey, Adelaide Hall, Cleo Laine, George Lamming, V. S. Naipaul, and Sam Selvon.

This idealistic vision drew only the brief reply: "Although I admire your energy in trying to promote television work for unemployed Commonwealth artists, I doubt whether the present planning of BBC-TV will allow much room for the sort of programme you have in mind."[111] Its "planning" was soon to change, however, as the Corporation began to rethink its *laissez-faire* approach to "minority" content; in fact the Connors' idea anticipated the BBC's approach to its migrant audience by a few years. For instance, in 1964 the Corporation's General Advisory Council suggested the power of the BBC to accelerate the integration of all immigrants into British society, "not only through the content of its programmes but also by using coloured immigrants as announcers and in other programme capacities." Soon after the Board of Governors conferred with various West Indian communities and centrally acknowledged "the need to educate the white host community to accept coloured citizens."[112] The first programs (on radio, designed for the Indian and Pakistani population) were broadcast in November 1965, more than three years after Edric Connor Limited's timely pitch.

In 1962, communications between the Connors and the BBC soured considerably. Not only was their pitch for a fortnightly program of international talent dismissed, but in October suspicions grew that the BBC was boycotting Edric Connor Limited and hiring international actors through other agencies. Such suspicions may have been unfounded, but they were harbored by working actors as well as Pearl Connor, who wrote irritated letters to producer Alan Bridges and Head of Drama Bookings Holland Bennett: "I was told that rumour is running rife amongst the company

---

110 "Memorandum on Television Services for the West Indies and Commonwealth Countries," Edric and Pearl Connor, Edric Connor Limited to Eric Maschwitz, February 15, 1962; TVART 1—Edric Connor File I (1946–62), WAC.

111 Letter, Eric Maschwitz to Edric Connor, February 19, 1962 ; TVART 1—Edric Connor File I (1946–62), WAC. Interestingly, Maschwitz was the man behind the creation of the extraordinarily popular and long-running *Black and White Minstrel Show*, which regularly featured white performers in blackface. Despite continued high ratings, it was removed from the schedule in 1978 due to charges of racism. In the 1930s he wrote a hit song for Leslie "Jiver" Hutchinson, called "These Foolish Things." According to Leonard Miall, he was still earning £1,000 in annual royalties from the song in the 1960s. See Miall, *Inside the BBC: British Broadcasting Characters* (London: Weidenfeld and Nicolson, 1994).

112 General Advisory Council, *Minutes*, October 21, 1964; Board of Governors, *Minutes*, July 22, 1965 quoted in Briggs, *The History of Broadcasting*, 590–91.

[of an all-colored musical], that in so far as the BBC casting of coloured people is concerned, <u>our Agency is out</u>."[113] Although both Bridges and Bennett expressed their dismay at the situation and laid it down to a series of misunderstandings surrounding the casting for their program *A World Inside*, Connor's fears were not paranoia.

Opportunities for West Indian and other foreign artists were scarce enough that her agency could not simply wait for casting calls but had to be aware of upcoming productions likely to cast their clients. They also had to possess a strong relationship with production companies that would keep them in touch. Most of the agency's clients freelanced through multiple agencies in order to secure as much work as possible. Thus it was informal connections that gave talent agencies the upper hand, and Pearl Connor took those connections seriously:

> We had to have information, you know, that was a problem we had, lack of information. I mean the technology we have nowadays, we didn't have it. ... So we had to wait on the grapevine, and our grapevine was kind of good. We had connections with people who actually let us know what was happening.[114]

In her interview for *Black and White in Colour*, Pearl Connor aptly summed up the boundaries and limitations of their role within mainstream institutions like the BBC:

> Edric always believed that if you get something into your head, an idea, a dream, something magical could happen. I think there is some magic nowadays, but magic eluded us at that time. We were in the struggle, or what we called the struggle—fighting for recognition, fighting for people to know who we were and to accept our talent. That's where we stood then.[115]

Pearl has mentioned on more than one occasion the degree to which she and her clients depended on the BBC for small contracts and appearances, but as her comment above shows, the process was a continual fight. Until the BBC changed its view of West Indian artists in Britain, recognizing them as more than an exotic, niche interest, small contracts were for the most part all these artists ever got.

---

113 Letter, Pearl Connor to Holland Bennett, October 4, 1962; TVART 1—Edric Connor. File I (1946–62), WAC.
114 Pearl Connor-Mogotsi, *Blackgrounds* interview.
115 Pearl Connor interview in Pines, *Black and White in Colour*, 40.

"I Got Type Cast as a Calypso Singer":
Cy Grant

Cyril Grant was born and raised in British Guiana, a mainland colony of the British West Indies. He became perhaps the most recognizable "colored" West Indian in Britain in this period, singing the news calypso-style on the hit television program *BBC Tonight*. His career at the BBC overlapped with Edric Connor's and, due to the limited range of acting roles open to West Indians, they co-starred in several productions. In fact, they were very different performers, with different career goals. For instance, although Grant routinely supported the West Indian community in London, appearing at charity events, dances, and even the first Caribbean carnivals in Notting Hill, he was not nearly as fervent in his promotion of Caribbean artists and causes. According to Pearl Connor, Grant "wasn't part of us in the sense that Edric was. When I say 'us' I mean our black community, the Caribbean community; the Afro-Caribbean community. Cy wasn't identified in that at the beginning."[116] However, like Connor, Cy Grant would become frustrated with the options available to him at the BBC after several years of support and success. His great success on *Tonight* served to pigeonhole him as little more than a genial calypso minstrel, and more often than not Grant had to look outside the Corporation for more challenging and rewarding work.

When Grant began working for the BBC in 1949, he had already gained some remarkable experiences, artistic and otherwise. Raised in a respectable "colored" (mixed-race) middle-class family in British Guiana—Grant called his upbringing "Victorian"—he, like so many other early postwar migrants to Britain, was educated in a classical English manner. His mother taught music, so Grant received classical training in piano, while absorbing the eclectic influences of British Guiana: "we had all the music of the world there because you have African drumming ... all the Indian festivals; we are near to South America so you have all the Latin American music; we are near to America and so we had all the jazz ... so I grew up with a very catholic taste in music."[117]

According to Grant, his education, as well as his knowledge of the hierarchy of color that still prevailed in British Guiana, made him feel "very much trapped," with no future of particular distinction.[118] The war offered him a chance to escape: "I felt that I wanted to see a bit of the

---

116 Pearl Connor interview by Stephen Bourne, 1993; Stephen Bourne Interview Collection, NSA.

117 Cy Grant interview by David Johnson, May 7, 1997; Special Collections 9704092/A, *Blackgrounds* oral history project on the experience of Black Theatre and Black Theatre professionals, TMA.

118 Ibid.

world, I couldn't have afforded to have gone to university, and joining the air force was one way of getting out of Guyana and seeing the rest of the world."[119] He joined the RAF in 1941, becoming a flight navigator and later, a prisoner of war. It was in the officers' POW camp that he decided to study law in London. He qualified for the bar in 1951 but, unsatisfied with the work available to him, he turned to acting, where he was more successful. ("The fact that I was a qualified barrister-at-law and had been an officer in the RAF didn't help me to find a job—that tells you a lot about racism in those days.")[120] Grant's biggest professional achievement prior to his BBC career was his membership of the prestigious Olivier Company at St James's Theatre, with which he toured from London to New York City.

Like most of his colleagues from the West Indies, Grant's early years at the BBC were dominated by work in radio, particularly on the General Overseas Service, on *Caribbean Voices* and *West Indian Diary*. He was quickly involved in a variety of different series, but the range of his performances suggests that he was used as an almost generic Caribbean "type." As well as shows with a British Guianese theme, he did programs on Bermuda (*This is Bermuda*), Jamaica (*Jamaican Folk Songs*), and Trinidadian calypsos. He was hired on at least one occasion to perform African and English folk tunes. Such variety was nonetheless a measure of his versatility.

Most of Grant's early radio and television jobs were vocal performances. He possessed a smooth, warm singing voice well-suited to the folk and popular music featured on the Overseas Service and the Light Programme. Although calypsos always figured prominently in his repertoire, and would later bring him fame, some of his admirers within BBC radio felt that his "great quality" was as "a lyric balladeer." One producer described him as "a West Indian singer of some versatility, managing straight sentimental ballads, French patois songs and calypsos with ease and great charm. I must say that of all the facets of his varied singing, I prefer him in straight songs with guitar accompaniment. In these he really excels."[121]

Grant's natural, kindly presence also appealed to Children's Hour producers; in 1953 its head W. E. Davis wrote, "He turned out to be a charming young man with a delightful baritone voice and just the right quiet intimate approach that one needs for songs to the guitar." Throughout the years, children's programming was a dependable staple of his work. Of course, one cannot enchant everyone, and one BBC staffer felt that he "crooned rather revoltingly." This was a decidedly minority viewpoint, and

119 Cy grant quoted in Phillips and Phillips, *Windrush*, 20.
120 Cy Grant interview in Pines, *Black and White in Colour*, 44.
121 Memo, H. Rooney Pelletier, Chief Assistant, Light Programme to Edward Nash, Assistant Producer, Light Programme, November 25, 1954; confidential report, Nash to Head of Light Music, December 3, 1954; RCONT 1—Cyril Grant Artist's File I (1946–57), WAC.

throughout the 1950s, Grant felt his "relationship with the B. B. C. [had] on the whole been of the friendliest."[122]

Thus, despite his background in drama, Grant became most well known at the BBC as a singer, albeit one with acknowledged acting talents. Part of the reason for this was, according to Grant, the dearth of good material for "colored" actors: "That's one of the reasons I wanted to sing, it gave me a chance to choose my roles, you know, I wouldn't play a part which I didn't want to play."[123] Fortunately, he could rely on his vocal skills and physical attractiveness to pick up the coveted few dramatic parts that emerged. At the BBC, these were starring roles in radio dramas like *The Blackamoor Dandy* (Third Programme, 1958) and *My People and Your People* (Home Service, 1959), although he did step out of type briefly to play a nerdy encyclopedia salesman in an episode of the TV series *They Met in a City* (1961), a move that puzzled at least one enamored agent: "I was sad ... to think that the hero should be played by somebody so palpably attractive and desirable ... one smile and one succumbs, and his walk is enough to make girls turn their heads in the streets!"[124]

Despite his growing fame, Grant's only roles were in dramas specifically calling for a West Indian or other "colored" actor. In this practice the BBC was no different from any other contemporary producer, although at least a few realized the possibly detrimental consequences of the practice. In a 1959 letter to James Davidson, Assistant Head of Light Entertainment, Grant's agent noted, "I entirely share your opinion that so far his career has been handled with too much consciousness of his being a coloured man with a guitar."[125] Outside the Corporation his career flourished and, no doubt aided by his Harry Belafonte-style good looks, he landed a Hollywood role co-starring with Richard Burton and Joan Collins in the film *Sea Wife* (1957). As early as 1956, Grant also broadened his horizons by establishing his own nightclub.

As significant as these ventures in music, radio, and film may have been, Grant's fate was sealed in 1957 when he became a fixture on *BBC Tonight*. In many ways, it was a perfect fit. *Tonight* was about as hip a program as the BBC could manage for an adult audience in 1957. It combined news, current affairs, and entertainment with young, fresh personalities— an innovative mix at a time when these were considered strictly separate

---

122 Memo, W. E. Davis to John Lane, Assistant, Children's Hour, November 20, 1953; note for circulating from unknown BBC staff, September 29, 1953; ibid. And letter, Cy Grant to Patrick Newman, Head of Booking), April 7, 1959; RCONT 1—Cyril Grant Artist's File II (1958–62), WAC.

123 Cy Grant *Blackgrounds* interview.

124 Letter, Margaret Ramsay, play agent to Hal Burton, producer, January 5, 1961. TELI/C/955/8877—Drama, They Met in a City (The Encyclopaedist), B/C 4-4-61, WAC.

125 Letter, Richard Armitage to James Davidson, July 7, 1959; RCONT 1—Cyril Grant Artist's File II (1958–62), WAC.

genres. Everything took place in a live atmosphere that kept the mood spontaneous and relaxed. Grant's calypso news contributed greatly to the lively and inviting mood:

> The tone was set when Cy Grant appeared on the screen singing topical calypsos ... He was one of the first black faces to be seen on the screen, and at a time when there was the first talk of Britain becoming a multi-cultural society, his attractive presence was reassuring.[126]

Tonight gave Grant tremendous visual exposure, more than most entertainers—black or white—could expect in an entire career. It was one of the BBC's most successful programs, drawing nine million viewers daily by 1960; and Grant appeared on it regularly.

Grant's charisma was not lost on others inside the BBC. When he went on a two-month hiatus from the program to shoot another film in the Caribbean, *Tonight*'s producer, Donald Baverstock, tried to engineer a scenario with Enalpa (the film's production company) in which Grant would shoot short clips on location that could be featured on *Tonight* in his absence. Although his fees for the show were moderate, ranging from fifteen to seventeen guineas per episode, his fees for non-*Tonight* appearances rose considerably; his next BBC TV performance—*Starlight*, August 1, 1958—paid him a forty-guinea performance fee. Kenneth Adam (Controller of Programmes, Television), for one, felt that his potential could be more effectively exploited: "Watching Cy Grant last night in *Tonight*, I thought:—can we not do something which will make more of this very attractive singer? I think he could be encouraged perhaps in a fifteen minute series? Or as an element in a big show—he acts very well, of course."[127]

Grant felt just the same way. Six months later, in May 1959. he wrote to Adam expressing his first inklings of a desire to strike out on his own:

> I feel I am over-exposing myself on the Tonight Programme, and in a way which does not show me to my best advantage.
>
> I am aware of course that I owe a great deal of my popularity to the "Tonight" Programme, but I never get much chance to do a finished or produced job, or more important, to sing the songs I like to sing.[128]

Despite his temptation to leave the show by the end of the month, he stayed on for more than a year (and even longer on a more intermittent

---

126 Briggs, *The History of Broadcasting*, 163.

127 Memo, Kenneth Adam to Head of Light Entertainment, Television, November 19, 1958; TVART 1—Cy Grant File I (1952–62), WAC.

128 Letter, Cy Grant to Kenneth Adam, May 1, 1959; TVART 1—Cy Grant File I (1952–62), WAC.

basis), perhaps waiting for other opportunities to arise. With the exception of a few one-off appearances, nothing came along, despite the professed good intentions of powerful BBC individuals like Adam, Tom Sloan, and Eric Maschwitz. Although he conceded Grant's talents and wide following, Maschwitz felt that "it might be some months before we could even contemplate giving him a show of his own, on the other hand I will recommend him warmly to all my producers for guest spots." Almost before his eyes, Grant could see much of his support evaporating, and he said as much to Adam, who had earlier offered to help promote him to producers: "I did not think it necessary to bother you as several producers had indicated their willingness to use me when I was no longer appearing on 'Tonight' every night. Things have not turned out quite like that and your benevolent interest would be welcome."[129] Reflecting on his experiences years later, Grant noted, "I never got asked to play dramatic parts any more. ... If *Tonight* had lasted for just six months it would have been great, maybe. But I got type cast as a calypso singer. So I paid a price for staying on the programme so long."[130] Grant's agent, Richard Armitage, fully sympathized with his client's frustration at being pigeonholed and supported Grant's desire to reinvent his image. To Maschwitz he wrote:

> Although I do not think that the new look we are bringing about in Cy Grant has yet reached its logical limit there is no doubt that his three programmes for you and his new cabaret act at the Savoy have caused a considerable stir.
>
> I believe passionately that he has been one of the most persistently under-rated men in the country. Nobody with such a tremendous dramatic and vocal range should be looked upon as a reliable fill-in.
>
> I do wish that you and Tom [Sloan] would give thought to a series for him, but not one in which he is expected to alternate Creole burial laments with topical calypsos.[131]

As this letter mentions, three unnamed, possibly trial, variety programs were planned for Grant, with Travers Thorneloe producing. They were broadcast in June 1961 but, besides his contract (his fee was seventy-five guineas per episode), there remains no trace of them; certainly no regular series was initiated.

---

129 Letter, Eric Maschwitz, Head of Light Entertainment to Richard Armitage, December 7, 1960; letter, Cy Grant to Kenneth Adam, December 12, 1960; TVART 1—Cy Grant File I (1952–62), WAC.

130 Cy Grant interview in Pines, *Black and White in Colour*, 47.

131 Letter, Richard Armitage to Eric Maschwitz, June 22, 1961; TVART 1—Cy Grant File I (1952–62), WAC.

It is probable that producers simply did not know how to position Grant within BBC programming. He was certainly considered an asset to any program, and all the circumstances suggested that he was "leading man" material—he was handsome, charming, and versatile, skilled as both a singer and an actor, with extensive experience in radio, television, film, and theater. Stage director Ned Sherrin enthused that "Cy had a great sort of feeling of matinee idol about him."[132] Perhaps most crucially, *Tonight* had made him famous—one of the few famous colored performers working in Britain—and his face was therefore a valuable commodity. However, likely because of his colonial, mixed-race roots, BBC producers and administration simply could not envision him at the center of his own variety series, or in a broader dramatic capacity; they conceived his image narrowly, as little more than an appealing singer of West Indian folk songs. Tom Sloan, by this time Head of Light Entertainment, stated pessimistically, "We all know everything there is to know about Cy Grant but it is difficult for us to consider using him on any large scale—particularly in view of the dearth of musical programmes."[133]

Cy Grant did not stop working for the BBC—far from it. He continued making fairly regular appearances, though mostly on radio, and never on a serial basis. The Overseas Service, which became the World Service in 1966, remained a steady source of jobs. But one cannot help thinking that his stint on *Tonight* was a mixed blessing; it brought him distinction, but only as a singing sidekick. Looking back, Grant observed:

> In a sense ... it interfered with ... my acting career quite considerably ... When I came back [after shooting a film] I went back to my programme just thinking that this was a nice beautiful little stop gap in between my career, which was doing very well at the time. I had made two films from either side of '56 ... '58 I'd been in 2 very big television plays, so my career as an actor had been quite established, but I found that people saw me purely and simply as a calypso singer. At the time I resented it very much you know because it ... devalued what I ... wanted to do.[134]

Grant's disillusioning experiences eventually led him, in 1974, to co-found the Drum Arts Centre, to provide emerging black artists an outlet for training, networking, and performing.[135]

---

132 Ned Sherrin interview by Stephen Bourne, 1993; Stephen Bourne Interview Collection, NSA.

133 Memo, Tom Sloan to Stuart Hood, Controller of Programmes, Television, October 8, 1962; TVART 1—Cy Grant File I (1952–62), WAC.

134 Cy Grant *Blackgrounds* interview.

135 Subsequently, Grant rejected the idea of an oppositional black culture, and his work in the arts focused on encouraging aspiring performers from all ethnic backgrounds.

*

Despite its tendency toward a narrowness of vision, the BBC remained one of the more supportive British cultural institutions in terms of the employment of West Indian artists. Moreover, it accepted their creative input, particularly on subjects dealing specifically with West Indian culture. It was less the particular prejudices of individual producers, and more a tacit and unquestioned assumption about the genres suitable for colonials and non-whites, which funneled them into certain programs. Many West Indians shared these assumptions and, for example, auditioned only for race-specific roles—although this practice likely had more to do with the presumed expectations of white English producers and directors. Thus, despite its good intentions, BBC programming often reinforced a handful of West Indian stereotypes (positive or otherwise), and frustrated the efforts of individuals like Edric Connor, Pearl Connor, and Cy Grant to break the Corporation of its white- and Anglocentric habits.

Chapter 3

London Calypso

Within the history of black Britain, the 1948 Pathé newsreel of calypsonian Lord Kitchener about to disembark in Tilbury from the *Windrush* is emblematic of the excitement and optimism of the postwar generation of West Indian migrants to Britain. He shyly serenades the reporter with a calypso he composed during the voyage, "London is the Place for Me." The clip is now famous. And while Kitchener's appearance now stands as a symbol of New Commonwealth migration, it also announced calypso's relevance in the culture of postwar London. Like the West Indian settlers who settled into the moods and patterns of London life, the calypso creatively adapted itself to new surroundings without sacrificing its essence or social function.

This chapter evaluates those calypsos that were originally recorded and performed in Britain by Lord Beginner, Lord Kitchener, Lord Invader, and others. It argues that these artists used their craft to articulate a generous late-imperial vision of national belonging in the 1950s. This vision encompassed their new English audience as well as recent settlers from the West Indies who represented both the New Commonwealth and a newly self-conscious multiracial Britain. Their calypsos, written and performed in an urban English context, were light-hearted and upbeat, but collectively they presented an imperially conscious perspective on British society and identity. Their lyrics referred sympathetically to the cultural and historical ties between Britain and the West Indies—public virtues like loyalty to the Crown, fair play, and adherence to British social rules and codes; the empire as a natural component of greater Britain; and the idiosyncratic experience of living in London, which native Britons and West Indian settlers had in common. These components made up a flexible but sturdy conception of what it meant to be British in the 1950s, a conception that, significantly, depended neither on race, ethnicity, nor birth in the British Isles. From the musical repertoire emerges a vision of Britain that is multicultural, cosmopolitan, and honestly in touch with its own history. Most strikingly, these calypsos posit, sometimes even *assume*, the existence of a British community that is optimistic and proactive about facing contemporary social changes—including, but not limited to, the influx of Britons from the Commonwealth.

This chapter is in two sections. The first places the calypso in its postwar British context, with consideration of the terms of production, audience, and cultural significance, and the second examines the calypsos themselves—those relatively few that were recorded for posterity. Through their compositions and performances, which emerged on the cusp of decolonization and the birth of a more visibly multiracial Britain, migrant calypsonians performed the difficult work of assembling a British identity that would be viable in the decades to come.

Calypso in Britain

This study's focus on postwar calypso in Britain requires some artificial trimming for two reasons. First, just as the postwar Caribbean migrants to Britain were not the first, so calypso's establishment in the city dates back to the interwar period (at least). Marc Matera in particular has shown the prewar and wartime origins of much postwar calypso, for example in the recordings and live performances of Cyril Blake and Freddy Grant. Second, calypso music in Britain was never separable from other "black sounds" that filtered in from the Caribbean, South America, Africa, and the United States: although Cyril Blake had his Calypso Serenaders (the band), he was also a jazz musician, and calypso, jazz, and swing were routinely performed as a jumble. Matera cites the Caribbean Club, once a venue for modern jazz performance, which later became "associated almost exclusively with calypso, albeit calypso performed with the addition of African hand drums and Latin American percussion instruments such as the maracas, bongos, and congas."[1]

Whatever its hybrid, interwar London past, the calypso genre ultimately became associated in the British media with the first wave of Caribbean settlers in general (despite its predominantly Trinidadian profile). The association began, as scholars have often noted, with the Pathé newsreel of Lord Kitchener on the *Windrush* in 1948 (noted at the outset of this chapter) and was epitomized in Britain by Cy Grant's nightly serenades on the *Tonight* program. The BBC, of course, regularly included calypso music in its programming related to West Indian themes, such as Errol John's "Federation Calypso," broadcast after coverage of Princess Margaret's visit to the Caribbean in the spring of 1958.[2] (John was also a talented playwright and actor, and his name appears on occasion throughout this

---

1 Matera, *Black London*, 180–81.
2 See Errol John Artist's File (1951–57), WAC.

book.) Dramas featuring West Indian characters, like the BBC's *A Man from the Sun* (1956) and Granada Television's *You in Your Small Corner* (1962) included calypso soundtracks, while the credits for the feature film *The Heart Within* (1957) rolled to bongo and steel pan music before fading into an opening shot of London Bridge. BBC radio also ran a series entitled *Calypso Calling* in 1957, with Edric Connor acting as resident folklorist and content advisor. His thank-you note from the producer remarked, "I think the series proved that Calypsos, for a short while, will have their place in the sun."[3] In 1962, the Theatre Royal's "all-Negro" musical *Do Somethin' Addy Man* had a generous repertoire of calypso, all of it composed by George Browne, otherwise known as Young Tiger.[4] Trinidadian writer Sam Selvon suggested calypso's commercial potential at this time in his vignette "Calypso in London," in which a down-on-his-luck St. Vincentian cajoles his Trinidadian friend to put his lyrics to music: "Hotboy, I have an idea here for a calypso that is hearts. ... We might even get it play by the BBC."[5]

The media saw calypso's vibrancy, spontaneity, and topicality mirrored in the West Indian settlers themselves, and used the genre to bring out the cultural impact of first-wave migration on London life, for better or worse. For example, one London paper covered the inaugural social of the South Kilburn Club, "designed to bring people of all races together socially," and stated that things "got off to a slow start ... with a barn dance, but when the coloured folk arrived with their own records, calypsos put a real swing into the proceedings." Similarly, when the *Kensington News* ran an article on the loneliness of migrants settling in London, its interviewee from the Migrant Services Division explained:

> The West Indian gets a feeling of claustrophobia living in an English house ... So he opens the door of his room ... the noise of the radio, maybe the smell of food spreads to the rest of the house ... take it a bit further ... on a fine evening he might go out on to the doorstep, or under the nearest lamp-post, like a tree at home—except that here he can't sing a Calypso as someone might think it was a disturbance of the peace—and people look on these gatherings at the street corners with suspicion.[6]

---

3   Letter, unknown (probably David Miller, producer), to Connor, May 16, 1957; RCONT1 Edric Connor - Artist's File 3 (1955–62), WAC.
4   See posting in the *West Indian Gazette*, September 1962, 3.
5   Sam Selvon, "Calypso in London," in *Ways of Sunlight* (1957; New York: Longman, 1987), 116.
6   "Good Start for Inter-Racial Club," paper unknown (June 5, 1959), and "Friendship is Number One Problem for West Indians—More than Housing," *Kensington News* (May 20, 1960); Clump no. 2, Press Clippings, ACC/1888/116, London Council of Social Service Correspondence File, LMA.

These two instances are revealing—the first uses the playing of calypsos to illustrate the Caribbean community's enlivening effect on London society, while the second uses it to highlight their behavior as foreign and even suspect. In general, however, calypso had the effect of putting a positive gloss on the phenomenon of colonial migration in this period, even when its controversial aspects were front and center. At a 1956 conference on the theme of "Problems arising in London as a result of West Indian Migration to Britain" (discussed in Chapter 1), one presenter discussed the unsatisfactory state of black employment but concluded "on a cheerful note with a couple of lines from one of Lord Beginner's calypsos."[7] In short, calypso served as the innocuous and fun-loving face of a social transformation with which many Britons were profoundly and increasingly uncomfortable.

Its commercial potential and jovial mood, however, in no way tarnished the authenticity and critical capacity of London calypso. Cultural critic Michael Eldridge's perspective is refreshing in this respect:

> Every generation of commentators both in and outside the Caribbean ... has ritually clucked its tongue over calypso's supposed betrayal of its authentic folk roots, its self-sullying absorption of nonindigenous commercial influences. Yet calypso in its modern incarnation ... has always been commercially oriented, always Creole and cosmopolitan, always "compromised," shaping and reshaping itself according to bourgeois imperatives and market forces; this is in great measure what *made* it "modern."[8]

Calypso's very flexibility allowed it not only to adapt itself admirably to the context of an emerging—and increasingly tense—multiracial London, but to express social criticisms and West Indian pride without positioning itself in opposition to white English listeners. Calypsonians in mid-century Britain utilized the genre's traditional musical and stylistic elements (which had emerged at the turn of the century) to extemporize on issues—fashionable or political—that were specifically pertinent to London society.

---

7   London Council of Social Service, conference report, "Problems Arising in London as a Result of West Indian Migration to Britain," ACC/1888/116, London Council of Social Service Correspondence File, LMA.

8   Michael Eldridge, "There Goes the Transnational Neighborhood: Calypso Buys a Bungalow," in Annie J. Randall, ed., *Music, Power, Politics* (New York and London: Routledge, 2005), 173–93. Although Eldridge's article is an examination of calypso in 1930s America, his observation applies equally to mid-century London.

The Definition of Calypso

Like so many other examples of indigenous Caribbean art and culture, calypso is essentially a heterogeneous concoction of international historical influences, a fact that paradoxically reinforces its regional authenticity. Thus Raymond Quevedo, calypso historian and calypsonian (Atilla the Hun), unabashedly writes that

> [calypso] is a particular form of folksong undeniably African in origin which was brought by the African slaves to the West Indies. Conditioned historically by its new environment and by French acculturation, the kaiso developed most distinctively in Trinidad into a form of mass art in song and dance uniquely or typically West Indian.[9]

Although its specific origins are unclear, it is generally understood that some of the genre's main attributes—syncopated rhythm, extemporaneous singing, and call-and-response variation—derive from West Africa, whence slaves brought it to the Caribbean region in the seventeenth and eighteenth century. There, it gradually combined with European and American elements; for example, it incorporated the rhythms of the Venezuelan *paseo*, and early Caribbean calypsos were sung in French patois, although by the turn of the twentieth century English had established itself as the dominant calypso language. There are a myriad hypotheses concerning the origin of the term "calypso," but the most commonly accepted is that it is a mutation of "kai-so," an African word meaning "well done" (it has no connection to the Greek goddess of the same name). Quevedo has written that "every competent writer on the subject is agreed that the term calypso is a misnomer,"[10] but it has long been accepted over "kaiso." (Musician and orchestrator Rupert Nurse, who played with Lord Kitchener in Britain through the 1950s, claimed that calypso was a mutation of "Caruso," the name that approving fans would yell out at Trinidad performances in homage to the famous Italian tenor Enrico Caruso.)[11] At any rate, it is clear that calypso's roots go back at least 150 years, and that it had assumed its modern form by the late nineteenth century, when "chantwells" in Trinidad began preparing verses in association with the annual Carnival. The intimate connection between calypso and Carnival

---

9   Raymond Quevedo, *Atilla's Kaiso: A Short History of the Trinidad Calypso* (St. Augustine, Trinidad and Tobago: University of the West Indies, Department of Extra Mural Studies, 1983), 2. Raymond Quevedo was formerly the great calypsonian Atilla the Hun, and he originally wrote this history between 1956 and 1958, although it was only published twenty-five years later.

10 Quevedo, *Atilla's Kaiso*, 3–4.

11 Rupert Theophilus Nurse interviewed by Val Wilmer, NSA.

in Trinidad persists to this day; most calypsos are written exclusively for performance at Carnival competitions.

Musically, the genre continues to evolve. Near the middle of the century calypso arrangements began borrowing much from the dance styles of popular swing and jazz bands, which doubtless enhanced their popularity among American soldiers stationed in Trinidad—and later among Americans in general. Again under America's influence, the musically distinct soca—soul plus calypso—developed in the 1970s; and in the 1990s, as the number of calypsonians of South Asian descent increased, they successfully incorporated Indian-style melodies and instrumentation into their calypsos. Although these musical innovations irritated purists, they have in fact kept calypso vibrant and socially relevant, so that it continues to attract new generations of listeners inside and outside the Caribbean.

This is important, for calypso is most fundamentally a public and performative poetry, in which the lyrics play the central role. All the musical variations mentioned above share this lyrical focus. Certainly one of the most prized skills of the true calypsonian is extemporaneous composition, and it is this talent that often distinguishes the calypsonian from the commercial calypso singer. However, over the course of the twentieth century, as calypsonians increasingly gained fame through their performances in the tent competitions during Carnival, they spent more time constructing and preparing eloquent, clever, and timely verses weeks in advance. The result was the emergence of more sophisticated and socially conscious calypsos, although the ribald variety of calypso has always thrived; the former comprise the bulk of the works examined here. As calypso scholar Keith Q. Warner has explained, "It seems logical that the calypso should have evolved with more emphasis being placed on lyric than on melody, since its role as some sort of mouthpiece was always predominant."[12]

Finally, when considered as a body of work, calypsos constitute not only an artistic progression, but more than a century of oral history on the West Indies and the bulk of its people.[13] This characteristic, too, can be traced back to the roots of calypso: "Six hundred years ago *griots* of [the African Mandingo people] held an esteemed place among the nobility. They

---

12 Keith Q. Warner, *The Trinidad Calypso: A Study of the Calypso as Oral Literature* (London: Heinemann, 1982), 20.

13 Keith Warner has rightly questioned the representativeness of the calypso in Trinidad, with its large population of Asian descent: "the fact that the overwhelming majority of calypsonians were, and still are, of African descent has led to a situation in which calypso is seen by the Trinidad and Tobago public as first and foremost 'a black man's thing', and this despite the very cosmopolitan make-up of the society." See Warner, "Ethnicity and the Contemporary Calypso," in Kevin A. Yelvington, ed., *Trinidad Ethnicity* (London: Macmillan Caribbean, 1993), 277. Nonetheless, despite its not-quite-universal relevance, calypso remains a valuable historical tool.

were the repositories of their country's history, of its music, dances and poetry. They were the antecedents of the Trinidad calypsonian."[14] It is thus reasonable to conclude that British calypso was also an earnest attempt to express the excitement, apprehensions, and complaints of those West Indian migrants newly adjusting to urban life, rather than a commercial, ersatz portrayal of Caribbean culture performed for the amusement of native English audiences. In other words, it was "an accurate indicator of the people's pulse on matters of national concern."[15]

There is a recognizable musical and lyrical difference between the work of the above calypsonians and the more commercialized calypso sounds that gained widespread appreciation on both sides of the Atlantic in this era. In the United States, the Andrews Sisters, Harry Belafonte, and folk groups like the Kingston Trio both popularized and in some ways diluted the genre, crooning smooth, generic sounds with a pop sensibility. Although the distinction could be fuzzy at times, much of this commercial output was not considered "authentic" calypso in the West Indies. Learie Constantine, for one, characterized true calypso as more emotionally potent: "Anyone who has heard, as I have, the Calypso of the West Indies sung in its natural setting and by its own people—not by hired bands for the amusement of thrill-sated tourists!—has felt that same quiver of the heart-strings that a Spiritual causes."[16] Still, as Keith Warner notes, "Trinidadians considered Belafonte a 'Johnny-come-lately' who sang calypsos 'in good English,' but his contribution [to the internationalization of the genre] cannot be totally ignored."[17] Belafonte and his ilk most likely aided the careers of the bona fide performers in Britain, the United States, and elsewhere beyond the Caribbean.

A central distinction can be made here between a *calypsonian*, who writes all of his own material, and a calypso singer who simply sings existing compositions. (Cy Grant, for example, who sang calypsos on the BBC, was not a calypsonian.) Authentic Trinidadian calypso was rawer, both in overall sound and lyrical content. Instead of the glossy production values of the Andrews Sisters and Belafonte, Lords Kitchener, Beginner, and Invader had a rough and decidedly un-pretty vocal style. Although their recordings contained the occasional simple string arrangement (and indeed there was a string band tradition in the West Indies), their standard instrumental setup was piano, guitar, and three saxophones (alto, tenor, and baritone).[18]

---

14 Errol Hill, "The Calypso," in Michael Anthony and Andrew Carr, eds, *David Frost introduces Trinidad and Tobago* (London: Deutsch, 1975), 73.

15 Ibid., 83.

16 Constantine, *Colour Bar*, 175.

17 Warner, *The Trinidad Calypso*, 22.

18 Rupert Theophilus Nurse in interview with Val Wilmer, H6090 BD1, NSA.

Most significant, the subject matter for the roots calypso composition tended to be either satirical, moral, or downright bawdy and filled with sexual double entendres; hardly material for mass American consumption in the early postwar period. Authentic calypso, the kind composed for Carnival and live performance, was nothing if not politically incorrect and even at times disreputable. C. L. R. James recollected of his youth:

> I was fascinated by the calypso singers and the sometimes ribald ditties they sang in their tents during carnival time. But, like many of the black middle class, to my mother a calypso was a matter for ne'er-do-wells and at best the common people. I was made to understand that the road to the calypso tent was the road to hell, and there were always plenty of examples of hell's inhabitants to whom she could point.[19]

Although Lord Kitchener did not record it until 1967, at least a decade earlier he had composed a scathing indictment of "what he perceived as the lapsed standards of calypso writing."[20] He was in fact targeting his talented rival Mighty Sparrow—hardly a musical imposter. Still, his lyrics give a sense of the native Trinidadian aesthetic:

> Bring more bounce especially, less bars in your melody
> Don't stray all entirely from the correct harmony
> Change that voice in which you sang, get that real calypso twang
> And perhaps you'd like to know, then you singing calypso.[21]

It is inapt in many ways, though, to draw too stark a division between "authentic" and "commercial," because calypso was *premised* on the virtue of reflecting and appealing to the people, broadly conceived. As Quevedo remarked about the inevitable decline of his generation of calypsonians:

> The Old Brigade still had their followers who supported them fully, and a visit to the tents revealed the Old Brigade was patronised by what was called the better class of people, and herein lay the evidence of their ultimate defeat, for after all in the final analysis the people are always right.[22]

In Britain, the same rule applied, and "authentic" calypsonians enthusiastically molded both their performances and recordings to their newly conceived

---

19 James, *Beyond a Boundary*, 25–26.

20 Timothy White, "Lord Kitchener: Once and Future Monarch of the Mas," liner notes, *Klassic Kitchener Volume Two*, Ice Records 941002, NSA.

21 Aldwyn Roberts (Lord Kitchener), "No More Calypsong," *Klassic Kitchener Volume Two*, NSA.

22 Quevedo, *Atilla's Kaiso*, 88.

audience or market. This was nothing new; all musicians performing in London had to make some of the same concessions. Cardiff-born Don Johnson, who sang with Ken "Snakehips" Johnson's West Indian Orchestra beginning in 1937, recalled that the musicians had to "subdue themselves" to conform to commercial tastes and big audiences. They would thus play one-and-a-half to two hours of straightforward commercial hits each night, with little creative alteration or improvisation, then perhaps one or two numbers in which they would really "go to town."[23] For players trained for live performance in the jazz tradition, this practice was the norm.

The Calypsonians

To get to London, Aldwyn Roberts (Lord Kitchener), Egbert Moore (Lord Beginner), and Rupert Westmore Grant (Lord Invader) trod the path—between Trinidad, New York, and London—that other West Indian performers had before them. Once they arrived in London, they took up with those versatile musicians already established in the jazz and popular music scene, and by 1950 had contributed to a calypso upsurge similar to that which had been occurring in the United States, beginning before the war. The commercialization of calypso in America, indicated by the rise of stars like Harry Belafonte, as well as increasing migration from the West Indies to Britain, helped build a diverse core calypso audience in London.

Calypso colleagues Beginner and Kitchener voyaged together on the now-historic *Empire Windrush* that docked at Tilbury on June 21, 1948, but they were intersecting at different moments in their histories. Lord Beginner already had an active career behind him. Starting out as a vaudeville artist (as other calypsonians had done), he first shot to calypso fame in 1929, and sealed his reputation as one of the "greats" by remaining among the top-ranked calypsonians for over fifteen years, performing as part of the famous "Maginot Line" (a calypso tent that also featured Atilla the Hun, Lion, Lord Invader, and others), and writing memorable and crowd-pleasing tributes to labor leader Arthur A. Cipriani and cricketer Learie Constantine. Also a favorite among American troops stationed in Trinidad beginning with the war, Beginner performed there in the double-role of calypsonian and vaudevillian. He traveled twice to the United States, in 1935 and 1945, where he performed and recorded.[24] He was already a Trinidadian legend when he stepped off the *Windrush* in 1948.

---

23 Don Johnson in interview with Val Wilmer, "History of Black British Jazz," part one, B9244, NSA. "Snakehips" Johnson was the foremost West Indian performer in London before 1945, and his orchestra was the most visible West Indian presence in the London music scene. Snakehips died when the club in which he was performing was bombed in the Blitz of 1941.

24 See Quevedo, *Atilla's Kaiso*, 98–100.

His fellow passenger Lord Kitchener was, by contrast, just rising to prominence. He had debuted in Port of Spain as a relative unknown in 1944, but aficionados quickly spotted his potential, and in 1947 he founded a new tent of emerging calypsonians. The "Young Brigade" positioned themselves as rivals to the Old Brigade of established stars, including Beginner: "Everyone knows or have been told / That the young bound to conquer the old / So tell them we are not afraid / We're going to mash up the Old Brigade."[25] Raymond Quevedo (Atilla the Hun), a former Old Brigade member, notes that Lord Kitchener was a leading spirit in this revolt, which shifted the emphasis away from lyrical topicality and toward melodic innovation. Even Quevedo concedes, "The lyrics may be a bit innocuous, if not silly, but all this was redeemed by the change in the melodic pattern and the musical energy."[26] Gordon Rohlehr, though, questions the assumption that the Young Brigade uniformly avoided political substance in favor of more ribald subjects:

It was not true that the Young Brigade were indifferent to current events. Their method of dealing with them was different, and they were almost entirely free of the moral self-righteousness of an earlier generation of singers, some of whom could celebrate an easy libertinism in one breath and preach the most moral sermon in another.[27]

This will become apparent below in an examination of Kitchener's numerous London calypsos that manage, with subtlety and humor, to throw light on some of the most politicized aspects of race relations in that city. As soon as Kitchener established himself as a leading light in Trinidad calypso having toured Curaçao, Aruba, and Jamaica, he sailed to Britain. He would eventually return to Trinidad and Tobago in 1963, winning Road March and Calypso King titles throughout the 1960s.

According to Quevedo, Lord Invader was one of the most traveled calypsonians of his era, working stints in both London and New York City, especially Harlem. Originally from San Fernando (like Beginner), he performed as a calypsonian in Port of Spain with some success from 1935, but real fame came in the early 1940s with "Cat O' Nine Tails" (discussed below), and he easily maintained his stature in the years following.[28] He was perhaps the best-known authentic Trinidadian calypsonian of his generation, for he penned the lyrics to "Rum and Coca-Cola," which the American trio the Andrews Sisters made a huge hit during the Second

---

25 See Gordon Rohlehr, *Calypso and Society in Pre-Independence Trinidad* (Port of Spain: Gordon Rohlehr, 1990), 458–59.

26 Quevedo, *Atilla's Kaiso*, 85.

27 Rohlehr, *Calypso and Society in Pre-Independence Trinidad*, 465.

28 Quevedo, *Atilla's Kaiso*, 112.

World War. (The melody had been more or less perpetually recycled from other calypsos and folk tunes since as early as the 1890s.) It was an American entertainer, Morey Amsterdam, who initially took credit for the lyrics, but Invader successfully sued for the song's royalties later that decade.[29] When he came to London in May 1956, *Melody Maker* knew him well, and commemorated his arrival with an article, "Invader is Here!" "Rum and Coca-Cola" had helped make him famous, even though it was never played on the BBC ("advertising, you know"): "Soon, he will be recording in Britain. The titles? No idea yet. 'They'll come to me when I want 'em. I get an idea—and there it is.'"[30]

There were certainly other Trinidadian calypsonians traveling in and out of London during these years, such as Roaring Lion, Young Kitchener, the Mighty Terror, and Young Tiger; a few of their compositions are considered below. But Kitchener, Beginner, and Invader were the most prolific in their reflections on life in Britain, and it is their calypsos that comprise the bulk of the following analysis.

Calypso Production and Reception in London

It is not easy to pin down the exact size and profile of the British calypso audience, but making the effort is worthwhile, for it demonstrates calypso's currency in a variety of milieux: Caribbean music and jazz clubs, large dance halls, and mainstream radio and television. It had listeners throughout the British Empire. Most apparent was the growth of the consuming West Indian public in London, as well as in cities like Birmingham and Manchester. Until the end of the Second World War, audiences at clubs featuring calypso and other Caribbean music were tiny and specialized; when Parlophone recorded Cyril Blake's band live at Jig's Club in 1941, the "audience comprised West Indians—some recently arrived to assist in the war effort—and British jazz enthusiasts." Likewise, when *Melody Maker*—then a jazz-oriented publication—first introduced calypso to its readers (as late as 1938), it presented the genre and its artists as "curios."[31]

That West Indian music catered to a tiny niche market in Britain is reflected in the fact that prior to 1945, almost all recordings produced in

---

29 Donald R. Hill, *Calypso Calaloo: Early Carnival Music in Trinidad* (Gainesville: University Press of Florida, 1993), 234–36.

30 "Invader is Here!," *Melody Maker* (May 5, 1956), 8.

31 Cyril Blake was a veteran music of calypso and other Caribbean and Latin American styles, and had been resident in Britain since at least the 1930s. He was the bandleader on Lord Kitchener's early London recordings. See John Cowley, "West Indian Gramophone Recordings in Britain, 1927–1950," in Rainer Lotz and Ian Pegg, eds, *Under the Imperial Carpet: Essays in Black History 1780–1950* (Crawley: Rabbit Press, 1986), 249.

Britain and the United States were for export. Both British Decca and Parlophone issued calypso and other West Indian recordings throughout the 1930s and '40s. In some cases, record agents traveled to Trinidad to recruit particular artists, but most of the time it was visiting musicians and calypsonians who were recorded, in London and especially New York. This music was then released as part of the label's "foreign" or "West Indian" series. Its classification of foreign and domestic releases was imperial: "British Decca had already built an empire of international music beginning in the 1920s (consisting of roughly a dozen different genres, precision targeted at as many different colonial markets)."[32] A few American recordings were issued in Britain in the 1930s and '40s, and the odd British release was planned to coincide with a string of appearances by a West Indian artist, but these were rare, and most musicians gained a name for themselves in music circles by performing live in urban clubs.

The production of calypso recordings for colonial markets, largely by Parlophone and the newly established Melodisc label, continued apace after 1945. The West Indies were the obvious first destination for this "Caribbean jump-up music,"[33] but West Africa was another. Lord Kitchener's "Birth of Ghana" (Melodisc), for instance, celebrated the forthcoming independence of the Gold Coast: "Ghana is the name / We wish to proclaim / We will be jolly, merry, and gay / The sixth of March, Independence Day."[34] The tune was undoubtedly both crafted and marketed with the West African audience in mind; the region had already established itself as a profitable market for Trinidadian calypso, and copies of "Birth of Ghana" doubled as souvenirs of independence. Years later, at a 1996 symposium on West Indian journalist and activist Claudia Jones, Alex Pascall recalled, "Britain used calypsos at that time to sell to Africa and the Caribbean as part of its economy after the war. Calypso never took off here at all."[35] Indeed, in terms of record sales, it remained a tiny niche market; but its British visibility and reach was greater than Pascall's comment suggests.

In addition to consumers in the colonies, Melodisc and Parlophone benefited from the rapidly growing pool of West Indian music listeners settling in Britain. In fact, Melodisc, a postwar creation, depended in its early years on the domestic calypso market. Its co-founder, Jack Chilkes, was a jazz devotee, but he increasingly produced records by Lords Kitchener and Beginner, and came to very much admire the musicianship of calypso players like guitarist Freddy Grant, who arranged and performed on several

---

32 Eldridge, "There Goes the Transnational Neighborhood," 190 (footnote 2).

33 This term was used to describe Shake Keane's up-tempo calypso at a National Sound Archive lecture, "The History of Black British Jazz," part two, B9245, NSA.

34 Aldwyn Roberts (Lord Kitchener), "Birth of Ghana," *London is the Place for Me*. Originally recorded for Melodisc, 1956.

35 Alex Pascall, symposium comment, in Sherwood et al., *Claudia Jones*, 208.

Melodisc sides. Chilkes has claimed that it was only the calypso Melodisc releases that really sold well—a direct result of the influx of West Indians to Britain.[36]

The extent of calypso's native English (and overwhelmingly white) audience was variable and scattered—it consisted, at times, of casual television viewers and radio listeners, but also of urban club-goers and dancehall patrons. Calypsonians like Beginner, Kitchener, and Invader took up with those versatile musicians already established in the jazz and popular music scene, and by 1950 had ushered in a minor calypso upsurge. Their activities fortuitously coincided with a mainstream calypso trend, with the rise of stars like Harry Belafonte and (in Britain) Cy Grant. Kitchener and his colleagues certainly shaped some of their calypsos to suit the perceived preferences of white audiences at London shows. Despite the growth of the calypso recording business in urban centers during these years, calypsonians' bread and butter remained live performance.

Jazz lovers and those who frequented downtown clubs and dancehalls would have been exposed to West Indian musicians and musical styles due to the cross-pollination that took place among jazz, swing, calypso, and popular music—Lord Kitchener himself suggested their relationship in his tribute to the newest jazz trends, "Kitch's Bebop Calypso." In it, he extolled the virtues of bebop greats like Dizzy Gillespie ("It really enchanted me just to hear him play 'Anthropology'") and modern jazz in general ("It sends you in a dancing heat with the drums that give you the Afro-beat.")[37] A glimpse of the Caribbean Club in a 1947 newsreel showed a predominantly black audience dancing along to back-to-back sets of calypso and Harlem-style jazz. The narrator of the newsreel, which also featured shots of the ritzier Coconut Grove Club, introduced: "London's Basin Street, where the dark folks meet—but no blues. Here, Britain's most famous coloured musicians often drop in and take a seat with the band in the haunting sung language of the Indies—calypso."[38] The English jazz singer Beryl Bryden, who was still a student during wartime, remembers one of her first forays into the urban jazz scene—to Jig's Club, then considered by *Melody Maker* to be one of London's best rhythm clubs:

> So we turned up there and found this very little dark alleyway—we were all a bit worried about the sort of area because it didn't have a very savoury reputation in those days—and we tapped on the door, and there was a little hole in the door, and it slid back, and all you could

36　Interview with Jack Chilkes, date unknown, H6808, NSA.

37　Aldwyn Roberts, "Kitch's Bebop Calypso", *London is the Place for Me: Trinidadian Calypso in London, 1950–56*. Originally recorded for Melodisc, 1951.

38　"London's Nightworld—Reel 2," Pathé newsreel (1947): http://britishpathe.com/record.php?id=75093; accessed September 20, 2009.

see was two large eye whites and black pupils! And he said "Yes?" ...
And we went in, and there's this not very big room, almost half of it
is this huge billiard table; I should think about eighty percent coloured
people—West Indians, mostly—and there in the corner is this wonderful
little jazz band ... And oh it was absolutely fabulous because we'd never
heard any live coloured jazz before apart from records, and we really
had a ball. ... Very exciting club, full of atmosphere. ... The club was
rather dark, and very smoke-filled; a real America-type club ... a lot of
talking, a lot of noise, people dancing in a little corner. And the band
of course, was very very good swing music in those days. ... Everybody
danced, jitterbugged very well in there.[39]

Bryden made this visit during wartime, but her description gives an idea of
the specialized market to which many jazz records and publications catered.
And although the paper *Melody Maker* focused most enthusiastically on
jazz, it also covered and reviewed calypso artists and recordings. Denis
Preston, who became intimately involved with calypso and calypsonians in
Britain, worked with producers like Jack Chilkes to get calypso on record
and wrote a feature for the magazine, "CALYPSO: the jazz of the West
Indies," designed to woo jazz fans into the calypso fold: "You're probably
wondering why the 'MM' should devote valuable space to discussing
something as (apparently) unjazzlike as the Trinidadian calypso. ... [But]
true calypso and raw jazz have more in common than, at first hearing,
you might imagine."[40]

Certainly by the early 1960s authentic Trinidadian calypso and Jamaican
steel pan music had gained a certain cachet among young jazz enthusiasts,
those 115,000 fifteen- to twenty-five-year-old "boys and young men" whom
Francis Newton identified as jazz's white, British demographic in 1959.[41]
Kitchener himself has discussed how his early audiences, mixed between
black and white, caught on to the calypso swing. After losing his first job
performing for an all-white audience that could not "understand a word
that I'm saying,"

I went to the Sunset Club, and there was a mixture of people. And I
started singing this song. "Kitch come go to bed, I have a small comb
to scratch your head." Of course, the Caribbean people understood the
song and they explain it to their white friends. So, most of the people
understood the song, and then the song became very popular. It was

39 Beryl Bryden, interviewed by Stephen Bourne, 1993; Stephen Bourne Interview
   Collection, NSA.
40 Denis Preston, "CALYPSO: The Jazz of the West Indies," *Melody Maker* (February
   25, 1950), 3.
41 Francis Newton, *The Jazz Scene* (1959; New York: Da Capo Press, 1975), 236–37.

so popular until I was in three night clubs in one night. ... So, after this, I had no more worries. I was living like a king at that period.[42]

By the 1960s, Newton's young "minority public" was dancing to calypso and steel pan at swinging London coffee houses and the Cambridge May Ball.[43]

The Calypsos

Despite the professed rivalry between the Old and Young Brigades, in fact the calypsos of Kitchener, Beginner, and Invader were thematically similar in their views about life in London. These calypsos addressed diverse aspects of English society from a broadly populist perspective; specifically, they criticized or satirized particular practices and events while simultaneously praising or reaffirming England's historical reputation and symbolic institutions. Calypsonians working in London had several reasons for adopting such a stance, not all of them motivated by patriotism for the mother country. Furthermore, they combined their Anglo-enthusiasm with an awareness of, and passionate support for, Trinidad, the West Indies, and British colonies in Africa. Thus their calypsos expressed a catholic patriotism that fused the interests of English pride with those of an independent, prosperous Commonwealth.

> Cricket lovely cricket
> At Lords where I saw it
> Cricket lovely cricket
> At Lords where I saw it
> Yardley did his best
> But Goddard won the Test
> With those little pals of mine
> Ramahdin and Valentine.[44]

Although applauded for their critical coverage of everything from high politics to sexual politics, calypsonians were probably best known in Britain for their cricket calypsos, which they usually wrote in reference to particular players or test matches. More than any other sport, cricket exemplified the shared cultural ground of Britain and the West Indies. What was considered

---

42 Aldwyn Roberts quoted in Phillips and Phillips, *Windrush*, 94.

43 See, e.g., Pathé newsreels "Two Tempo Restaurant" (1965): http://britishpathe.com/record.php?id=1955 and "The Questioning City" (1963): available at http://www.britishpathe.com/record.php?id=81580; accessed September 20, 2009.

44 Egbert Moore, "Victory Test Match," lyrics quoted in Phillips and Phillips, *Windrush*, 95, and featured on *London is the Place for Me*. Originally recorded for Melodisc, 1950.

the most English of games was also the most imperial, and its appeal was democratized in the Caribbean. C. L. R. James has most famously written about the imperial and racial dimensions of cricket in the autobiographical *Beyond a Boundary*. Also a Trinidadian, James describes himself "in my teens at school, playing cricket, reading cricket, idolizing Thackeray, Burke and Shelley," and he goes so far as to state that "There is a whole generation of us, and perhaps two generations, who have been formed by [the cricket ethic] not only in social attitudes but in our most intimate personal lives, in fact there more than anywhere else."[45] West Indian enthusiasm for the game carried over into the neighborhoods of the early migrants; along with boxing, cricket was the sport most covered in the pages of local papers like the *West Indian Gazette* and the *West Indies Observer*.

Likewise, the cricket-themed calypso reflected all the national, imperial, and social fissures that the game suggested.[46] According to some, the West Indian presence in England was forcibly asserted for the first time at the Lords Test Match in 1950, where England lost to the West Indies for the first time on its own turf. It is significant that both Beginner and Kitchener were present, along with another two or three dozen migrants, cheering and rattling cans. Immediately following the West Indian victory, Beginner spontaneously composed the commemorative "Victory Test Match," while Kitchener led a raucous, Carnival-like procession from Lords: "I think it was the first time they'd ever seen such a thing in England. And we're dancing in Trinidad style, like mas, and dance right down Piccadilly and dance around Eros. The police told me we are crazy."[47] It was an important triumph, because it demonstrated that West Indians had an equal claim on the culture of the game, despite the colonial snobbery that deemed it the preserve of Englishmen. The match was, to an extent, a battle of nationalisms.

Nevertheless, composers of cricket calypsos honored the gentlemanly spirit of the game, and filled their songs not with gloating criticisms of England or the English team, but with praise for particular players and skills, and, more generally, with reverence for the institution of cricket itself. Lord Kitchener's tribute to the 1964 Test Match in the West Indies began by extolling the level of play as well as the psychic significance of the contest:

This was cricket at its best
At Lords the second test

---

45 James, *Beyond a Boundary*, 15, 49.

46 These tensions, incidentally, have not disappeared, as the controversy over the national preferences of British sports fans has demonstrated. The feeling that a fan's national identity can usefully be determined by the national cricket or football team for which he cheers has persisted.

47 Aldwyn Roberts quoted in Phillips and Phillips, *Windrush*, 103.

It is said by everybody
It is the greatest in history
Well, it was war with two countries
England versus the West Indies
What a miracle
With the champions doing the impossible.[48]

Like all calypsos, these told a story, recounting the important plays by both sides as well as the attitudes of the spectators:

West Indies was feeling homely
The audience had them happy
When Washbrook's century had ended
West Indies' voices all blended
Hats went in the air
People shout and jump without care, so
At Lords was the scenery
It's bound to go down in history.[49]

Player name-dropping was frequent, and the verses were designed to recreate the excitement of the game for true cricket fans. Thus, although the calypsonian boasted of West Indian supremacy on the cricket pitch, in fact he endorsed the rules of the cultural game, embracing the shared history of England and the West Indies.

"Victory Test Match" also remarked on the presence of George VI among the viewers ("He saw the King was waiting to see / So he gave him a century"), and indeed the monarchy was another prominent calypso theme. This was perhaps appropriate, because it represented the positive gloss of empire and Commonwealth and was presented in the colonies as a symbol of imperial unity; West Indian schoolchildren paid their respects to the king and queen daily, and royal colonial tours were public spectacles on a grand scale.[50] Overall, calypso (whether written from a London or Trinidadian perspective) served to buttress the prestige of English royalty, even when, like today's gossip magazines, it light-heartedly speculated on their personal lives. However, these songs rendered the monarchy as the symbolic head, not of England, but of the British Empire and Commonwealth. Like the cricket calypsos, they represented Britain's and the West Indies' *shared* culture and thus underscored the former's imperial identity and responsibilities.

---

48 Aldwyn Roberts (Lord Kitchener), "Cricket Champions," *Klassic Kitchener Volume One*, Ice Records release 931102, NSA. Originally released *c.* 1964.
49 Lord Beginner with the Calypso Rhythm Kings, "Victory Test Match."
50 See, e.g., Rush, *Bonds of Empire*.

By the 1950s, royal themes were a bona fide calypso tradition. From the early days of calypso's ascendancy in the West Indies (prior to the First World War), it was common for calypsonians to pledge their loyalty to the Crown, and the practice persisted into the postwar period. Lord Executor's "Reign of the Georges" celebrated the hallowed history of the Georgian monarchy and was written in time for George VI's coronation in 1937; likewise, Roaring Lion wrote "Royal Tour" about Elizabeth II's 1954–55 Commonwealth tour, and in fact most royal calypsos commemorated major events like these.[51] George Browne, more commonly known as Young Tiger, was in London in 1953 when Elizabeth was crowned, and wrote his own musical account of the Coronation—actually recorded prior to the June event, in order to boost its sales as a souvenir on the day. It is a detailed, play-by-play description of the procession and its personnel: all the military divisions, Royal Horse guards, Lords of the Admiralty, "physicians and surgeons all in good stead," and the representatives from the colonies and dominions, rattled off like a shopping list. The new queen got special mention of course:

Her Majesty looked really divine
In her crimson robe furred with ermine
The Duke of Edinburgh, dignified and neat
Sat beside her as Admiral of the Fleet
He was there (at the Coronation)
I was there (at the Coronation).[52]

Every verse ends with this refrain, and serves to give Young Tiger a place in the historic event, along with those in the procession, and the English spectators: "Millions of people, all happily / Shouting three cheers for Her Majesty / They were there (at the Coronation) / I was there (at the Coronation)."[53] Here again, the West Indian migrant is positioned at the center of a shared imperial—not exclusively English—culture, enjoying its traditions and national celebrations equally with other Britons.

Reverential calypsos like this one commingled with saucier ones that were nonetheless very topical. In "Princess and the Cameraman" (1961), the legendary Mighty Sparrow expressed his perplexity at Princess Margaret's decision to marry commoner and photographer Tony Armstrong Jones (Lord Snowdon). The princess probably enjoyed the joke. She was herself a calypso fan and once attended a smoky London club to hear Lord

51 Lord Executor, "Reign of the Georges" (1937), and Roaring Lion, "Royal Tour" (1954), featured on BBC Radio 2 program *Queso Calypso*, part three, H6501, NSA.

52 Young Tiger with Cyril Blake's Calypso Serenaders, "I Was There (at the Coronation)," *London is the Place for Me*. Originally recorded for Parlophone, 1953.

53 Ibid.

Kitchener perform. Her favorite tune was "Kitch, Come Go To Bed," and she allegedly bought a hundred copies of the record when it was released.[54] (Incidentally, it was not only the British royal family that fell victim to the calypsonian's wit; Lord Invader poked fun at the end of Monaco's Prince Rainier's bachelor days after he became engaged to Grace Kelly.)[55] Whatever personal speculation went on in these works, none of them expressed substantial criticism; indeed, they almost invariably reiterated the calypsonian's admiration for the monarchy. However, royal calypsos in general—and declarations of loyalty in particular—declined with the onset of colonial independence struggles, although older calypsonians continued the practice to a degree.[56]

Calypsonians on both sides of the Atlantic composed songs about royalty, but those residing in Britain tailored many calypsos to purely English situations, reflecting their own experiences and impressions. More than anything else, the calypso is topical. This is true to such an extent that in most cases, "once a calypso serves its purpose for one year, if it is not recorded, it hardly surfaces again in the repertoire of the performer."[57] While this inevitably entails the unfortunate forgetting of good songs, it ensures the vigilance of the calypsonian and the creation of timely lyrical compositions designed specifically to resonate with the prevailing public mood:

> [T]he calypsonian constantly monitors what is happening around him and uses the platform of the calypso to expose to his listeners a point of view that is not only his personal one, but more often than not is indicative of what the man in the street is thinking about a particular situation.[58]

Errol Hill has referred to "the ancient role of the calypso" as that of the "poor man's newspaper."[59] The calypsos that Kitchener, Beginner, and Invader wrote in Britain were centrally concerned with the life around them. In Sam Selvon's vignette "Calypso in London," published in 1957, the year after the Suez crisis, Mangohead tries out his mediocre lyrics on a Trinidadian friend, Hotboy, who rebukes him, "You think we still in

---

54 *Queso Calypso*, part three, BBC Radio 2, H6501, NSA.

55 Lord Invader, "Prince Rainier," National Sound Archive Soundserver, British Library, London.

56 As late as the 1990s, Mighty Sparrow's "London Bridge Is Falling Down" was actually lamenting Britain's international decline and yearning for the days of its imperial greatness. *Queso Calypso*, H6501, NSA.

57 Warner, *The Trinidad Calypso*, 4.

58 Ibid., 59.

59 Errol Hill, "Foreword," in Quevedo, *Atilla's Kaiso*, viii–ix.

Trinidad? This is London, man, this is London. The people want calypso on topical subject":

> And Mango, as if he get an inspiration, start to extemporize on Nasser and Eden and how he will give them the dope—the best thing is to pass the ships round the Cape of Good Hope.
> "Like you have something there," Hotboy concede, and he begin to hum a little tune.[60]

The tendency to dedicate calypsos to commonplace English phenomena and current events—the police, the strength of the pound, riding the underground, shopping with ration books—was an important part of calypso's established social function. The calypsonian "acts as a mirror for the society and provides the population with a voice and a platform. He also interprets that which is new, puzzling, controversial or foreign."[61] So it was in London as in Trinidad, and recent migrants to the city would have related to their descriptions of ordinary London life.

Calypsonians' observations quickly became more biting. Kitchener's sanguine "London is the Place for Me" may be among the most remembered of postwar calypsos, but it does not accurately reflect the tone of most others. Lines like "To live in London you are really comfortable / Because the English people are very much sociable" and "I cannot complain of the time I have spent / I mean my life in London is really magnificent," were clearly wishful thinking on Kitchener's part, for he wrote them before the *Windrush* had even docked in England. Edric Connor noted in his memoirs that "our calypsonians seldom hand out bouquets,"[62] and Kitchener and his colleagues quickly grew wise to the realities of life for West Indian migrants, translating their increasingly ambivalent assessments into somber or humorous critiques. By 1952, Kitchener had quite literally changed his tune:

> Many West Indians are sorry now
> They left their country and don't know how
> Some left their jobs and their family
> And determined to come to London city
> Well, they are crying, they now regret
> No kind of employment that they can get
> The city of London they have to roam
> And they can't get the apartments to go back home
> So darling Jamaica, Jamaica

---

60 Selvon, "Calypso in London," 116–17.
61 Warner, *The Trinidad Calypso*, 87.
62 Connor, *Horizons*, 71.

We want to remember darling
Jamaica, Jamaica
Our heaven and saviour.[63]

Kitchener and others often harbored very specific reservations about getting by in London. Lord Beginner's "Dollar and the Pound" (1950), for example, complains of the sterling crisis and the weakness of the pound against the American dollar: "So Stafford Cripps who did explain / That the pound will climb back again / But I want them to realize / that the dollars have me too paralyzed."[64] Calypsonians' foremost irritation seems to have been rationing, however, due to the meager allowances ("the weekly ration is so small / In a day or two you can sure eat all") and curbed spending power ("If you want a suit or you want a tie / You just cannot walk in a store and buy").[65] Sensitive to the hardships created by rationing, Beginner dedicated a thoughtful composition to English housewives (although he recycled the lyrics from an earlier paean to Caribbean housewives):[66]

These women when they're shoppin' they walk miles a day
To see their home and children in a happy way
From the grocer's to the butcher's stall, goodness knows,
Some of them don't leave until the markets close
If they can't get the meat they will get the fish
Those who love the horse, they will make a dish
That's why the son and daughter, grandma and dad
Say housewives really workin' hard.[67]

Most interestingly, calypsonians bravely and candidly addressed the elephant in the room, the issue of race and color in postwar Britain. Although light-hearted, bawdy, and silly calypsos abound, it is the social or political calypso that is most cherished by calypsonians and aficionados, and that most rewards historical analysis: "Entertainment value ranks high in judging

---

63 Aldwyn Roberts (Lord Kitchener), "Sweet Jamaica," *London is the Place for Me: Trinidadian Calypso in London, 1950–56*. Originally recorded for Lyragon, 1952.

64 Egbert Moore (Lord Beginner), "Dollar and the Pound," 1950, National Sound Archive Soundserver, British Library.

65 Aldwyn Roberts, "Sweet Jamaica." The second quotation is from a private recording that features an alternative verse (Matrix RJG 4); 0508W, NSA.

66 See Gordon Rohlehr, "Images of Men and Women in the 1930s Calypsoes: The Sociology of Food Acquisition in a Context of Survivalism," in Patricia Mohammed and Catherine Shepherd, eds, *Gender in Caribbean Development* (Kingston: Canoe Press University of the West Indies, 1999), 223–89. Sincere thanks to Alwyn Harrison for bringing this article to my attention.

67 Egbert Moore, "Housewives," *London is the Place for Me: Trinidadian Calypso in London, 1950–56*. Originally recorded for Parlophone, 1950.

the great calypso, but its worth must also depend partly on moral insight and observation, on the ability of the composer to aim, however obliquely, at understanding or improving the human condition."[68] This is nowhere more apparent than in those calypsos that made reference to race relations and identity, both in Britain and multiracial Trinidad itself, where at this time color prejudice was widely practiced but rarely openly acknowledged. As late as the 1990s, Trinidadian calypso scholar Louis Regis noted, "Race is a taboo subject in public polite discourse in our society but not for the calypsonian. All but one of the major calypso controversies since independence have had to do with race relations."[69] In 1959 Kitchener exposed the persistence of color prejudice with his calypso "If You're Brown": "If you're brown they say you can stick around / If you're white—well everything is all right / If your skin is dark no use you try / You've got to suffer until you die."[70] At least a decade earlier, however, he knowingly contrasted this elaborate West Indian pigmentocracy with the much cruder racial differentiation that prevailed in Britain. "If You're Not White You're Black," recorded in London in 1953 for Melodisc, voiced the perspective of a dark-skinned West Indian chastising an educated, middle-class, lighter-skinned associate:

> You jet along the thoroughfare
> You shape your ways like Fred Astaire
> And when you see me passing by
> You watch me with a crooked eye
> And yet you speak to Mr. B
> Who does not want your company
> In every way you endeavor
> To show yourself superior
> No, you can never get away from the fact
> If you not white, you considered black.[71]

The snob targeted in the song is clearly unacquainted with social categories dominant in the metropolis, where all non-whites, including those of Asian and South Asian descent, were lumped together as "black." Elsewhere in the calypso, Kitchener accuses him of hating his own race, and identifies not England, nor the West Indies, but Africa as his true homeland: "You hate the name of Africa / The land of your great-grandfather / The country where you can't be wrong / The home where you really belong."[72]

---

68 Hill, "The Calypso," 82.

69 Louis Regis, *The Political Calypso: True Opposition in Trinidad and Tobago* (Kingston: University of the West Indies Press, 1999), xi.

70 Aldwyn Roberts, "If You're Brown," *Klassic Kitchener Volume One* (Ice Records 931102, 1993), 1CD0110865, NSA. Originally recorded for Melodisc, 1959.

71 Aldwyn Roberts, "If You're Not White You're Black."

72 Ibid.

What is most striking about this calypso, however, is that it contains no explicit criticism of English attitudes. The focus is instead on the shallowness of a West Indian migrant persisting under the illusion that his relative lightness would have any significance in a mostly white society. The song thus engages most with the particular concerns of the West Indian community (or perhaps the non-white community more generally). Indeed, the bulk of recorded calypso customers in London would have been expatriate West Indians, though the club-going contingent was probably much more diverse. Nonetheless, where most English-produced commentaries on the subject of color prejudice in Britain would certainly have dwelt upon the question of white racism, in "If You're Not White You're Black" Lord Kitchener confined himself to issues unique to the West Indian experience.

This does not mean that calypsonians made no comment on white racism, although when they did, they tended, like many white liberals at the time, to ascribe overtly racist behavior to an unreconstructed minority within British society, and not to cast it as an essential ingredient of British (imperial) identity itself. Lord Invader's response to the racial violence of Teddy Boys is an example, with Caribbean roots. Invader consolidated his fame in Trinidad in the early 1940s with a rhythmic suggestion to the government to quell a recent outbreak of hooliganism by bringing back the "old time cat-o-nine":

Hit them hard and they bound to change their mind
Is to send them to Carrera
With licks like fire
And they bound to surrender.[73]

Faced in London with Teddy Boy violence, he wrote a new calypso, and simply replaced "Carrera" with "Dartmoor." "Teddy Boy Calypso" denounced the Teds for "causing panic in Great Britain" but, like most of the white majority, he did not openly interpret their actions as symptomatic of a broader racism. Invader even singled out the police for particular praise: "The police is working harder and harder to see this thing go no further / Every night they on duty to save gatherers from violence and robbery."[74] In years to come, the police would be acknowledged as intimately complicit in the swelling of racial antagonism in London neighborhoods, and accused of doing little to prevent the particular inflammation of North Kensington and Notting Hill in 1958.

Lord Kitchener's timely "My Landlady" is equally surprising in its

---

73 Lyrics quoted in Quevedo, *Atilla's Kaiso*, 112.
74 Rupert Grant (Lord Invader), "Teddy Boy Calypso (Bring Back the Old Cat-O-Nine)," *Kings of Calypso* (Castle Communications MC 244, 1992), NSA.

circumlocution of the issue of English prejudice. In the 1950s and '60s, landladies were notorious for their rejection and exploitation of migrants on racial grounds. As one settler recalled of his first "little room," "I wasn't allowed to take no visitors at all, even the couple of friends that I know, they couldn't come and meet, we got to meet in the street." Another remembered, "You move around a lot because people didn't give you a lot of time. You say thirty bob a week, somebody would come and say two pounds. And, of course, when your wages is about five or six pounds a week, to pay two pounds, that's a lot."[75] Kitchener accurately notes the common prohibitions against visitors, early curfews, lack of basic amenities (like hot water) and furnishings, and extortionate rents, but he refrains from exploring the slanted motivations for such actions. His landlady is simply callous and mean with money: "And she has the audacity / To tell me I'm livin' in luxury."[76]

Contrary to appearances, perhaps, this approach to the London calypso reflected neither a lack of racial consciousness nor a pre-political orientation toward the issue of white racism in Britain. Rather it was a comparatively subtle way to insert the concerns of the West Indian community into a popular musical genre enjoyed by a London audience that was decidedly mixed. As stated above, the calypsonian's task was to mirror the sentiments of his listeners, not alienate them. Invader's suggestion that violent racism was a fringe phenomenon confined to hooligan youths, for example, was not merely a capitulation to English listeners or authorities. Like the other London-oriented calypsos discussed above, Invader's calypsos posit a vision of society in which he figures as both a member and a mouthpiece—that such an imperial, cosmopolitan society could be fundamentally color-prejudiced was illogical.

The notion that Kitchener and his peers were meekly pandering to the prejudices of white listeners is a conclusion roundly countered by their other compositions. Lord Beginner's "Mix Up Matrimony," for example, was a boldly celebratory observation of mixed marriages, recorded in a context where such unions were viewed with marked anxiety if not hostility:

The races are blendin' harmoniously
White and colored people are bindin' mutually
It doesn't take no glass
To see how it come to pass
Colored Britons are risin' fast.[77]

---

75 Quoted in Phillips and Phillips, *Windrush*, 89–91.

76 Aldwyn Roberts, "My Landlady," *London is the Place for Me*. Originally recorded for Melodisc, 1962.

77 Egbert Moore, "Mix Up Matrimony," *London is the Place for Me*. Originally recorded for Melodisc, 1952.

Throughout this song Beginner repeatedly promotes the idea of interracial marriage, with no reference to the fact that such unions were overtly frowned upon in the mother country.

Even saucier was the Mighty Terror's "Women Police in England." I have not here dwelt upon the long tradition of sexual humor and double entendre in the calypso canon, because this substantial body of work makes little reference to topical events in Britain or elsewhere. But "Women Police in England" is a good illustration of the degree to which calypsonians were unconcerned with social taboos or political correctness. In this song, Mighty Terror—Fitzgerald Henry, a member of Kitchener's famed Young Brigade at Trinidad Carnival—marvels at the existence of female officers in London, then professes his willingness to commit a misdemeanor in order to get himself arrested by one:

> If I do anything as to get arrest
> To the inspector I'm makin' a request
> Please don't send any male policeman for me
> Because the magistrate would not find me guilty
> But if he send the lovely blondie one
> When she comes I would throw myself on the ground
> And if she bend down to arrest me
> Man, I'm peepin' as far as me eyes could see.[78]

In a climate where male West Indian settlers were often stereotyped as oversexed bachelors, and the "liberal" media were pumping out their own gentle, clean-cut counter-stereotypes in the mold of Earl Cameron and Cy Grant, these lewd compositions reflected a lively irreverence for social taboos that was part of calypso's heritage. While the result in the above lyric is that the West Indian narrator (Terror himself) comes across less as a sexual predator than comic relief, its swaggering references to the sexual attractiveness of respectable white women was gutsy in the British context, because it made no concessions to proprietorial English masculinity. As Val Wilmer, an English woman who came of age in the mixed-race milieu of the British jazz and rhythm-and-blues scene, noted, even performing music could come across as a black masculine threat to Britain's covert racial hierarchy:

> Once Black people became more vocal and challenging by their presence, the fantasy atmosphere created by the music's liberal chroniclers began to sour. It is, after all, a world in which macho values dominate. Alongside the good humour and exuberance the musicians are making

---

78 Fitzgerald Henry (Mighty Terror), "Women Police in England," *Kings of Calypso* (Castle Communications MC 244, 1992), NSA.

a statement of intent that can be daunting to men from outside the culture. Indeed the music itself threatens notions of white supremacy and Black subservience.[79]

This was no mean feat in the years of mounting white anxiety over West Indian migration, and mounting West Indian frustration at their treatment as second-class citizens in the mother country. As a result of its reputation as a playful, easy-going, impish performance genre, calypso had the potential to mask social and racial tensions beneath its seemingly innocuous observations on British society and current events. In 1948, before Kitchener had even got off the boat, his "London is the Place for Me" expressed a

fleeting moment before the idealism of Caribbean immigrants turned sour. Here are the twitchings of giddy possibility, the utopianism many migrants feel when embarking upon new chapters of their lives. The optimism of Kitchener's calypso makes the viewer nostalgic for a time when black and Asian people genuinely believed their mother country was happy to see them, a time when they could anticipate the future with relish.[80]

However, over the next few decades, Lord Kitchener and his fellow émigré calypsonians Beginner and Invader used the traditional narrative conventions of satire, flattery, and double entendre, as well as their own personal charisma, to artfully place loaded political issues—imperial loyalty, white violence, cultural connections between the West Indies and Britain, the nature of racial xenophobia, and the significance of Commonwealth status—onto the agenda of British calypso.

---

79 Wilmer, *Mama Said There'd Be Days Like This*, 45.
80 Sukhdev Sandhu, *London Calling: How Black and Asian Writers Imagined a City* (London: HarperCollins, 2003), 317–18.

Chapter 4

Ronald Moody,
from Primitive to Black British

In 1982, when Ronald Clive Moody was seventy-two and in the last years of his life, he received a letter from a young student working on a personal study project for her A-levels. Her chosen subject was black artists in Britain, and she wrote to ask Moody for information about his life and work. In his response he immediately stated, "First I would like to be the artist first and then, what colour you prefer, if I am any use to you in your A level."[1] Too few critics of Moody's work have heeded his request.

This chapter examines Moody's art and career from his own perspective, as reflected in his art, radio scripts, lectures, drawings, literature, interviews, and personal correspondence. This perspective, like that of all artists, was "informed by education, class, regional custom and the pressure of friends" as well as "unstated physical, economic, political and moral constraints."[2] It therefore changed over time.

One must also consider the perspectives of those who have assessed and presented Moody's work to the public: galleries and curators, art critics and the media, as well as academic scholars. No less than Moody, these institutions and individuals were (and continue to be) informed by custom, economy, politics, and are therefore changeable too.

The story below, then, runs along two tracks that run parallel, intersect, and diverge as they chart Moody's career and legacy. Such intersections and divergences are historically vital to any assessment of the sculptor's significance to British culture as both a colonial *and* a British artist. I argue

---

1   Letter, Moody to Marlene Smith, January 12, 1982. TGA 956, Box 3, Professional Miscellaneous L–Z, Hyman Kreitman Research Centre, Tate Museum, London (HKRC).

2   Margaret Garlake, *New Art New World: British Art in Postwar Society* (New Haven and London: Yale University Press, 1998), 4.

here that while art critics, institutions, and historians have, on account of his race and colonial status, positioned Moody variously as a representative of "primitive," Caribbean, and Negro (later Black or Black British) art, these labels do not reflect the totality of Moody's history and artistic evolution. In fact, a closer evaluation of his experiences in Jamaica, England, and France, his grappling with the politics of race and colonialism, even his aesthetic inspirations, highlights the extent to which he was a product of, and contributor to, British and European artistic traditions since the 1930s. Like many of the other subjects in this book, Ronald Moody operated within a British and European cultural world, and used it to express his own dynamic aesthetic, intellectual, and political priorities—priorities that often had little to do with the color line over which postwar British society agonized.

At the same time, he very much resisted categorizing himself as a part of any national or aesthetic school. Leon Wainwright has written of Guyanese painter Aubrey Williams that "his biography entwined spaces that art history has treated as largely disconnected," and that his allegiance to no particular country or region frustrated "the demand of audiences who assumed easy 'connections' to any single visual heritage."[3] Much the same could be said of Moody. Like Williams, his formative years were not spent in one place—for Moody it was Jamaica, Paris, and London. Each place left its imprint on his work, but not in discrete, classifiable ways.

Over the years, as Moody grappled with aesthetic and political questions that were similar not only to Aubrey Williams's, but Henry Moore's and Barbara Hepworth's, the universalist spirit of his sculpture did not diminish. What did change was the critical and political context. His career began when the extent of the British Empire was at its peak, and ended in late-century postcolonial London. His recognition and placement in the British artistic canon shifted accordingly.

Moody's career spanned from his days as a student of dentistry in London, through his early success in cosmopolitan Paris, his unusual and harrowing experience of the Second World War; then to the surge in Caribbean migration to Britain in the 1950s, the campaigns for colonial independence, and the creation of a self-consciously "black British" identification in the 1970s and 1980s. In the midst of these changes, Moody perpetually struggled to articulate his own politics and to question its influence on his sculpture. He struggled, too, to reconcile his cultural politics with his shifting social and professional place in British society and the European art world. It is the struggle that is historically interesting.

The literature on Ronald Moody portrays him as "the doyen of Caribbean artists in Britain,"[4] and indeed his relatively early arrival in London and

---

3   Leon Wainwright, *Timed Out: Art and the Transnational Caribbean* (Manchester and New York: Manchester University Press, 2011), 36–37.

4   Anne Walmsley, "The Caribbean Artists Movement, 1966–1972: A Space and a Voice

interwar success made him something of a father figure for aspiring West Indian artists after 1960. His place within the Caribbean canon is both appropriate and assured, but such a description, on the surface, elides vital aspects of his work, aesthetic philosophy, and the important changes that took place in his professional status over the years. Moody's current image as a black British and diasporic artist constitutes only the most recent incarnation. For *at least* the first thirty years of his career, Moody operated exclusively in a European, metropolitan world. His aesthetic approach developed in much the same way as that of other European artists at this time, even as he rejected Europe's artistic legacy in favor of non-Western, pre-Columbian art. As he told Anne Walmsley,

> Each of us has to delve within himself and really begin to find out what he is. I definitely was never influenced very much by European art. My influences came from Egypt, India and Africa; and gradually a kind of inner fight had to take place, throwing away so much I had learned at school. ... And this was a very, very difficult kind of long pilgrimage. I think that is the fundamental thing that the West Indian is faced with.[5]

In order to bring out the historical richness and significance of Moody's "pilgrimage," I will attempt to transcend the binary distinction between the cultures of the "colonizer" and "colonized," and emphasize instead the dialectical relationship at work in Moody's artistic and political development.[6] Doing so implicitly involves a repositioning of categories of "primitivist," "colonial," and "black British" art.

for Visual Practice," in Mora J. Beauchamp-Byrd and M. Franklin Sirmans, eds, *Transforming the Crown: African, Asian and Caribbean Artists in Britain 1966–1996* (New York: Franklin H. Williams Caribbean Cultural Center/African Diaspora Institute, 1997), 48.

5   Ronald Moody quoted in Anne Walmsley, *The Caribbean Artists Movement: A Literary and Cultural History* (London and Port of Spain: New Beacon Books, 1992), 181.

6   Here I follow the examples of Leon Wainwright's "Francis Newton Souza and Aubrey Williams: Entwined Art Histories at the End of Empire," in Simon Faulkner and Anandi Ramamurthy, eds, *Visual Culture and Decolonisation in Britain* (Aldershot: Ashgate Publishing Limited, 2006), 101–26; Rasheed Araeen, *The Other Story: Afro-Asian Artists in Post-War Britain* (London: Arts Council, 1989); Catherine Hall, "Histories, Empires, and the Post-Colonial Moment," in Iain Chambers and Linda Curti, eds, *The Post-Colonial Question: Common Skies, Divided Horizons* (London: Routledge, 1996), 65–77.

Revelatory Moments in the British Museum

As he later recalled on more than one occasion, Ronald Moody's formative moment as an artist occurred in 1928 on a visit to the British Museum, when he "turned left instead of right" and happened upon a room filled with monumental sculptures from ancient Egypt.[7] As he gushed to broadcaster Una Marson in 1943, "I can't tell you what a thrill it was when I first discovered Egyptian art for myself."[8] The "tremendous inner force, the irresistible movement in stillness" of these giant stone statues is what struck him most, and it was these characteristics of Egyptian, Indian, and African art that profoundly informed his own work.[9] In writings and interviews, Moody made much of this first fateful visit to the Egyptian section of the British Museum. He meant to suggest how his work was fundamentally influenced by non-Western—African, Indian, Chinese—precedents, and not the European tradition to which he was exposed in his (British-style) colonial education.

Nonetheless, it is not incidental that this galvanizing episode occurred in London, mediated by an institution made great, in large part, by Britain's history of imperial domination. Moody's discovery of so-called "primitive" art was, in this sense, a distinctively European, even British, experience, one that was likely shared by other young artists and students in interwar London, and was certainly shared by one—Henry Moore, who was two years Moody's senior. The celebrated Yorkshire sculptor also found an immediate and enduring inspiration in the collections of the British Museum. He became one of the foremost exponents of "primitivist" sculpture in interwar Europe, and in 1941 he wrote, "Excepting some collections of primitive art in France, Italy, and Spain, my own knowledge of it has come entirely from continual visits to the British Museum during the past twenty years." And Moore was fascinated for much the same reason as Moody. His 1958 book *Heads, Figures and Ideas* contained a postcard of an eighteenth-dynasty Egyptian head of a woman, on which were scribbled the words, "I would give everything, if I could get into my sculpture the same amount of humanity & seriousness; nobility & experience, acceptance of life, distinction, & aristocracy with absolutely no tricks no affectation no self-consciousness looking straight ahead, no movement, but more alive than a real person."[10]

---

7 Quoted in Cynthia Moody, "Ronald Moody: A Man True to his Vision," in *Third Text: Third World Perspectives on Art and Culture* 8–9 (1989), 5.

8 Broadcast transcript, "Calling the West Indies: Close-Up" (interview with Ronald Moody by Una Marson, broadcast West Indies Service January 31/February 1, 1943), 2. Box 7, TGA 956—Ronald Moody, HKRC.

9 Quoted in Cynthia Moody, "Ronald Moody", 5–6.

10 Peter Stansky and William Abrahams, *London's Burning: Life, Death and Art in the Second World War* (London: Constable, 1994), 11.

Incidentally, Moore's contemporary Barbara Hepworth also attributed her first urge to sculpt to her exposure to Egyptian art, though in her case the exposure came from a school lecture.[11] Like Moore, Hepworth, and other British and European artists fascinated by the creations of non-Western, pre-Columbian societies, Moody was first exposed to his monumental, ancient inspirations through the filter of cosmopolitan London.

I have mentioned Moore's experience because there seems to be a knee-jerk tendency to relate some black artists' *aesthetic* interest in non-Western precedents to a more fundamental *political* rejection of European values, and to regard this rejection as the basis of a "colonial" school or approach. As Veerle Poupeye has observed, "It is a common notion … that authenticity in Caribbean art is measured by its independence from the Western artistic canons."[12] This is especially the case because most of the art under discussion dates from the late twentieth century, during the aftermath of decolonization, the Black Power and civil rights movements of the 1960s, and the first wave of large-scale colonial migration to Britain. In the Caribbean, "Most national schools originated in the decolonization process, for instance, and the resulting quest for cultural identity has remained a unifying concern."[13] Moody, born near the turn of the century, belonged to a different generation, and while he rejected many of the formal concerns of the Renaissance tradition, his initial reasons for doing so need to be interrogated; he did not explicitly connect them to his self-identification as a black subject but echoed, in fact, the sentiments of young men like Moore.

It is also worth recalling that, prior to his sailing across the Atlantic, Moody, like so many others who were inspired by the "primitive" in Europe, had little to no exposure to indigenous Caribbean art; his artistic life appears to have truly begun in England. Although this would change in the decades to come, Moody observed that both in Britain and the West Indies, his compatriots displayed either indifference or hostility to indigenous artists and art. As late as 1960, Moody wrote a letter to the editor of the *Barbados Sunday News* lamenting the poor turnout for a local exhibition by one of his fellow Caribbean artists and asking, "As I am aware that when a European artist gives an exhibition in the West Indies, it is usually a great success financially, why isn't local talent more generously supported?"[14] For Moody, this indifference was at least partly a result of the Eurocentrism of West Indian society and the middle-class

---

11 Matthew Gale and Chris Stephens, *Barbara Hepworth: Works in the Tate Gallery Collection and the Barbara Hepworth Museum St Ives* (London: Tate Gallery Publishing, 1999), 9.

12 Veerle Poupeye, *Caribbean Art* (London: Thames & Hudson, 1998), 9.

13 Ibid., 10.

14 Letter, Moody to Editor, *Barbados Sunday News* (December 12, 1960).

education of which he was a product. And while London sparked Moody's interest in ancient and (eventually) Caribbean art, it did not have the same effect on most of his colonial peers, whom he repeatedly criticized for their indifference to the cultivation of a distinctive, indigenous tradition of fine art within which young artists could develop:

> In the West Indies, the cultural heritage had been destroyed during successive occupations, and the slave trade and indentured labour brought new races to live on the islands. When I really began to get interested in sculpture, I found this attitude of indifference made me feel a little isolated. Though everyone, including myself, worked hard and many passed their exams with distinctions, I knew it was useless to suggest a visit to a Museum or contemporary exhibition.[15]

To explain Moody's relative cultural isolation among his peers we need to look closer at his background among the West Indian middle class from which he and so many other colonial students sprang. He was born into a family of growing affluence in Kingston, Jamaica, on August 12, 1900, part of the expanding black middle class "able to pay for their children to attend secondary schools and the private preparatory schools that catered to them." (It should also be noted that by the first half of the century, most schools in Jamaica were open to students of all colors.)[16] His father, Charles Ernest Moody, was a prosperous local chemist. Ronald had six siblings, most of whom, according to his niece Cynthia, "lived up to what was expected of them" professionally.[17] Notably, his eldest brother, Harold Moody, trained as a physician at King's College, London, and in 1931 founded the League of Coloured Peoples, a prominent multiracial and Christian organization that worked to protect the rights of colonial people in Britain and to support various pan-African and colonial initiatives internationally. Harold Moody was part of a prewar British circle of radical black intellectuals that included Marcus Garvey, George Padmore, and C. L. R. James. He epitomized the ambitions and professional trajectories of many middle-class sons of the British colonies in the first half of the twentieth century: schooling at a reputable colonial institution, followed by a prestigious education (often on scholarship) for a solid profession, perhaps a period of public service in Britain, and then a return home to a profitable career, sometimes in politics, and a leading position in the community.

The connection between class status, professional ambition, and political commitment is worth emphasizing here; both David Killingray and Anne Spry Rush have examined this pattern as it applied specifically

---

15 Ronald Moody, "Caribbean Survey: An Exile Looks Back" (BBC typescript).
16 Rush, *Bonds of Empire*, 26–27.
17 Cynthia Moody, "Ronald Moody," 5.

to Harold Moody. Rush in particular demonstrates that English notions of middle-class respectability profoundly informed the rhetoric and style of Moody's political activism.[18] West Indian students who had the good fortune to study in Britain were expected to become the colonial leaders of tomorrow, and they often did. As Anne Walmsley notes, "going to Britain was the only option for ambitious young men from black middle-class homes and the best colonial secondary schools."[19] The Secretary of State for the Colonies, Lord Swinton, noted in 1931 that black people in Britain were "men who either have already made their mark and are men of influence in their own lands, or young men who will go back and have influence in their own countries, and through whose eyes thousands of their fellow countrymen will see England."[20] This trend was strongest prior to the Second World War, when education was one of the few passports to Britain, but it persisted into the early postwar period. For those who chose not to return to their home colonies, professional status and political activism still commingled. The League of Coloured Peoples, for example, drew strength and status from the connections Harold Moody cultivated as, among other things, a Cambridge graduate, physician, member of the Congregational Church, and chairman of both the Colonial, and later the London, Missionary Societies.

Ronald Moody, eighteen years Harold's junior, grew up in a similar environment of Anglocentric expectations. He received a "sound classical education" at Calabar College,[21] and his memories of that experience, like C. L. R. James's, might have belonged to any middle-class English boy: "I remember the intense discussions and preparations for the inter-schools football matches, as I was in the first eleven. I still possess a medal from the Jamaica Football Association, 1921–22. Dare I admit that I was never drawn to Cricket?"[22] He felt compelled to follow in the respectable path trod by his four older siblings. As Anne Walmsley notes, he made this decision "more because professional training was open to him and expected of him

---

18 See David Killingray, "'To Do Something for the Race': Harold Moody and the League of Coloured Peoples," in Bill Schwarz, ed., *West Indian Intellectuals in Britain* (Manchester and New York: Manchester University Press, 2003); Rush, "Imperial Identity in Colonial Minds." Gentlemanly conduct—along English lines— was central to the acceptance of West Indian men in respectable British society. So much so that Marcus Collins has suggested that the "hard task" of West Indian men in the 1950s was "severing the association between British gentlemanliness and masculine respectability." See Collins, "Pride and Prejudice: West Indian Men in Mid-Twentieth-Century Britain," *Journal of British Studies* 40 (July 2001): 417–18.

19 Anne Walmsley, *The Caribbean Artists Movement*, 1.

20 Sir Philip Cunliffe-Lester (Lord Swinton), quoted in Moody, *The Colour Bar*, 2–3.

21 Cynthia Moody, "Ronald Moody," 5.

22 Ronald Moody, "Caribbean Survey: An Exile Looks Back" (BBC typescript; broadcast West Indies Service, January 12, 1953). Box 7, TGA 956—Ronald Moody, HKRC.

as the youngest of a prominent, middle-class Kingston family, than because he was enthusiastic about this or that career."[23] His motives were unrelated to the arts. This was not unusual; a great many West Indians who earned creative success in the British scene originally migrated in order to pursue other occupations, especially (during wartime) in the military, but also in medicine, law, and engineering. Moody's avowed motivation was to study dentistry, "because I thought it was an easier profession than medicine, and one thing I did know, was that I wanted to get away from my environment and really think."[24] So in 1923, like Harold before him, Ronald began his studies at King's College. (Later in life, his dentistry skills would serve him well; in lean times, he picked up appointments through the National Health Service.)

Nonetheless, despite treading the path carved out by his older brother and so many others, young Ronald Moody was uncomfortable with the politicized atmosphere of his circle of radical colonial students and intellectuals in London. These educated, ambitious young men were keenly interested in race politics, but Moody was ambivalent about his own commitment to the cause. He observed that among his fellow West Indian students, politics was

> endlessly discussed; so was the colour problem. I met students who were so embittered by the injustice of the colour bar, that the whole of their outlook was warped. This seemed to me too dear a price to pay, for it showed that they had become the victim of the very thing they were fighting.[25]

Increasingly drawn to cultural and philosophical questions, he felt alienated from the strictly political priorities of his peers.

In light of the ingrained expectations placed upon colonial students from the Caribbean, one can better grasp the less-than-enthusiastic response of Moody's family to his decision to switch careers:

> Well, it caused such a hullabaloo and there was such a row about it, I was fortunate to be 5,000 miles away, and so untouched. When, eventually, I sent home some cuttings and things, they began to think it was—well, still dreadful, because no artist really works—but, "Well at least you are working a bit". And so, for a very long time, I was simply, the black sheep of the family—and that was that![26]

---

23 Walmsley, *The Caribbean Artists Movement*, 1.
24 Cynthia Moody, "Ronald Moody," 5.
25 Moody, "Caribbean Survey: An Exile Looks Back" (BBC typescript; broadcast West Indies Service, January 12, 1953). Box 7, TGA 956—Ronald Moody, HKRC.
26 Transcript of Sylvia Moore interview with Ronald Moody for the World Service, Radio Nederland, Hilversum, July 29, 1977. Box 7, TGA 956—Ronald Moody, HKRC.

There is evidence to suggest that Moody believed this attitude to be endemic in Jamaica, and among West Indians more generally.

Such a conviction was perhaps borne out by the coverage of Moody's career in the Jamaican news, which praised above all the *British* nature of his success. For instance, in 1951 Moody joined a small group of London artists known as the Seven Dials, and the *Jamaica Daily Gleaner* boasted, "Jamaica-born Ronald Moody is the only Colonial member of the 'Seven Dials Group', a newly-formed painters' and sculptors' club in London."[27] Here Moody was recognized for his achievements *outside* the colonial framework, for his success within a British cultural world.

For his part, although Moody always preferred non-Western inspirations for his creative work and later committed himself to recovering a Caribbean "idiom" in his sculpture, he acknowledged that the cities of Europe were far more congenial to artists. He remarked in a 1951 interview that "in the West Indies, a man who is not a member of the leading professions" had "little or no status," and he went on to explain that

> colonial painters, sculptors, musicians and writers have an unpredictable future in the colonies. Consequently most of those who have been to European countries, prefer to make their homes there. They may not be a financial success there, but if their work shows merit, they are, at least, accorded some recognition which is absent in colonial societies.[28]

Life in London represented a refreshing alternative to the stultifying attitudes prevalent in Jamaica. In fact, Moody paradoxically felt that a more cosmopolitan environment could work as a corrective to the Eurocentrism of West Indian society:

> The West Indian is born with one eye trained on Europe or America. The other vaguely scans his homeland. Education strengthens the Euro-American eye and tends to make the other more myopic. If he does eventually reach these countries he MAY be fortunate enough to recover the proper use of his eyes and begin to see his home and to understand his own and his country's difficulties. This involves a long and often painful process of revaluation.[29]

Of course, such a statement, as well as his own life choices, reveals Moody's own metropolitan orientation. Hence, although both his artwork and

---

27 "Ronald Moody Joins The 'Seven Dials,'" *Jamaica Daily Gleaner* (January 20, 1951). TGA 956—Ronald Moody. Box 5, HKRC.

28 Moody quoted in E. B. Timothy, "Future of Art in the Colonies," *East African Standard* (May 30, 1951). TGA 956—Ronald Moody. Box 5, HKRC.

29 Moody, "Art in the Caribbean" (date and publication unknown, probably late 1940s). TGA 956—Ronald Moody. Box 9, HKRC.

aesthetic philosophy embodied a reaction to the Western tradition, they were made possible, as we shall see below, by Moody's European activities; he thrived in both the London and Parisian art scenes and appeared never to consider returning permanently to Jamaica.

Thus, at an early age Moody felt himself to be at one remove from the educated, politically active, colonial middle class of which he was a member, and his decision to pursue art professionally was an expression of this. That is not to say that Moody did not become increasingly committed, in his way, to colonial politics and social justice, which will be discussed in greater detail below. But his metropolitan orientation and partial rejection of the values of his middle-class colonial peers greatly influenced his early professional and artistic choices.

European Primitivism

As argued above, the relationship between Moody's art and politics was not straightforwardly anti-colonial. Veerle Poupeye has astutely observed that "assumptions about a purely oppositional relationship" between colonial and European art "fail to recognize the complexity and dialectic nature of the relationship between Caribbean and metropolitan Western culture."[30] One must bear this in mind when considering Moody's mid-century work and philosophy, which contains parallels to other Caribbean primitivist work but was at least as closely connected to European precedents.

Among the most fundamental of these European influences were his personal experiences in France between 1938 and 1941, and his permanent return to London in the middle of the war. Moody moved to Paris in July of 1938 after his first two major exhibitions—in Paris (which opened October 29, 1937) and Amsterdam (which opened January 8, 1938)—proved to be considerable successes.

Prior to this move, Moody's trips to London museums and galleries became more frequent, and triggered his growing preoccupation with sculpture, which expressed itself in early models shaped from Plasticine and even dentist's plaster. He immersed himself in texts of Chinese and Indian philosophy and religion, which in turn informed his sculpture and inspired for the first time a sustained interest in the arts as they related to his colonial background. Upon his graduation from dental school, Moody set up a practice but continued to pursue sculpture after hours. In 1934 he moved into a flat with an adjoining greenhouse that became his studio. In this greenhouse Moody created his first large woodcarving, the expressive, questioning head *Wohin*, which he later sold to the English art critic Marie Seton, who became a lifelong friend and promoter of his work. *Wohin*

---

30 Poupeye, *Caribbean Art*, 10. Also see 22–23.

also brought him his first one-man show in Paris in October 1937, and it was at this point that Moody left dentistry to pursue his craft full-time.

Moody's early woodcarvings conveyed universalism and worldly equipoise; their apparent non-material spirituality meant they were often classified as part of the school of "primitive" art, although they do not explicitly reference a particular regional or historical aesthetic. As Moody himself stated, "I do not wish us to attempt to put the clock back. A return to first principles would not and cannot re-create the outward form of medieval or primitive art."[31] Like the giant Egyptian structures that he first saw at the British Museum, Moody's forms expressed a powerful serenity and introspection that was challenging in the context of mid-century European modernism and expressionism. In 1940, the reputable art critic Max Osborn wrote:

> He carves from blocks of wood, with a robust yet delicate chisel, figures and heads of a very personal character. How this calm, meditating young artist attacks the noble living material, grasping its planes and volumes with the hand of a master, re-echoing the hidden forces of the soul in faces of exotic expression not consciously evoked is truly extraordinary.[32]

Moody's first major sculpture, *Wohin*, suggested this eternal calm, and made no explicit political statement; even its title, meaning "whither" in German, was taken from a title in Schubert's song cycle *Die Schöne Müllerin* (the work's only obvious European referent). Its buyer, Marie Seton, found that it conjured very individual responses:

> After this striking head, symbolic of man's search for truth, came into my possession, many people would stand in front of it and relate what it called up in their minds. Was it a man striving for sainthood; was it some god of the distant tropics; what was it? Some people found it so provocative that they could not bear to sit in the same room with it.[33]

This kind of reaction was likely just what Moody wanted; he meant his imposing carvings to trigger responses that highlighted the shared humanity of the viewers.

---

31 Moody, "The Artist's Education," BBC typescript (pre-recorded August 2, 1946), 6. TGA 956, Box 7, BBC Transcripts Talks, HKRC.

32 Max Osborn quoted in the catalogue for a solo exhibition at the Woodstock Gallery, London (July 25–August 13, 1960). TGA 956, Box 4, Exhibitions Catalogues, HKRC. Originally published as a review in the *National-Zeitung*, Basel, Switzerland (January 25, 1940).

33 Marie Seton, "Prophet of Man's Hope: Ronald Moody and his Sculpture," *The Studio* (January 1950), 26. TGA 956, Box 5, Press Cuttings, HKRC.

In one sense, his carvings pose a contrast to much modern European sculpture of the period, which Seton described as being "preoccupied with new concepts of form or with capturing the topical features of our period."[34] Moody spoke often of his distaste for so much of the Western tradition in art and philosophy as it had developed since the Renaissance; about the latter he once wrote that Italy was "the mother of this over-confident, arrogant and self-willed child."[35] His disinterest stemmed largely from his belief that modern European art was disproportionately preoccupied with conveying external beauty, that it was less concerned with the expression of "profound truths" than non-Western cultures, where the accurate representation of nature was not a priority. Mary Lou Emery has described Moody's massive *Johanaan* as "a Spiritual Man" possessing "an intense and even rigid physical strength shaped in the warm, heavy matter of wood out of which arises the visionary head with its gaze directed beyond the material world."[36] According to Moody, this focus on technical mastery at the expense of spiritual or universal meaning in fine art continued to thrive in Europe, reaching its impoverished nadir just prior to the turn of the twentieth century: "The research into the nature of appearances which began at the time of the Renaissance, towards the end of the nineteenth century, resolved itself into a technically perfect but lifeless imitation which denied the very reason for the existence of art."[37] It is clear that Moody did not view the evolution of European art as essentially progressive; rather the opposite. Furthermore, he believed that such artistic and philosophical impulses persisted into his own time, manifesting themselves in a multitude of repugnant aesthetic "isms" (such as modernism and surrealism).

And yet many prominent British and European artists shared Moody's critique of European modernism during the interwar period, especially those who were influenced by ancient or primitive sculpture. They too wanted to distance themselves from the proliferation of willful, abstract trends jockeying for position in the European art scene. The British Seven and Five group, for instance, which counted a young Moore and Hepworth among its members, declared in a public statement from the 1920s that "they are not a group formed to advertise a new 'ism'. They feel that the gladiators of the present warring sects are often concerned more with the incidental politics and temporary eddies of art than with its essential

---

34 Ibid.

35 Moody, *Calling the West Indies*, "Renaissance Art," BBC typescript (pre-recorded July 25, 1950), 1. TGA 956, Box 7, BBC Transcripts Talks, HKRC.

36 Mary Lou Emery, *Modernism, the Visual, and Caribbean Literature* (Cambridge: Cambridge University Press, 2007), 89.

37 Moody, *Calling the West Indies*, "Modern Art," BBC typescript (pre-recorded August 10, 1950), 1. TGA 956, Box 7, BBC Transcripts Talks, HKRC.

realities."[38] Hence this facet of Moody's anti-Europeanism paradoxically placed him at the cutting edge of the European art scene.

Moody's rejection of the liberal notion of progress, cemented by his experience of twentieth-century warfare, also triggered his re-evaluation of dominant notions of the "primitive" art with which his own work was associated. "Primitive" was in some ways a catch-all term used after the turn of the century to describe not only ancient or pre-modern artifacts, but also modern art that presumably expressed a similar spirit; in other words, art that referenced non-European or non-rational artistic precedents. The aesthetic celebration of primitivism was spearheaded by members of the European avant-garde such as Pablo Picasso, Henri Matisse, and Man Ray, who incorporated African artifacts or motifs into their paintings and photographs.

This designation was, of course, implicitly racial, an expression in part of the negrophilia of interwar, metropolitan Europe. In cities like Paris, "Academic theories about origin, evolution, function and meaning merged with Dadaist, surrealist and other avant-garde thinking which promoted the primitive as central to modern life."[39] The European focus on primitivism thus positioned non-Western art as both a critique of, and an antidote to, the worst parts of Western civilization.

The reception and positioning of artists of color within this context was ambivalent and is undergoing a gradual historical revision (of which this treatment of Moody is a small part). On the one hand, these artists were often accepted and praised by art dealers, gallery owners, and audiences as more in touch with the "primitive" search for essential truths, purely because of their race or colonial background. This was despite the fact that "the educated Caribbean middle classes, to which most artists and cultural theorists of the [interwar period] belonged, were nonetheless socially and culturally isolated from the masses."[40] That so many of these artists, particularly before the Second World War, were (like Moody) not professionally trained, served to bolster this assumption. Colonial primitivism thus gained a certain prominence.

For decades, art history reflected this implicitly racial classification, which had the effect of categorizing artists primarily as proponents of colonial primitivism or national art. This was all to the good insofar as the artists viewed themselves as proponents of a distinctly "black" or colonial art. (Edna Manley did so, though even in this case "her Jamaicanness

---

38 Seven and Five manifesto quoted in Richard A. Born, *From Blast to Pop: Aspects of Modern British Art, 1915–1965* (Chicago: The David and Alfred Smart Museum of Art, The University of Chicago, 1997), 10.

39 Petrine Archer-Straw, *Negrophilia: Avant-Garde Paris and Black Culture in the 1920s* (London: Thames & Hudson, 2000), 60.

40 Poupeye, *Caribbean Art*, 51.

was always contested by others because of her foreign birth and ostensible whiteness"—Manley was of mixed parentage and very light-skinned.)[41]

But for those who did not, the tendency has been to cleave Caribbean artists from their foundational experience within the European art world and evaluate them as something other than modern artists.[42] Art historians now stress, for example, the extent to which painter Wilfredo Lam's "engagement with Africanizing forms and ostensibly primitive imagery was *learned*, not instinctual," cultivated in part through his engagement with European circles. Moody, too, was highly educated, and his primitivism, like that of his European-born counterparts, was both emotional and intellectual. His generation was able to buttress their visual art with a thoroughly informed and articulated critique of the West.[43]

As Lowery Stokes Sims avers, colonial artists and intellectuals "were able to recuperate an appreciation of their 'native' cultures as a result of the favorable—if flawed—reception those cultures gained in vanguard circles in Europe."[44] However, although there was no coherent or cohesive West Indian *school* of painting or sculpture at this time, questions of authenticity and colonial identity were on the minds of several artists from the region after the First World War. Even artists who produced radically dissimilar work in visual terms often approached it from a similar angle. British Guianese painter Aubrey Williams, who produced abstract representations of everything from Amerindian people and landscapes to outer space, shared many of Moody's cultural convictions, for example a detestation of the proliferation of aesthetic "isms" in the twentieth century and a fascination with ancient non-Western art. Both made their homes in London.[45]

Commonalities among Caribbean artists existed despite the fact that they worked in isolation from each other. Poupeye, while stating that "Moody's work was not guided by the nationalist agenda of his Jamaican-based contemporaries," still maintains that "his early work is nonetheless

41 Veerle Poupeye, "Jamaican Art and the Changing National Imaginary: From the Affirmative to the Critical," in Deborah Cullen and Elvis Fuentes, eds, *Caribbean Art at the Crossroads of the World* (New York: El Museo de Barrio and Yale University Press, 2012), 186.

42 Leon Wainwright, *Timed Out*, 54.

43 Michele Greet, "Inventing Wifredo Lam: The Parisian Avant-Garde's Primitivist Fixation," *Invisible Culture*, 5 (2003): http://ivc.lib.rochester.edu/inventing-wifredo-lam-the-parisian-avant-gardes-primitivist-fixation/, accessed January 12, 2017. See also Colin Rhodes, *Primitivism and Modern Art* (London: Thames and Hudson, 1994), 196.

44 Lowery Stokes Sims, *Wilfredo Lam and the International Avant-Garde, 1923–1982* (Austin: University of Texas Press, 2002), 8.

45 See Box 2001/12, (Aubrey) Williams—Writings and Publicity Material and Video, HKRC.

stylistically akin to the contemporary carvings of [Edna] Manley and [Alvin] Marriott, with whom he shared his mastery of woodcarving."[46] Over the years Moody would become increasingly aware of the connections between his own creations and those of his West Indian colleagues, but until well after the Second World War, his stylistically colonial or "West Indian" idiom evolved almost entirely inside a European incubator.

It is certainly possible that Moody's early achievements outside Britain, particularly in France, were colored by the interwar Parisian avant-garde's enthusiasm for what it viewed as genuine "primitive" art. In December 1939, for instance, he exhibited at the Galerie Tropiques Billet Vorms; in Holland, he formed an artistic alliance with Nola Hatterman, a Dutch painter who specialized in black and colonial subjects and with whom he later collaborated (in 1950) on a dual exhibition at London's Galerie Apollinaire.

Moody did not discard the "primitive" label, with its implications of colonial backwardness, even as it applied to himself. But he was no imperial apologist; nor was he apolitical. In a 1949 talk for the BBC program *Calling the West Indies* entitled "What is Called Primitive Art," he emphasized that particular notions of primitivism had to be discarded:

> The first is that the primitive artist was technically and artistically inferior, and that with the gradual passing of time there has been a sort of evolution and consequently an improvement. ... No! There has been no evolution or development. Nowadays the painter can buy his colours already made up and the tools of the sculptor can be bought at a shop. But what real advantage do these things give to modern art? There has only been the change that each age shows in expressing itself.[47]

By actively interrogating and debunking dominant and condescending notions of the "primitive" in art, Moody posed an implicit challenge to the supremacy of his own imperial, Anglocentric education as well as the colonial system that reproduced such convictions.

Again, however, it is essential to remember that while Moody's embrace of primitivism reinforced the colonial challenge to European cultural hegemony, it was famously shared by (white) European artists like Picasso, Matisse, and Henry Moore, whose sculpture appropriated non-Western themes and motifs with great faith and care.[48] Like Moody, Moore

---

46 Poupeye, *Caribbean Art*, 79.

47 Moody, *Calling the West Indies*, "What is Called Primitive Art," BBC typescript (pre-recorded December 14, 1949), 2–3. TGA 956, Box 7, BBC Transcripts Talks, HKRC.

48 Alan Wilkinson has remarked that "the influence of primitive art—prehistoric fertility goddesses, African, Oceanic, Peruvian, Inuit, and, above all, pre-Columbian sculpture—had, in my opinion, a more sustained impact on Moore's work than on

appreciated this art that made "a straightforward statement" and concerned itself with "the elemental," in contradistinction to a comparatively empty Western approach: "It is art before it got smothered in trimmings and surface decorations, before inspiration had flagged into technical tricks and intellectual conceits."[49] And Moody, too, cultivated and promoted his philosophy and art in London and Paris, the centers of two global, albeit crumbling, empires. It was in these imperial cities that he first gained success, not in the colonial West Indies.

Notwithstanding this association of Moody's work with artistic primitivism, early criticism of his work was complimentary but notably free of references to his racial, or even national, origin. Reviews from the late 1930s appeared primarily in newspapers and art publications that had no specialized interest in colonial art, primitivism, or race issues more generally—publications like *Beaux Arts*, *Nouvelles Littéraires*, *De Telegraaf*, and *Algemeen Handelsblad*, which ran what Moody considered the best analytical criticism of his work. In Paris he exhibited at a range of shows including at the Salon des Tuileries (in June 1938 and 1939) and the Galerie Matières et Formes (in April 1939 and 1940). When Elsie Cohen, an early patron of Moody—he made a bust of her—penned a ringing letter of endorsement to the British Council on his behalf in 1942, she wrote:

> Moody is, in my opinion, one of the most talented Sculptors of our time and this was, I know[,] the opinion of many European critics. ... I was present at his first show in Paris which created quite a little furore. ... The exhibition in Holland was an outstanding success and several commissions arose out of it. ... He is of quite exceptional talent which I think particularly at this time should be fostered.[50]

Cohen made no mention of Moody's racial background, simply his abilities and achievements as a European artist. Max Osborn, in his 1940 review, did note that Moody was a "negro" who hailed from "an old family of lawyers and doctors in Jamaica," but located him, as an artist, not within a particular colonial or racial tradition, but as a representative of "the growing generation of artists ... dominated by a yearning for great forms and strong expression."[51] If Moody was cast as an authentic proponent of primitivism,

---

the work of any other major twentieth-century painter or sculptor." See "Moore: A Modernist's 'Primitivism,'" in Dorothy M. Kosinski, ed., *Henry Moore, Sculpting the 20ᵗʰ Century* (New Haven: Yale University Press, 2001), 33.

49 Moore, "Primitive Art," in Jack Flam and Miriam Deutch, eds, *Primitivism and Twentieth-Century Art: A Documentary History* (Berkeley: University of California Press, 2003), 267.

50 Letter, Elsie Cohen to A. A. Longden (Director of Fine Art, British Council), November 13, 1942. TGA 956, Box 3, Professional Miscellaneous A–K, HKRC.

51 Max Osborn quoted in the catalogue for a solo exhibition at the Woodstock

it was not an oppressive label—he later reflected that although he did "not want it to be thought that England or the Continent is a paradise for the Negro," he had exhibited his work in Paris, Amsterdam, and London, and "the interest shown was in its merits and not because of my race."[52]

War and Universalism

The catastrophe of the Second World War had a fundamental effect on Moody's sculpture and his philosophy of art. He gave form to his extraordinary wartime experiences through an increasingly explicit commitment to universalism in his work.

Moody was still living in Paris when the war broke out, and he continued to carve and exhibit even as more and more galleries closed; his last show opened on April 11, 1940. Exactly two months later he and his English wife Helene (whom he had married in 1938) fled Paris, just two days before the Germans arrived. They spent the next twelve months trying to escape France, during which time Ronald contracted pleurisy, a condition that would plague him intermittently for the rest of his life. They often traveled on foot: "For days [about a fortnight, between Pau and Marseille] we walked miles and miles, sleeping under hedges. My feet felt like Shredded Wheat, and my wife's feet were bleeding profusely, not only underneath, but on top, too."[53] Helene made it to Glasgow in July 1941, but Ronald—being a British male of military age—only made it back to Liverpool in October. He never again resided in France but remained in London for the rest of his life.

Moody's experience of war, and the bombings of Hiroshima and Nagasaki in 1945, shaped his own perspective on modernism and thus his individual creations. For most of the war Moody was unable to carve anything, not only during his eighteen months on the run, but also afterward, because he was recovering from his illness and because of the wartime dearth of material, especially wood. He did manage to acquire an oak beam that he carved into *Levels of Organisation* (also known as *Three Heads*) in 1945; he first exhibited it as part of a one-man show at London's Arcade Gallery. *Levels of Organisation* was an undisguised critique of Western scientific advance, inspired by the immediate example of the war and its nuclear resolution. It featured three faces representing different stages of

---

Gallery, London (July 25–August 13, 1960). TGA 956, Box 4, Exhibitions Catalogues, HKRC. Originally published as a review in the *National-Zeitung*, Basel, Switzerland (January 25, 1940).

52 Moody, letter draft for *Ebony* magazine, undated (1950). TGA 956, Box 9, Articles and Papers RM Typescripts, HKRC.

53 Moody in discussion with Una Marson, BBC transcript, *Calling the West Indies*, "Close-Up," (broadcast January 31–February 1, 1943, West Indies Service), 4. TGA 956, Box 7, Interviews and Discussions, HKRC.

human enlightenment, and with it Moody explicitly drew attention to the ambivalent inheritance of Western science: "It is interesting to note the three symbols of the top head, a test-tube left, a book middle and a bomb right: then the face, intelligent yet enormously helpless, not really master of itself, despite its knowledge."[54] Moody viewed the atrocities of war as a legacy of the scientific spirit of the European Renaissance:

> Like all movements of this kind the good as well as the bad were sacrificed. New slogans such as, "Humanism," "Evolution," "Progress," "Individualism" began to grip the imagination. Undoubtedly all these have a place in the scheme of things, but neither separately or collectively do they explain the whole of existence. It appeared as if man had become tired of the ceaseless search for first principles and decided to concentrate on what was nearest at hand. This "specialisation" has led him helplessly on to the atom bomb.[55]

Moody's universalistic philosophy remained remarkably consistent over the decades, and while he was keenly interested in the colonial condition, he rarely brought race into his discussions and was fond of remarking that "Man is equally foolish and equally wise." In a 1946 draft of a talk entitled "Art at the Crossroads," he expressed the hope that mankind could "look forward to a time when a universal belief, so characteristic of the great cultures of the past, will be restored."[56] If anything, Moody's views hardened throughout the 1950s and 1960s, during which time he retained the interest in non-Western philosophy—the "great cultures" of ancient China, India, and Africa—that he had first cultivated in dental school. Only now, he was a part of conversation with other artists, journalists, and critics engaged with similar questions.

One aspect of these ancient societies that particularly attracted Moody as he blossomed into a full-time sculptor was their treatment of the artist. He argued that there was little or no distinction in these societies between the artist and the craftsman; both were considered technical masters of their medium, and both created works that expressed the values of their

---

54 Moody quoted in ibid., 14.

55 Moody, "The Artist's Education." Famed cricketer and West Indian transplant Learie Constantine argued that precisely because of new global anxieties like the prospect of nuclear war, "Negro art" was becoming more relevant to Europeans: "In the complacent Victorian yesterday, white folks could not understand the Negro's sorrows and fear. But now that the obscene shadow of the atom bomb spreads steadily across the world, touching the faces of all our children, mistrust and doubt chill the hearts of humanity. In such an atmosphere, the eternal sadness of Negro art can be best understood." Constantine, *Colour Bar*, 177.

56 Moody, "Art at the Crossroads," typescript, January 31, 1946, 26. TGA 956—Ronald Moody. Box 9, Articles and Paper Typescripts, HKRC.

people. But most importantly, the artist was seen as an interpreter of the society's culture, politics, and mores, and as such was widely respected and fully integrated into the mainstream of the community. That Moody admired these features is not surprising, given his belief that the twentieth-century West Indian artist was ignored by and alienated from his modern homeland. He in fact applied his ancient lessons explicitly to the case of the Caribbean's nascent artistic renaissance, urging his colonial peers "to avoid making [the artist] something peculiar by encouraging his idiosyncrasies; but try to link [him] more with the life of the people."[57] And when he addressed the question of an authentic West Indian culture, he referred most to the Carib mythology that predated the arrival of Europeans, Africans, and (East) Indians. For Moody, the role of the artist was universal, applicable to all cultures and eras; in an ideal world, the artist would "once again resume his role of interpreter, and in the dress of his age, grapple with the problems which in essence remain ever the same."[58]

Black in Britain

After his return to London, Moody repeatedly declared his resistance to the "black artist" label. Regardless of his own reluctance, however, after the Second World War art critics, promoters, and the media increasingly viewed Moody as first and foremost a "negro" artist associated with Africa and the West Indies—despite the fact that virtually his entire artistic development occurred in a European context. He tolerated the "black artist" mantle, at least in part because it opened up opportunities to participate in numerous high-profile exhibitions organized around the themes of race, empire, and Africanness. He was never entirely comfortable in the self-conscious role of black artist, but by the middle of the 1960s his own interest in West Indian art had grown, and it had become more difficult to maintain the delicate distinction between the aesthetics of colonial identity and the politics of blackness.

In Britain Moody was most highly regarded as a portrait sculptor and a "Negro" artist. Even before the war, carvings like *Wohin* and *Johanaan*, which Moody felt "all important" and which formed the basis of his continental exhibits, were marginalized in London galleries. In fact, Moody was included in only two British (group) exhibitions before the war. In early 1935, for example, he had displayed one piece, *Head with Superimposed Mask*, as part of an exhibition at the Adams Gallery that featured a hodgepodge of

57 Moody in discussion with Una Marson, BBC transcript, *Calling the West Indies*, "Close-Up," (broadcast January 31–February 1, 1943, West Indies Service), 9. TGA 956, Box 7, Interviews and Discussions, HKRC.

58 Moody, "Art at the Crossroads," 26.

ethnographical (or historical) Negro works, contemporary Negro works, and contemporary English works "inspired by an interest in negro life or art." The curators hoped that in juxtaposing these pieces, "a relationship between them is made more vividly apparent."[59] In 1944 Moody's presumed roots again took precedence over his European career when he was asked to participate in a London conference of foreign artists. The invitation acknowledged that "your connection with Jamaica and the West Indies has been somewhat severed by your living here and in France for so long," but nonetheless wished Moody "to say something about the artists of the West Indies, and the existence or absence as the case may be of artists' societies or organisations in the West Indies or the need for them here."[60] It is unlikely that Moody was equipped to provide such guidance given his relative separation from the Caribbean artistic community. Thus, even before war's end, Moody was beginning to accumulate, in a professional context, racial and colonial labels that were not a function of the art itself.

This tendency sharpened after mid-century. The twin phenomena of decolonization and Commonwealth migration were accelerating in these years, and gaining increased public and media attention. Partly as a result, the number of exhibitions addressing colonial and West Indian themes grew, on both the local and international levels, and these actively solicited Moody's sculpture. A typical example of this impulse was the Leicester Festival of West Indian Art and Craft, which sought to make a "contribution towards the improvement and consolidation of race relations in Great Britain, and to acquaint the British Public with some aspects of West Indian culture."[61] Fifteen years later the University of Leicester's Black Cultural Society similarly wished "to depict black culture in the way it has expressed itself abroad and at home."[62] (Moody politely refused their request for a contribution.) In 1962, he contributed pieces to an art exhibition held in conjunction with the annual rally of the Standing Conference of West Indians in Britain. And although Moody received most of his portrait commissions from individuals of European descent, his most recognized work was the bust of his brother Harold, which was exhibited as part of a Human Rights exhibition in the crypt of St. Paul's Cathedral in 1968, along with his depiction of Paul Robeson. Internationally, Moody took part in the historic First World Festival of Negro Arts in Dakar, Senegal,

59 Catalogue, "Negro Art" exhibition, Adams Gallery, London, January 19–February 16, 1935. TGA 956, Box 4, Exhibitions Catalogues, HKRC.

60 Letter, R. Ch. Graetz (Joint Secretary for Artists Regional Groups and International Artists Organisations) to Ronald Moody, April 17, 1944. TGA 956, Box 3, Professional Miscellaneous A–K, HKRC.

61 Letter, George B. Greaves to Ronald Moody, October 19, 1959. TGA 956, Box 3, Professional Exhibitions L–Z, HKRC.

62 Letter, Roy N. Francis to Ronald Moody, January 16, 1975. TGA 956, Box 3, Professional Exhibitions L–Z, HKRC.

in 1966 in an exhibition whose aim was to "reflect the unity and originality of the present-day negro world, through its most representative works of art. It is open to all black African artists, as well as to artists of negro descent."[63] Moody, a black Jamaican artist with years of experience and a small foothold in the urban European art world, but with an independent aesthetic and a taste for non-Western forms and precedents, was a perfect candidate for these local British and black international events at a time when West Indian and colonial populations were more confidently asserting their cultural presence.

The media too viewed Moody largely through the lens of race and empire in the 1950s and 1960s. As Moody's archives suggest, the BBC employed Moody to write and narrate numerous lectures on the subject of art and his experiences as a colonial artist in London for broadcast on the West Indies Service, as well as sitting for personal interviews. As late as 1973, he loaned the Corporation five pieces for use in the television program *Full House*, which was devoted entirely to the subject of West Indian culture in Britain.

Journalists in Britain and abroad grappled with the racial implications of his work. Valerie Wilmer, whose photographs of black musicians and artists in Britain during these years remain a valuable scholarly resource, interviewed Moody for the magazine *Flamingo* in 1964. In the article she simultaneously rejected and affirmed that cultural productions could be racially characterized: "No particular influences are evident in his work which is not essentially negroid, but as with all artists there is always some influence in the initial thought behind their work."[64] The Jamaican *Gleaner* had been both more forthright and less specific a few years earlier when it declared: "the definite form of Moody's art comes from the unconscious and profoundly racial memories which come from his birth-place."[65]

In the United States, although Moody received little attention from the press in general, *Ebony* magazine was particularly fascinated by his status as a black artist working wholly within a European artistic milieu. Moody's longtime friend and advocate Marie Seton, who coordinated the *Ebony* article, warned him that *Ebony*, "not being an art magazine, want 'angles' on people. Here negro artists take 'negro themes', the 'angle' on you is that you don't and aren't compelled to [adopt such themes] under European conditions."[66] Although American race relations were certainly more dichotomized than those in Europe, Moody was not as free from the

63 First World Festival of Negro Arts, copy of regulations, November 8, 1965. TGA 956, Box 3, Professional Exhibitions L–Z, HKRC.

64 Valerie Wilmer, "Meet Ronald Moody," *Flamingo* (November 1964), 32–33. TGA 956, Box 5, Press Cuttings, HKRC.

65 Rudolph Dunbar, "Ronald Moody—Sculptor of Distinction," *The Gleaner* (September 17, 1961). TGA 956, Box 5, Press Cuttings, HKRC.

66 Letter, Marie Seton to Ronald Moody, February 9, 1950. TGA 956, Box 7, Marie Seton to Ronald Moody, 1940–1980, HKRC.

imagined linkages between race, culture, and reputation as *Ebony* might have hoped.

Moody's perspective on the racial politics surrounding his own work was ambivalent. On the surface it seems that, in the decades after the war, he rejected the notion that his race had any bearing on his reputation as an artist. Initially, too, he professed little personal allegiance to the West Indian community in Britain, in contrast to many artists and entertainers—including many of those discussed in this book—who felt a particular obligation to serve as public representatives of Britain's black settlers. As late as 1976, when the Anglo-Caribbean Society belatedly asked to borrow a few of Moody's sculptures for display during its annual seminar—positing that they "would be good for the promotion aspect and also helpful in the projection of black Artists and their Art"—Moody drafted a testy reply: "Painting and sculpture, in my view, deserve more than a casual glance whilst attending to the really important reason for your gathering. ... I have exhibited here and abroad over the years and had 'task making' invitations only from my fellow West Indians. Why?"[67] Clearly Moody felt no obligation to serve particular groups on the grounds of regional affinity.

Nonetheless, Moody did tentatively reflect upon the connections that others drew between his racial origins and his creative output. This process had begun in response to his intermittent association with primitivism. In a 1943 interview he professed interest in the critical contention that

> although I have lived in Europe for at least half my life, my work always shows that I have remained faithful to my racial origin, and my early environment. I haven't consciously aimed to be what is known as "Primitive", but I find that my work undoubtedly shows some of the qualities which are usually associated with the peoples of my race.[68]

His declarations on the racial dimensions of his own work were never more explicit than that and most often, as we have seen, he phrased his aesthetic philosophy in geographic or cultural terms, for instance when he stated, "At first I was very much influenced by Egyptian art. ... Later I became very much interested in the art of Africa and the East and I suppose my background lies somewhere in the middle."[69] Most importantly, Moody was not very preoccupied with his black African heritage, which distanced

---

67   Letter, W. Wilkie (Anglo-Caribbean Society) to Ronald Moody, November 18, 1976, and undated draft response, Moody to Wilkie. TGA 956, Box 3, Professional Exhibitions A–K, HKRC.

68   Moody in discussion with Una Marson, BBC transcript, *Calling the West Indies*, "Close-Up," 3.

69   Moody quoted in Wilmer, "Meet Ronald Moody," *Flamingo* (November 1964), 33. TGA 956, Box 5, Press Cuttings, HKRC.

him from the radical black politics of the 1960s. While the desire to discover or formulate a tradition, or "language," that they could call their own was widespread among West Indian intellectuals at this time, most looked to Africa as the main alternative to the Western tradition. Moody had acknowledged this in 1951 in discussion with writer and intellectual John Figueroa: "The trouble with us West Indians, I think, is not having some kind of philosophy. And I think there are three influences there from what I can see—the West, the East (China and India), and Negro Africa. And some kind of synthesis will have to be found." At this point Figueroa remarked, "I think at the present time they are very much remembering the negro part of it; but I don't think they ever think of the Eastern part."[70] Thus, despite the degree to which Moody carefully articulated his own aesthetic philosophy, there is little evidence that he connected it explicitly to the question of racial identity *per se*. This was perhaps a recognition of his notably European artistic experience.

Regardless of his artistic position on the growing prominence of race politics, Moody the private individual was nonetheless vocal in his distaste for the everyday injustices that arose on account of colonial and racial prejudice. In 1944 he refused a flat because the lease stipulated that certain colored people were not welcome—although he had presumably "passed the colour and cultural test." He voiced his outrage in a letter to the *Picture Post*:

> As a Colonial and British subject, who has lived for many years both in England and on the Continent, I would like to know why so much blood is being spilt in fighting Nazism and the creed of racial discrimination implicit in its doctrine, when at home it is still very much alive? This letter would be far too long if I allowed myself to deal with the larger issues such as the effect a creed like this will inevitably have on the politically conscious colonies, who are determined to look after their own affairs in the near future.[71]

Later he wrote letters to the editors of various papers, several of which were printed; a few others were perhaps too biting in their sarcasm for publication. He also became involved in a published altercation with other writers in the *New Statesman and Nation* concerning their imperialist and racist sentiments on the independence struggles in Kenya and elsewhere. He signed all these letters "A Presumptuous Native."[72]

---

70 Transcript, Moody in discussion with John Figueroa, *Calling the West Indies*, "The Artist in the Community" no. 1 (broadcast February 15, 1951), 11. TGA 956, Box 7, Interviews and Discussions, HKRC.

71 Letter, Moody to Editor of *Picture Post*, November 27, 1944 (published in 9 December issue of *Picture Post*). TGA 956, Box 7, Interviews and Discussions, HKRC.

72 See Moody, letters to the Editor ("The Voice of the Settler"), *New Statesman and*

There is also very occasional evidence to suggest that Moody responded to certain professional challenges with a similarly sharp sense of colonial injustice. For example, in 1949, he learned that artists who lent their work to a big exhibition without the intention of soliciting sales were customarily paid a fee by the sponsoring institution. He asked the League of Coloured Peoples to make this demand to the Colonial Office, which was organizing an exhibit of colonial art: "why should colonial artists be exploited when the exhibition is supposed to show the kindly and beneficent rule of our betters!"[73]

At mid-century, then, Moody was neither unaware of nor hostile to questions of racial identity and politics; he simply opted not to use this language to express the relationships between himself, his art, and his environment. Increasingly in the 1950s and '60s, however, he gave more active consideration to the significance of his Jamaican background, and to specific questions about West Indian identity and its relationship to English culture and history—by reaching out to other West Indian artists and searching for a Caribbean "idiom" in his sculpture.

Finding a Caribbean Idiom

What distinguished Moody from his white, European-born counterparts was the urge to apply his aesthetic values, which he felt were particularly vulnerable to corruption by the Western artistic tradition, to the West Indies. In this way, he politicized his aesthetic approach, linking it to the issue of the Caribbean's *cultural* independence. In the process, his work became a model for fledgling West Indian artists because it posed an alternative to a blind mimicry of nineteenth-century European ideals.

It was thus Moody's long-standing critique of the Western tradition that facilitated his entry into the postwar discussion of colonial art. Moody wished colonial, especially West Indian, artists to avoid the fate of Europeanization just at the moment when he felt they were beginning to visualize an indigenous artistic vision of their own. He emphasized this danger repeatedly in his writings. Referring to what he viewed as the spiritual poverty of much prominent twentieth-century art, he noted, "I hope, perhaps in vain, that the Colonial artist will be spared the present experience of his European counterpart." Moody made explicit his belief in the hegemony of Western aesthetic principles, which, more importantly, he viewed as an outgrowth of political imperialism: "It is ... inevitable that

---

Nation (November 8, 1952 and July 25, 1953). TGA 956, Box 7, Interviews and Discussions, HKRC.

73 Letter, Moody to J. Malcolm Mitchell (League of Coloured Peoples), July 31, 1949. TGA 956, Box 3, Professional Exhibitions A–K, HKRC.

when a race has been forced to accept alien customs and a way of thinking foreign to its psyche, its iconography will suffer. If this continues for a long time, there follows a period of degeneration and possible death of its art."[74]

Not surprisingly, then, he also emphasized the direct link between political and artistic independence in the colonies: "The deep spiritual desire for independence in the colonies is perhaps a way of preserving the soul of the race and consequently its iconography or idiom."[75] For Moody, a community or nation's artistic idiom, which visually expressed the "soul of the race," was unique and unified. European cultural and political imperialism had thus far prevented the healthy cultivation of a distinctive idiom, which, given the polyglot nature of the Caribbean population, was an inherently difficult task. Moody recognized an imperative:

> The Paramount responsibility of non-European artists, and in this article I address myself to the African and those of African descent, is to resist this new and sinister form of domination by every means in his power, sinister because the victim willingly invites his own destruction under the false conviction that equality implies keeping up in every way with his European-Joneses.[76]

At mid-century, such a rejection of European standards was still radical, and Moody was expressing a position distinct from many of his peers, who had acquired status by successfully *conforming* to the social and professional standards set by Europe—in terms of education and cultural tastes, for example—rather than deviating from them. By the 1960s, however, black and colonial artists would espouse such ideas with enthusiasm.

An even trickier issue was that, especially in the years before Jamaican independence, there was no obvious dividing line between the Western and the colonial "idiom." As much as he associated the Western canon with a spiritual or existential vacuum, even Moody was both continually inspired by European creative precedents and fundamentally shaped by his own European training. It is not clear that he was even in contact with other Jamaican or Caribbean artists between the 1930s and the 1950s— he circulated entirely within the Western European art world. Moody recognized that British culture was a part of Jamaica's inheritance, and that the West Indian artist could not simply claim African ancestry and assume its aesthetic mantle. When in a 1943 BBC interview Una Marson mentioned the growing artistic consciousness in the West Indies, Moody

---

74 Moody, "The Colonial Artist and his Idiom," typescript (undated, probably mid-century), 3. TGA 956, Box 9, Articles and Papers Typescripts, HKRC.
75 Ibid., 6.
76 Moody, "The Responsibility of the Artist," typescript (undated, mid-century), 2. TGA 956, Box 9, Articles and Papers Typescripts, HKRC.

voiced his interest in seeing the resulting work, stating, "I feel that we'll produce a culture that is neither African nor English, but will be something which, for lack of a better name, we shall call West Indian."[77] This is a rich statement; with it Moody suggested, first, that West Indian culture was a thing to be consciously constructed, and moreover that it was still in the making. Second, he implied that West Indian art would be more than a simple hybrid of transplanted traditions, that it would take shape as something distinctive—a recognizable and coherent idiom.

In 1966 Moody became a co-founder of the fundamental Caribbean Artists' Movement (CAM), a decision that cemented his connection to the West Indian creative community.[78] Between 1966 and 1972, when it disbanded, CAM boasted as members the cream of West Indian artists and writers working in Britain, including C. L. R. James, John La Rose, Andrew Salkey, Edward Kamau Braithwaite, Aubrey Williams, Stuart Hall, and Linton Kwesi Johnson. Through the movement, these individuals "sought to discover their own aesthetic and to chart new directions for their arts and culture; to become acquainted with their history"; and "to reassert their own tradition in the face of the dominant tradition."[79] In these ways, CAM's aims corresponded with Moody's search for a colonial idiom and his belief "that when a race has been forced to accept alien customs and a way of thinking foreign to its psyche, its iconography will suffer."[80] CAM constituted a productive reaction to English, and even Western, cultural standards, the kind of artistic work that Moody had been doing for years.

It is nonetheless vital to remember that CAM appeared at a historically fraught moment that "bridged the transformation of Britain's West Indian community from one of exiles and immigrants to black British."[81] The movement's personnel embodied this shift (sometimes as much imagined as real), and so its members held a range of political positions that clashed spectacularly at times. While CAM's Visual Arts Symposium was not subject to this kind of conflict, Moody did attempt to reckon with the vocabulary of "blackness" and "Caribbeanness" being bandied about in the other symposia. Ultimately, however, he remained true to a more universal perspective that implicitly rejected black or West Indian exceptionalism: "Well I think the important thing is that [the West Indian artist] is seeking to find himself and within that context he lives in the Caribbean, he's

---

77 Moody in discussion with Una Marson, BBC transcript, *Calling the West Indies*, "Close-Up," 3.

78 In fact, Moody had one young West Indian protégé in London, fellow sculptor Namba Roy.

79 Walmsley, *The Caribbean Artists' Movement*, xvii.

80 See footnote 37. Moody, "The Colonial Artist and his Idiom," typescript (undated, probably mid-century), 3. TGA 956, Box 9, Articles and Papers Typescripts, HKRC.

81 Walmsley, *The Caribbean Artists' Movement*, xviii.

black and all that sort of thing. He faces the same problems as any other similar country going through the same difficulty." This was a response to a questioner's observation that the artists in the room seemed less preoccupied with "Caribbean consciousness" than other CAM collectives, perhaps because "art today is very international in outlook."[82]

Moreover, as fine artists they had worked in greater isolation than, for example, the entertainers in CAM: "The groups in which Moody and [Aubrey] Williams exhibited until 1967 were international or Commonwealth. Each essentially worked alone in his studio—Moody in Chelsea, Williams in Hampstead—with few contacts with other Caribbean artists and intellectuals."[83] At the Visual Arts Symposium, Jamaican artist Karl "Jerry" Craig observed with some astonishment, "it's the first time that we have ever been together collectively. I happen to have known two people before we came together. So I mean, it's not a case of knowing each other's paintings and being influenced by each other."[84] However, like others at the symposium, Craig felt that they all shared a common approach, despite their physical separation. Williams noted a "special Caribbean slant," but he emphasized overall "a great respect for humanity[,] and man's acquaintance with his environment seems to be in all the work."[85] Moody's search for universal first principles in his art was still taking place, but within a movement that defined itself regionally. His questions, after all, had always been West Indian questions too.

One sculpture in particular came to symbolize Moody's particular orientation toward the West Indies by the 1960s. This is *Savacou*, a seven-foot aluminum bird-like sculpture whose home was the Epidemiological Research Unit of the University of the West Indies (it was commissioned by the Unit's sister institution in South Wales). For this project, Moody "was determined that [the subject] should be innate to the West Indies and 'not something in origin thousands of miles away.'"[86] The bird character that he subsequently created was his interpretation of "the Carib god called *Savacou*, who came down to earth and looked after the storms and the sea and, after doing his stint, as it were, for a number of years—many, many years—returned to heaven and became a star."[87] He chose the common West Indian parrot as formal inspiration. *Savacou* was officially unveiled on August 21, 1964, and was displayed outside the Commonwealth Institute in London before moving to its permanent home in Jamaica.

---

82 Transcript, Symposium on the Visual Arts: West Indian Artists, June 2, 1967, 28–29. CAM 5/3/4, George Padmore Institute, London.

83 Walmsley, *The Caribbean Artists' Movement*, 32.

84 Transcript, Visual Arts Symposium, 24. CAM 5/3/4, GPI.

85 Ibid., 18.

86 Cynthia Moody, "Ronald Moody," 19.

87 Transcript of Sylvia Moore interview with Ronald Moody for the World Service, Radio Nederland, Hilversum, July 29, 1977. Box 7, TGA 956—Ronald Moody, HKRC.

Ronald Moody at the Commonwealth Institute, London,
with *Savacou*, 1964. Photograph by George R. Hales.
© George R. Hales/Getty Images 2015.

The sculpture both addressed and transcended contemporary political
issues about colonialism and race by taking pre-colonial Carib mythology
as its subject. On the one hand, it was deeply tied to West Indian history;
it was fundamentally political in that it articulated resistance to colonial
oppression by using an alternative narrative to situate West Indian culture;
it was one facet of a "continual development of a symbolic discourse

characteristic of the Caribbean."[88] It was also a fitting symbol of CAM's search for a positive route out of Europe's cultural shadow. Thus when CAM, after starting a chapter in Jamaica, decided to launch a journal, it chose the title *Savacou*. CAM also used the sculpture as a logo, the design later adopted (in 1979) by the Caribbean Universities' Press.

Conclusion: Moody's Posthumous Legacy

This examination of Moody's career has tried to show the historical shift in the exhibition and reception of his work as it spanned the heydays of interwar European primitivism, mass Caribbean migration, colonial independence, and the consolidation of a black British arts community with the establishment of CAM. This chapter has also emphasized how Moody stands out not only as a representative of Caribbean art, but also as a complex and fascinating proponent of European modernism and primitivism. Moody's multifaceted professional character and cultural politics demand an engagement with his artistic work, to be sure, but also an engagement with the shifting context in which his work was received. This context continues to shift; today, Moody is finally taking his place within the pantheon of postwar British art, full stop (a development that the present study reflects). Like his Caribbean-born contemporaries Frank Bowling and Aubrey Williams, in Britain his "most successful episodes of visibility have been posthumous."[89]

Moody continued to work actively until the end of the 1970s, when illness and the death of his wife made it difficult for him to sculpt or exhibit consistently. (He died at Westminster Hospital on 6 February 1984.) While he eventually reconsidered his long-standing practice of keeping his art separate from his identity as a black or colonial artist, he did so in a way that did not limit the scope or significance of his sculpture. *Savacou* was a perfect synthesis in this respect. It provided an independent West Indian voice, but persisted in making an inclusive claim to spiritual roots that reached deeper than those of empire or even race. Moody had a lively interest in and sense of connection to Africa, but his blackness, in itself, was never central to his artistic or political perspective, a fact that distinguished him from others in CAM, especially its younger members and those black British artists who came of age after the Second World War and were more intimately engaged with black nationalist movements all over the world.

88   Patrick Taylor, *The Narrative of Liberation: Perspectives on Afro-Caribbean Literature, Popular Culture, and Politics* (Ithaca and London: Cornell University Press, 1989), 230.

89   See Chambers, *Black Artists in British Art*, 16.

Long after Moody's death, at the turn of the 1990s, a few London art critics nicely grasped Moody's brand of artistic and political consciousness on the occasion of a major retrospective of black British art at the Hayward Gallery that ran from October 1989 to April 1990. The exhibition, entitled "The Other Story: Asian, African and Caribbean artists in Post-War Britain," featured works from the late 1940s through the 1980s, and Moody's sculpture was well represented. However, the exhibit was "contentious," in the words of distinguished art critic Marina Vaizey, precisely because:

> the organisers seem to want unqualified acceptance for the artists simply because of their origins, claiming that they have been ignored—although the facts speak differently—just because of their origins. ... The overall impression of the exhibition is that the artists have been chosen for their biographies rather than their art.[90]

Moody might have been in agreement with this verdict, especially considering the vast chronological and aesthetic scope of the exhibition. Lest one conclude that Vaizey's interpretation was unduly conservative, art historian Petrine Archer-Straw also argued in *Art Monthly* that the

> privileging of a political agenda over an aesthetic one works more comfortably with the more recent section devoted to the sixties, seventies and eighties, in line with the growing self-consciousness of the painters as being combatants of political and racial oppression. ... For the most part artists such as Ronald Moody ... appear blissfully unaware of it within the context of the fifties.

Archer-Straw still recognized the political potential of these works, but asserted that Moody and his peers "perceived their position in the narrower terms of the coloniser-colonised syndrome. ... Rather than being considered political there is an underlying strain of universalism which runs through the works of the fifties and sixties."[91] This assessment is astute, but the foregoing study has attempted to demonstrate that Moody's perspective was not necessarily any "narrower" than the perspectives adopted by younger black British artists. On the contrary, it proved to be a "robust yet delicate chisel" that Moody could subtly manipulate to shape his remarkable sculpture.

---

90 Marina Vaizey, "Why Partiality Does not Tell the Whole Story," *The Times* (December 10, 1989). TGA 956, Box 10, Folder 4—Press Cuttings, HKRC.
91 Petrine Archer-Straw, "Exhibitions: The Other Story," *Art Monthly* (February 1990). TGA 956, Box 10, Folder 4—Press Cuttings, HKRC.

Chapter 5

The Race Relations Narrative in British Film

Writing a story of postwar British culture that takes better account of the contributions of West Indian and other New Commonwealth settlers involves throwing light upon people, productions, and communities that have been invisible historically: the theater groups and underground plays, for example, that were independent from the mainstream.[1] Some artists were successful enough to operate to some extent *within* the mainstream, however, with theaters and producers that targeted a broader audience, especially in the 1950s and early 1960s. The next two chapters, then, are about West Indian writers and actors who constituted the roots of the West Indian artistic community in postwar Britain. But they are also about the British producers they worked with and the productions that they collaborated to create. History has tended to define the British cultural canon in one way, while positioning black British culture as a counterpoint or (at worst) an alien interloper. The stories that follow showcase a more organic meshing of so-called "white" and West Indian cultural priorities in postwar London.

The day after the ITV drama *Hot Summer Night* first aired on British television, in 1960, Jamaican Lloyd Reckord thought his acting career was made. His name was in the newspapers, all because of one provocative scene in the previous evening's dramatic teleplay—Britain's first onscreen interracial kiss, with actress Andrée Melly:

The first time a black man is on the white stage and he kisses a white girl and there were big pictures and there were bloody newspapers

---

1 Roland Rees, ed., *Fringe First: Pioneers of Fringe Theatre on Record* (London: Oberon Books, 1992); Owusu, *Storms of the Heart*; Owusu, *The Struggle for Black Arts in Britain*; Stephen Bourne, *Black in the British Frame: The Black Experience in British Film and Television* (London: Continuum, 2001).

all over the place and I thought, God, I'm made! You know, the next thing is Hollywood, that sort of bull. Several leading roles on television happened after this, but, they were more or less the same part. You know, where I was always in love with this white girl, I was either beaten up or kicked or embraced by the father or the mother. But it didn't matter, it was the same part.[2]

Upon breaking into the world of mainstream British drama, Reckord discovered the boundaries of that world for West Indian (and other black) actors, not to mention writers and directors. Yet, despite the frustrations of being pigeonholed and stereotyped by producers and audiences, they were not marginal to that world. In fact, the presence of a growing West Indian community in Britain, and of West Indian creative and dramatic talent in the studios, was an integral part of the changes beginning to occur in British cinema in the late 1950s.

This chapter is the first of two to examine the evolution of the race relations narrative in British drama, as expressed by both mainstream British producers and West Indian playwrights and directors. It focuses in particular on film, while the next chapter focuses on theater, the rise of the Royal Court, and three plays by Barry Reckord (Lloyd Reckord's brother). This chapter argues that mainstream filmic representations of what I call the British race relations narrative used the provocative themes of interracial romance and conflict as vehicles to highlight the films' fundamental preoccupation with white English prejudices, insecurities, and domestic relationships. This does not mean that they marked a turgid, forgettable contrast to the more challenging "social realist" films that began appearing at the end of the 1950s; as MacKillop and Sinyard suggest, "cracks in [mid-century] complacency are discernible some time before the appearance of the New Wave."[3] This study thus looks at the race relations film in the context of an evolution that began, not in the early 1960s, but in the 1950s. It shows how West Indian migration to the United Kingdom, and the growth of that community, provoked both a greater engagement with the issues of imperial/Commonwealth migration and racism, and a distinct *change* in the representation of race relations during the twenty years following the end of the war. Youth culture, working-class mobility, and West Indian (and African) migration did not merely provide the backdrop for British "social problem" and New Wave films; they were also the historical forces that pushed more radical themes and approaches onto the cinematic agenda. The distinction may seem fine, but scholars have not

---

2   Transcript, Caribbean Artists' Movement Symposium on West Indian Theatre, November 10, 1967, 28, CAM 5/5/1, George Padmore Institute.

3   "Introduction," in Ian MacKillop and Neil Sinyard, eds, *British Cinema of the 1950s: A Celebration* (Manchester and New York: Manchester University Press, 2003), 7.

sufficiently acknowledged that mid-century, middle-class British films were shaped by these developments, as much as they shaped their representations of them. Although many, if not all, of the films under discussion here can be—and usually are—grouped together under the "middle-class liberal" heading, they in fact represent an evolution of approaches to the question of race and migration in the British cinema.

West Indian artists were a part of this rapid evolution of filmic treatments of race relations and British society more generally in these years. Earl Cameron and other actors, for example, have not been sufficiently acknowledged for the degree to which they shaped the image of the black Briton—as that figure became, for the first time, a fixture of British cinema. Mainstream films produced by the Rank Organisation, at mid-century Britain's largest film production conglomerate, and Ealing Studios certainly privileged white middle-class perspectives, but this does not mean that West Indian actors were not important contributors to the development of the genre.

Even more ambitious at the time was the work of actor and director Lloyd Reckord, who adopted a more nuanced approach to the issue of race relations in Britain. As film scholars Barbara Korte and Claudia Sternberg have noted, while the 1950s and '60s "marked a time of stereotyping blackness in the mainstream media," they "also saw the first attempts by black film-makers to introduce different modes of representing people of colour in Britain," for example through short film.[4] These works demonstrated both a greater engagement with the predicament and challenges facing West Indians and often a more sophisticated interpretation of the politics of black-white relations, for example by looking more closely at the economic dimensions of racism.

Although their approaches diverged from mainstream filmmakers, they should nonetheless be viewed as part of, and even anticipating, the shift to greater social realism by the turn of the 1960s. While West Indian artists of this period are acknowledged as precursors to the flowering of black British drama and film in the 1980s and 1990s, they have not been given a place within the history of British drama in general. Like other dramatists and filmmakers, however, they too engaged with the social issues of class identity and generational conflict that had so influenced cutting-edge film and theater in the two decades after war's end.

The concept of the race relations narrative, as I use it here, refers to the dominant narrative that emerged in the postwar period to dramatize and interpret the contemporary phenomenon of New Commonwealth settlement in Britain. The narrative *ostensibly* revolved around an interracial romance, usually, but not always, between a young West Indian man and a young English woman. By choosing to focus on miscegenation, the

---

4   Korte and Sternberg, *Bidding for the Mainstream?*, 51.

race relations narrative highlighted what was considered to be the most controversial consequence of migration.[5] But the true narrative conflict lay in the white family's reaction to the romance, and involved one family member or another betraying the "real" reason behind his or her irrational prejudice. This was usually a domestic or sexual neurosis. These were stories, essentially, about white British families. Jim Pines cites the 1970s as a major watershed in black British film history, because it was then that cultural practitioners moved away from a preoccupation with the race relations narrative, freeing themselves from the "otherwise omnipresent white figures in the narrative."[6] Actor Johnny Sekka acknowledged this—from his own perspective—during his work in *Flame in the Streets* in 1961: "All too often in plays about the colour bar the negro artist is not asked to portray a character, only a racial symbol, the action centres around him but he is not allowed to express his feelings."[7]

The race relations narrative framework provided the scaffolding for dozens of plays, television dramas, and films in the 1950s and 1960s, some of which are examined in other chapters. The present chapter examines three cinematic examples: *Pool of London* (1950), *Sapphire* (1959), and *Flame in the Streets* (1961). I have chosen to focus on these three films for a few reasons, not least because of the existence and availability of archival records. In addition, they were among the highest-profile expressions of the race relations narrative and demonstrate a good deal of continuity in terms of their production and content values; *Pool of London* and *Sapphire* were both Basil Dearden and Michael Relph productions, while *Flame in the Streets*, though directed by Roy Ward Baker, still conforms to the liberal themes and "realistic" tone set by the first two. Finally, Earl Cameron took on major roles in all three films. These continuities of subject matter, production, and casting not only allow us to sketch out the characteristics of the race relations narrative on the silver screen but also, crucially, reveal the degree to which the genre evolved over the years, in response to changing social conditions in British society and the changing tastes of British audiences.

This chapter deals with filmic representations of domestic race relations while the next deals with theater, but the worlds of film, television, and theater were closely intertwined. Writers, producers, directors, actors, and technicians all moved freely between them, sharing themes, technical

---

5   A September 1958 Gallup poll, for instance, found that while only seven percent of respondents objected to their children having colored classmates, seventy-one percent objected to mixed marriages. Gallup, *The Gallup International Public Opinion Polls*, 478.

6   Jim Pines, "The Cultural Context of Black British Cinema," in Houston A. Baker, Jr., Manthia Diawara, and Ruth H. Lindeborg, eds, *Black British Cultural Studies: A Reader* (Chicago: University of Chicago Press, 1996), 185.

7   Johnny Sekka quoted in *Flame in the Streets* promotional booklet (March 1961), 39, Special Collections, British Film Institute (BFI), London.

experience, and aesthetic sensibilities as they went. Lloyd Reckord, for example, appeared as Sonny Lincoln in the ITV television drama *Hot Summer Night*, which was then adapted for the big screen and renamed *Flame in the Streets*. He directed a collaborative Sunday Night production at the Royal Court, and appeared onstage there in *Flesh to a Tiger* and *You in Your Small Corner*, both of which were written by his brother Barry. He also directed one of the earliest "black British" short films, *Ten Bob in Winter*. But Reckord's diversity of experience was the rule, not the exception, in postwar Britain, especially within the "social problem" and New Wave genres that garnered such critical attention at the time. For this reason, individual people and productions will recur periodically in both chapters.

Film critics and historians alike have characterized the 1950s as a "cusp" moment for British cinema, situated between the defining documentary-style wartime productions and the provocative British New Wave. It is perhaps for this reason that several contemporary scholars have struggled to rescue mid-century British film from those critics who cast it as artistically uninspired in production and socially outmoded in perspective. Raymond Durgnat was one of the first to do this in his influential *A Mirror for England*, where he argued that "many of the middle-class movies are richer in nuance, in tension, in honest doubt and sophisticated misgiving, than they have had credit for in circles influential simply because uniquely institutionalized."[8] Similarly, Ian MacKillop and Neil Sinyard have suggested that although the 1950s is "perhaps the most derided decade in British film history," it was also a decade in which "British cinema was connecting with its home audience more successfully than at any time in its history, culminating in the quite extraordinary statistic (almost inconceivable today) that the top twelve box-office films of 1959 in Britain were all actually made in Britain."[9] Finally, John Hill bestowed critical legitimacy upon the "social problem" films of the 1950s by placing them in the same scholarly framework as the pathbreaking realist dramas of the early 1960s. He pointed out that the two genres not only shared a similar historical context, but that, like the New Wave, the social problem film "was generally applauded for its determination to tackle such contemporary issues as juvenile delinquency, homosexuality and racial tension."[10] In short, scholars have assessed the authenticity of these films more sympathetically within their mid-century context.[11]

Such perspectives are even more valuable in the context of more recent criticism that employs textual analysis. Scholars such as Lola Young and

---

8   Raymond Durgnat, *A Mirror for England: British Movies from Austerity to Affluence* (New York and Washington: Praeger, 1971), 3.

9   "Introduction," in MacKillop and Sinyard, *British Cinema of the 1950s*, 2.

10   John Hill, *Sex, Class and Realism: British Cinema 1956–1963* (London: BFI Publishing, 1986), 2.

11   On this subject, see also Burton et al., *Liberal Directions*.

Carrie Tarr have provided close readings of films like *Sapphire* (1959) that revolve around the categories of race and sexuality, and tend to excoriate these works for reinforcing contemporary white, male assumptions and power.[12] Their analyses are sensitive and smart but they do not engage rigorously with the historical context of film production and reception, and draw no distinction between these filmic representations of race and those that came before and after. Meanwhile, black film collectives of the 1980s and 1990s shed a stark light on the conservative, white-centered character of earlier mainstream efforts, but applying their sophisticated questions of black identity and representation to the films of the 1950s and 1960s (even those of black writers and directors) results in a perceptive but historically skewed interpretation of the race relations drama. As Jim Pines has suggested, racial imagery in the British media did not become a "panic-stricken" legitimation of racism until sometime after the mid-sixties. Prior to this, it "was certainly less institutionalized" and "exhibited a strong tendency towards humanism with definite undertones of anti-racism."[13] This is certainly not to argue that negative racial stereotypes did not abound in the early postwar period— they did—but such images ought to be evaluated as part of an evolution of cinematic representations stretching across the twentieth century.

Some explanation of terms is necessary here. Terms like "New Wave," "social problem film," and "middle-class liberal" pepper the historiography, sometimes in contradistinction, sometimes overlapping. The British (as opposed to French) New Wave in cinema was a direct product of the same movement in theater, which is discussed at length in the following chapter. All of the films associated with this movement, which flowered in the late 1950s and early 1960s—notably *Room at the Top* (dir. Jack Clayton, 1958), *Look Back in Anger* (Tony Richardson, 1959), *Saturday Night and Sunday Morning* (Karel Reisz, 1960), *A Taste of Honey* (Tony Richardson, 1961), and *This Sporting Life* (Lindsay Anderson, 1963)—were adaptations of contemporary novels or plays. Their documentary-style realism attempted to capture the nuances of life in a usually northern, urban, working-class setting. Although directors like Richardson and Anderson did not seek to make grand political statements with their work, they did operate in aesthetic opposition to the so-called middle-class values that saturated much postwar cinema, including the social problem genre.

British "social problem" films—like Basil Dearden's *Sapphire* (1958, discussed below)—enjoyed their commercial heyday between about 1945 and 1965, when British film studios began portraying provocative social

---

12 See Lola Young, *Fear of the Dark: "Race", Gender and Sexuality in the Cinema* (London: Routledge, 1996), especially chapter four, "'Miscegenation' and the Perils of 'Passing': Films from the 1950s and 1960s"; Carrie Tarr, "*Sapphire, Darling* and the Boundaries of Permitted Pleasure," *Screen* 26, no. 1 (1986): 50–65.

13 "Introduction," in Pines, *Black and White in Colour*, 9–10.

issues—juvenile delinquency, prostitution, working-class education, official corruption, and interracial romance—within a conventional melodramatic framework. Like those of the New Wave, these films took their inspiration from current social events and the drama of "ordinary" life. But, unlike the New Wave, the social phenomena they represented served primarily as a sensationalist backdrop to the formulaic drama unfolding on the screen; social problem films were mainstream in the sense that commercial considerations were paramount in the selection of themes and plots. Thus *"Beat"* *Girl* (1959), about a teenager turned stripper, is a pulpy sexploitation picture; *Sapphire* is a crime drama; and *Victim* (1961), about homosexuality, is really a melodrama involving blackmail. Directors and screenwriters developed the cautionary moral of these stories to a greater or lesser extent.

Thus the biggest difference between the characterization of social problem films and the New Wave is that the latter have been viewed as a rebellion against the liberal, mainstream Establishment, while the former are viewed as an endorsement of it. Basil Dearden, who directed two of the three studio films under discussion in this chapter, is generally portrayed as a quintessential representative of this mid-century liberalism. He worked for much of his film career at the legendary Ealing Studios, which became famous during the Second World War for producing realistic dramas and witty comedies that focused on the ordinary lives and communities of British people of all classes. Michael Balcon, production head at Ealing between 1938 and 1959, described himself as a "Gladstonian Liberal" and, as Jeffrey Richards argues, this penchant for "tolerance, restraint, decency, stern moralism and sexual Puritanism, service and duty" was shared by others in the studio:

> [W]e were a group of liberal-minded, like-minded people ... middle-class people brought up with middle-class backgrounds and rather conventional educations. Although we were radical in our points of view, we did not want to tear down institutions ... We were people of the immediate post-war generation, and we voted Labour for the first time after the war; this was our mild revolution.[14]

Dearden and Michael Relph—and Roy Ward Baker, who directed *Flame in the Streets*—shared Balcon's outlook as it applied to their productions. Relph has reflected:

> We believed in the message of the film, although now it seems a bit over-benign, but at that time we were still very service-minded after the

---

14   Michael Balcon quoted in Jeffrey Richards, "Basil Dearden at Ealing," in Alan Burton, Tim O'Sullivan, and Paul Wells, eds, *Liberal Directions: Basil Dearden and Postwar British Film Culture*. Trowbridge: Flicks Books, 1997, 14.

war ... Basil had a very strong sense of the importance of films and influencing public opinion, and he thought that films should always be about something and have some sort of theme.[15]

Relph's service-mindedness echoed Balcon's, for whom the war, as Christine Geraghty notes, "meant allying the British film industry with the high ideals of creating a national identity and seeking to put the cinema at the service of the war effort."[16] It is possible to see a continuation of these ideals in the 1950s because social problem films, even the most sensationalist, often doubled as cautionary tales that suggested the price paid by those who engaged in acts of social deviance, regardless of the injustice of their suffering. As Balcon remarked, "Nothing would induce us to do anything against the public interest just for the sake of making money."[17] They also had clearly delineated heroes and villains, the former usually characterized by the open-minded liberalism and decency valued by the filmmakers themselves. Already by the turn of the 1960s, this cohort of respected and professional filmmakers came under critical attack for their value system, their formulaic directorial approach, and the very tasteful nature of their output; such criticism persists to the present.[18]

The liberalism championed in many Ealing films had its counterpart, of course, in British society. This is worth remembering when we return to the social and political context of the evolving "race relations narrative" in British drama. Many improving middle-class liberals in the 1950s, black and white, expressed a particular perspective on the racism that was becoming increasingly active in response to increased colonial migration to Britain. They felt strongly that the majority of those who harbored such prejudices did so out of ignorance, out of a lack of knowledge about the backgrounds and cultural habits of New Commonwealth settlers. It followed that education and awareness were the most effective long-term solutions to white racism in the country.

The result was the organization of a plethora of locally sponsored, and explicitly labeled citizens' advice bureaus, interracial dances, clubs, picnics, and public performances discussed in Chapter 1. (A precursor of the postwar initiatives, of course, was Harold Moody's League of Coloured

15 "Interview with Michael Relph," in Alan Burton, Tim O'Sullivan, and Paul Wells, eds, *Liberal Directions: Basil Dearden and Postwar British Film Culture*. Trowbridge: Flicks Books, 1997, 246.

16 Christine Geraghty, *British Cinema in the Fifties: Gender, Genre and the "New Look"* (London and New York: Routledge, 2000), 4.

17 Balcon quoted in Pam Cook and Mieke Bernink, eds, *The Cinema Book*, second edition (London: BFI Publishing, 1999), 84.

18 For a good overview of criticism of Ealing methods and outlook, see "Introduction," in Alan Burton, Tim O'Sullivan, and Paul Wells, eds, *Liberal Directions: Basil Dearden and Postwar British Film Culture*. Trowbridge: Flicks Books, 1997, 1–13.

Peoples, established in 1931, which brought public attention to instances of discrimination in Britain but also cultivated an image of moral uprightness and middle-class respectability that put it in line with interwar liberal internationalism rather than more radical black organizations.)[19] In the year following the outbreak of the Notting Hill riots, the district of Kensington organized a "Goodwill Week" of planned activities in Holland Park, with racial amity as its primary goal. The local *Kensington News* promised an "anti-slavery exhibition, a large dance at Porchester Hall, plays at the Twentieth Century Theatre, displays in Holland Park and the appearance of Paul Robeson."[20] Part and parcel with this optimistic faith in education and propaganda, however, was mid-century liberals' blindness to the existence of institutionalized forms of racism and reluctance to explore the historical roots of white prejudice and xenophobia, above all in the empire.

As we shall see below, this brand of liberalism, as manifested in connection with the race relations debate, fundamentally shaped the films under consideration here by confining the cause of white hostility to personal, domestic ignorance or neurosis. As Hill argues throughout *Sex, Class and Realism*, mid-century films' focus on domestic tension and individual ethics tended to obscure the economic and political causes of racial animosity, the existence of a more deep-seated institutional racism, and official complacency.[21]

The film analyses below give a sense of the continuities and evolution of the race relations narrative in the postwar period and emphasize the role of West Indian artists in this evolution, especially through an examination of the cultural work of Earl Cameron and Lloyd Reckord. They managed, in particular ways, to integrate their own perspective into British film at a time when the form was at its most insular and inward looking.

Pool of London

In *Pool of London* (1950), West Indian seaman Johnny confides to his white female friend:

> You know, when you're at the wheel of a ship at night, far out at sea, and nothing else to do, you think about a lot of things you don't understand. You wonder why one man is born white, and another isn't. And how

---

19   On the League, see, for example, Rush, "Imperial Identity in Colonial Minds."

20   "GOODWILL WEEK IS NOW A FACT: First news of Big Programme for Race Unity," *Kensington News and West London Times* (May 8, 1959), 1. This announcement came only nine days before the fatal stabbing of Antiguan Kelso Cochrane in the Paddington area of London.

21   See Hill, *Sex, Class and Realism*, 5–31.

about God Himself? What colour is He? And the stars seems so close, and the world so small in comparison with the other worlds above you … It doesn't seem to matter so much how you were born.

This awkwardly inserted reflection on race prejudice signaled the appearance in mainstream British drama of a new character type: the upright colonial migrant to London, simultaneously a good man and a sexual threat. And Johnny's character was not the only new element. The first feature to examine and acknowledge the existence of white British prejudice, in many respects *Pool of London* set the parameters of the race relations narrative that predominated for the next fifteen years. And it did this prior to the largest influx of West Indian migrants after 1954—Johnny's character was not even a permanent settler.

Although it clocked in at just eighty-five minutes, *Pool of London* was not a "quota quickie," but a high-profile Ealing Studios film directed by Basil Dearden and distributed by Rank. It was not a quintessential social problem film, but it foreshadowed that genre's concern with topicality and authenticity in its portrayal of setting and character. The film won critical praise for its extensive location shooting at the London dockside, at a time when Ealing relied, in general, on studio production.[22] Documentary filmmaker Paul Rotha wrote, "Ealing Studios are trying very sincerely, I believe, to build up a school of authentic British cinema and are certainly in the attempt taking their cameras out and about, that fact in itself is welcome."[23] *Pool of London* was a clear attempt to match gritty, realistic sets and sequences with equally gritty, realistic subject matter, even if it was less than successful: "Where the scene, and much of the activity (the waterfront bustle, the work of the river police, and the car chases) are so authentic, a correspondingly high degree of authenticity in the playing is looked for. And this is where some disappointment is quickly felt."[24]

Even taking into account its awkward intersection of themes and unwieldy plot, however, the film is an early example of Ealing's tentative move away from an unambiguous moral code; as Tony Williams has remarked, it "does not contain an ideologically satisfying harmonious resolution like previous Ealing narratives. … *Pool of London* is less remarkable as a typical Ealing Studios film but more as a work expressing tensions that will emerge later in British society."[25]

---

22 Cook and Berninck, *The Cinema Book*, 84.

23 Paul Rotha in *Public Opinion* (March 2, 1951), quoted in Alan Burton and Tim O'Sullivan, *The Cinema of Basil Dearden and Michael Relph* (Edinburgh: Edinburgh University Press, 2009), 113.

24 Philip Hope-Wallace, "Films of the Month: Pool of London," *Sight & Sound* 19, no. 12 (April 1951), 474.

25 Tony Williams, *Structures of Desire: British Cinema, 1939–1955* (New York: State University of New York Press, 2000), 184–85.

The film tells the story of two seaman, friends Dan (white) and Johnny (black), who inadvertently get mixed up in a diamond theft and a related murder while on a short leave in London. Dan, as a small-time smuggler, is responsible for their involvement, as he gets a completely unsuspecting Johnny to deliver the package of diamonds, although he too is initially unaware of the parcel's dangerous contents. Although Dan, out of fear, is tempted to let Johnny take the rap for the crime, his new love interest perceives Dan's essential decency and persuades him to go to the police. Meanwhile, Johnny, a gentle, honest young man from Jamaica, falls for a sweet and genuine cinema cashier, Pat, when she defends him against the racism of others and later shows him friendship. Dan's and Johnny's storylines are imperfectly united by the themes of loyalty and decency and by their separate experiences with "good" women.

Earl Cameron played Johnny with a wistful, almost virginal purity, and with his wide eyes and open face he looked the part. Johnny embodies several of the elements that marked later incarnations of West Indian and other black characters in later British films. First, and most importantly, he is impeccably moral and upright, demonstrating common courtesy, good English manners, and responsibility. The film's first scenes reveal him as a hard worker aboard the SS *Dunbar* and, unlike Dan and his other colleagues, he takes no part in the petty smuggling of cigarettes and pantyhose. The prevailing British stereotypes of "colored" or "foreign" seamen and residents—for instance, their association with crime, interracial sex, prostitution, and seedy "hot" jazz clubs—are all assiduously overturned in the character of Johnny, who is even uncomfortable in the dancehall that he and Pat are "swept" into one evening. (He leaves quickly, although Pat, a regular, remains with her friends.)

Moreover, he is a perfect gentleman toward Pat. After she defends him against the hostility of the prejudiced theater commissionaire, he gives up his place in the bus queue for her so that she does not have to wait in the rain. As their acquaintance blossoms, he makes no advances despite his attraction. In fact, he appears in the film as longing but almost passionless in his goodness.

Thirdly, Johnny's character is self-improving but humble and deferential, even self-effacing. For most of the film he betrays no hint of anger or aggression, despite the racist invective hurled at him from various corners. It is always white people who attack him, and it is always white people who come to his aid, like Pat and Dan outside the cinema—he never stands up for himself. Even when he speaks of his personal achievements and goals, the film uses the moment to showcase his extreme humility. He confides to Pat:

> I like the sea, but not for all my life. Spent a lot of hours on it, thinking about things. Getting ambitions, and all sorts of high and mighty ideas. Now I've saved a bit of money, I want to go back to school. See if I can turn them into something. I may not have brains, but at least I'd like to find out.

Pool of London's politics are loosely anti-racist, but in order for this position to come across clearly and convincingly, Johnny has to be a saintly young man. Not only does Johnny's lack of assertiveness showcase the unreasonable hostility of many of the bit characters, but also positions him as the moral compass of the entire film. The presence of "bad" players is signaled by their expression of prejudice against Johnny. When Dan's first girlfriend Maisie witnesses Johnny about to give a pair of coveted nylon stockings to Pat, she remarks, "Hm! You must be hard up to go with <u>him</u> to get them." Maisie's ignorant racism and materialism sets her in contrast to the loyal—and unprejudiced—Sally, who cultivates Dan's better self at the film's end. When she learns that Dan is considering letting Johnny get caught with some stolen diamonds, she pleads, "You can't do that! If they wouldn't believe you, they'd never believe him. You know that."

Most importantly, Johnny's presence encourages the audience to believe in the main protagonist, Dan. Despite his involvement in petty crime and his dubious choice of Maisie as a girlfriend, the script's character sketch notes that "underneath all this, he is a decent person. This is indicated by his relationship with JOHNNY, the coloured seaman. He looks upon himself as his big brother, and protects him against any evidence there might be of the colour bar."

Pool of London's credentials as a "progressive" film are assured by treating anti-racism as a primary signifier of moral substance, a fact satirized by at least one reviewer, who suggested:

> Ealing Studios should be awarded the good citizenship badge First Class for its unswerving devotion to its conception of the London way of life. ... [The film] self-consciously skirts any of the main issues of the Negro problem but [it] will no doubt succeed in getting the film banned south of the Mason and Dixon line.[26]

Nevertheless, even acknowledging the presence of commonplace racism in Britain was a courageous leap for Basil Dearden and Michael Relph, at a moment when "the English were congratulating themselves on their infinite fair-mindedness," especially in film.[27]

Yet, *Pool of London* was a film very much of its time, a time when West Indian settlers were still arriving in relatively small groups and before the sharp racial tensions of the late 1950s and 1960s. First of all, what I am calling the race relations narrative was almost incidental to the film's plot and action. As *Sight and Sound* noted, "The colour question hardly rears its head, though the Bermudan gives off some mild and rather sententious

---

26 Milton Shulman, "So this is the London Way of Life (or is it?)," *Evening Standard* (February 22, 1951), 9.
27 Durgnat, *A Mirror for England*, 105.

opinions about intolerance on Greenwich Hill, while the young person simpers politely."[28] Although Johnny gets embroiled in the diamond heist, he never realizes it, and his own story—his relationship with Pat—operates on an entirely separate plane from the film's central conflict.

Pool of London is essentially an action and crime drama, and it is Dan's redemption, not Johnny's, that provides the central emotional drama. The viewer's report that Rank distributed to cinemas, to give exhibitors a sense of the genre, content, and likely audience for the film, classified it as a "London Crime Drama" and noted "scenes aboard a merchant ship and in dockland, as well as pubs, dance halls, music halls and river. A motor car chase through Rotherhithe tunnel is one of the high spots of the climax." Apart from describing Johnny as "coloured," the report made no mention of him or his story; the theme of racism is ignored, perhaps in order to more effectively market the film as "Good strong, holding entertainment for all classes."[29] Years later, Rank films like *Sapphire* and *Flame in the Streets* would do a better job of integrating questions of race into their central conflicts. Nonetheless, *Pool of London* is of a piece with later British productions in that it employs the controversy of race relations as a tool to highlight the emotional journeys of its white protagonists.

Johnny's West Indian character is not only incorruptible, but his status as a racial or sexual threat is systematically neutralized, first, because despite his enjoyment of London, he clearly has no plans to settle in Britain; instead he declares his intention of pursuing his education in Jamaica. Even more important, *Pool of London* does not problematize Johnny and Pat's relationship, because neither of them seriously considers the prospect of an actual romance. The movie implicitly suggests that their color divide—and not other factors—makes a future between them impossible. When Johnny makes his final heartfelt farewell to Pat, he intimates both his feelings for her and the impossibility of acting on them: "I wanted to go home, Pat, like I told you, I wanted to go home. But now I don't. I want to be coming back again. Back to the Pool. Back to London. But because I do, I can't." It is clear that *Pool*'s producers were acting on unquestioned assumptions here; as Tony Williams has said, "despite the attraction both feel to each other, the studio cannot approve of their union."[30] Even the script's character sketch notes that while Johnny "is carried away by her friendship," "he realises that nothing can come of it." Thus the producers limit the progressive or radical potential of both the film and the society it is representing. This is articulated when, after Pat protests that one's race "doesn't matter," Johnny

28 Philip Hope-Wallace, "Films of the Month: Pool of London," *Sight & Sound* 19, no. 12 (April 1951), 475.

29 General Film Distributors Viewers' Report for *Pool of London*, dated "trade shown" February 14, 1951, Special Collections, BFI.

30 Williams, *Structures of Desire*, 185.

gently counters, "It does you know. Maybe, one day it won't any more [*sic*], but it still does. Come on ... We can't put the world right." The British Film Institute's indifferent review in its *Monthly Film Bulletin* called the love story "the film's least successful element," and complained that "The relationship is treated as an interlude which can have no outcome, but is not handled with that feeling or sympathy which would justify its part in the film."[31] The review placed the lion's share of the blame for this on Dearden's cold and detached direction.

Meanwhile, the film left unexplored the question of Pat's own feelings for Johnny. His romantic regard is clear, but though she is perhaps especially attentive to him during their few days together, the audience remains unsure whether this is a reflection of her own attraction or her natural friendliness and generosity. In hindsight, this may seem a very conservative depiction, but the explosive controversy over miscegenation in London during the Second World War and the tarring of the reputations of white women who socialized with African-American or West Indian servicemen was probably too fresh in the minds of viewers to allow for a more liberal approach, especially given that Pat's own character was meant to be unblemished. Neil Wynn has drawn attention to the ambiguous reception of black American and West Indian servicemen in wartime England; although many were welcomed by the locals, both the American and British military discouraged interracial relationships, especially marriages, and the mixed-race children of these unions were stigmatized in the media and sometimes in their communities.[32] Thus in 1950 and 1951 (when the film ran in theaters), many viewers would still have seen interracial relationships in Britain within this framework, and not in the context of postwar immigration. In this sense, *Pool of London* is unique among the films under review, and as will be seen below, the treatment of interracial romance altered dramatically over the next fifteen years.

There was, however, one way in which *Pool of London* complicated—perhaps even subverted—its own liberal intentions in its portrayal of Johnny. Unexpectedly given an extra evening in London due to investigations into the diamond theft, he rushes off to see Pat again but is intimidated when he finds her at the dance hall surrounded by her many friends and admirers. Suddenly gripped with despair at the thought that he and Pat can never be together, Johnny spends the rest of the night at a seedy bar, where he encounters more racist remarks and accusations from the uncouth patrons. Drunk, and finally fed up with the abuse, he gets involved in a brawl, is ejected from the establishment, and falls asleep in the rubble of a bombed-out building. By losing his self-control, Johnny does

---

31   Review, *Pool of London*, *Monthly Film Bulletin* 18, no. 206 (March 1951), 230.
32   Neil A. Wynn, "'Race War': Black American GIs and West Indians in Britain During The Second World War, *Immigrants & Minorities* 24, no. 3 (2006): 338–39.

Johnny in despair. Earl Cameron in *Pool of London*, 1951. © Moviestore
Collection/REX Shutterstock 2015.

indeed end up embodying several of the negative stereotypes attributed
to his race at the time. As a result, the white bystanders who witness the
scene shrug and classify him as just another "colored" troublemaker. At
any rate, such behavior starkly exposes a dangerous weakness in Johnny's
otherwise unimpeachable character, and again, the film's tone is ambivalent.
Is his fall from grace to be blamed on the unjust *status quo* that keeps him
and Pat apart, or simply on his own colonial inferiority complex? When
juxtaposed to Dan's personal epiphany at the church, followed by his moral
redemption, Johnny's weakness comes across most darkly.

Bermudan Earl Cameron was well cast as the seaman Johnny, and his
gravity and charisma guaranteed him many more such roles in the future.
(He in fact earned prominent credits in three of the four cinematic features
under examination here, as well as in "race relations" television features
including *A Man from the Sun* (BBC, 1956) *The Dark Man* (BBC, 1960),
and *A Fear of Strangers* (ATV, 1964).) As one of the most recognizable
West Indian faces in mainstream British cinema, as well as in television
and theater, he personally did a great deal to *define* the image of the
dignified West Indian in London. In the context of 1950, he was perfect
as would-be lover Johnny, but in subsequent productions from the late
1950s and early 1960s, when the immigration issue became more visible

and provocative, he most often played less passionate, usually older and more old-fashioned roles. In this sense, although he played a variety of characters, Earl Cameron came to represent an earlier, less radical generation of Caribbean settler. And mainstream British film tended to portray this cinematic "type" the most sympathetically, sometimes in marked contrast to the more independent and aggressive youths coming of age in the 1960s.

Cameron's apparently unusual entry into show business in many ways typifies the unpredictable experiences of West Indians and other non-white performers trying to make a living in London. Born in Pembroke, Bermuda in 1917, Cameron sailed to England in 1939 as a worker on board a ship called the *Warhead* (his experience here gave him some insight for his role in *Pool of London*). He had virtually no experience or training when, while working as a dishwasher in 1942, he landed his first part in the chorus of *Chu Chin Chow*, which was running at the Palace Theatre. It was not raw talent that created the opening for him, but rather the fact that his friend Harry Crosman was in the chorus when another player fell ill: "So he took me over to see Robert Atkins [the director], he looked me up and down and said, Yeah, Harry, I think he'll do."[33] Later that same year he appeared as Joseph in the inferior (as Cameron has described it) production *The Petrified Forest*, again not for his inherent quality as a performer, but "mainly because his Bermudan accent sounded American."[34] After this, Cameron worked as an actor for the Entertainments National Service Association, traveling to Calcutta with the well-known Leslie Hutchinson's band (also West Indian). But it was not until his return that his career took off. A few elocution lessons later, Cameron became one of the most successful West Indian actors in Britain, appearing in over thirty films between the 1950s and 1970s.[35]

Although the vast majority of struggling entertainers (black and white) in London experienced nothing like Cameron's luck, the sheer randomness of his big break was in fact the norm for colonial performers. As the next chapter will discuss, West Indian actors like Cameron were most often hired—or rejected—on the basis of their appearance and accent, with little to no regard for their lack of—or often quite substantial—professional experience. It is likely no coincidence that although *Pool of London*'s Johnny is a merchant seaman from Jamaica, he betrays no trace of a Jamaican accent; he is foreign but not *too* foreign.

---

33 Transcript, conversation with Earl Cameron and David Johnson, May 29, 1997, London, 9704094/A, *Blackgrounds* oral history project, TMA.

34 Carl Daniels, Earl Cameron biography, Screenonline, available at http://www. screenonline.org.uk/people/id/475450/index.html, accessed July 6, 2006.

35 Cameron can still be seen occasionally in small film and television roles, most recently in Christopher Nolan's *Inception* (2010) and Stephen Frears's *The Queen* (2006).

And yet Cameron's influence on the contours of the British race relations drama should not be underestimated (or ignored, as has more often been the case). Again, this is not necessarily because of his consummate acting skills; in fact, the *Monthly Film Bulletin* particularly noted Cameron's inexperience as an actor, although it remarked significantly on his "pleasant personality" on screen.[36] His open and guileless manner (for Cameron largely a natural trait that comes across in interviews recorded decades later) became part of the template for the dignified West Indian "type" noted above, which was often portrayed by Cameron himself. Although Johnny's willingness in *Pool of London* to have white allies defend him from racist antagonism suggests subservience and passivity, his character could have suffered far worse in the hands of another actor. Cameron may have been inexperienced, but he was not wooden, and he instilled in Johnny a warmth and humanity that immediately wins the viewer's sympathies, in much the same way as Cy Grant did on BBC's *Tonight* program.[37] He made a potentially one-note role believable. It was, presumably, this quality that Dearden and Relph valued most in the portrayal. Furthermore, in white liberal representations of British race relations for years to come, it was this stock character—natural, respectable, moral, and dignified—that was repeatedly calculated to be the most sympathetic to mainstream British audiences, in contrast to other West Indian stereotypes that emerged, such as the immigrant with a chip on his shoulder and the underworld hustler. (However, Johnny's character also anticipates a fourth type when his feelings of alienation lead him to drink: that of the naïve settler who, after enduring a few hardships, is easily drawn into wrongdoing.)

Sapphire

Seven years later, Relph and Dearden teamed up again to explore anew the issue of race, but this time in a dramatically different context. In the intervening years roughly 100,000 West Indians had migrated to Great Britain, settling mainly in England's urban areas, and especially in London.[38] Although the presence of colonial and foreign people in London was certainly nothing new, in the late 1950s racial tensions were heating up, with some complaining about high concentrations of black people in neighborhoods like Kensington, Notting Hill/Dale, and Brixton, and others calling for a limit on (non-white) immigration from the empire and Commonwealth. Only months before the cameras began rolling on *Sapphire*, three days of violence broke out between white and black residents

---

36 Review, *Pool of London*, *Monthly Film Bulletin* 18, no. 206 (March 1951), 230.
37 It is perhaps no coincidence that Grant was also considered for the part of Johnny.
38 For annual migration estimates in the 1950s, see Fryer, *Staying Power*, 372.

in Notting Hill. It was the first significant sign that white racism was not confined to a handful of Teddy Boys and extremists; some people even commuted to the neighborhood to observe or take part in the agitation. (One eyewitness reported: "As I turned into Bramley Road I saw a mob of over 700 men, women and children stretching 200 yards along the road.")[39] Although newspapers and officials denounced the riots, it was clear that the issue of race in Britain would become more, not less, significant over the next few years.

Audiences and critics by this time had developed a taste for realism in their films, at least in terms of production values, and hence more prestigious movies began featuring scenes shot on location instead of fabricated inside a film studio. What had been novelty in *Pool of London* was still a mark of distinction in *Sapphire* (1959). Basil Dearden, no doubt desiring to portray his race relations story more "realistically," shot several of the film's scenes on location in Hampstead and other London neighborhoods. The Rank Organisation had declared its intention to film in Notting Hill, but was met with public opposition. The Association of Cinematograph, Television and Allied Technicians, whose secretary called the decision "tactless," objected to "anything likely to make the recent trouble start all over again." The article added that the union "would welcome the script if it were objectively done and helped people understand the problem."[40] (In November Relph confirmed that there was to be no shooting at Notting Hill Gate.)[41] But even before this skirmish, Dearden and Relph had battled considerable opposition from inside the Rank Organisation to their film. Producer Michael Relph revealed years later:

What was interesting really, was the attitude of Rank to the subject. John Davis[42] had a deputation of all the Mayors of the London boroughs asking him not to make the film. He desperately did not want to make the film, but had agreed that we could make it if we got the budget down to a certain point. We failed to do so by a relatively small amount, but he dug his toes in on this, because he saw a way of getting out of the predicament. ... Earl St John[43] was on his way up to the Rank board

---

39 Colin Eales, "Witness to Violence," *Kensington News and West London Times* (September 5, 1958), 1.

40 "Tactless to Film in Notting Hill," *The Times* (October 11, 1958), 3.

41 "Film Not to Be Shot at Notting Hill," *The Times* (November 15, 1958), 12.

42 John Davis was a studio executive at Rank at this time, and has been described as "one of the most influential and unpopular figures in the British film industry"; he "famously advocated clean 'family films,'" "but always disclaimed—disingenuously perhaps—any wish to interfere in the creative aspects of film-making." See Brian McFarlane, ed., *The Encyclopedia of British Film*, revised edition (London: Methuen, 2005), 171.

43 Executive Producer at Pinewood Studios, which produced the film.

meeting to cancel the project, and I stopped him at the gate and said "Basil and I will make it for nothing". This was a way of meeting the budget figure, so they had to let us make the film. We believed implicitly in the message of the film.[44]

These instances of internal and media controversy are illustrative. They reveal both the public's heightened sensitivity to the issue of race and racism, and the producers' commitment to bringing this out in their film, to somehow get at the dynamics of the issue, even going so far as to film at one of London's racial battlegrounds. Though we may question Relph and Dearden's approach to many aspects of the film's production (discussed below), it is clear that their commitment was sincere.

Of all the mid-century films that deal with the contemporary issue of colonial migration and racism, *Sapphire* has been examined most, but scholars often overlook the extent to which the film responded to changing popular attitudes about race. The 1950s and early 1960s in Britain did not constitute a single "moment" of domestic or imperial history,[45] and we can see this in the considerable difference in the treatment of interracial romance in *Pool of London* and *Sapphire* eight years later. *Sapphire*, for all its middle-class liberalism, represented a new treatment of the race relations narrative, different in so many respects from *Pool of London*, with its hermetically sealed love story and unthreatening Jamaican protagonist. Dearden and Relph had the foresight to see that such a filmic treatment of interracial relationships was simply unconvincing in 1958, and that *Sapphire* would have to delve more deeply into current controversies. And it did so—not just frankly, but sensationally. The film dealt with interracial romance, but also dive bars, hustlers, racial "passing," police prejudice, and white racism of the most virulent and destructive kind. A far cry from *Pool of London*.

On the other hand, *Sapphire* clearly conformed to several of the narrative and aesthetic contours introduced in *Pool*. Not only did it share a similar creative team, but it too was presented as a progressive film meant to disrupt ordinary Britons' complacency and interrogate their innermost prejudices. Furthermore, the race relations theme in *Sapphire* is again partially submerged in the plot and action for it is essentially a mystery and a crime drama, although here the two approaches are tightly and more successfully integrated. Nonetheless, like *Pool*, it is the dilemmas of the central white characters that constitute the film's main focus. A final similarity between the films is that they both partly sabotage their progressive credentials by presenting scenes in which racial stereotypes are affirmed instead of overturned. And so *Sapphire* was both a departure from, and a continuation of, the race relations narrative established in *Pool of London*.

---

44 "Interview with Michael Relph," 247.
45 See, for example, Young, *Fear of the Dark*, chapter 4.

Sapphire's title refers to young Sapphire Robbins, a music student who never appears in the film alive. Her body is discovered one morning dumped on Hampstead Heath, and Inspectors Hazard and Learoyd are charged with finding her killer. They discover that she was engaged to be married to an upwardly mobile working-class architecture student, David Harris, who had planned to study in Italy until he learned that Sapphire was pregnant. The case quickly becomes more complicated and sinister when Hazard and Learoyd discover that Sapphire was "passing" for white, her fair skin and hair allowing her to conceal her mixed-race parentage. David's family had learned of this only very shortly before her murder, which places them all under suspicion.

As stated above, the creative producers of *Sapphire* clearly meant it to be a tough, provocative, and "realistic" representation of London's racial dynamic. In her quest for authenticity, screenwriter Janet Green apparently made several outings to West Indian and black neighborhoods in an attempt to get a feel for the lifestyle of the new settlers, as well as the attitudes of the white people around them. One American interview with her, adopting a recognizably American perspective, reported:

> Miss Green tackled the subject [of the "race problem" in Britain] because there was so little admission of racial prejudice in Britain—and yet, plenty of prejudice exists there. Her technique was to explore with her husband the black ghettos of London "dozens of times" until "we actually heard lines that would fit right into the script."[46]

Green heard one white woman say to her friend, upon observing a black man enter a club, "I see they've let the jungle in." Her attitude was that of an absolute outsider—she remarked to the journalist quoted above that "I got to like Negroes, at least the ones I met"—but her desire to expose an issue she felt was swept under the carpet paralleled both Dearden's liberal intentions and the style of the "social problem" films just coming to prominence.

In a program printed for the film's regional charity premiere in Newcastle, Michael Relph described *Sapphire* as a "contemporary detective story in which the futility of racial prejudice is exposed for the irrational thing that it is." Likewise actor Nigel Patrick, who played Superintendent Hazard in the film, stated blandly that it was "about modern people having modern problems." However, Yvonne Mitchell, who portrayed David's forlorn sister Mildred, most accurately summoned the contemporary cinematic mood when she remarked that *Sapphire*'s quality lay in the fact that "it is a picture of life in England as it is lived today. I believe

---

46 "Took 'Murder' to Tell Race Issue," *San Francisco News-Call Bulletin* (February 6, 1960), 7. Interview with Janet Green.

that every country makes its best films about its own people and places and problems."[47] Mitchell's short comment both acknowledges England's changing demographic makeup, and positions this change as problematic. These comments from the film's major creative players suggest that *Sapphire* was a self-consciously modern film, meant to provoke reaction like *Room at the Top* (1958) or *Look Back in Anger* (1959), both of which were at the forefront of the New Wave.

And yet while the desire of producers and actors to highlight real-life injustice was prominent, *Sapphire*'s plot, characterization, and action were highly contrived and melodramatic; it was a tight, methodical production and the story and visuals were engineered to heighten the viewer's every sensation and assumption, sometimes affirming, sometimes contesting, the suspicions aroused.

The most obvious manifestation of the film's carefully constructed sensationalism was the fact that it was, as the Rank viewer's report classified it, a "murder and colour bar drama"[48]—a film with an earnest liberal theme but a Hollywood vehicle. Screenwriter Green, according to the same interviewer, "decided the best way to discuss the 'problem', cinematically, was 'by writing a rattling good murder story.'"[49] Although she might have found this combination useful, it was not clear to everyone that a police investigation was the most productive way to highlight the injustice of urban racism. *The Times*'s critic found it impractical:

> A good whodunit needs confident pacing and a strong narrative drive, but in order to deal tactfully with all shades of opinion in a controversial issue one has to stop, underline a point here or skate rapidly over a difficult subject there, and these two opposite requirements are almost impossible to reconcile.[50]

Variety concluded that "concession to the boxoffice [*sic*] makes 'Sapphire' a near-miss": "though obviously inspired by last year's outbreak of color-bar riots in London and Nottingham, it ducks the issue, refusing to face boldly up to the problem ... [and] eventually adds up to merely another whodunit."[51] Even Michael Relph, in hindsight (and no doubt chastened by years of critical excoriation), conceded:

---

47 Michael Relph, Nigel Patrick, and Yvonne Mitchell quoted in cinema program for the Newcastle premiere of *Sapphire* (1959), 5, 16, 17, JG/8/5, Janet Green Collection, Box 5, Special Collections, BFI.

48 Rank Viewers' Report for *Sapphire*, dated "trade shown" April 17, 1959, Special Collections, BFI.

49 "Took 'Murder' to Tell Race Issue," 7.

50 "Thriller and Social Study: An Awkward Film Mixture," *The Times* (May 8, 1959), 6.

51 Review of *Sapphire*, *Variety Film Reviews* (April 29, 1959).

We "sugared the pill," too commercially. Take a film like *Victim* [1961], for example, which we made after Ealing, when we were able to find our own feet. We reckoned that rather than making an esoteric film which would reach only a limited number of people, that we should wrap up the homosexual issue in a really watertight thriller format, which would have the capacity to reach out to a general film-going public. A lot of people thought that that was cheapening the idea too much, and that by wrapping it up in this commercial sugar coating, we were commercialising the themes and not treating them with sufficient seriousness.[52]

The *Monthly Film Bulletin* coolly stated: "The film is undoubtedly meant in earnest; its failure, consequently, seems twice as sad, though there are doubtless many who will be impressed by the politeness of its 'liberal' gesture."[53]

There were. *Sapphire* won critical praise on both sides of the Atlantic, eventually winning Best British Film from the British Academy of Film Arts. In a review entitled "Can London Really Be Like This?" the *Evening Standard* admired its "almost tangible reality" and declared that "Sapphire brings every member of the audience face to face with the appalling revelation [of the 'colour problem']. It demands that everyone should have an attitude, and thereby does a service."[54] *Sapphire* also earned rave reviews in the United States, where its tackling of the theme of racism appeared even bolder, and just as relevant. Archer Winsten wrote in the *New York Post*, "Not to beat around the bush, this picture deals with race prejudice on half a dozen authentic levels in a way that is so outspoken and knowing that it has no equals. ... Not everyone will like it, but no one will be left cold or disinterested."[55] Likewise, in a review efficiently titled "'Sapphire' Thriller with Moral," the *New York Mirror* wrote that "'Sapphire' is terse, tense and exciting because of its detective-story elements—yet thoughtful without preachment because it holds a mirror to circumstances we encounter almost every day."[56] Thus in many cases, the movie's reception confirmed the success of its overall "message," despite its delivery in a glossy, melodramatic package.

Although the creative team behind *Sapphire* effectively communicated its serious moral intentions, they were nonetheless aware of the power of

---

52 "Interview with Michael Relph," 244.
53 Review of *Sapphire*, *Monthly Film Bulletin* (June 1959), 69.
54 John Waterman, "Can London Really Be Like This?" *Evening Standard* (May 7, 1959), 10.
55 Archer Winsten, "'Sapphire' Glitters at the Sutton," *New York Post* (November 3, 1959), 44.
56 Justin Gilbert, "'Sapphire' Thriller with Moral," *New York Mirror* (November 3, 1959), 24.

race when effectively dramatized to draw mainstream viewers into the cinemas as well as send a message. The New York *Sunday News* reported that it took Janet Green "two years to sell her story to a producer,"[57] and this may well be true, but Rank certainly had faith that it would be a commercial success. Throughout the 1950s, the organization adopted a more aggressively commercial policy toward its filmmaking, focusing heavily on distribution and exhibition, those facets of the industry that were most lucrative. Accordingly, its engagement with film production decreased dramatically; it produced only a handful of movies in the second half of the 1950s.[58] Those it *did* produce must therefore have been viewed as profitable investments. Michael Balcon, the famous head of Rank, had assured at least one investor, the Schlesinger Organisation, that it would receive an estimated ninety percent return; after the film's release, the profits suggested even more.[59] Moreover, *Sapphire*'s executive producer at Rank, Earl St. John, wrote to Green, "If you get any ideas that you are very keen about and feel that they have some sort of a gimmick[,] this is needed today, please get in touch with Joyce Briggs."[60] Race prejudice was *Sapphire*'s particular "gimmick," and over the next few years Green would oblige Earl St. John and Rank with two other such films, *Victim* in 1961, another crime drama exploring the issue of homosexuality, and *Life For Ruth* in 1962, which examined religious fundamentalism.

Sapphire's profile in this respect places it squarely within the tradition of the melodramatic social problem film. Its screenplay played up such melodrama, especially at its climax, when David's sister Mildred, revealed as *Sapphire*'s killer, breaks down and delivers a disturbing tirade:

> She didn't care. Ruining David's life. Ruining Dad's dream. When I said she'd better watch out ... [that] David might prefer to give her ten bob a week for the yellow brat ... and keep his scholarship ... she laughed in my face. And said David didn't care what colour the baby was or what colour she was. He wanted her and I'd forgotten what that was like. I'd forgotten what it was like to be wanted. She was taunting me with Sid never coming home. ... There was a knife on the counter. And then there was blood.

---

57 Kate Cameron, "The Sutton Presents Unusual Murder Film," *Sunday News* (November 3, 1959).

58 See Durgnat, *A Mirror for England*.

59 The profit margin was helped by the fact that *Sapphire*'s production costs came in under budget, at approximately £145,000. Profits (excluding the western hemisphere) were estimated at about £81,000. See letters to Michael Balcon, June 26 and 29, 1959, MEB/I/227a, Aileen and Michael Balcon Collection, Special Collections, BFI.

60 Earl St. John to Janet Green, May 12, 1959, JG/8/3, Correspondence, Janet Green Collection, Special Collections, BFI.

Dearden also enhanced the melodramatic potential of *Sapphire* visually, especially in his emphasis on color, likely to highlight not only the "colorfulness" of multiracial London, but also the social importance of skin color, especially in regards to the central character. One of the first clues to Sapphire's true identity, for example, is the clothes she was wearing when she died. A promotional booklet set the scene:

> Detective-Superintendent Robert Hazard, gazing down at the still figure, noticed first her beauty. Then something unusual challenged his attention ... in contrast to her quiet beige and brown clothes she wore a chiffon petticoat of vivid flame-red. ... It was a Sapphire of the night-time—a gay girl who haunted dance clubs and whirled her dancing way in the arms of coloured men.[61]

In the film, when Hazard wonders aloud about "red taffeta under a tweed skirt," Inspector Learoyd replies, "Yes, that's the black under the white all right." The cover of the promo book itself was an image of a club scene painted on a black background in bright, jazzy colors and impressionistic brushstrokes. Even Yvonne Mitchell imbibed *Sapphire*'s descriptive language when she described it as "a 'whodunit' which throws a spotlight on those vivid parts of London where negro and white people mix."[62]

And, indeed, Relph made these locations look and feel more colorful than the spaces of white domesticity, in particular David's home. The scene in Tulip's shady club is particularly striking, distinguished by dim mood lighting, dancing, numerous close-ups, and quick cuts between various figures and body parts, with Johnny Dankworth's Orchestra providing a rhythmic jazz soundtrack.

Tulip's is also presented in opposition to the respectable environment of the International Club, also an arena of interracial socialization. (One cynical character, the African student Paul Slade, refers to it as "One of those 'get together, let's be brothers' places.") At the International Club, Hazard and Learoyd witness nothing but mild conversation and table tennis, although they discover from a former acquaintance that Sapphire had stopped hanging around with that circle because "The rhythm at the club; it wasn't hot enough for her. So Paul Slade used to take her to the Tulip's." The convention of crime investigation allowed Dearden to showcase a cosmopolitan variety of urban locales, with particular attention on those presumably unseen landscapes, those "vivid parts of London where negro and white people mix." More importantly, the film juxtaposes

61 Promotional booklet for *Sapphire* (undated, probably 1959), JG/8/4, Janet Green Collection, Special Collections, BFI.

62 Yvonne Mitchell quoted in cinema program for the Newcastle premiere of *Sapphire* (1959), 17, JG/8/5, Janet Green Collection, Special Collections, BFI.

the liberal, controlled space of the International Club—a space the white detectives inhabit with ease—and the more marginal, uncontrolled space of the nightclub, which Hazard and Learoyd discover only by word of mouth, and where their presence is much more conspicuous.

Even Sapphire herself, based on those elements of her character that are revealed to the viewer, presents a contrast to many of the other players, especially as she is the only one who fits comfortably on neither side of the social divide drawn in the film, a living but ultimately impossible embodiment of her mixed race. It was that much easier for her to serve as a symbol since, being dead, she has no voice of her own: "Unable to answer the question of her identity herself, she is bound by the whodunit into a position of passivity, silence, absence. Yet the fascination which she exercises erupts into the film through the intrusion of sexual imagery."[63] Indeed, Sapphire's youthfulness and liveliness are definitely out of place in David's rather drab home and family life, and contrast most with her murderer, Mildred, mother of two, whose husband has virtually abandoned her. Mildred herself draws the contrast when describing her last conversation with Sapphire: "She sat on the counter all the time I was tidying up. Sweeping, doing Lily's work. Swinging her legs and laughing." It is unclear where exactly the viewer's sympathy should lie in this case, with Sapphire or her killer, because Sapphire appears almost sinister in her innocence and disregard for the social consequences of her actions. The viewer also learns, for instance, that Sapphire dropped friends in her effort to integrate herself more fully into a white social milieu. Thus, despite her personal charms, her morality remains questionable, and her pregnancy begins to look like a deception, although all of this remains purposefully ambiguous in the film.

In fact, one of *Sapphire*'s main tricks is to play with the supposed racial preconceptions of its mainstream, white British audience. The most important example of this, of course, is that although Hazard and Learoyd spend much of the film pursuing black juvenile delinquents and petty criminals, Sapphire's true killer turns out to be white and female, a mother of two young children—and a respectable, doting mother at that. One of the best scenes features the suspect Johnny Fiddle, played with perfect pitch by Harry Baird, being chased and then questioned by the police. His frantic awareness of the realities of racism in Britain have him so panicked that he in fact appears guilty. But, of course, this assumption—made by both the police and the audience—proves groundless. Likewise, the wealthy black barrister Paul Slade (played, in another powerful performance, by Gordon Heath) takes care to mention to Hazard and Learoyd that his father is a prominent African bishop, but it later comes out not only that he was Sapphire's first dance partner at Tulip's, but also that he is embittered and cynical about Hazard's courtesy toward him. To his girlfriend he

---

63   Tarr, "*Sapphire, Darling* and the Boundaries of Permitted Pleasure": 55–56.

complains, "Sanctimonious ... ! Always so careful to have his hand out first," to which she replies, "I know, 'we're all the children of God'. Forget it." More generally, almost all of Sapphire's non-white contacts turn out to have excellent credentials: Paul Slade is a barrister, her old friend Mary is a nurse, her own brother is a doctor, and the rest are students. Only the lowlifes at Tulip's, like the crime boss "Horace Big Cigar" (what a name), conform to the worst stereotypes of non-white settlers.

The educational and professional background of David's family seems inferior in comparison; David, the prize-winning architecture student, is their great hope. It is in fact class more than race that defines the characters in *Sapphire*. Durgnat observes of the film that "if London's now a racial jungle, the intention probably isn't alarmist; for according to the Relph-Dearden line, established later, all characters who drop their aitches need to have their lives sorted out for them, or their heads knocked together, by the British bobby and his social superiors."[64] Indeed, it is the aspirational but still working-class Harrises who unsuccessfully attempt to conceal their racial neuroses, while the professional Dr. Robbins unfailingly keeps his cool despite the fact that his sister has just been murdered in an act of racial violence.

Dr. Robbins, like his predecessor Johnny in *Pool of London*, is the quintessential contradiction of the image of "black ghetto" life conjured up by Tulip's. Again Earl Cameron's soft-spoken charisma was perfectly suited to portraying the "quiet, respectable brother" in contrast to his impulsive, outgoing, and much lighter-skinned younger sister. The oft-repeated descriptor in the reviews was *dignified*; *Variety Film Reviews* singled out Cameron for bringing "immense dignity" to the secondary role, *The Hollywood Reporter* described the role as "dignified and sympathetic," and to these may be added similar evaluations of Cameron's characters and acting style in *Pool* ("a restrained and dignified performance") and, later, in *Flame in the Streets* ("played with dignity and assurance").[65] The continuities in these reviews are suggestive of the continuities in these roles and of Cameron's distinctive onscreen presence. When, in 2002, an interviewer asked him whether that was "your personality coming through there," Cameron replied:

> I was extremely lucky. Most of the parts were dignified parts. I must say that when I got a script that showed black people in a derogatory way I would say, "No, I am not going to do it" or I would tell the director

64   Durgnat, *A Mirror for England*, 65.

65   Review of *Sapphire*, *Variety Film Reviews* (April 29, 1959); Jack Moffitt, "'Sapphire' Focuses on Interracial Rows in London," *The Hollywood Reporter* 156, no. 16 (August 11, 1959), 6; review of *Pool of London*, *Variety Film Reviews* (February 28, 1951); review of *Flame in the Streets*, *Variety Film Reviews* (June 28, 1961).

to change things about it. Sometimes they did, sometimes they didn't. Fortunately, most of the parts I did I am proud of.[66]

David's family, more conscious of his dark skin than his manner, are markedly uncomfortable in Dr. Robbins's presence, and both David's mother and sister appear to take exception to his even being in their home to participate in the investigation. It is his *touching* of her children's toys that finally sets Mildred off on her maniacal confession—she can no longer conceal her utter disgust. Mildred's is not the cultural racism that decried loud West Indian neighbors, confusing accents, or charges of job theft. It is the lurking, repressed, and shameful biological racism that feared miscegenation—the racism that UNESCO's *Statement on Race* had delegitimized in 1950. It is no accident that Sapphire, at the time of her murder, is pregnant with a mixed-race child, or that her killer is a mother. Sapphire, being already dead at the film's outset, serves primarily as a symbol of deeply felt but repressed white, British fears: of the biological impact of black migration and assimilation, in the form of a mixed-race nation, and of the social consequences of racial "passing," dramatized here in working-class David's sacrifice of his scholarship and social mobility. The film's expectation was that Mildred's buried hatred would, on some level, resonate with British viewers. As Gavin Schaffer states in his history of racial science in Britain, at this time the Eugenics movement, which professed such biological fears, "was marginal not because people did not agree with many of its ideas but more because, in the wake of Nazism, it was politically unfashionable."[67]

Again, like Johnny in *Pool*, Dr. Robbins (he is never referred to by his first name, probably to emphasize his status) remains passive and stoic throughout Mildred's vituperative display. But unlike Johnny, he does not romantically ponder the reasons for the inequality of man. His experience in London has made him hard-headed and unafraid to express his feelings. When Hazard assures him that he will find Sapphire's murderer, Dr. Robbins replies, "There is no assurance for me or my kind, Superintendent. I've been black for thirty-eight years, I know. She may have looked white but Sapphire was coloured." Only moments later, however, Dr. Robbins apologizes for his cynicism because it impugns Hazard's professional integrity. This exchange illustrates that Robbins has learned to be very wary of the police in general, but that he is not embittered (in contrast to the dandified Paul Slade, who neither recognizes nor appreciates Hazard's sincerity). It also helps explain his failure to respond to Mildred's outburst at the film's end. Unlike *Pool*'s Johnny, he is not standing down out of shock or meekness, but because,

---

66 Earl Cameron in conversation with Dylan Cave, National Film Theatre, London, September 16, 2002. Interview originally published at http://www.bfi.org.uk and accessed July 12, 2010 but since removed.

67 Schaffer, *Racial Science and British Society*, 157.

as a respectable man, he refuses to engage such a blatantly unenlightened, hysterical individual. By 1959, his dignity has given him moral stature, at least in the movies.

It should be reiterated that, like *Pool of London*, *Sapphire* occasionally inadvertently chips away at the anti-racist edifice it so painstakingly constructs. This is not a new observation, and Marcia Landy goes so far as to attribute this unsettling penchant to the social problem genre as a whole: "What is memorable about the films is not their dissection of a particular social problem so much as their exposure, mainly unconscious, of their failure to resolve the problems they pose."[68] The most glaring instance of this occurs in the symbolically loaded scene at Tulip's where the barman, motioning toward a fair woman moving in rhythm to the music, remarks that "you can always tell" when someone is really "coloured" by the way they react to the beat of the bongos, and the direction does not contradict this assumption the way it does so many other pernicious clichés in the film. As one contemporary reviewer astutely noted:

> [A]n unprejudiced observer will be surprised to find no evidence that Janet Green, who wrote the screenplay, questions certain misconceptions such as that the murdered girl owes to her racial background rather than her individual taste or lack of it a disposition to wear flamboyant underclothes under "sensible" British tweeds or to respond instinctively to bongos.[69]

This, combined with the film's distinctly ambivalent portrayal of Sapphire and her pregnancy, dulls the effectiveness of the liberal message.

The shakiness of *Sapphire*'s moral message is also implicit in Dr. Robbins's characterization. As noted above, Cameron imbued this role with a greater strength and confidence than he did *Pool of London*'s Johnny. This is only possible, however, because his moral fiber is unimpeachable, and clearly superior to the Harrises. He is, in fact, Frantz Fanon's "Negro doctor," the successful black professional held to impossible standards: "As long as everything went well, he was praised to the skies, but look out, no nonsense, under any conditions!"[70] Cameron's Dr. Robbins is all gravitas.

Sapphire was very much of its time insofar as it presented white racism in Britain as an individual, moral problem, and not an official or systemic weakness. The film was not so much about the black community it portrays as about the Harris family and the dark prejudices they harbor. Thus,

68 Marcia Landy, *British Genres: Cinema and Society, 1930–1960* (Princeton: Princeton University Press, 1991), 437.
69 Paul V. Beckley, "Sapphire," *Tribune* (November 3, 1959), JG/8/6, Janet Green Collection, Special Collections, BFI.
70 Frantz Fanon, *Black Skin, White Masks* (New York: Grove Press, 1967), 117.

although it showed a wider range of non-white characters and settings than *Pool of London*, it retained a basically white focus; it is Mildred's—the killer's—struggle that we are shown, not Dr. Robbins's, and certainly not Sapphire's. This preoccupation with the white domestic conflict is perhaps more disappointing because Inspector Learoyd's character creates an opening for the film to explore the institutional aspects of British racism, in this case within law enforcement. By 1960 speculation of police complicity in violence against minorities and colonial settlers was already rife within Britain's urban neighborhoods, and it would seem that Learoyd's presence in *Sapphire* is a brave acknowledgement of this. Ultimately, however, Learoyd's prejudice is pictured as merely a personal problem that exists in stark juxtaposition to Superintendent Hazard's own even-handedness. Moreover, Learoyd himself is reformed by the film's end, a development that suggests, again, that his frailties are his own, and not engendered by the institutional racism of the police itself.

Another avenue by which the taint of racial discrimination within British officialdom might have been illuminated was also closed in a later revision of the shooting script. Originally, the final scene occurred not within the walls of the Harris home, but in a courtroom where Mildred is being sentenced, presumably for manslaughter. The jury takes only twenty minutes to deliberate her case, and she receives just five years in prison.[71] The leniency of the sentence makes one wonder again whether the viewer's sympathy is meant to lie with Sapphire Robbins or Mildred Harris. At any rate, including the scene would have conjured still more questions about the existence and danger of racism in official quarters; this was perhaps one of the reasons it was cut. Ending the film within the bosom of the Harris family reaffirms the film's overall suggestion that prejudice is borne of individual weakness and ignorance, and is exacerbated by seemingly unrelated emotional conflict.

In this respect, just like *Pool of London*, the film offered no possible resolution to the problem of British racism beyond perhaps the gradual education of the population into non-racialist patterns of thinking. This is confirmed by *Sapphire*'s concluding exchange between Hazard, Learoyd, and Dr. Robbins:

[Hazard:] We haven't given you very much to take back, have we, Doctor?

[Dr. Robbins:] No. But then I see all kinds of sickness in my practice, Superintendent. I've never yet seen the kind you can cure in a day.

[Learoyd:] Cases don't get solved without somebody getting hurt, you know that.

---

71 See JG/8/1, Box 5, Janet Green Collection, Special Collections, BFI.

[Hazard:]　　　We didn't solve anything, Phil. We just picked up the pieces.

Racial prejudice is here posed as a deeply personal, albeit widespread, "sickness" that presumably attacks either those individuals most mentally or emotionally vulnerable, or those who are simply ignorant. Mildred, the abandoned mother, is the most extreme example of the former, while Learoyd, who quickly wises up, is an example of the latter. The fact that *Sapphire* does not explore the possible systemic dimensions of British racism should not be viewed, however, as a sign of its fundamental conservatism. In 1959, the majority of so-called "liberals" or "progressives," black and white, still felt that racism, at least the overtly hostile variety, was the province of the two categories of persons mentioned above. The attitude was that little could be done about the small, unbalanced minority who perpetrated acts of violence and abuse, but that the much larger, uneducated group could be enlightened over time. *Sapphire*, in fact, can be read as an effort to do just that, particularly with the sharp distinction it draws between "rational" and "irrational" responses to London's black settlers.

Finally, what is most striking about *Sapphire* from the perspective of this study is its total failure to acknowledge the imperial dimensions of British race relations at the close of the 1950s. The audience learns almost nothing about the personal histories of the non-white characters (i.e., whether they are British-born, or have migrated from British colonies, or from elsewhere), and they all have an English accent. Only one very minor character, a young woman from the International Club, remarks to Hazard that although she is studying child welfare, she "shan't bother with it." When Hazard asks why, she replies, "I want to get married, stay here. I like the English." This indicates that she is in fact an international student who has made plans to settle in England permanently, but, along with Paul Slade's unsympathetic appearance, this is one of the film's few glimpses of the migrant experience, and it remains detached from the central characters and storyline.

That *Sapphire* is a film about race relations, but decidedly not about immigration or empire, is initially puzzling, especially as the recent Notting Hill violence had done much to put the issue of curbing non-white imperial migration on the table. Indeed, only two years later, agitation had grown to such a pitch that the first Commonwealth Immigrants Bill was passed. One would expect a film with such liberal intentions to take care to emphasize the shared bond of empire among the black and white players; as argued elsewhere in this study, it was precisely this strategy that West Indian artists adopted in an effort to make a place for themselves in the world of British arts and entertainment. Yet, in order to frame the race relations narrative within a personal, white, domestic (in both senses of the word) rubric and keep the melodrama tight and contained, *Sapphire*'s creative producers removed from view the history of imperial relations leading up to postwar migration and settlement. If they had not, the explanation for British prejudice would extend far beyond the parameters of the ignorant individual or the troubled English home, and call forth uncomfortable questions about Britain's historical—and current—relationship to its colonies at a time when the British Commonwealth and empire were meant to be evolving into an enlightened partnership among equals. Viewed in this light, the severance between domestic racism and its imperial implications facilitated the production of a tidier film, one that would not alienate mainstream viewers by disrupting their claims to the moral high ground on the issue of race relations.

Flame in the Streets

Roy Ward Baker's 1961 melodrama *Flame in the Streets* was the most sensationalist, but in many ways the most radical, treatment of the race relations narrative to come out of mainstream British cinema in this period. More than its predecessors examined above, it harshly interrogated the racial anxieties of "ordinary" Britons, both economic and sexual. More importantly, it did so partly through the voices of its black characters, who had evolved into more assertive and self-reliant folks in the two years since the release of *Sapphire*. Nevertheless, despite its more active and thorough engagement with the "world" of London's black settlers, *Flame in the Streets* still adhered to the central tenets of the narrative set out in *Pool of London*: a dramatic conflict revolving around apparently ordinary but actually vulnerable white folks, usually in a domestic setting; a fundamental investigation not of black communities, nor even predominantly of black-white relations, but of white racism; and an implicit assumption that the most subversive consequence of non-white settlement in Britain, for both the film's characters and its audience, is the threat of miscegenation.

The film ultimately had trouble negotiating the boundaries among consensual Ealing-style liberalism, progressive social documentation, and sensationalism. A ninety-page information booklet compiled by the studio explained that

> [*Flame*] does not produce a nice neat solution to this problem. It shows the arguments on both sides. It shows parents who face either the loss of their daughter or the addition of a negro to their family circle. It shows ordinary people grappling with a problem that has no immediate solution. And these are not unreal people created for cinema entertainment.

This measured summary only appears on page 66, however. The introductory synopsis proclaims:

> A flame sears through the streets of London—a flame kindled by hatred. Men hurl abuse at other men and sometimes they hurl more than words.

There is violence, bitterness and fear. The flame is ugly—its name is prejudice.

And the words too are harsh and ugly. They are whispered at street corners, shouted at a retreating back, screamed as fist meets flesh— "Spade!", "Nigger!"[72]

One glowing review tried hard to stress the film's direct but tasteful treatment of interracial romance—"Instead of coyly skirting round the physical attraction ... it brings it out into the open—though without over-stressing it sensationally"—but concludes with the rhetorical, "what better exploitation angle could you ask for?"[73] As this confusing appraisal suggests, *Flame in the Streets* challenged and upheld Britain's racial *status quo* in similar measure.

Like so many of the movies, teleplays, and documentary programs of the 1950s and 1960s, *Flame in the Streets* asked the question, "What would *you* do if your daughter wanted to marry a Negro?" (it was in fact adapted from the ITV television drama *Hot Summer Night*, which aired the previous year.) It tells the story of an active and committed trade unionist, Jacko Palmer, who prides himself on, among other things, his belief in the fair and unbiased treatment of all workers, regardless of race—early in the film he persuades an ambivalent union to vote for a capable West Indian, Gabriel Gomez, as a factory chargehand. Only moments later, he learns from his panicked wife that his daughter Kathie is engaged to another West Indian, Peter Lincoln. He is unsettled by this news, but his wife Nell reacts hysterically; like Mildred in *Sapphire*, it is the female characters in *Flame in the Streets* who feel the threat to domestic stability most keenly. The story provides a starkly revealing picture of Jacko's home life and failings as a husband, and glimpses at the harsh domestic fortunes of interracial couples.

Earl Cameron stars yet again as Gabriel Gomez, "a hard-working negro known to his mates as 'Gabe,'" and again this character is the quiet, dignified type that Cameron had perfected in film and on television. He is gentle and well-liked by his peers, but, like Johnny and (to an extent) Dr. Robbins before him, Gabe is extremely non-confrontational, to the point where he means not to attend the union meeting at which his promotion will be determined; again, it is a white man, Jacko, who pushes for his advancement. But in *Flame in the Streets*, Gabe's stoicism and meekness are not portrayed in a wholly favorable light. Rather, his wife Judy, who is white, berates him for not standing up for himself and his achievements, and it is her passion that eventually persuades him to show up—late—to the union meeting. Gabe's quiet acceptance of his situation and treatment

---

72 *Flame in the Streets* information booklet, 5, 66, Special Collections, BFI.
73 Review of *Flame in the Streets*, *The Daily Cinema* 8466 (June 2, 1961), 7.

Ann Lynn and Earl Cameron as Judy and Gabe Gomez in *Flame in the
Streets*, 1961. © Everett Collection/REX Shutterstock 2015.

are now represented less as a sign of dignity, and more a sign of weakness;
in fact, he is almost an anachronism, as the British Film Institute notes in
its summary of the film: "Rather than seize his opportunity, [Gabe] would
prefer others decided his fate. To a large extent, this perception of West
Indians died with the Notting Hill Riots."[74]

By the time Teddy Boy-inspired racial violence flares up on Guy
Fawkes Night, at the end of the film, Gabe has learned that there are times
when he must show solidarity with other black people and face the fight.
Likewise, Peter Lincoln comes to the aid of Jubilee, his exploitative black
landlord, when the latter faces attack from white hooligans. Race pride
has finally entered the cinematic frame, and not unsympathetically. When
Pool of London, *Sapphire*, and *Flame in the Streets* are taken together,
one can trace the evolution of Earl Cameron's cinematic type from a

74 "Flame in the Streets (1961)," http://www.screenonline.org.uk/film/id/475471/index.
    html; accessed July 6, 2006. In 1964 Cameron would leave meek characters like
    Gabe behind with his portrayal of a cool, mustachioed jazz musician accused of
    murdering a white lover in ATV's *A Fear of Strangers*.

naïve, even helpless, outsider to a soft-spoken but independent citizen who harbors no illusions about the prejudices of the society of which he is an active part.

The fortunes of Gabe and Judy illustrate the fate of two respectable people in a mixed marriage. In Gabe, the viewer sees the unfair attitudes of his coworkers despite his proven abilities. In his marriage, we see the residential discrimination that afflicts non-white people and those who live with them. And in Judy, we see the alienation of English women who choose to marry outside their race, ultimately belonging to neither community. As the script summary describes, Judy laments "how difficult marriage is when the partners have different coloured skins, how you are shunned by your 'friends.'"

The real drama occurs within Kathie's family, and in particular between Jacko and Nell; it is *their* relationship, not Kathie and Peter's, that is truly the subject of the film's exploration. Jacko, upon hearing of Kathie's decision to marry Peter, thinks first of how "this problem is now about to affect his own family," while Nell displays a virulent, knee-jerk prejudice. When she realizes with horror that Kathie will eventually bear mixed-race children, she implores, "Kathie! You don't know how they live. Like animals. Have you seen them? Six, eight, ten to a room. Is that how you want to end up? In one room with a horde of black children?" When Kathie, appalled, prepares to leave, her mother continues:

> You can't wait, can you? You're no better than the whores in the high street. You can't wait to be with him, that's the truth. All you want is one thing. … Go with him, then! Make your bed and lie on it! Go to your nigger! Go to your nigger!

This blatant display of meanness and sexual jealousy is all the more jarring against Kathie's deliberate sweetness—there is no hint that Kathie is anything less than a virtuous and respectable young lady. But the outburst also allows the audience to understand Nell's motivations. She is not simply attempting to preserve a family life she feels to be threatened by the social effects of a mixed-race marriage, she is revealing the emptiness of her own marriage to a workaholic; at one point she accuses her husband of making love to her "as if you were taking a quick drink." Jacko, astonished at this revelation, feels he must try to patch up his fraying domestic world by convincing the two young lovers not to marry.

Thus the interracial relationship, apparently the focus of the film, is in fact only a vehicle to provoke, expose, and eventually mend the fault lines of the white British family. A Rank Viewers' Report for *Flame* inadvertently makes this clear. In response to the increased sensitivity of the portrayal of the racial aspects of the drama, it comments only that the "supporting Jamaican types and the young white thugs, too, are realistically drawn, while a Guy Fawkes's night bonfire contributes to a sizzling climax."[75] Largely staying true to the genre of the social problem film, then, the social message is exploited for its commercial potential, while the crux of the emotional story remains the white family.

Despite the continuities between *Flame in the Streets* and its predecessors, and despite its sensationalist treatment of both Jacko and Nell's domestic troubles and the race question, the film demonstrates a surprising subtlety of feeling and attitude in its characters that was new for mainstream representations of the race relations narrative in Britain. This revealed itself to best effect in the penultimate scene when Peter responds angrily and forcefully to Jacko's advice against the proposed union with Kathie:

> Do you think I'm a fool, an ignorant man? Why do you talk to me like this? "There's the door," you say, "Find yourself a black girl," you say. Why do you talk to me like this? Only one reason, the old reason, this! [He holds up his hand.] This skin! Click, click, words out like bullets, don't say anything you black bastard, we don't want you in this family, get out! ... No! In other countries they have better ways. There they tell you: "Keep off, nigger, walk in the gutter, nigger." Signs up all the time. But here there's no signs, but we can tell. You smile at us never with the eyes, only with the mouth.

Jacko is abashed but calls Peter out on his own prejudices and suspicions about white people, arguing that despite his love and best intentions, Peter "might not be able to stop" Kathie from coming to harm, socially and economically.

It is significant that no clear "winner" emerges from this verbal sparring, neither in the movie itself nor in the audience's sympathies. Since both men are acting out of love for Kathie (this becomes clear in Peter's case despite his initial anger), the film does not delineate between "right" and "wrong" attitudes or "good" and "bad" individuals. This is an imaginative leap from *Sapphire*, filmed only two years prior, in which Mildred's prejudices render her mentally unstable, the troubled villain, and Inspector Hazard's careful even-handedness remains unchallenged, the perfect good guy. No such easy divisions appear in *Flame in the Streets*. In fact, the argument between Peter and Jacko was likely meant to serve at least two purposes. First, it captured, in a nutshell, the contemporary debate over miscegenation in Britain. Jacko became the mouthpiece for "ordinary" white Britons who did not consider themselves prejudiced—but retained serious misgivings about mixed marriages, especially within their own families. Second, the argument served to introduced a new element into the race relations narrative: justifiable black anger. Peter was a new character, at least as far

---

75 Rank Viewers' Report for *Flame in the Streets*, dated "trade shown" May 31, 1961, Special Collections, BFI.

as mainstream British film was concerned, although as we will see in the next chapter, he had his precursors in more cutting-edge drama from Barry Reckord and others.

Even Earl Cameron, widely recognized for the highly controlled, dignified, and fundamentally good characters he played, had his chance to play a righteous and angry man, in ATV's 1964 drama *A Fear of Strangers*.[76] This live production takes place almost entirely in a police interrogation room in Manchester, where jazz saxophonist Ramsay (played by Cameron) has been brought in for questioning by the obviously bigoted Chief Inspector Dyke. Unlike Cameron's roles in *Pool of London*, *A Man From the Sun*, *Sapphire*, and *Flame in the Streets*, Ramsay is not perfect. He lies to the police under interrogation, almost flaunts his brief fling with the murder victim, and doesn't work hard enough to exonerate himself. His behavior easily convinces Inspector Dyke that he is guilty, but of course he is not, and the usually insouciant Ramsay offers up a few moments of angry indignation that, because it is Cameron, still come across as justified.

A Fear of Strangers was actually written in 1958, making it contemporaneous with *Sapphire*, but the script was banned for six years on account of the police's abuse of Ramsay:

> The ban is curious, because it's difficult to be certain whether it reflected concern about compromising the integrity of police methods, or concern about the offence the racial abuse might cause to black viewers. One doesn't have to be a cynic to suspect that the former rationale carried the day.[77]

The combination of a reckless and racist policeman and a Caribbean protagonist who refuses to ingratiate himself with white viewers was apparently too much for the Independent Television Authority to stomach, and indeed its characterization is more extreme than *Flame in the Streets*, released the same year. Nonetheless, *A Fear of Strangers* still fits the mold of the race relations narrative, for its liberal message—along the lines of "don't judge a book by its cover"—is clear. In addition, like Mildred Harris and Nell Palmer, Inspector Dyke's psychological racism is explained away by a traumatic experience from his past: humiliation in the ranks of the Indian Army.

Like *Pool of London* and *Sapphire* before it, *Flame*, due to its domestic focus, offered no real resolution to the question of race relations because those characters who express the ugliest racist sentiments are actually

---

76 Herbert Wise, dir., "Drama '64: *A Fear of Strangers*" (ATV, May 10, 1964). National Film and Television Archive, BFI, London.

77 "A Fear of Strangers," *BFI Screenonline*: http://www.screenonline.org.uk/tv/id/501620/; accessed September 28, 2015.

giving vent to their own emotional traumas, unrelated to whatever race drama triggers them. Like *Sapphire*'s Mildred, Nell Palmer is an abandoned wife of sorts who views her daughter's controversial engagement as a threat to the integrity of what family she has left. Thus racial prejudice is presented as a symptom of unrelated problems with which the white characters are struggling. Such a presentation offers no fruitful strategy for ameliorating racial strife, because it ignores larger social or political forces. That the social problem is resolved in *none* of these films is a damning verdict on mainstream, "liberal" attitudes to the question of race and immigration in Britain at the time.

Interestingly enough, the studio's extensive information booklet, which was presumably used to provide copy for promotional materials, included several quotations from the film's lead black actors, Johnny Sekka and Cameron, that implicitly support the film's non-systemic approach to British racism. Both actors, in their published comments, professed an aversion for the politics of race. Sekka lamented the lack of voice offered to black characters in British drama, but then declared himself "sick of talking about" the "colour question." "And as for the question of mixed marriage," he added, "if you love someone you don't care if they are black, white or sky blue pink. You just love them."[78] He gave the impression that racism and its opposite were essentially functions of individual impulse, and shied away from larger societal explanations. Cameron, notwithstanding his position as perhaps the most visible representative of the "color question" in the country, also set himself apart from politics:

> Personally I am not a crusader. I have no time to worry about slights either imaginary or real. I want to get on with living and the things I enjoy most—acting, playing tennis and travelling. ... Frankly politics bore me. I take the world as I find it—as it affects me. Like most people I don't want to get involved in big issues. Things are as they are. Each person can do his or her level best to alter what affects them personally. But the world will not change overnight.

In these comments there is more than a touch of the high-minded placidity so visible in the characters Cameron portrayed onscreen, but this does not mean they were disingenuous. His remark—"I do not think of any marriage as being mixed. It is a marriage and the people who say that miscegenation should not happen do not annoy me. I regret their shortcomings"—is all the more powerful considering that Cameron had married a white Englishwoman only four years before.[79] It was, of course, no accident that his moderate, liberal, *laissez-faire* remarks made it into the booklet. In

---

78 *Flame in the Streets* information booklet, 39.
79 *Flame in the Streets* information booklet, 30–32.

drawing on the remarks of black actors like Sekka and Cameron, the film's promoters lent credence to the film's personal, psychological presentation of racial prejudice in Britain.

Flame in the Streets ends with Jacko, Peter, and Kathie returning home together to face the hysterical Nell, while Guy Fawkes bonfires and racial violence (in which Gabe is participating) rage in the background. Raymond Durgnat was unsatisfied with such an approach to the social problem of racism: "Of course we're all against thugs pushing people into bonfires; but the case for Liberalism is lost if it has to equate race prejudice with this."[80] And, indeed, the real tragedy of *Flame in the Streets*, the quality that makes it a sensationalist melodrama rather than a substantial social critique, is its refusal to look beyond the realm of its characters' personal fears and insecurities, however carefully articulated.

Ten Bob in Winter

As illustrated above, over time mainstream engagement with the subject of race developed a narrative structure and common themes that recurred in different ways over the years. Although their treatment of particular character types and attitudes evolved over the same period—for example, the representation of black pride or righteous aggression—certain themes remained remarkably static. Common to both film and television productions was the use of the interracial romance as a vehicle to dramatize domestic white neurosis and conflict; the presence of a virtuous black male hero (who may or may not be in the role of the would-be lover) and at least one irrational white racist; and a voyeuristic orientation toward the "colored" spaces of London, for example jazz bars, gambling dens, and run-down tenement buildings. Lloyd Reckord, as discussed in the introduction to this chapter, was a visible player in the race relations narrative as it ran its course on stage, television, and in cinemas. In a 1991 interview he recalled:

> I was usually cast as a nice young West Indian in love with an English girl. I usually got beaten up by teddy boys, or quarrelled violently with the girl's parents, or some other similar situation. I must have done about six of these plays [in just over a year], and I was becoming rather suspicious and tired of the stereotyped role. But then it petered out.[81]

Lloyd Reckord's short films *Ten Bob in Winter* (1963) and *Dream A40* (1965) did not overturn or contest the thematic or narrative tendencies that he found so tiresome, nor did they challenge white, mainstream

---

80 Durgnat, *A Mirror for England*, 62.
81 Interview with Lloyd Reckord, in Pines, *Black and White in Colour*, 54.

representations of race relations or racism in Britain. What is intriguing is the fact that they did not engage *at all* with these provocative issues, which is a tantalizing suggestion of how far the cinematic priorities of white British filmmakers and audiences might have differed from those of the West Indian community. Of course, it would be unwise to allow two short films to speak for the sensibilities of an entire artistic community, but it is nonetheless suggestive of important differences in perspective, especially considering that Reckord's first work was centrally concerned with race relations and the personal motivations behind race prejudice.

Ten Bob in Winter, a black-and-white short narrated in the first person, was financed in part by the British Film Institute and featured a score by black British jazz musician Joe Harriott. It follows one man, a black man, through the streets of London, after he borrows ten shillings and then attempts to recoup that same amount from an acquaintance. This friend, a musician, must in turn procure the money from a local pawn shop. While the friend is inside negotiating with the shop owner, the first man waits outside uncomfortably, slightly embarrassed to be seen in front of such an establishment. His embarrassment increases as he encounters a third acquaintance, light-skinned and wealthy, who treats him with a certain amount of contempt and disdain. But our protagonist persists in his efforts to impress this man, and his actions backfire when he willfully ignores his—much darker-skinned—musician friend who emerges from the shop and attempts to hand over the ten shillings. Both men eventually depart, and the central character curses himself for both his toadying behavior and his resultant financial mess. In the end, however, the poor musician returns the money despite the fact that he was snubbed, demonstrating his superior dignity and maturity.

Ten Bob in Winter was, then, vitally concerned with the social politics of skin color in London, but from a decidedly non-white perspective, and in several ways a West Indian perspective. This is not only because Lloyd Reckord himself was Jamaican, but also because the film's main character is so aware of gradations of skin color, an issue that had less visibility and weight in Britain, and even Africa, than it did in the Caribbean (and especially Jamaica). Although the production was set in London, the few white individuals to appear do so briefly; they are looking for a day's work, like the protagonist, but when the employer states that he only needs two men (there are three), the protagonist allows the other two men to take the work, in exchange for a loan of the ten bob of the title from one of the white men. But they are peripheral to the true action of the story, and in this scene interracial tensions and politics are absent (a situation that would be rare in a mainstream British film dealing with race, in which prejudice lurks around every corner).

What emerges out of the production is a different race relations narrative, one in which native white Britons do not figure (except, perhaps, as off-screen members of a social system that privileges lightness over darkness). In this narrative, racial prejudice certainly exists, and it manifests itself in a few ways. For instance, not only does the socially mobile, light-skinned man smirk at the protagonist, contemptuous of his attentions, but the latter accepts such treatment, and goes out of his way (unsuccessfully) to earn favor, at the expense of his worthier but dark-skinned companion—the only one of the three who does not alter his actions according to prevailing prejudices.

However, a purely racial explanation of the social dynamics of *Ten Bob* is too reductive; as Barbara Korte and Claudia Sternberg have pointed out in their study of black and Asian film in Britain, "The film's central concern is not race- but class-related."[82] Indeed, each of the three individuals is defined at least as much, if not more, by their apparent economic status than by their skin color. His profession alone would likely position the musician nearer the bottom of the social scale, and he is least self-conscious about depending on the pawn shop as a part of his financial planning. The protagonist exists somewhere in between the musician and the well-dressed gentleman and is clearly uncomfortable with this position. He would like to fancy himself above the former but realizes that he is not only indefi-nitely unemployed, but that he too operates on borrowed cash. It is this that he is so unwilling to reveal to the second man. Thus, although skin color acts to a certain extent as a signifier, it intersects in important ways with questions of class and status. (In fact, the struggle of *Ten Bob*'s hero is reminiscent of the historical struggle of the emblematic lower middle-class Briton, the Leonard Bast figure who desperately clings to respectable status but is never secure enough to be convincing.)[83] Although it is possible to see some of the same intersections in more mainstream productions, especially with some of the characters in *Sapphire*, their significance is less explicit and less important; whatever the economic distinctions among the characters, they are far less influential than their *perceived* race, their whiteness or non-whiteness—not their actual skin color. In other words, in *Ten Bob in Winter*, racial distinctions are finer and more loaded, and economic appearances much more vital, than in mainstream cinematic productions in Britain.

Ten Bob in Winter was well received on the whole, and it made the rounds of various film festivals in Britain. The next year, Reckord wrote a very different script for another short film entitled *Dream A40*, which he produced and released in 1965 (and which starred David Hemmings, the young English actor who had appeared in Barry Reckord's play *Skyvers* at the Royal Court, and who came to fame a year later as the swinging fashion photographer in Michelangelo Antonioni's *Blow-Up*). *Dream A40* was less linear as a narrative than *Ten Bob in Winter*; it was a more avant-garde

---

82 Korte and Sternberg, *Bidding for the Mainstream?*, 55.
83 E. M. Forster, *Howards End* (London: Edward Arnold, 1910).

production with a homoerotic subject that placed it beyond the pale of mainstream exhibition, although, according to Reckord, "the few reviews it got were quite good":

> Some people were not so excited when they read the script for *Dream A40*, because it had to do with a relationship between two young men which was sort of sexual. Sex wasn't brought obviously into it, but certain people were scared, I think, because of the homosexual theme. They certainly didn't dare show it.[84]

It is an obvious point, but both of Reckord's short films, produced on his own initiative, were entirely unconcerned with the race angle that larger British companies for film and television were peddling, and with which they had pigeonholed Reckord as an actor. As he has noted, Reckord did not expect these films to bring him notoriety, but he hoped that they would act as proof of his initiative and potential as a director; he wanted the chance to direct for television, but this did not materialize: "They fobbed me off with comments like 'Well, a film is all very well and good. But a television play, now that's different, you see, that takes a different intelligence.'" Reckord eventually returned permanently to Jamaica in 1968, where he founded the National Theatre Trust: "I'd had enough."[85] He had tried strenuously to prove himself as an actor and budding director, and to escape the limited professional role that had brought him his initial success—the black lover in the classic race relations narrative. In this his aims were frustrated.

Conclusion

This chapter has tried to demonstrate the important role played by West Indian artists and the phenomenon of West Indian settlement in the history of mainstream British film in the 1950s and early 1960s, and specifically in the development of a distinctive race relations narrative that found expression in literature, theater, radio, and television, as well as film. Moreover, the examination of three major films in the genre suggests that when these productions are viewed in chronological order, one can identify an evolution. Critics, usually analyzing a single work, have often been struck most forcefully by the one-dimensional, stereotypical portrayal of non-white figures in the story, and the persistence of the themes of racial and sexual trespass and taboo so characteristic of prewar race narratives in Europe, America, and the British Empire. Such a perspective is not inaccurate, but it is partly misleading in that it ignores the fact that these

---

84 Interview with Reckord, in Pines, *Black and White in Colour*, 54.
85 Ibid., 55.

characters, and their relationships with the white individuals with whom they come into contact, become increasingly independent, socially aware, and assertive—a response to the changing social situation "in the streets" of London, and the growing sensitivity of British audiences to the debate about immigration and race. Over the course of the 1950s and 1960s, British audiences became well-versed in the race relations narrative as a genre, and thus received a particular liberal education on the subject, with all its inconsistencies and buried assumptions.

It is also important to remember that it was West Indian actors, and Earl Cameron especially, who gave shape and humanity to characters that, on paper, were often shallower than the white protagonists. Their motivations, and the motivations of their white counterparts, come under much heavier interrogation in *Sapphire* than in *Pool of London*, and more so again in *Flame in the Streets*, although this undoubtedly came at the price of greater sensationalism. This development suggests the growing salience and sophistication of the race relations/immigration debate in British society at large.

I have also, however, tried to show the limits of any thematic radicalization in mainstream British film. However earnestly creative producers like Relph and Dearden, Roy Ward Baker, Janet Green, and Ted Willis grappled with the possible ramifications of British racism, the neurosis of white prejudice remained their main object of enquiry, while the priorities of people of color were ignored, or assumed to be the same. In fact, as Lloyd Reckord's *Ten Bob in Winter* shows, the race relations narrative could take on a dramatically different form, while remaining authentically situated in the English metropolis. Efforts like Reckord's, in a small way, added depth to the representation of West Indians in multiracial London. The productions of his brother Barry did the same in the realm of theater, the subject of the next chapter.

Chapter 6

Barry Reckord,
the Race Relations Narrative,
and the Royal Court Theatre

This chapter's subject is Jamaican playwright Barry Reckord. Despite their current obscurity in the historical canon, Reckord's plays deserve visibility within the history of postwar British theater for at least two reasons. First, they mark one early postwar instance of a fruitful, creative relationship between a West Indian artist settled in London and an influential British cultural institution. Reckord's plays are best evaluated not simply as "West Indian" drama, but as a part of the Royal Court's tradition of socially aware alternative theater. Reckord's desire to create drama that tackled the thorny issues of colonialism, race identity, and repression dovetailed with the Royal Court's own mandate to produce fresh, topical, and challenging British plays. This shared mandate allowed Reckord to create a complex picture of West Indian migration and race prejudice that took into account the effects of British imperialism, social conditions, and especially class identity. It also allowed him to position the issue of migration and racism not as a special, foreign "problem," but as just one element in a matrix of domestic British ills.

Secondly, Reckord's work engaged with, and contested, two of the era's defining dramatic themes and narratives: the dominant "race relations" narrative of racial transgression and domestic neurosis, discussed in the previous chapter on postwar film; and what was perhaps the Royal Court's most cherished subject and aesthetic, working-class social realism or the "kitchen sink" drama. Both of these themes were, in large part, the creations of white, British-born writers and producers. Reckord used his own distinctive perspective not to reject them as a framework for his plays, but to reshape them. In the process, he expanded the scope, texture, and subtlety of the Royal Court's *oeuvre*. Reckord's plays in this sense encourage a re-evaluation of the postwar British theater story. It was, to be sure, a story about representing new class identities and engaging frankly with the dilemmas of postwar society, but Reckord's plays show that London's West Indian settlers and, indeed, the West Indies themselves, were active shapers of that story as well. In other words, Reckord understood that questions of class were also questions of race.

Barry Reckord wrote five plays for the Royal Court between 1958 and 1974 on wildly different topics, but each one resonated in some way with that theater's penchant for the radical, the political, and the subversive. The three that fall within the purview of this study each criticized a facet of the British social or political *status quo*. *Flesh to a Tiger*, although set entirely in an impoverished Jamaica balm yard, was a decidedly unromantic (and, one could argue, elitist) look at the effects of racial stratification and European imperialism on the sensibilities of ordinary West Indians. *You in Your Small Corner* (1960) also explored racism, but this time in a metropolitan context that both imitated and challenged the parameters of the dominant and familiar British race relations narrative. Reckord's third and most successful play for the Royal Court, *Skyvers* (1963), took critical aim at the British education system by focusing on one student's merciless discouragement by his teachers and his peers. Taken as a whole, these plays represented a challenge to the dominance of the race relations narrative in British drama.

Each of these plays was resolutely contemporary in subject and setting; in the context of their production by the English Stage Company, they made transparent Reckord's political, rather than aesthetic, motivation. As he summed up years later, "The whole point is that you have ideas, you have something you want to say about something and you invent the characters and the dialogue and the plot that's going to help you say this."[1] Some of the Royal Court's most celebrated playwrights had a similar attitude toward writing for the theater, one that transformed postwar British theater into a place where the old certainties of the class, gender, and generational order were subjected to unflinching reappraisal. This chapter historicizes Reckord's first three plays for the Royal Court in the context of the English Stage Company's penchant for issue-based social realism and the existing narrative of race relations (discussed in the previous chapter) circulating in television and film. The Company actually produced six of Reckord's plays, but the last three, *A Liberated Woman* (1970), *Give the Gaffers Time to Love You* (1973), and *X* (1974), reflect a very different historical moment in British drama and fall outside the frame of this study. Finally, a word should be said about my evaluation of the "success"—or lack thereof—of Reckord's plays: I am talking here of *critical*, not commercial, success. Of the three, only *Skyvers* garnered a modest profit for the Royal Court during its initial run.[2] This, however, was the norm for Royal Court productions;

---

1   Barry Reckord in conversation with David Johnson, April 22, 1997.
2   The box office details for *Flesh to a Tiger*: twenty-nine performances, 22% seats,

English Stage Company manager George Devine complained that "except for obvious successes," "far more people in London support the English Stage Company as an idea rather than buy seats at the box office."[3]

That may have been so, but the Company, and its house at the Royal Court, was a force to be reckoned with from the 1950s. It was a pioneer in more ways than one. The Royal Court is most famous, of course, for producing the work of unknown playwrights and tackling contemporary British themes, for being a writer's theater, and for acting on the belief that theater is an "essential part of society, a major educative force, a potential agent of political change, a temple of ideas and a cultural necessity."[4] It was a lightning rod of reaction to the lightweight drawing room fare that had dominated London theater for decades.

But, whatever its box office receipts, the Court was also a major player in the redefinition of mainstream theater in postwar Britain. While in the immediate postwar era theater operators perpetuated the star system of dramatic acting and were largely resistant to innovation, the success of *Look Back in Anger* established the Royal Court "as a major venue for new writing and, furthermore, a venue that learnt from the outset the necessity of transferring production into the commercial theatre in order to survive economically."[5] Crucially, its fresh vision of the purpose of theater—that it could be a challenging, educative force for mainstream audiences—had the approbation and concrete support of the state in the form of substantial Arts Council funding. In the 1950s and early 1960s, this ranged from between five and eight thousand pounds a year.[6] This annual subsidy alone placed the Royal Court firmly within the new theatrical mainstream, despite its reputation for daring productions. In short, the Court enjoyed both a cutting-edge reputation and mainstream visibility. By 1962 the English Stage Company and its theater were a force to be reckoned with, with a recognizable pedigree and a committed direction for the future.

The Court was in this respect an ideal incubator for the dramatic work of Barry Reckord. Born Barrington John Reckord in Kingston, Jamaica,

---

15% box office, production cost £2,783, box office takings £1,196. *Skyvers*: twenty-two performances, 33.5% seats, 22.5% box office, production cost £1,422, box office takings £1,710. (No data are available for *You in Your Small Corner*.)

3 George Devine, *English Stage Company*, quoted in Marcus Tschudin, *A Writer's Theatre: George Devine and the English Stage Company at the Royal Court 1956–1965* (Bern and Frankfurt: Herbert Lang and Company Limited, 1972), 63.

4 Richard Findlater, ed., *At the Royal Court: 25 Years of the English Stage Company* (Ambergate: Amber Lane Press Limited, 1981), 10.

5 John Bull, "The Establishment of Mainstream Theatre, 1946–1979," in Baz Kershaw, ed., *The Cambridge History of British Theatre, Volume 3: Since 1895* (Cambridge: Cambridge University Press, 2004), 336.

6 Ruth Little and Emily McLaughlin, *The Royal Court Theatre Inside Out* (London: Oberon Books, 2007), footnote, 455.

in November 1926, he was in some sense an archetype of those early postwar settlers whose migration was a result of intelligence, talent, and great ambition. His longtime partner and friend, editor Diana Athill, wrote in her memoirs that "Barry, having been educated by English schoolmasters at his Jamaican school and by English dons at Cambridge, used sometimes to say that his fellow Jamaicans saw him as 'a small, square, brown Englishman.'"[7] He was born into a middle-class family and received a middle-class education, distinguishing himself as an unusually gifted student at Kingston College and later St. Peter's College, where he studied theology—a pursuit that likely fueled the ideas behind his first play, *Della*. He won Jamaica's Issa Scholarship in 1950, which funded his first migration to England and his university education at Emmanuel College, Cambridge.

Reckord's attitude toward his early education in Jamaica appears to have been ambivalent; he was an intellectual at heart, something that his education certainly fostered, but he was frustrated with the content of his English-style education, and once stated that he turned to dramatic writing in England as a way to draw attention to problems relevant to modern society: "I was at school writing a play in iambic pentameters about William of Orange, a most extraordinary thing to do ... Imagine a Jamaican schoolboy bothering with that."[8] There are moments, looking over Reckord's observations in interviews, when it seems that he became a playwright almost by accident. By most accounts, it was not he, but a friend at Cambridge who first submitted *Della* to the Royal Court for consideration:

> I had no background in theatre. The only theatre that I knew in Jamaica I was fairly contemptuous of ... it was either English pantomime where I dressed up and played the lion and was ashamed of myself or it was ... Bim and Bam, which was broad slapstick, not very funny, except when it was very rude Jamaican comedy ... I knew a little bit of both those worlds but neither of them impressed me so I can't understand why I got wrapped up in theatre.[9]

In 1997 he was, it seems, equally skeptical of contemporary commercial drama on television and in film. When interviewer David Johnson asked his opinion on the future of black theater in Britain, he lamented that "it couldn't be worse. I mean my advice to any intelligent young black writers [is] 'Get out as soon as you can.'" And about British television's offerings for

---

7   Diana Athill, *Somewhere towards the End: A Memoir* (New York and London: W. W. Norton and Co., 2008), 28.

8   Barry Reckord in conversation with David Johnson, April 22, 1997.

9   Barry Reckord in conversation with David Johnson, April 22, 1997.

black actors, including *Porkpie* and *Desmond's*,[10] he remarked: "Channel 4 should be put in front of the firing squad for putting on this stuff."

Whatever his cynicism about the state of theater past and present, Reckord employed creative means to express the social and political ideas that were his primary concern. At Cambridge in the early 1950s, he wrote short stories, at least three of which were broadcast on the BBC's *Caribbean Voices*.[11] Then there was *Della*, first performed at Kingston's Ward Theatre in 1953, and then staged by Barry's brother Lloyd in London the following year under the title *Adella*. In other words, Reckord had been functioning within the arts community in both Jamaica and London before his relationship with the Royal Court Theatre began—while he was at university and later when he was a teacher on both sides of the Atlantic. He went home to Jamaica shortly after graduating, but returned to London when the English Stage Company accepted *Della* for production.

Flesh to a Tiger

Consistent with his declared fidelity to ideas over aesthetics, *Della* "was written from political motives rather than a specific desire to express himself in terms of theatre,"[12] and his concern in this first play was the ill effects of religious superstition, poverty, corruption, and racial stratification in contemporary Jamaican society: "I hated the business of Jamaica being a place where you had a tabernacle [and a murder] on every street corner and I was politically interested in religion. ... I wasn't really interested in theatre, but that's why I wrote the play."[13] *Della* is thus political: it trades on context more than character, and its plot is a function of the ideas close to Reckord's heart. It is concerned with the use of religious belief and fear to exercise power and the effect of British imperialism on racial identity in postwar Jamaica. Della is a young Jamaican mother attempting to extricate herself from the clutches of Shepherd, a powerful local figure who uses obeah rituals to frighten the villagers and thus maintain his own power and prestige. Toward women, he is callous and domineering. In her efforts to free herself from both Shepherd and the superstition around her, Della turns to her English doctor, who warms to her romantic advances but ultimately "forces [her] to feel that she is inferior." In effect,

---

10　These were British sitcoms that ran from the late 1980s to the mid-1990s, and revolved around the fortunes of a group of ethnic West Indians living in Peckham. *Desmond's* was very successful, but its spinoff *Porkpie* only ran for one season.

11　RCONT 7—Barry Reckord. Copyright Contributor Clumps (1951–53). BBC Written Archives Centre (WAC), Caversham, Reading.

12　THA/273/712/358. Undated bio for Barry Reckord (*c.* 1960)—X, August 1974. Royal Court Archive, Theatre Museum Archive (TMA), London.

13　Barry Reckord in conversation with David Johnson, April 22, 1997.

Della desperately tries to pull herself, and her community, out of bondage; she "sees herself and her people trapped between the inferiority and the superstition of the balm yard,"[14] but she is offered no direction or support. In the end, she resorts to tragic violence—the murder of her child—to lash out at Shepherd and the doctor.

Della's preoccupation with contemporary social ills, its tone of political engagement, is precisely what made it so attractive to the English Stage Company. Although critics have found fault with the plays produced by the English Stage Company for their lack of dramatic momentum or the weakness of their story arcs, they have acknowledged their cultural importance as social documents. These plays marked a change in the British theater's treatment of contemporary society and political events—in fact, they were often praised for broaching these subjects *at all*, at a time when most West End fare consisted of safe drawing room comedies, Shakespeare revivals, and American musicals. The Royal Court offered an alternative for audiences who did not view theater as an escape from, but a mirror of, the "burning questions of the day."[15] Its plays were valued at least as much for their political and social content as for their aesthetic qualities.

In this respect, the cultural and political aims of not only Reckord, but many West Indian artists and writers in Britain, mirrored those of the English Stage Company. Their music, literature, or visual art often conjured an image of postwar society that was, to mainstream audiences, *new* (although it was usually the context within which these artists had grown up or operated). This newness was usually the result of the inclusion of colonial or non-white individuals in the British social picture, but was also due to the intermingling of imperial or other "foreign" themes with domestic British concerns. Thus, the cultural productions of West Indian artists in Britain projected a similar sensibility to the productions of the English Stage Company: they implicitly or explicitly contested the domesticated, consumer-oriented ideal of postwar society celebrated at the time by much of the mainstream media and Conservative politicians like Harold Macmillan.

As Taylor marveled, "writers who fifty, fifteen or even five years before would probably have adopted the novel as their chosen form ... now, all of a sudden, were moved to try their hand at drama and, even more surprisingly, found companies to stage their work and audiences to appreciate them."[16]

14　Synopsis from dress rehearsal program, Royal Court Theatre—*Flesh to a Tiger*, general Royal Court Archive. TMA.

15　It was Lord Tyrell who, as President of the British Board of Film Censors, boasted in 1937 that there was "not a single film shown today in the public cinemas of this country which deals with any of the burning questions of the day." The same might have been said of theater.

16　John Russell Taylor, *The Angry Theatre: New British Drama* (New York: Hill and Wang, 1962), 9. Published in Great Britain under the title *Anger and After*.

Although he perhaps overstates the immediacy and magnitude of this shift, postwar repertory theater was in several respects perfectly suited to the work of politically minded West Indian artists like Reckord.

Some subjects of the new theater, however, captured the public's attention more than others. In the case of the New Wave of British dramatists, one of these subjects was undoubtedly the continued currency of class identity and class tensions in "affluent" Britain. Although almost unnoted at the time, the gendered character of much New Wave or "angry" writing has received much scholarly attention in the last thirty years.[17] On the other hand, even today, the presentation of the domestic race relations debate and the decline of empire on the small and silver screens remains less discussed. Reckord was not the only one who alluded to the relationship among colonialism, race relations, and other social divisions; postwar uncertainty around the issues of empire and race constitute part of the backdrop to the dramas of Osborne and others. It was certainly not an invisible issue at the Royal Court.

It was director Tony Richardson's idea, for example, to change the play's title from the nondescript *Della* to the more evocative *Flesh to a Tiger*, a choice that draws attention to the play's politically charged themes. Reckord himself acknowledged that he was motivated to write by his concern with "ideas" over aesthetics, but even if he had not, the play's dialogue made his intentions clear enough. When, to take just one example, Della attempts to persuade Shepherd to use his clout to engender pride in his black followers, Shepherd tersely replies, "Trust meself to black people, I fall to ground. Root meself to obeah, I stay high. Sweet breeze blow on me."[18] Here Reckord makes explicit his belief in the corrosive power of superstition on a population already made vulnerable by colonialism and endemic poverty, and he reiterates his ideas through the voices of all his characters. The title itself comes from a line in the play; the neighbor's warning that "black to white is like flesh to a tiger." Of Reckord's concern with political content, one unimpressed reviewer for the *New Statesman* wrote, "The earnest sincerity of the author is obvious enough: it kills almost every scene stone dead."[19]

---

17 See, e.g., John Hill, "Working-Class Realism and Sexual Reaction: Some Theses on the British 'New Wave,'" in James Curran and Vincent Porter, eds, *British Cinema History* (London: Weidenfeld and Nicholson, 1983), 301–11; David Castronovo, *Blokes: The Bad Boys of British Literature* (New York: Continuum, 2009); Micheline Wandor, *Look Back in Gender: Sexuality and the Family in Post-War British Drama* (London: Methuen, 1987); David Ian Rabey's discussion of *Look Back in Anger* in "John Osborne: Just Like a Man," in Rabey, *English Drama since 1940* (London: Pearson Education Limited, 2003), 32–36.

18 PLAYS REC Barry Reckord, *Della; or, Flesh to a Tiger*, prompt script, 2-I-3 (Act Two, Scene One, p. 3). Royal Court Archive. TMA.

19 T. C. Worsley, review of *Flesh to a Tiger*, *New Statesman* (May 31, 1958). THM/273/7/2/13, *Flesh to a Tiger* press cuttings, Royal Court Archive. TMA.

The Royal Court opened *Flesh to a Tiger* on May 21, 1958, two years after its original performance of *Look Back in Anger*. Like *Look Back*, *Flesh to a Tiger* was a first play by a young, unknown playwright who had mailed his script to the English Stage Company in response to an advertisement in *The Stage*. Also like *Look Back*, it was a contemporary play more concerned with issues—in this case, insecurity and religious superstition exacerbated by the colonial relationship—than with narrative arc or dramatic structure; it dismissed the old-fashioned English concern with the "well-made play" in favor of poetic language and mood. Finally, like the cadre of dramatists attached to the Company at the time—John Osborne, Arnold Wesker, Ann Jellicoe, and N. F. Simpson—the Royal Court supported many of Reckord's subsequent efforts almost regardless of their box office success.

But instead of gaining the critical momentum and acknowledgement that would have positioned it within the "angry" postwar theatrical tradition, *Flesh to a Tiger* got brief media attention as a "West Indian play," received tepid reviews, and was then simply forgotten. Analysts of postwar British theater and the heyday of the Royal Court in the late 1950s and early 1960s give Reckord barely a passing mention, despite the fact that during this historic period the theater produced two more of his plays, in 1960 and 1963, both to considerable success and critical praise (and another two later, in 1973 and 1974).

The popular conception of the "angries" was firmly in place by the time *Flesh* premiered in May 1958, and several observers did not hesitate to position it firmly within that genre of new theater, albeit with a consciousness of Reckord's West Indian background; a *Daily Sketch* reviewer complained that "the author has been too violent—too unrelenting—an Angry Young Negro, with no humour to lighten his passion," while the *South Wales Echo* wrote that the Cardiff production "is positively the latest angle on the Angry Young Man—the Angry Young Black Man."[20] This perceived connection is especially interesting in light of the fact that, of all Reckord's work for the Court, *Flesh to a Tiger* was perhaps the most unusual, with its Jamaican setting and conflicts and its positioning of Della, a struggling mother, as the outcast anti-hero—far different from the aggressive masculinity exhibited by Reckord's later plays.

A second way that *Flesh* appealed to the English Stage Company's sensibilities was through its emphasis on language and imagery. English Stage Company general director and guiding spirit George Devine was particularly concerned that the Royal Court should be a "writer's theatre"; not only would it seek out fresh work from fledgling unknowns, but

---

20 Harold Conway, "Cleo the Actress Hits the High Notes," *Daily Sketch* (May 22, 1958); "New Angle," *South Wales Echo* (May 1, 1958). THM/273/7/2/13, *Flesh to a Tiger* press cuttings, Royal Court Archive. TMA.

Cleo Laine as Della and Edgar Wreford as the Doctor in the Royal Court
production of *Flesh to a Tiger*, May 1958. Photograph by Tony Marshall.
© Tony Marshall/Associated Newspapers/REX Shutterstock 2015.

it would nurture their talent, so that they would be "allowed to fail,"
profits be hanged. In addition—and this was unusual at the time—writers
were encouraged to attend rehearsals and contribute to production and
performance decisions, so that they might become more familiar with
the process of translation from page to stage. Michael Hallifax, who was
the Royal Court's stage director (general stage manager) in these early
years, remembers that Devine was so adamant about the primacy of the
playwrights that he instructed him to refer to all productions by the writer's
surname. For example, *Flesh to a Tiger* was called "the Reckord."[21] And the

---

21   Michael Hallifax, *Let Me Set the Scene: Twenty Years at the Heart of British Theatre
     1956 to 1976* (Hanover: Smith and Kraus, 2004), 9.

play was a good candidate for Devine's writer's theater because of its focus on language, despite the critics' distaste for Reckord's style.

Reviewers in general attacked *Flesh*'s prose for two contradictory reasons: either it was too flowery and failed to authentically replicate Jamaican dialogue, or its West Indian phrasing was *too* authentic for native English audiences to understand. The *Evening Standard*, to take a typical example, noted that "Mr. Reckord makes an almost reckless use of language which is a curious amalgam of naïve West Indian slang and lush Elizabethan imagery. He reaches for poetry but only touches its hem."[22] Similarly, a reviewer for *The Lady* confessed "an odd feeling that sultry West Indian dramas are going to be fashionable. If so, I hope they will be more theatrically efficient than this one, which depends mainly on atmospherics."[23] The play was indeed thick with ornate metaphors and exotic monologues. The already famous jazz singer Cleo Laine, who played Della in her first dramatic stage role, was saddled with lines like:

> How Shepherd moved through his women with no reverent feeling, mashed them in his mouth like ripe bananas to fill a maw that soon emptied out again. Any tenderness he dropped was only seed to lure me to a dry spring. His eye pitched on no beauty he wouldn't swallow, flesh and bone and feather.[24]

Play readers at BBC Radio—Reckord submitted the play for consideration as a radio production not one, but three times—were in agreement that the language of *Flesh* was among its central characteristics, although they were divided as to whether the extravagant dialogue was an asset or a liability. One found it to be "strange and vigorous," another found it "intensely dramatic," a third, "spasmodic."[25]

Many in the public also had difficulty understanding the West Indian accents of the actors themselves. Michael Hallifax noted that "although the actors in the group were speaking English, it was a dialect that English audiences found nearly incomprehensible."[26] On this subject, however, Reckord had definite views. He believed it a shame that colonial actors in Britain were so often forced to soften or erase their accents for white

22 Review of *Flesh to a Tiger*, *Evening Standard* (May 27, 1958), 6. Royal Court Theatre—*Flesh to a Tiger*, general Royal Court Archive. TMA.

23 Review of *Flesh to a Tiger*, *The Lady* (May 5, 1958). THM/273/7/2/13, *Flesh to a Tiger* press cuttings, Royal Court Archive. TMA.

24 PLAYS REC Barry Reckord, *Della*; or, *Flesh to a Tiger*, prompt script, 1-I-4. Royal Court Archive. TMA.

25 Respectively, Helena Wood, memo (November 15, 1955); John Gibson, memo (February 16, 1956); J. Robin Midgley, memo (July 11, 1958). RCONT 1—Barry Reckord. Scriptwriters File 1 (1955-62), WAC.

26 Hallifax, *Let Me Set the Scene*, 65.

audiences, even when they were playing African and Caribbean roles. He felt that an actor

> would, in fact, lose his substance as a person the minute he started on stage to do that. He would, in fact, become a mimic and stop being an actor. And this is the tragedy [for] African actors. The moment they have to spend too much time, pay too much attention to this articulation they become dead and dry.[27]

The play's "atmospherics" were apparently just what the English Stage Company, and the play's director, Tony Richardson, were looking for; Reckord remarked that Richardson "liked the poetry of the play."[28] Richardson said as much himself in his memoirs, remarking: "Clumsy in its construction, *Flesh to a Tiger* had at moments a passion of language which was extraordinary." Although he ultimately felt unable to translate this passion to the stage on performance night, "the attempt to make it work was wonderfully worthwhile."[29] Not only did Richardson accept *Flesh to a Tiger*, with all its poetic language, but he enhanced its exotic and dramatic potential in several ways. He let the Jamaican dialect stand, for instance, with minor adjustments that reflected the audience's unfamiliarity with some terms, such as using the word "child" instead of "pickney." Editors also cut a few sexually explicit comments that would presumably have offended the sensibilities of the Lord Chamberlain, who reviewed and licensed all theater scripts until 1968. In addition, Richardson included calypso pieces in the play, and reproduced "voodoo" or obeah rites onstage, complete with a live goat. Loudon Sainthill's striking set was impressionistic, consisting largely of hanging rags and artfully placed debris that suggested rather than reconstructed a West Indian slum.[30] All these efforts heightened the drama of Reckord's already flamboyant script. Finally, it is arguable that its purple prose was necessary to convey the issues with which the play was concerned. Yvonne Brewster saw the play when she was a young drama student at Rose Bruford College, and the poetry and atmosphere apparently worked for her. She has noted that "hearing the once familiar drums, cadences and accents of my people seeing and feeling the power of

---

27 Barry Reckord, roundtable discussion, "African Writing—Discussion about the Problems Confronting the African and West Indian Writer Particularly Regarding Writing for the Stage and the Cinema," *African Writers' Club*, British Broadcasting Corporation (December 6, 1965). *African Writers' Club*, British Library website: http://sounds.bl.uk/Arts-literature-and-performance/African-Writers-Club/024M-C0134X0015XX-0200V0, part of the British Library Sound Archive, London.

28 Barry Reckord in conversation with David Johnson, April 22, 1997.

29 Tony Richardson, *Long Distance Runner: A Memoir* (London and Boston: Faber and Faber, 1993), 98–99.

30 *Flesh to a Tiger* Photograph File (2), TMA.

their body language, was an altogether empowering experience. The play's message for me lingers still."[31]

There was thus a great convergence between Reckord's reasons for writing *Flesh to a Tiger* and the English Stage Company's reasons for staging it. Ethically and aesthetically, play and company complemented each other. Moreover, despite the initial "outsider" status of Reckord and the English Stage Company, they shared a desire to use cultural productions to educate their English audience, much like many West Indian artists and the BBC. (The form this education should take was, however, a matter of debate.) Entertainment was to have "the appearance of contemporary relevance and [appeal] to audiences who were unwilling to use the theatre as an escape from the problems of the time"—including continuing social inequalities in Britain and her empire.[32] Reckord and the English Stage Company were radical and ferocious in their pursuit of this agenda.

In light of the Royal Court's desire to challenge and even educate British audiences about issues of contemporary relevance, did *Flesh to a Tiger* "educate" English audiences about race relations domestically or internationally, and if so, how? It was not set in England, and so might be expected to offer little in the way of a reimagining of the domestic race relations narrative as it was being established in film and television. In fact, Reckord returned to Jamaica soon after writing the play, and *Della* was first performed there, at the Ward Theatre, Kingston, in 1953 and 1954. It also seems that it was performed by Barry's brother Lloyd, in London at that time, but Reckord did not move back to England until he heard the play was to be produced at the Court. (He remained there almost uninterrupted until his old age.) Diana Paton has suggested that Jamaican playwrights like Reckord "had half an eye on international audiences while writing [their plays] even while attempting to create a nationalist theatre."[33]

But in effect, *Flesh to a Tiger*'s London production widened the frame through which West Indian migration and English racism might be viewed. At a time when the newspapers were reporting on growing numbers of West Indian migrants to Britain's urban neighborhoods and instances of racial discrimination and violence, *Flesh to a Tiger*, along with Errol John's *Moon on a Rainbow Shawl*, presented a timely colonial perspective on these domestic phenomena—they opened in May and December respectively, bookending the late-summer riots in Notting Hill.

Both productions are also widely considered to be the first two "straight" West Indian dramas produced in London—not a surprise in light of the scarcity of Caribbean playwrights in 1958 London. *Flesh to a Tiger* drew

31 Yvonne Brewster, ed., *For the Reckord: A Collection of Three Plays by Barry Reckord* (London: Oberon Books, 2010), 13–14.

32 Arnold P. Hinchcliffe, *British Theatre 1950–70* (Oxford: Basil Blackwell, 1974), 48.

33 Diana Paton, unpublished article (2012).

different lessons from its squalid Caribbean setting than did *Moon on a Rainbow Shawl*, but critics for both made the mental leap from British colony to imperial heartland: "White folk who get hot under the collar about the 'coloured' problem often thoughtlessly ask: 'Why don't the Jamaicans stay in their own country?' This fine play by a 30-year-old Jamaican playwright gives at least one clue."[34] Taken in the context of the heated and even violent controversy surrounding colonial migration and settlement in 1958, both plays expanded the terms of the debate by providing a colonial perspective.

Indeed, one of *Flesh*'s most important contributions to the genre of English "race drama" was its privileging of a West Indian perspective. The audience is never exposed to the inner landscape of the play's one white (English) character, the Doctor, even though his actions help move along the plot. At the same time, all the other central characters systematically provide a different viewpoint on late colonial race relations and economic depression in Jamaica. Della's eldest son, Joshie, is an example of a new generation growing up to despise its race and to associate skin color with degradation: "All I know is that our people ugly, nasty, ignorant and smell."[35] Her gossipy neighbor, Lal, is a well-intentioned but conservative community member whose poverty has taught her to fear change. She warns Della, "You let wishing confuse you. Nothing in this world better than the safety of the yard."[36] Shepherd and Della are more complex characters, but they too play carefully defined roles. The ironically named Shepherd coldly exploits the weaknesses and insecurities of the Trench Town inhabitants in order to maintain his local authority. He accuses Della of preaching white supremacy in order to turn his followers against her "when the power of God is living black."[37] Here, he shamelessly employs the language of both obeah and black pride to sway his supporters when, in fact, he possesses no religious faith and no concern for the degradation of his own people, many of whom he ruthlessly controls, especially women.

Della, on the other hand, is aware of all the above dynamics at play in Trench Town, and, as the play's ostensible heroine, is most concerned with finding an alternative to what Reckord would call "superstition" on the one hand, and allegiance to white colonialists on the other: "I hate White Wolf and feel abomination for Shepherd. Between them must lie a way."[38] Her attempt to recover her independence and dignity from both Shepherd and the doctor clearly parallels the challenge that Reckord sees facing West Indians in general. Della's failure, and her despairing murder of her own

---

34 "From Jazz Singer to Tragedienne," *Hampshire Telegraph Post* (May 9, 1958). THM/273/7/2/13. *Flesh to a Tiger* (1958). Press cuttings. Royal Court Archive. TMA.

35 PLAYS REC Barry Reckord, *Della; or, Flesh to a Tiger*, prompt script, 1-IV-7. Royal Court Archive. TMA.

36 Ibid., 1-III-5.

37 Ibid., 2-VIII-2.

38 Ibid., 1-III-5.

child, are perhaps a gauge of Reckord's own political pessimism about the issues he raises in *Flesh*.

Such a play, produced in London and elsewhere in Britain—it enjoyed a run in Cardiff—could not help but suggest the connection between domestic and imperial tensions at a moment when immigration and racial tension were being discussed frequently in the media. Cleo Laine's appearance as Della, for instance, drew attention to the domestic ramifications of the race question. Not only did her considerable fame as a singer garner much publicity for the play, but her status as the daughter of a white English mother and a black Jamaican father led to questions from the press loosely connecting her situation with the one portrayed in *Flesh*. Apparently, Laine did not see any of her own experience reflected in Della's struggle: "Cleo says that she has strong feelings on discrimination of any nature. But then she shrugs and says: 'Not that I'm worried. I've never been the victim of discrimination.'"[39] Such a remark may sound astonishing to today's ears, but it certainly reflects the different politics of the time, and presumably Laine's own perspective as a successful jazz singer.

Finally, although West Indian playwrights were relatively rare in London, West Indian writing in general was more common and gained much critical attention in the postwar period, especially novels set in the Caribbean. Critic Derek Granger described this blossoming of West Indian literature in the *Financial Times* as "one of the most recent and certainly happiest by-products of the great West Indian influx to Great Britain."[40] Combined with the West Indian presence in other media and literature, British audiences were more prepared for the "authentic picture of the poverty and squalor in which some Jamaicans are living"[41] than they would have been ten or fifteen years before.

Thus, while *Flesh to a Tiger* was not a reflection of the British situation, its thematic connections to current events in Britain gave it a contemporary domestic relevance that the English Stage Company must have noticed and appreciated. And, indeed, as "the first in a long line of 'ethnic' plays at the Court," *Flesh* and *Moon on a Rainbow Shawl* laid the foundations for the Royal Court's reputation as a venue that gave "opportunities to African and West Indian authors and actors unequalled by any other British theatre."[42]

At the same time, Reckord anticipated the more general aims of West

---

39 Charles Bayne, "Miss Laine Takes a Dramatic Turning" *Illustrated* (April 26, 1958), 24–25. Royal Court Theatre—*Flesh to a Tiger*, General Royal Court archive. TMA. Incidentally, Laine's experience contributed to her giving her son (with Johnny Dankworth) the middle name Tamba, after the young actor Tamba Allen, who portrayed Della's son in the production.

40 Derek Granger, "Flesh to a Tiger," *Financial Times* (May 22, 1958), THM/273/7/2/13.

41 "Miss Laine Hopes to Combine Two Careers," *Financial Times* (May 22, 1958), THM/273/7/2/13.

42 Findlater, *At the Royal Court*, 46.

Indian actors and writers in the late 1960s and 1970s. At a 1967 theater symposium held by the CAM, actor Ram John Holder declared that West Indian theater should be focusing on "our lives now" including "the church and state and government. ... We will be doing a disservice if we don't apply our arts to this thing."[43] The social and political awareness of many colonial artists, including Reckord, complemented the English Stage Company's philosophy.

In spite of the shared aesthetic and political goals between Reckord and the English Stage Company, the former acknowledged, in a way, his strange disconnection from the Royal Court's renown:

> When I came, when my play was on at the Court, they were saying, "Let's find you a flat," you know, "You're going to be rich." ... So we walked along King's Road and we, we saw these new ... house agents saying, "No blacks, no dogs, no children." ... They were going to find me a rich flat because that was what's going to happen to me ... and the play flopped and I was living in a boarding house.[44]

This feeling of alienation of course became a trademark of Royal Court culture and its writers. It was not only his plays, but Reckord himself, that possessed some of the key traits that characterized the most famous "angry young men" of the period. The general scholarly consensus is, of course, that it is impossible and misleading to place such disparate figures as Osborne, Amis, or Arden within a single creative school, when in fact their styles and literary concerns were so disparate. Following this rationale, it would be equally foolish to place Reckord himself in this camp, when his plays differed in important ways. That being said, scholars have continued to analyze these writers as a "New Wave" collective, even while acknowledging their creative differences. At the very least, New Wave writers were united "in their antagonism to a dour, restricted national culture and a political establishment that several of them rapidly joined."[45]

Barry Reckord shared this antagonism and, unlike Osborne and Amis, who famously took a conservative turn in the 1960s and 1970s, Reckord continued to raise eyebrows throughout his career. A self-described "rabble rouser," in his 1997 interview with the Theatre Museum, he was still taking aim at everything from black actors to the Royal Court to the state of television. Actor Don Warrington, who performed in a BBC

---

43 CAM 5/5/1, transcript of CAM symposium on West Indian Theatre (November 10, 1967), 7. George Padmore Institute, London.

44 Special Collections 9704095/A. *Blackgrounds* oral history project on the experience of Black Theatre and Black Theatre professionals. Barry Reckord in conversation with David Johnson, Primrose Hill, London, April 22, 1997. TMA.

45 Lacey, *British Realist Theatre*, 5.

TV production of Reckord's *Club Havana*, wrote that his best trait was irreverence: "Nothing was beyond question, everything, whatever it was, for its own sake, and ours, needed to be tested from time to time. Barry lived his life in that fashion."[46] Even Yvonne Brewster, who remarked that Reckord wrote "six brilliant plays," added that he unfortunately became "obsessed with sex," a trait that marred his later material.[47] He remained a marginal, contrarian figure, even within the stable of outspoken Royal Court writers, never named among those actively involved in the Writer's Group, or in the marches for nuclear disarmament. As Reckord recollects, at the opening of *Flesh to a Tiger*, "Gregory" Poke (he was likely referring here to Greville Poke, a member of the Royal Court's board of directors) apparently ran his hands through Reckord's hair and remarked, "I love this stuff." When Reckord replied, "'Yes, my barber tells me that,' ... he took vast offence... he used to have Sunday breakfasts for Royal Court writers and I was never invited." On why the English Stage Company chose his play to produce in 1957, he blithely stated: "I think the Court did it because it was exotic and the language was poetic and this is what they expect from black people."[48] These comments give some indication that Reckord didn't feel as much a part of the Court scene as, for example, Osborne or Ann Jellicoe. Nonetheless, he was an outsider in an outsider's theater, and he consistently turned out dramatic material that jibed perfectly with the theater's political and artistic direction, and the theater, in turn, never rejected one of his scripts.

This disconnection from the theater's fame has, by and large, been replicated in current histories of the Royal Court, which confine their evaluation of Reckord's plays to a few lines, if indeed they mention them at all. Philip Roberts's administrative history of the theater sums up the impact of *Flesh to a Tiger* by stating that it "lasted for only twenty-nine performances at a disastrous 15 percent box office. A brave and adventurous work simply did not appeal." (Never mind that Ann Jellicoe's *The Sport of My Mad Mother* and Harold Pinter's *The Birthday Party*, which ran at the Court in the same year, performed even worse, in both critical and financial terms. They are now celebrated in the dramatic histories.) Meanwhile, the passing decades have only intensified the mythical aura surrounding the Royal Court and four or five of the playwrights it launched, whose works, good and bad, popular and unpopular, are subjected to repeated scrutiny—*Look Back in Anger* most of all. Theater historians writing with

---

46 Don Warrington, "Meetings with Barry Reckord," in Yvonne Brewster, ed., *For the Reckord: A Collection of Three Plays by Barry Reckord* (London: Oberon Books, 2010), 248.

47 Yvonne Brewster quoted in Michael Reckord, "Jamaica's Gifts to British Theatre," *The Jamaica Gleaner* (March 15, 2009), http://mobile.jamaicagleaner.com/20090315/ent/ent1.php; accessed May 12, 2010.

48 Ibid.

a twenty-first-century awareness of Britain as a multiracial nation now mention both Barry Reckord and Errol John, usually with a brief congratulatory note about the Royal Court's pioneering role in the production of black or ethnic plays.[49] But while the English Stage Company certainly deserves to be acknowledged for investing in these productions when many theaters would not, the critical practice of consigning Reckord's works to the status of "West Indian" or early "Black British" plays not only erases their individuality, but also marginalizes them to a realm outside domestic British culture. Besides, if *Flesh to a Tiger* was an "exotic" play, Reckord's next two were much more intimately bound up with distinctively British problems. They were also more closely allied to the Royal Court's distinctive dramatic preferences.

You in Your Small Corner

The affinity between Reckord's and the English Stage Company's approaches to social drama was implicit in *Flesh to a Tiger*, but it was startlingly apparent in his second play, *You in Your Small Corner*. To understand just how much, we need to compare it to what was undoubtedly the Sloane Square theater's most famous production: the May 1956 premiere of its third play, John Osborne's *Look Back in Anger*. About a young man dissatisfied with the hypocrisy and complacency of the society in which he lives, *Look Back in Anger* soon became a symbol of the new turn in British theater, and made the Royal Court England's seminal "writer's theater" in the process. Critic John Russell Taylor wrote, "The whole picture of [dramatic] writing in this country has undergone a transformation in the last five years or so, and the event which marks 'then' off decisively from 'now' is the first performance of *Look Back in Anger* on 8 May 1956."[50] Even reviewers not wholly in favor of the play tended to acknowledge its youthfulness, contemporary political sensibility, and radical potential.

In short, *Look Back in Anger* was, and continues to be, hailed for tapping into popular disillusionment, especially among the young, with the dominant, conservative vision of postwar Britain that emphasized economic prosperity, social harmony, and continued international supremacy, ignoring the slippage of Britain's imperial status and the persistence of social inequality. A runaway success, it is commonly credited with revolutionizing postwar British drama.

Despite all that might be said in favor of English theater before the apparent watershed of 1956, it was limited in terms of its audience and its subject matter—both were predominantly middle class, both were attentive

---

49 Billington, *State of the Nation*, 119. See also Findlater, *At the Royal Court*.
50 Taylor, *The Angry Theatre*, 9.

to long-standing literary/aesthetic/theatrical conventions, and neither wished to explore the harsher realities of postwar British life. And it was in precisely these areas that the new theater, as represented by the Royal Court, flourished. Even the first reviews for *Look Back in Anger*, which were decidedly mixed, declared that while the play's writing and execution were flawed in various ways, it was undeniably different, new, and "young, young, young."[51] Just as important, it retrained audiences and critics to identify and appreciate these different qualities—raw feeling, and a willingness to tackle timely social and political issues. John Elsom explains:

> The success of *Look Back in Anger* ... destroyed several inhibiting myths about plays: that the theatre had to be genteel, that heroes were stoical and lofty creatures, that audiences needed nice people with whom to identify. Even the recognized clumsiness of Osborne's plays were [*sic*] indirectly encouraging to other dramatists, for it seemed to prove that passion and dramatic substance mattered more than obedience to the rules. ... [Osborne] had also given the first telling expression in modern British theatre to the theme of social alienation.[52]

The revolutionary significance given to the Court's early productions— Osborne, Pinter, Arden, Jellicoe—masks their important differences; as assaults on the "Establishment," these productions displayed flashes of (oft-quoted) articulate social *criticism* but did not represent a systematic social or political *critique*. In terms of their larger political or social import, they were small reflections—or refractions—of a still disparate public feeling.

Nonetheless, the British dramatists who made a home at the Royal Court in these years began, brazenly but in a piecemeal fashion, to develop a self-consciously alternative theatrical tradition in Britain, consistently drawing on contemporary society for characters, setting, and thematic substance. In this project, they were undoubtedly successful, even though only a small minority of productions achieved commercial success, or even solvency.

You in Your Small Corner was a humbler production than *Flesh*, firstly because it made its premiere at the Royal Court as a Sunday Night "production without décor," and secondly because its focus was more limited and personal in nature.[53] Despite its low-budget production and

51 John Barber, "This Bitter Young Man—Like Thousands," *Daily Express* (May 9, 1956), quoted in Dominic Shellard, *British Theatre Since the War* (New Haven: Yale University Press, 1999), 54.

52 John Elsom, *Post-War British Theatre* (1976; London: Routledge and Kegan Paul, 1979), 80, 81.

53 The Royal Court produced about a half-dozen Sunday Night productions per year during George Devine's tenure as artistic director. The production budget was not

unknown cast, however, *You in Your Small Corner* was, at least according to the critics, a much more satisfying story from a better-crafted script. In fact, its Sunday Night performance on October 23, 1960 went over favorably enough to warrant a proper run on the Court's main stage the following March.[54] But however much the play exceeded its predecessor in quality, it also conformed thematically and structurally to the kind of drama for which the Royal Court had by that time become famous. In addition, it consciously used and manipulated the template of the race relations narrative repeatedly cultivated in British films and teleplays. For both these reasons, critical English audiences had more familiar material—and a more familiar politics—to sink their teeth into, despite the play's modest scale.

With *Flesh to a Tiger*, Barry Reckord had established himself as a West Indian playwright concerned with West Indian issues. *You in Your Small Corner*, ostensibly about race and West Indian migration, established him as a playwright concerned with contemporary class issues. Indeed, the play does not merely follow Osborne's exploration of class; it complicates it by incorporating the equally current conundrum of racial and imperial relations. Moreover, in Royal Court fashion, it is about the lived experience of class in the personal or cultural sense, and focuses in particular on the lives of two young people operating within fixed familial boundaries.

Dave Jordan, the play's protagonist, is a Jamaican student who has just moved to England to attend Cambridge. His mother, already settled in Brixton, runs a successful West Indian club but harbors higher hopes for her son. She is none too pleased when he begins a relationship with Terry Jamieson, the working-class daughter of her white neighbors. Dave, for his part, is less confused by his romantic feelings than by his racial and class identity, a confusion that breeds antagonism toward Terry. When she protests her love, the snobbish Dave rejects the significance of love for the likes of them: "When we're low what we have is never love. Just an everlasting instinct to avenge our lowness."[55] The parallels between Dave Jordan and Osborne's Jimmy Porter in *Look Back in Anger* are obvious here, in particular their feelings of helplessness against social forces deemed beyond their control, and the way their frustrations are directed against their long-suffering female

to exceed £500, and they served multiple purposes: "They could provide a means whereby promising writers could see and hear their work and profit by it; they could be used to try out work about which there was a certain unease; and they could be quite ruthlessly used to fob off work which could not simply be dismissed." See Philip Roberts, *The Royal Court Theatre and the Modern Stage* (Cambridge: Cambridge University Press, 1999), 58.

54 Although the Sunday Night was originally to be the play's first performance, it did a one-week run just before in Cheltenham, produced by the Cheltenham Everyman Theatre Company.

55 English Stage Company 1962/W/16. *You in Your Small Corner*, prompt script, 3-I-12. Royal Court Archive. TMA.

partners, who appear less troubled by such intangible concerns.[56] Reckord's second play is not a story of star-crossed lovers; it is about the psychic damage endured by those living under conflicting hierarchies of color and class (and in this sense, at least, it is not so different from *Flesh to a Tiger*).

In effect, *Corner* turns the race relations narrative discussed in the last chapter on its head, because it is Mrs. Jordan, and not Terry's mother, who opposes the relationship. The reasons for this are economic, cultural, and class-related, not racial. Dave is less concerned with race than upward mobility, while Terry is not seeking to rise in the social order. Even at the play's outset, before he has gone off to Cambridge, he is better educated and presents himself as such. The telltale indicator here is accent—Terry and her family *talk* working class, while Dave, even with his Jamaican accent, speaks "proper" English, and the contrast is especially marked in comparison to his mother's turns of phrase. Reckord wrote these differences right into the script; Terry's brother Georgie drops aitches constantly: "What I'm sayin' is she's 'ad enough of bein' mucked about and I 'ope she's settled wiv you now."[57] Dave attempts to "teach" Terry better speech and manners, and gets frustrated when she shows little motivation to "improve" herself: "Listen to my mother talk, then listen to me. I came from no bloody place. You can do it but you won't try."[58] That Reckord uses accent as a key signifier in the play demonstrates his desire to emphasize the continuing and decisive importance of class as a cultural barrier, perhaps even more than race.[59] It is a fascinating and, I would argue, deliberate inversion of the mainstream race relations narrative in which race is everything.

English audiences would have recognized *Corner*'s troubled protagonist, Dave Jordan, for he was a young, alienated anti-hero despairing over his lack of place in contemporary British society. This is partly a result of his race, but also a result of his educational and social background. His feelings of isolation are thrown into sharpest relief in his relations with the play's young female characters. Although he and Terry, for instance,

---

56 *Look Back in Anger* goes further in its expression of misogyny; Jimmy goes so far as to wish that Alison "could have a child, and it would die," so that she might "wake" out of her "beauty sleep." John Osborne, *Look Back in Anger and Other Plays* (London: Faber and Faber, 1993), 34.

57 English Stage Company 1962/W/16, *You in Your Small Corner* prompt script (1962), 2-I-3. Royal Court Theatre Archive. TMA.

58 Ibid., 3-I-12.

59 It should be noted that no visual or sound recording of the Royal Court production exists, although we can perhaps assume that the idiom of the script was faithfully rendered on the stage by Pearl Nunez (Connor), a Trinidadian by birth. Interestingly, Ida Shepley, who played Mrs. Jordan in the Granada Television production, did not employ a West Indian accent. See "Play of the Week: *You in Your Small Corner*," Granada Television May 23, 1962, National Film and Television Archive, BFI, London.

are instinctively attracted to each other, Dave is constantly bothered by her unselfconscious lower-class ways. On multiple occasions he denies her the unqualified acceptance that she gives him. When her brother Georgie insinuates to Dave that she has had other lovers, Dave explodes, interpreting it as a racially motivated attack upon himself: "If she's mucked around, I'm just about good enough is that it? You know you're hell bent on me bein' not quite equal, and I'm tempted as hell to say, know your place, man."[60] Again, on one level his outburst suggests that he is most sensitive about his status as a black man dating a white woman, but it simultaneously suggests a certain reactionary snobbery, as though he is most outraged because Terry's family treats him as their equal instead of their social superior. Mrs. Jordan's rather crude attitudes only increase his confusion over his sincere feelings for Terry. She views Terry as nothing more than a passing fling: "Yes, mek him learn off her so that when he meet one of his own class he will know how to handle himself." Dave's insecurities and angry hypersensitivity closely resemble Jimmy Porter, who is also given to unwarranted explosions of bitter indignation when he feels slighted.[61]

This leads us inevitably to the handling of gender in *You in Your Small Corner*, in terms of Dave's type of masculinity and Terry's role as his romantic partner. Both fit, to a remarkable degree, the template laid down by *Look Back in Anger*. There is no doubt that it is general circumstances rather than particular attacks that wound Dave's sense of independence and manliness; the play presents virtually no instances of outright or hostile racism directed against him. Rather, his heightened awareness of his own difference gives him a chip on the shoulder. When, for instance, he has a brief encounter with a university-educated upper-class woman, Jill Kendrick, and she invites him to a party, he feels like a novelty that she is showing off to her friends. While this may be true (and the audience does not know for certain), it is also clear that his interest in her is similarly superficial. It is her class and social status that he finds temporarily attractive, but there is no chemistry of the kind that he has with Terry. And yet it is Terry, the strongest character emotionally, who receives the sharp end of his masculine insecurity. Like Jimmy's Alison, she is made to suffer her lover's infidelity before a reunion can take place. In addition, like *Look Back*, the resolution of *Corner* revolves around Terry's ultimate acceptance of Dave's weaknesses. Referring to his dalliance with Jill, she states, "We'll have more of last night but I swear I'll bear it, bear it till you stop wanting it." He responds that he loves her "with my head and my heart," which suggests a kind of coming-to-terms with his own identity.[62] Like the ending of *Look Back*, this

60　English Stage Company 1962/W/16, *You in Your Small Corner* prompt script (1962), 2-I-3. Royal Court Theatre Archive. TMA.

61　See Osborne, *Look Back in Anger and Other Plays*, 33.

62　Ibid., 3-IV-8, 3-IV-9.

conclusion is neither satisfying nor convincing, and yet it is closure of a sort: the protagonists' mutual resolve to commit to each other and work out the vagaries of race and class in postwar London together.

It would be doing a disservice to Reckord's legacy, however, to evaluate *You in Your Small Corner* purely as a counterpoint to *Look Back in Anger*. Indeed, from an historical perspective, the production and reception of this play are fascinating because they illustrate the complexities, the gray area, of a West Indian man writing an interracial romance in 1962, when attitudes about race, sex, and success were both in transition and fraught with anxiety. It is a very simple story. But with it, Reckord neatly and unobtrusively brought several of British society's gray areas to the fore.

It is not clear how conscious Reckord was of the structural and thematic similarities between *Corner* and *Look Back*, or the Royal Court's reputation more generally. He was, however, keenly aware of the particular challenges of being a colonial, West Indian writer producing plays for a predominantly white English audience. Diana Athill has remarked that of all his plays, this one "was closer to his personal experience than anything else he wrote."[63] Furthermore, it is clear that his plays after *Flesh to a Tiger*, especially *Corner*, conform much more closely to the trajectory of alternative British theater in these years, as discussed above. It is not easy to find a thorough contemporary record of his creative approach, but in 1965, he participated in a round-table discussion on the BBC radio program *African Writers' Club*. The topic of discussion was "writing for an English audience." While the other participants, all African fiction writers, emphasized the challenge of describing and interpreting African history and culture for the foreign reader, Reckord immediately stressed the issue of perspective:

The problem is this, that if your films are for European audiences, or white American audiences, what they tend to want is to see coloured people in terms of problem; I mean, in terms of their relationship to white people. ... If you say to a white film producer that "I want to write plays about black people just as human beings," he'll say, "I can have plays about white people as human beings; I'm not interested in that. I'm interested in them if you're going to show them to me as wide boys, or show them to me in an exotic, entertaining sort of way, in a way to entertain white people, but if you're going to just show them as human beings having human emotions, then I can see that in white people."[64]

---

63 Diana Athill, "Prologue," in Yvonne Brewster, ed., *For the Reckord: A Collection of Three Plays by Barry Reckord* (London: Oberon Books, 2010), 9.

64 Barry Reckord, roundtable discussion, "African Writing—Discussion about the Problems Confronting the African and West Indian Writer Particularly Regarding Writing for the Stage and the Cinema," *African Writers' Club*, British Broadcasting

Reviewing the subject matter of British plays, programs, and films involving West Indian characters and dilemmas in this period, it is hard not to agree with Reckord's interpretation. The mileage and durability of the British race relations narrative in popular drama is itself a testimony to his conclusions.

You in Your Small Corner is so interesting, therefore, because Reckord managed to both satisfy the perceived thematic/aesthetic tastes of the Royal Court audience and critics, *and* manipulate the classic race relations narrative to highlight the perspective of West Indian characters, rather than the domestic concerns of white families. Despite Reckord's apparent reliance on pre-existing dramatic patterns—the race relations narrative, the "angry young man" elements introduced by Osborne—he departed from, or combined, these conventions in daring ways that made *You in Your Small Corner* a brave play.

Most obviously, the play was unorthodox in the degree to which it made the sexual relationship between (the unmarried) Dave and Terry explicit. This is a play about youthfulness and sex, as well as race and class, and the idea of interracial romance still sat uncomfortably with many viewers.

The first on-stage interracial kiss came in 1958 with the performance of Ted Willis's *Hot Summer Night*, and one year later that same kiss came to the small screen with the play's adaptation for ITV's *Armchair Theatre*. The kisser was Barry's brother Lloyd. But in *Corner*, Reckord implied much more than an innocent courtship between his two young protagonists. If the 1962 Granada Television production is anything to go by—and presumably it was no more scandalous than the stage production—the characters of Dave and Terry engage in everything from passionate kissing to behind-the-scenes premarital sex; scenes include Dave touching Terry's breast (over her dress) and Terry sitting up in bed wearing only her bra, talking to a shirtless Dave dressing in the corner. The teleplay also featured a fantastic line that wasn't in the stage script: Terry's mother telling her daughter, "If you ask me, Dave's only class is in his mouth; he's like a black BBC."[65]

Reckord in fact shopped the story to the BBC's Sound Department for radio production, and internal correspondence concerning his script highlights both the reactions from more conservative quarters *and* the potential shift in sensibilities at the dawn of the so-called "permissive" era. The first reader commented, "Unbelievably coarse and nauseating to read.

Corporation (December 6, 1965). *African Writers' Club*, British Library website: http://sounds.bl.uk/Arts-literature-and-performance/African-Writers-Club/024M-C0134X0015XX-0200Vo, part of the British Library Sound Archive, London.

65 "Play of the Week: *You in Your Small Corner*," Granada Television, May 23, 1962, National Film and Television Archive, BFI, London.

Far too realistic for my sophisticated taste. All this wallowing in sex seems highly unadult to me!" The second reader declared it to be "an exercise in literary perversion." The third, future director Richard Cottrell, disparaged the script for technical reasons, but wrote in his memo:

> Help, help, young people do "wallow" in sex, it's important, it's demanding, it's frightening; "the heart of another is a dark forest" etc. and there's a lot of pain before one can accept that humbly. Or else forget that people have hearts at all of course. The play may be coarse, but people <u>are</u>. Tough, i'n't it?[66]

The ability of *You in Your Small Corner* to stir up such debate in the early 1960s, in a genre—the race relations drama—that was already beginning to lose its bloom, indicates the extent to which Reckord was pushing the envelope, at least with regard to the play's suggestion of interracial sexuality. It is worth noting that Reckord submitted all three of his early Royal Court plays—*Flesh to a Tiger, You in Your Small Corner,* and *Skyvers*—to the BBC for consideration as radio plays. They were all rejected, the first for its purple prose and violent conclusion; the second for its sexual content and language; the third for its obscene dialogue. Although readers like Richard Cottrell seemed more receptive to such daring material, the BBC's repeated rejections suggest the gulf between the priorities of the Royal Court Theatre/English Stage Company and those of more mainstream institutions like the BBC.[67]

Reckord also departed from the mainstream race relations narrative in his characterization of Dave Jordan. Although quintessentially Osborne-esque, this characterization was even more radical when applied to a young West Indian man. In 1960, when theater, cinema, or television presented West Indian migrants, the result (for the most part) was either unambiguously negative or positive. *Sapphire* (see previous chapter), which many contemporary observers on both sides of the Atlantic viewed as gritty and audacious, provides a good example.

Dave Jordan, on the other hand, is an unsettlingly human combination of traits. Indeed, he is unlikeable in many ways. He is a snob, who at

---

66 Respectively: memos, Cynthia Pughe to John Tydeman (September 20, 1963); David Close-Thomas to John Tydeman (September 30, 1963); and Richard Cottrell to John Tydeman (October 31, 1963). RCONT 12—Barry Reckord. Scriptwriters File 2 (1963–67), BBC Written Archives, Caversham, Reading.

67 In 1975, a dozen years after its rejection of *You in Your Small Corner,* BBC radio broadcast Reckord's "Club Havana," a play strikingly similar to *Corner* in terms of plot, characterization, and dialogue. The only real difference appears to be the names of the characters and the setting: the story takes place in Handsworth, Birmingham instead of Brixton. See RCONT 20—Barry Reckord. Copyright Contributor File (1970–74).

different moments betrays contempt for both Terry and his own mother. Lloyd Reckord, who played Dave Jordan on both the stage and small screen, employs a convincingly unappealing intonation and bearing to demonstrate the character's sense of cultural superiority. Even more significant, Dave's insecurities cause him to be angrily suspicious of others, especially white people—he even accuses sincere, affectionate Terry of looking down on him: "You've got a man and he's only bloody black so why should you try? ... You came down to Black Street for a rest. Here is the bottom."[68] This bitterness at times makes it seem that he will never be satisfied, in England or anywhere else. Dave has a chip on his shoulder, a quality that was stereotypically attributed to colonial immigrants who openly expressed resentment at their treatment as second-class citizens. This character type recurred in narratives for radio, television, film, and the stage, including *A Man from the Sun* (1956), *Sapphire* (1959), and *Flame in the Streets* (1964).

This stereotype of the "angry young black man" was typical, and high-profile black personalities in England rarely expressed frustration with the English social system, although some aired grievances with particular incidents or individuals. (These, however, were usually framed as isolated and *not* representative of public feeling at large.) The fact that Dave Jordan in many respects embodies the negative "chip-on-the-shoulder" image shows that Reckord was less concerned with political correctness and narrative convention than with exploring potential explanations for his hero's angry behavior. In short, the play persuaded audiences to sympathize with a protagonist who was not wholly good; not the "stoical and lofty creature" that John Elsom associated with British theater before *Look Back in Anger*, nor the stoical black settler played in these years by Earl Cameron.[69]

The search for answers in *Corner* resulted in its departure from the established British race relations narrative in another significant way—it privileged the perspective of its West Indian characters over that of its white English characters (although it touches on these too). Moreover, it does so without abandoning the classic narrative's familial parameters. Like *Sapphire* or *Flame in the Streets*, *You in Your Small Corner* situates the vast majority of its emotional drama within the confines of the home, and (even more specifically) in the emotional insecurities of its actors. But this time, it is not a white sister or sexually frustrated housewife who expresses the domestic threat posed by interracial marriage. In fact, in *Corner*, Terry's mother has no problem at all with her daughter's relationship with Dave; even Terry's prejudiced brother Georgie expresses no real qualms, although he does appear to be jealous of Dave's education and status. The real conflict

---

68   1962/W/16, *You in Your Small Corner* prompt script (1962), 3-I-12.
69   Elsom, *Post-War British Theatre*, 80.

takes place in Dave's psyche, and between him and his mother. And again, Mrs. Jordan's prejudices are an inseparable mixture of class snobbery and desire for her son to escape the stigma of Jamaica's racial hierarchy:

> Back in that stinkin' little island every little white or near-white gal in a clean frock and sandals is a queen, not matter where she came from. A decent black boy could never live long enough to hold one of them hand. That's why I say God bless this coloured immigration to England. You know why? Because our people come over here and see white people not as God on high but as servant. Sweep street. Clean people floor.[70]

Even Mrs. Jordan's employee, Jim, quietly tries to familiarize Dave with the new social ladder; of the West Indian club's clientele he remarks, "our boys not serious with this [Terry's] sort no longer you know, Mass Dave. When they come down here is wid good looking and good class English and continental."[71] For the purposes of the story, these sentiments increase Dave's uncertainty about his reasons for being with Terry; he confuses his sincere affection (and physical desire) for her with his inferiority complex. He fears that deep down, he considers himself unworthy of a better-educated or wealthier white woman. In this respect alone Reckord delved deeper into the psychological motivations behind prejudice than any of the "serious" productions of the mainstream British companies, even those released later in the decade. In addition, as we can see from Mrs. Jordan's observation above, Reckord's script drew a subtle but explicit connection between Jamaica's history and social system and the particular shape of the "colour problem" in Britain, a connection that the British race relations narrative largely ignored.

Finally, there is another kind of historical narrative about race in postwar Britain that Reckord overturned, though much later in life, through his comments in interviews and his reflections on the making of his plays. That is the narrative of a struggling but united black arts community. If he was an angry young man in the context of mainstream theater, then he was in for a penny, in for a pound: he was just as angry in the context of the expatriate West Indian community, with which he had a vital but complicated relationship, often taking issue with its racial politics and artistic strategies.

To talk of "West Indian theater" in 1950s and 1960s London is misleading— the phrase suggests a large, cohesive group, when in fact it barely existed. Reckord, Trinidadian Errol John, and Saint Lucian Derek Walcott were the

---

70 English Stage Company 1962/W/16, *You in Your Small Corner* prompt script (1962), 1-I-3.

71 Ibid., 1-I-7.

only three to gain any notice in London in this period.[72] Theater director Yvonne Brewster has singled out 1962 as a key year for black theater in London, due to the working presence of these three playwrights, as well as the Nigerian Wole Soyinka. Of these, according to Brewster, Reckord was the most popular at the time:

> In 1962, he had this incredible play, *You in Your Small Corner*, which was put on at the Royal Court Theatre. Then it transferred to the West End, to New Arts Theatre, and in a few months it was taken up by Granada Television in the "A Play for Today" series. Barry was doing what no white playwright was achieving at the time.[73]

Part of Reckord's achievement was providing material and employment for black actors, who were most often typecast or relegated to bit parts. Reckord's "intelligent and questioning"[74] drama provided weighty, straight roles that were the exception to the rule.

Reckord's undeniable influence and respect within the West Indian arts community, then and now, was tempered by his idiosyncratic political and intellectual disposition, as well as his articulate candor. He was an equal-opportunity critic, derogating mainstream entertainment, but also black actors and dramatists, at a time when they needed as much encouragement as they could get. In such a context, Reckord may have come across as less than sympathetic in the eyes of his peers. In his 1997 interview he complained about his West Indian colleagues on the set of *You in Your Small Corner*, including Pearl Connor, who at times acted as his agent, but in this context was an actress in his play:

> Pearl Connor was doing one of the parts and a boy called Neville Monroe ... was offered a part in a film called, "A Taste of Honey" by Tony Richardson. And here he was in my play and Pearl was his agent so she was encouraging him because the money was better to go into this film and to leave me stranded. ... It was a most bizarre situation. And I'm afraid this happens quite a lot in black theatre—people have more than two eyes, they have two in the back of their heads as well, and ... there is an enormous amount of screwing up that goes on.[75]

Reckord was displeased with what he viewed as the unprofessionalism of Monroe's and Connor's decisions. Connor, no doubt, was thinking not

---

72   Walcott is today considered a poet first—he was awarded the Nobel Prize for Literature in 1992.

73   Yvonne Brewster quoted in Michael Reckord, "Jamaica's Gifts to British Theatre," *The Jamaica Gleaner* (March 15, 2009).

74   Ibid.

75   Ibid. In fact, Neville Monroe did not appear in *A Taste of Honey*.

only of the better money and greater notoriety offered to Monroe by starring in *A Taste of Honey*, but also the potential for more and better dramatic opportunities for her West Indian and Commonwealth clients more generally. As she herself recalled years later, "Every day was a struggle, every day was a fight, for every penny an artist got. ... [W]e were trying to build reputations, trying to get people recognized."[76] Reckord did not seem to possess Connor's crusading spirit for the untrained West Indian actor attempting to win fame in London show business:

> I was talking to one [black actor] at a bus stop and he just got a part in a ... soap opera. He told me that he was going to be a star and I had to remind him, and he didn't know this, that every five years ... there is a West Indian actor who is going to be a star and they get this one part and it's going to make them king ... and it never does.[77]

Arguably, a remark like this reveals Reckord's bitterness about his own failure to gain lasting fame equal to the New Wave's most visible dramatists. But it also reveals his critical perspective on the real challenges facing young black actors in the British cultural mainstream, an outlook to which his experience producing *Skyvers* also contributed, as we will see.

Although his perspective on the state of the arts in Britain may have been bleaker than his colleagues, Reckord nonetheless did much to bring West Indian drama into the limelight through his connection to the Royal Court Theatre. He (and his brother Lloyd) worked continuously and energetically within that tiny scene, and his work laid a critical foundation for the efforts of other West Indian performers and writers trying to make it in London. Pearl Connor, whose work as a talent agent for colonial artists was so tireless and essential, remarked, "There was no representation for black and coloured people. I was inspired because it was a pioneering job, and two Jamaican brothers, Barry and Lloyd Reckord, were bulwarks of my efforts, one a writer, the other an actor."[78]

Despite a few technical and aesthetic qualms, English observers responded very favorably to *You in Your Small Corner*; much more favorably than to *Flesh to a Tiger*, even though they bestowed much less critical attention upon it. Their accolades, moreover, often dealt with Reckord's "original" emphasis on class as well as race—although such an emphasis could only be viewed as original in a "West Indian" play expected to address "West Indian" subjects. John Russell Taylor, in his 1962 book on the "new British drama,"

---

76 Special Collections 9704095/A. *Blackgrounds* oral history project on the experience of Black Theatre and Black Theatre professionals. Pearl Connor in conversation with David Johnson, Wembley, London, June 25, 1997, TMA.

77 Barry Reckord in conversation with David Johnson, April 22, 1997.

78 Connor-Mogotsi, "My Life with Edric Connor," 147–55.

wrote that with *Corner*, Reckord "showed a considerable advance in dramatic technique," and noted that "the story of a group of relatively wealthy West Indians living in Brixton and looking down on their 'low-class' English neighbours had a number of salutary surprises in store for the conventionally minded."[79] In the *Daily Express*, Clive Barnes reported:

> For the first few minutes I fidgeted in my seat, grimly prepared for yet another of those plays about colour prejudice where all the blacks are white and all the whites are dirty. But as Mr. Reckord's play got underway I became fascinated. Mr. Reckord has vitalized the hackneyed cliché of black and white by using it as a counterpoint to his main theme—prejudice between the classes.[80]

The *Daily Mail* found the play similarly refreshing, and praised Reckord for cutting "right through already hackneyed 'Would you let your daughter marry a negro' territory, to essay a most unusual and provocative drama about class."[81] In the context of the Royal Court's output, Reckord's "drama about class" was in fact not all that unusual, and it was provocative only in the sense that it suggested that in postwar Britain, class might be a more fundamental marker of social difference than race. By explicitly placing domestic considerations of race and class in the same frame, Reckord effectively made a more foreign subject—racism and imperial migration— familiar to an English audience, both in the theater and, later, on television. As legendary critic Kenneth Tynan wrote: "The real distinction of Mr. Reckord's piece ... lies in the ironic skill with which it weaves two separate problems—class-consciousness and colour-consciousness—into a single dramatic thread."[82]

Of all Reckord's plays for the Royal Court, *You in Your Small Corner* most closely resembled the other contemporary "social problem" dramas appearing in their scores in Britain. However, by obviously employing familiar conventions, those established by both the Royal Court canon and the race relations narrative, Reckord was able to create a more complex, and arguably more subversive, picture of postwar British society in terms of class, race, and gender. His next play, *Skyvers*, would stress some of these elements over others, surprising critics and cementing his reputation as a playwright in the Royal Court—and not simply "West Indian"—tradition.

---

79 Taylor, *The Angry Theatre*, 89.

80 Clive Barnes, "A Jamaican Changes the Old Theme," *Daily Express* (October 24, 1960). THM/273/7/2/63, *You in Your Small Corner* Press Cuttings (1960), Royal Court Archive. TMA.

81 Muller, "It's a Little Play with a Lot to Say," *Daily Mail* (October 24, 1960). Royal Court Theatre—*You in Your Small Corner* Production File (1960), Royal Court Archive. TMA.

82 Kenneth Tynan, "The Birth of a Snob," *Observer* (October 30, 1960), THM/273/7/2/63.

Skyvers

No one considered *Skyvers*—which premiered as a Sunday Night production "without décor" on April 7, 1963, and then graduated to a proper run at the Royal Court on July 23—to be a West Indian play. It was set in England. All the players were white. It made no mention of the British Empire, the West Indies, immigration, or even black people, with the exception of a vague reference to "makin' ten quid a week on a building site and havin' to fight off them blacks, and the Irish."[83] With this third effort, then, it seems that Reckord finally shook off the "West Indian playwright" label, graduating, in a sense, to simply "playwright." *Plays and Players* summed up his achievement:

> [F]inally—and really quite irrelevantly as far as this play is concerned— he has broken away completely from the "negro dramatist" tag. Even the most emancipated critics tend to suppose that as women dramatists should write "women's plays", so negro dramatists should write plays about negroes; but *Skyvers* is not a play about negroes, it is a play about people who just happen, this time, all to be white; it is ultimately, and triumphantly, just a play.[84]

In the process of shedding the "negro dramatist tag," however, Reckord transformed himself into a "Royal Court dramatist," as *Skyvers* incontrovertibly shows. It possesses a shopping list of thematic and aesthetic concerns associated with alternative postwar theater in Britain, of which the Royal Court was the most celebrated proponent.

The play is an indictment of the English education system and its tendency to alienate vulnerable youths (and budding citizens) instead of encouraging or enlightening them. Cragge, another working-class Royal Court anti-hero, spends the play torn between loyalty toward his apathetic peers, who are contemptuous of sincere ambition, and his own fledgling desire to learn, which is consistently quashed by his bitter and prejudiced teachers: "Pursuing his own course, he defies the authority of both [the school and the gang] and, as a result, is physically punished both by his contemporaries and his elders."[85] In Cragge, the audience gets a glimpse of the adult anti-hero's origins, the roots of his decision to opt out of contemporary social norms.

---

83 Barry Reckord, "Skyvers," in *New English Dramatists, Vol. 9* (London: Penguin Books, 1966), 86–87.

84 "First Nights: *Skyvers,*" *Play and Players* (September 1963). THM/273/7/2/115, *Skyvers* Press Cuttings, Royal Court Archive. TMA.

85 Michael Billington, introduction to "Skyvers," in *New English Dramatists, Vol. 9* (London: Penguin Books, 1966), 12.

Yet despite the play's focus on Cragge as "the natural outsider"[86] and critics' widespread praise for the "authenticity" of Reckord's dialogue, observers most often assumed that the villains of the piece were neither the teachers nor the hooligans, but rather "the stub-end schools that disfigure this country's education system," or (more vaguely) "conformity and mass education."[87] Thus Cragge, like Della, Dave Jordan, and Osborne's Jimmy Porter, is the dramatic "hero" only because he is more intimately aware of the social forces acting upon him, and not because he possesses any particular moral or behavioral superiority. Their personal flaws and transgressions are simply less significant than their own suffering in society.

John Sandilands, writing for the *Daily Sketch*, was one of the few critics who took particular notice of just how faithfully *Skyvers* conformed to these now-established conventions:

> If you attend the Royal Court long enough you get a very quaint impression of the lower income brackets.
>
> They are always revolting, in more ways than one. They are always being trampled by Authority and Authority is always either vicious, insensate or criminally indolent.
>
> And in Barry Reckord's "Skyvers" we are at it again. ...
>
> Only a Royal Court audience, schooled to catch every bitter innuendo, could applaud as they did last night.[88]

Sandilands's description, though unsympathetic, draws attention to another point—that by 1963, audiences (and especially critics) had learned the language of the Royal Court and, like *You in Your Small Corner*, *Skyvers* pleased because it spoke that theatrical language with accuracy and artistry. Viewers knew what conventions and subjects they were dealing with, much more so than they had with a more "foreign" play, like *Flesh to a Tiger*. This is not to say that *Skyvers* was not a better-structured and executed play than its predecessors; only that it was easier to celebrate as a piece of English theater. And, indeed, *Skyvers* was in the main widely and excellently reviewed.

Skyvers is a play about class; or, more specifically, that class of youth that is oppressed by the British school system and forced to either submit and perpetuate the system, or reject the values of the dominant culture and be punished for it. Cragge and his companions are universally expected to

---

86   Ibid., 11.

87   Reviews from Jeremy Kingston in *Punch* (September 15, 1971) and the *New Statesman* (August 2, 1963). THM/273/7/2/270 and THM/273/7/2/115. TMA.

88   John Sandilands, "Authority Wins Again," *Daily Sketch* (July 24, 1963). Royal Court Theatre—*Skyvers* (1963), General Archive. TMA.

drop out of the system as early as possible and, at best, move on to a job in an economy where steady but dead-end work is all that's available. Cragge understands and resents this. When one of his teachers asks him why he swears so much, he replies, "'Cos there's too many things make me puke. He'd [the headmaster] lose the manor for us swearin'—but no matter how little we learn he don't lose nothing. For 'avin' most of us leave 'ere content to do borin' dirty work 'e gets the Mayor praisin' him."[89] But again, like Jimmy Porter, Della, and Dave Jordan, Cragge does not fit comfortably within his group of rejects either; secretly he nurses a tender ambition to continue in school, demonstrated by his writing for the school newspaper. When he finally breaks with the gang by refusing to participate in a high-profile school prank, he is ultimately the one the headmaster blames for it. The play ends uncertainly, with the audience unsure what path Cragge will follow, outcast as he is from both "classes," here defined more in cultural than economic terms. The *Daily Telegraph*, in fact, declared *Skyvers* too inconclusive: "Did he [Cragge] see that rough justice had been done, and continue in the school as a reformed rake? Or did he—which seems more likely—run away and become a delinquent?"[90] In essence, he is one of the few to recognize that both groups, one embodied by the headmaster and the other by the vicious gang leader Brook, are similarly narrow-minded and conservative:

> The gang and the school 'ave a bit in common, 'aven't they? The headmaster drives that luxury liner and 'as 'is own parking space. Brook loves that. And at staff meetings, all of them teachers, two hundred blokes, shoot up when the headmaster comes in. Brook loves that again.[91]

Cragge's is furthermore a uniquely postwar dilemma in that he comes from a working-class background but *in theory* has the opportunity to advance if he applies himself at school—an option that would have been closed to most low-income youths a few decades earlier. What *Skyvers* reveals is the persistence of prejudice between classes and generations that disfigures the education system and makes Cragge's progress so difficult.

Reckord's portrayal of the play's female characters also contains echoes of earlier representatives of the multifaceted "angry young man" tradition. If anything, *Skyvers* is more brutal in its approach. Helen and Sylvia, fifteen-year-olds at the school, are at the mercy of the men, who treat

89 Reckord, "Skyvers," *New English Dramatists*, 105.

90 "First Night: Salvation of a Rebel Schoolboy," *Daily Telegraph* (July 24, 1963). Royal Court Theatre—*Skyvers* (1963), General Archive. See also W. A. Darlington, "Five Misfits at School: Inconclusive Play by Negro Author," *Daily Telegraph* (April 8, 1963), THM/273/7/2/121, *Skyvers* Press Cuttings (1963), Royal Court Archive. TMA.

91 Reckord, "Skyvers," *New English Dramatists*, 105.

them meanly. In fact, a major subplot revolves around their alleged rape by Brook and his cronies; significantly, Cragge attempts to persuade a nervous and frightened Sylvia not to go out with them, and is "wickedly beaten" as a result. Obviously, Sylvia and Helen's predicament provokes sympathy but, as with *Look Back* especially, there is an ambivalence in the play's tone. They are both unheroic representatives of the conformity that the story critiques, preferring Brook to Cragge and consistently bowing to the social pressure of the boys in the gang. In the first scene, Helen explains to Cragge that when Brook "Talks to a girl his hand ain't all sweaty to hold from being nervous," and states that "no girl would 'ave you if she could get him."[92] Later, he attempts to protect Sylvia from the gang's violent intentions at the graveyard in the evening after Brook remarks, "If they die from overwork we can bury 'em right there and then." But Sylvia is eventually swayed because she too prefers Brook, and in fact joins in when they jeer at Cragge for opting out.[93] In a sense, Reckord presents the girls as willing participants in their own degradation. This is further emphasized by the fact that the audience is never entirely sure whether Helen and Sylvia consented to the sexual relations at the graveyard, and Reckord never resolves this strand of the storyline. The play's uncertain portrayal of its female characters, as both victims and predators, also fit the Royal Court mold.

Newspaper critics, however, remarked only obliquely on the significance of class in *Skyvers*, and even less on the representation of gender roles. What struck most reviewers was the "authenticity" of Reckord's script, Ann Jellicoe's direction, and the acting of the young stars, especially David Hemmings as Cragge. The *Spectator*, for example, remarked on Reckord's "beautifully authentic dialogue," and the *Daily Worker* was so convinced by the first Sunday Night performance that it declared: "This play by Barry Reckord is electrifying because it is true, and deserves a run."[94] The *Queen* was rather more specific in its praise when it noted Reckord's ability to convey "the tenderness and mercilessness of youth without either propaganda, sentimentality or melodrama."[95] Part of *Skyvers*'s purported authenticity no doubt stemmed from Reckord's liberal use of obscenities and Cockney slang, and the Lord Chamberlain was apparently equally liberal in his cuts and modifications to the original script. When the Court's Theatre Upstairs restaged the play in 1971, it was with all curse words and phrases intact, and critics commented on the continued, and perhaps even enhanced, currency of theme and language; it was successful enough

---

92 Ibid., 81.
93 Ibid., 114–16.
94 Reviews of *Skyvers* ("Sunday Night" performance) in the *Spectator* (April 11, 1963) and *Daily Worker* (April 9, 1963), THM/273/7/2/121. Royal Court Archive. TMA.
95 "Skyvers," *Queen* (August 14, 1963), THM/273/7/2/115. Royal Court Archive. TMA.

Skyvers at the Royal Court Theatre, July 1963.
Photograph by Douglas H. Jeffery.
© Douglas H. Jeffery/Victoria and Albert Museum, London 2015.

that *Skyvers* transferred to the Roundhouse, and *Today's Cinema* wrote: "Reckord, who is a school teacher himself, has captured the vernacular of the young men and women he is writing about with amazing fluency and authenticity." The *Guardian* concurred: "The punchy cadences of the less frequently printed parts of our mother tongue, indeed, give the piece a fair amount of its culture-shock value and even more of its laughs."[96]

The set design, acting, and direction, moreover, all drew attention to the boys' language. The 1963 set was spare and static; a drab, minimalist classroom with windows that mimicked a prison cell. This uninspiring backdrop heightened the effect of the characters' own frenetic energy. In her capacity as a director, Ann Jellicoe's productions are remembered

---

96   Allen Kalman, "Revitalised at the Roundhouse," *Today's Cinema* (September 21, 1971), and the *Guardian* review (September 10, 1971), THM/273/7/2/270, *Skyvers* Press Cuttings. Royal Court Archive. TMA.

not only for their language but for their physicality, and *Skyvers* is no exception; archival photographs show the boys not simply sitting at, but standing and dancing on their desks, as well as putting their feet up, lying on tables, taking off their pants, getting into fights, throwing books, and riding bicycles.[97] Their physical dynamism echoed their colorful dialogue and convincingly reproduced an environment of teenage rebellion.

In all these ways, *Skyvers* was truly a play for a writer's theater. But a final word needs to be said about the seeming authenticity or realism of Reckord's dialogue; it was a means to an end, namely the powerful presentation of a social or political issue. Cragge's and Brook's words were not just a slice of life; they highlighted the persistence of conformity, prejudice, and the repression of individualism in postwar England—phenomena exacerbated by the structure of the comprehensive school system. As Reckord wrote in the preface to Penguin's publication of *Skyvers*:

> Although I have avoided any sort of artificially heightened language and kept within the range of cockney idiom, the language in this play is clearly invented. Schoolboys, on the whole, don't talk in the way I make them talk. Usually their talk is less interesting. But if the play sounds real it is because I've got down what these boys do in fact think and feel, although they are often too inarticulate to say it. This, to me, is the imaginative process—the whole business of writing.[98]

The *Daily Mail* contained one of the few reviews to acknowledge the skillful rendering of dramatic language that the English Stage Company would have prized:

> I am tempted to a rash use of the word "authentic" to describe the boys' talk, but, strictly speaking, I don't know whether it is authentic or not—I never heard talk like that at my public school.
>
> Still, if not authentic, the dialogue is absolutely convincing, and sits absolutely naturally in the boys' mouths.
>
> What is more, it has elegance and rhythm, and hot feeling below it; a compelling picture of thoughts struggling to be born in the mouths of the inarticulate.[99]

It is a testament to the quality of the writing that so few observers seem to have noticed the distinction between dramatic realism and social reality; the suspension of disbelief not only made *Skyvers* a critically successful

---

97 See THM/273/6/1/474, *Skyvers* (1963)—Photographs. Royal Court Archive. TMA.

98 Reckord, preface to "Skyvers," *New English Dramatists*, 77.

99 *Skyvers* review, *Daily Mail* (April 8, 1963), THM/273/7/2/121. Royal Court Archive. TMA.

play, but also convinced viewers of the "authenticity" of the social or cultural issues it addressed. Pam Brighton, who directed the Court's 1971 revival, rhetorically asked "How had Barry, a Jamaican teacher, in a London comprehensive, described so accurately the alienation and rage of south London boys?" then answered, "He had come to England, had gone to Cambridge but was black, radical and incapable of compromise. He had a ringside [*sic*] at what social alienation meant."[100] Thus, from Brighton's perspective, Reckord's disposition and personal fortunes—as well as, presumably, his experience as a teacher in London—gave him an empathetic perspective on a social question by which he was apparently untouched.

Incidentally, the play's authentic power has aged well. In the summer of 2006, the Royal Court's Theatre Upstairs did several readings of Court plays from that defining era of the late 1950s and early 1960s, *Skyvers* among them. An ailing Reckord attended with Diana Athill, who recalled that

> it was a glorious surprise when it turned out to be so well done that within minutes the full house forgot that it was watching an excellent full performance of the play. The audience was as responsive as any playwright could wish, and when at the end Barry had to go on stage to thank everyone concerned, and said in a choked voice (looking so small and old), "I never, ever, expected to see that play again," they rose to him.[101]

In terms of this chapter's concern with Reckord's use and manipulation of the race relations narrative, it seems initially that an analysis of *Skyvers* offers little to the discussion, as it featured no black or West Indian characters, and made no comment on the issue of race relations. But there are a few points to note. First, Reckord (and others, including his brother Lloyd) have stated that this third script was originally intended for a cast of black, not white, youths. The professed reasons for this differ in historically interesting ways. Reckord was unflinching in his appraisal of black dramatic talent in the 1950s and early 1960s; in his view, not only was it scarce, but it was often substandard in quality ("Good black actors weren't thick on the ground"). He claimed that he originally wrote *Skyvers* for a cast of young black actors, but apparently "couldn't find any … it was impossible to find at that stage … now you could find five hundred probably."[102]

In later years Reckord came under attack for his decision to abandon the racial theme in his play. In a published conversation with noted fringe

100 Pam Brighton quoted in Brewster, *For the Reckord*, 73.
101 Athill, *Somewhere towards the End*, 126–27.
102 Barry Reckord in conversation with David Johnson, April 22, 1997.

pioneers Mustapha Matura (who worked with the Royal Court in the late 1960s and 1970s), Oscar James, and Roland Rees, the following exchange took place:

> REES: Barry Reckord's *Skyvers* was produced with an all white cast because, as Barry said, the Royal Court could not find any black actors. By the late Sixties, we were doing InterAction's seasons and Mustapha's plays with black casts. What happened? What had changed? Did this seem to you the start of something new?
> JAMES: Listen, maybe the Royal Court and Barry did not look far enough! ... No black actors! That's an old excuse, which has been going on for ages.
> MATURA: If we are talking about change, that is the change. Where you, Roland, wanted to find black actors because you had some vision of truth or realism that had been introduced into the culture of the times. You determined to find West Indian actors, and the Royal Court and Barry Reckord were not interested.[103]

This conversation, which occurred in the early 1990s, demonstrates a lack of knowledge of West Indian theater and performance in England prior to the 1960s. Taking into account both Reckord's own comments, and the fact that he had written other plays (like *Flesh to a Tiger*) featuring predominantly black casts, it is reasonable to conclude that, for whatever reason, he was dissatisfied with both the quantity and quality of black acting in London's postwar theater scene. He recounted, for example, his frustrations with a lead he had hired for a comedic play:

> [H]e couldn't act. ... It was a frightful business starting to get on an actor's back because he isn't getting the thing right ... and watching him break ... and finally, two days before we were supposed to open, ... him grabbing his jacket and just fucking off out of the place. ... Oh God, that scene ... I mean it's a bad one. ... And we couldn't think instantly of finding another black actor.[104]

Barry Reckord's frank criticisms of his West Indian peers in London likely made him a contrary figure in the small West Indian artistic scene, as well as in the larger arena of London theater. It is, for example, unlikely that many West Indian actors, in his own or subsequent generations, would have sympathized with his observation that "I have always wondered about the element of racism in theatre and I think that ... mostly there is positive discrimination, that people are bending over

---

103 Roland Rees, *Fringe First*, 101.
104 Barry Reckord in conversation with David Johnson, April 22, 1997.

backwards to find writers that they can back, writers that they can put out."[105] Such a reflection was perhaps influenced by his own experience, but also, perhaps by his position on black politics. While he made the above remark during a 1993 interview, his views on race politics were equally contrarian in the mid-1960s, when the Black Power movement was gaining worldwide influence. Taking part in a BBC discussion on the question of the existence of a "brotherhood of black people," Reckord was at odds with his co-panelists when he declared:

> I resent very much playing the white game of making negroes a special problem. We are not a special problem. We are seeking status, and this is a universal business. People are trying to move from insignificance to significance ... *everybody's* status seeking, and so are negroes. For us to *continuously* regard ourselves as a special kind of status-seeker with a special kind of personality that needs years to sort out, is just to play this humiliating game.[106]

Reckord's brother Lloyd voiced similar criticisms, and came under attack from his West Indian colleagues in the CAM. The symposium itself, to which I refer again in the Conclusion, is a fascinating look at a transitional moment when the politics of the first generation of postwar migrants clashed with that of the newer arrivals, who were clearly more influenced by American black culture and politics than older European standards of drama. Symposium attendees had been praising Ram John Holder's play *Eviction Blues*, in part because it brought West Indian drama back "into the ghetto, where it began," and Lloyd Reckord rather cynically questioned its intrinsic quality: "You see, unfortunately, or fortunately, looking back over my whole theatrical career I can only think, Jesus Christ, hasn't most of this stuff been bad?" When a contributor from the floor protested, "If Ramjohn's play inside of the ghetto turns on people and they think it's beautiful, then by God it's beautiful!" Lloyd Reckord sharply retorted:

> NO! I have been in 50 plays and the peasants have come backstage to me and they've said, Lloyd, you're marvellous. And I knew that they were stupid bastards and I knew the play stank. Shakespeare has said, "the verdict of which one [*sic*] must outweigh a whole theatre of others,"

---

105 Ibid.
106 Barry Reckord, roundtable discussion, "Is There a Common Bond between Black People All Over the World; a Brotherhood of Black People?," *African Writers' Club*, British Broadcasting Corporation (date unknown, probably mid-1960s). *African Writers' Club*, British Library website: http://sounds.bl.uk/Arts-literature-and-performance/African-Writers-Club/024M-C0134X0015XX-0200V0, part of the British Library Sound Archive, London.

and I would rather what Shakespeare has said, this white man, than what you have said, with your great knowledge of theatre, thank you very much.[107]

Both Reckord brothers were in this respect again "angry young men," not only in relation to the British Establishment, but even, to an extent, in relation to the West Indian arts community in London. Lloyd clearly wished to transcend his educated but narrowly middle-class origins, but he was also, as this remark suggests, impatient with aspects of the black politics that emerged in the 1960s—which, to him, suggested its own narrowness.

Reckord's use of an all-white cast is significant too because it illuminated the parallels between the experiences of racial discrimination and class discrimination for young people growing up in postwar Britain. Although Reckord most likely revised his script for the new cast, the fact that he could easily envision such an adaptation is further evidence that the "West Indian" concern with the British race question, far from being marginal to the postwar British experience, was an integral part of it. Some observers inadvertently made this connection, even when they were unaware that *Skyvers* was originally intended for a black cast. *The Times* reported:

> Barry Reckord is a West Indian dramatist and his last play was about an immigrant West Indian boy's struggle to fit into the British tribal system. The hero of *Skyvers* is again an adolescent outsider in search of identity: the difference is that this time he is white. In Cragge, the 15-year-old comprehensive school malcontent, Mr. Reckord has created the first white Negro to appear on the British stage.[108]

According to this definition, however, it is arguable that the Royal Court had in fact presented a string of "white Negroes" on the British stage, beginning with the famous Jimmy Porter. In fact, Tony Richardson's film adaptation of *Look Back in Anger* features a small subplot revolving around the fortunes of Kapoor, one of Jimmy's fellow market vendors, a newly arrived immigrant from India. And Shelagh Delaney's play *A Taste of Honey*, adapted for the screen and directed by Richardson in 1961, contains a white teenager's brief relationship with (and impregnation by) a black sailor as its trigger incident. Thus the major difference between Cragge and Jimmy Porter is only that the former was created by a West Indian playwright *expected* to address colonialism and race in his productions. In fact, when *The Times* reviewed the first "Sunday Night" production, it commented,

---

107 Transcript, 1967 symposium on West Indian Theatre, CAM 5/5/1, George Padmore Institute, London, 22–23.

108 "An Outsider in Search of Identity," *The Times* (July 24, 1963), Royal Court Theatre—*Skyvers* (1963), General Archive.

"For once we are not offered any formula explanations about the deprived and under-privileged; the boys are what they are, for whatever reasons; they are here, at this point in their lives, with decisions to make, and we simply observe them doing it."[109] Reckord's intentions were not nearly so artless; his play is nothing if not a critique of the British school system and its tendency to extinguish ambition in working-class students. But the critic for *The Times*, along with several others, viewed the boys' situation as recognizable and naturalistic. If the play had featured a black cast, however, as originally intended, the critical conclusion would likely have been very different—in that case, *Skyvers* would have been a "coloured," "West Indian," or "Negro" play.

This is a third reason why it is useful to evaluate *Skyvers* in relation to domestic issues of race and immigration: although the play did not specifically address these issues, Reckord's status as a West Indian meant that critics often brought race into their reviews. In particular, his colonial or "foreign" background made his achievement of British social realism all the more remarkable: "One might expect a West Indian playwright to concern himself about problems of integration. What one does not expect him to do is to concern himself about the growing pains of a young Cockney ... But Barry Reckord does exactly this, and does it extremely well." Another review celebrated the play as a triumph of the cultural and geographic margins of Britain over the center: "It has taken a West Indian playwright and a director born in Middlesborough to lift the lid off the non-education that can go on in a comprehensive school in London."[110] In this sense, Reckord helped subvert the dominant race relations narrative by producing a work that ignored it—after being himself pigeonholed as a "West Indian playwright" concerned narrowly with race and empire. *Skyvers*, meanwhile, startled observers precisely because it was so "authentically" *English* in tone, content, and language.

Barry Reckord's next two plays for the Royal Court, *Give the Gaffers Time to Love You* ("Sunday Night" production, 1973) and *X* (Royal Court Theatre Upstairs, 1974), were similarly unconcerned with West Indian or racial themes, although they did expand upon questions of class oppression, youth, and sexuality. They also continued in the Royal Court tradition of controversial, issue-based productions. Reckord never lost his self-declared identification as a "literary socialist," and he remained committed to creating politically charged, content-driven drama. *X* in particular revolved around a frank discussion of sex and morality between a university lecturer

---

109 "Unwanted Year for Youth," *The Times* (April 8, 1963), THM/273/7/2/121. Royal Court Archive. TMA.

110 "Skyvers," *Daily Mirror* (July 25, 1963), and Molly Hobman, "A School of Scandal," *Bath and Wilts Evening Chronicle* (July 27, 1963), THM/273/7/2/115. Royal Court Archive. TMA.

father and his teenage daughter, with the latter at one point attempting to seduce the former. (In the theatrical context of the mid-1970s, this was not as shocking as it would have been ten years prior. In fact, while some critics found the play sensationalist or even pornographic, the majority carefully avoided questions of morality in their reviews, choosing instead to disparage the play on aesthetic grounds.)[111] *X*, owing perhaps in part to its provocative subject matter, was a significant success at the Royal Court's Theatre Upstairs, which twice extended its run.[112]

By this time, the particular race relations narrative so current in the 1950s and early '60s was played out. Mustapha Matura was exploring Caribbean themes at the Royal Court with productions like *Play Mas*, but he was building upon a theatrical foundation laid twenty years earlier. The *overtly* sexual interracial relationship that Reckord presented in *You in Your Small Corner* would never seem so bold again, and the abandonment of racial themes as exhibited in *Skyvers* would, in the future, merit little attention. Unfortunately, the cleverness with which he manipulated audience expectations about race relations—by working within the emerging Royal Court tradition—has also been forgotten. This chapter has endeavored to insert Reckord's forgotten work back into the historical narrative of postwar British theater, to show just how much issues of "West Indian" concern so neatly complemented the Royal Court's historic commitment to revolutionize British drama by staging critical, topical, socially aware productions that would resonate with, and educate, a new generation of audiences.

---

111 See THA/273/712/358. Press clippings—Royal Court, *X*, August 1974. English Stage Company Archive. TMA.

112 *X* ultimately ran from August 19 until October 12, 1974.

Conclusion

The foregoing history, though selective, gives a sense of the priorities of, and challenges facing, the first postwar generation of Caribbean artists in London. They all worked diligently to negotiate a meaningful place for themselves within the British cultural sphere—one that was commercially viable and that justified and naturalized the West Indian and colonial presence in Britain. The collective result was the formulation of a distinctive cultural politics shaped by, among other things, colonial independence, West Indian federation, mainstream success and struggle in London, white racism, and the cultural similarities between Great Britain and her imperial margins. By injecting this cultural politics into British television, radio, music, art, and drama (as well as literature), West Indian settler-artists redefined so-called "white" British culture after 1945, both progressive and mainstream.

Their historical obscurity, then, is partly a comment on the preoccupations—and blind spots—of both general accounts of postwar British culture and more specialized analyses of black British art. In the former, black artists appear in the nation's culture as destabilizing agents signifying the break-up of cultural consensus. The latter, until recently, have tended to begin their histories after the early postwar era. Further, these theory-rich and deeply political studies employ fundamentally conflictual frameworks that are perhaps not well-suited to the professional and artistic choices made by the subjects of this book.

This is because the careers of Ronald Moody, the Reckords, the Connors, Earl Cameron—and many other musicians, artists, writers, and actors who migrated from the Caribbean to London at this time—demonstrate the continued domestic currency of the British Empire well into the 1960s. Moreover, they demonstrate that imperial ties could be an integrative force; that, even after decolonization, the memory of the imperial past, combined with present-day collaboration and education, could render British culture both united and multicultural at the same time. They did not invent these ties or connections, but their work made them visible to British audiences.

In order to gain a professional foothold in London, these individuals exploited the intersections between their own skills and the preferences of native British audiences and institutions. This was easier for some than for others. The novelty of the Trinidadian calypsonians, and their ability to deftly tailor their craft to their new setting, assured them recording contacts and appreciative listeners, black and white. Lords Kitchener, Beginner, and Invader sang about the topical and quotidian—riding the underground, queuing for rations—things to which all Britons could relate. They also leveraged a shared set of imperial values, like fair play, a sporting attitude, and a respect for historic institutions like the monarchy, in order to emphasize their own fitness for inclusion in the British polity.

Edric and Pearl Connor utilized the BBC's external service, and its mandate to educate and uplift viewers and listeners, to promote Caribbean culture, history, and artists. Edric's singing and acting talents were a means to this end; meanwhile, Pearl channeled the Corporation's demand for colonial talent into the business of professionalizing and representing West Indian performers in London. She created opportunities for her clients by simultaneously helping expand their existing niche and persuading producers to cast black actors in a wider range of roles. Cy Grant, on the other hand, had the crooning voice, good looks, and personal charm to secure a long-running presence on the *Tonight* program. But he too, contrary to his own ambitions, compromised with producers who could not envision him as a universally acceptable "leading man" on account of his color. It was thus his West Indian identification that gave him prominence as a calypso singer and as an actor in dramas of migration and settlement.

Although sculptor Ronald Moody met with initial success in Paris, his most ambitious works were less recognized in Britain, where he found more commissions as a portrait sculptor. His increasing participation in exhibitions with a Commonwealth, Caribbean, or diasporic theme reflected his identification, by the 1960s, as a "black" or colonial artist. Although, as Val Wilmer has remarked, Moody "died in 1985 scandalously neglected by the establishment,"[1] his intellectual and professional quest to find a recognized place for himself in the metropolitan art world best illustrates the experience of talented colonial artists in postwar London, as its image shifted from imperial capital to multiracial city.

Very few opportunities were open to Caribbean-born actors in postwar Britain generally, but this was especially true in mainstream film; Pearl Connor put it best when she remarked: "Usually they wanted a black person who could show his teeth, roll his eyes, shake his bottom and move along the road."[2] Bermudan Earl Cameron was the exception, appearing

---

1   Wilmer, *Mama Said There'd Be Days Like This*, 106.
2   Transcript, Pearl Connor interviewed by Anne Walmsley, February 25, 1987, 18, CAM 6/14, George Padmore Institute, London.

in a number of leading roles in mainstream films by Rank and Ealing. His characters, however, were almost universally defined by their race. Hence, Cameron's common ground with the English film industry lay in successively dramatizing domestic race relations. Even when we consider that Cameron was not particularly politicized in his ideals, this degree of typecasting is distressing. But before we view his cultural work as entirely dictated by white film executives, it is worth remembering that, due not least to the sheer frequency of his appearances, Cameron did a great deal to determine the character of the "representative" Caribbean settler on the silver screen. Not only did he imbue his roles with warmth and dignity—he has said that "there's no one I have felt ashamed to play in theatre, film, or television"[3]—but he adapted their demeanor to reflect the changing tone of the color question between 1950 and 1965.

Finally, playwright Barry Reckord was fortunate in many ways to earn the patronage of the English Stage Company and the Royal Court Theatre early in his career, because they allowed him considerable flexibility in his choice of subject matter, and the leeway to write relatively radical plays for mainstream London theater. He was also fortunate to join the Royal Court cadre just as its star was rising. Nonetheless, Reckord remained sensitive to the tastes of both Company directors and English audiences, choosing, after his Jamaica-set *Flesh to a Tiger*, to feature more British-oriented settings in his plays (a Brixton neighborhood, an English secondary modern) and issues (the race relations controversy, working-class identity). In doing so, Reckord expanded the creative range expected of a "West Indian playwright" in London.

Despite the differences in professed political commitment among these artists, together their work presented a picture of British society that was multiracial, multicultural, and aware of its imperial (and later post-imperial) history and character. They showed that the British citizenship of West Indian settlers was more than a purely legal status; it was grounded in shared values, history, and cultural aims.

The attitude of British (and London-based) cultural institutions, producers, agents, and audiences toward the work of the West Indian artists discussed above was, for roughly the first fifteen years after the end of the war, amenable and cautiously optimistic. In the 1940s, many West Indian men in London were known and celebrated for their military service, and the Jim Crowism of the U.S. forces stationed in Britain earned public disapproval. Newsreels and papers that covered the arrival of the early migrants thus depicted Britain as the "mother country," and the new settlers as loyal sons (and a few daughters) of empire. Accordingly, artists

---

3   Earl Cameron in conversation with Dylan Cave, National Film Theatre, London, September 16, 2002. Interview originally published at http://www.bfi.org.uk and accessed July 12, 2010 but since removed.

and writers enjoyed some professional success creating music, drama, and performance that emphasized Commonwealth connections and Caribbean culture. They also had the opportunity to celebrate the merits of racial diversity, especially regarding London, painting colonial settlement in a positive light.

By the later 1950s, however, Commonwealth migration had lost, in the popular imagination, much of the historical and imperial prestige that it had possessed during wartime; new settlers became unwitting signifiers of job competition, deteriorating neighborhoods, and racial violence. Reflecting this social situation, the cultural establishment and white audiences expressed diminishing concern for the imperial priorities and character of West Indian art, writing, and performance; they began to view most of it through the lens of colonial settlement in Britain and the race relations debate—especially after the 1958 riots. Artists and entertainers were able, in some instances, to capitalize on the widespread interest in racial conflict, but had more and more trouble producing and promoting work that did not engage with this issue.

Shifts in attitudes and perspectives, whether among artists, producers, audiences, government officials, or the general public, were gradual, and therefore my decision to end this study in 1965—my assertion that this era of creative cross-cultural potential lasted for about twenty years—needs some explanation. We can view the mid-1960s as a fitting endpoint or watershed because of developments both general and specific.

Generally speaking, the shift of feeling described above, which was intermittent and unfocused throughout the 1950s, became explicit by roughly the mid-1960s. Events like the Notting Hill riots (1958) and especially the passage of the first Commonwealth Immigrants Act (1962) were huge blows to the belief, subscribed to by representatives of both the white and Caribbean communities, that cultural production and education could heal racial tensions in Britain. West Indians received the news of the Commonwealth Immigrants Act, in particular, as a slap in the face, a crudely race-based rejection of the New Commonwealth connection. When the bill was first introduced in 1961, the *West Indian Gazette* fumed under the headline "Butler's Colour-Bar Bill Mocks Commonwealth": "It is to the shame of our Commonwealth—to the shame of England that such a measure was even introduced! There is no excuse for this Bill."[4] On the cultural front, many Caribbean artists felt their professional prospects dwindling rather than expanding; we can see evidence of this in the frustration of Pearl Connor, Lloyd Reckord, Cy Grant, and Errol John, and in the entrenched typecasting of established performers like Edric Connor, Grant, Earl Cameron, and even, in his own way, Ronald Moody.

---

4   Claudia Jones, "Butler's Colour-Bar Bill Mocks Commonwealth," *West Indian Gazette* (November 1961), 1.

There is no definitive event that marks out 1965 (or any other year) as *the* watershed, but there are a few specific occurrences that are suggestive of change. The first two are political actions in that year by the Labour government: a white paper that reduced the number of immigration vouchers available and enforced the immigration rules issued under the 1962 Act more strictly; and the near-simultaneous passage of the first Race Relations Act, which legally prohibited incitement to racial hatred and public discrimination. The immigration white paper did not have the bombshell impact of the first Commonwealth Immigrants Act, but it was the nail in the coffin for the Caribbean settler community because a Labour government had passed it. Throughout the postwar period a large majority of West Indians consistently voted Labour, and representatives of that party voiced considerable opposition to immigration restriction back in 1961. Thus, the 1965 amendments indicated that the "Labour Party had completed a U-turn on immigration policy,"[5] and that the two largest political parties were now united in favor of stricter controls, and in opposition to the ideal of a New Commonwealth open to all British subjects regardless of race or color.

At the same time, the 1965 Race Relations Act signaled a loss of faith among the Labour elite in the education-based, *laissez-faire* approach to the amelioration of white racism and public discrimination. For the most part, historians have explained the significance of the Act in terms of its connection to Labour's white paper on immigration, interpreting it as the party's transparent and unsuccessful panacea for the black colonial population. The settler community, for its part, found the provisions of the Act to be toothless—the first successful charge of incitement to racial hatred was actually against Trinidadian radical Michael X— and the gesture contemptible. Conversely, it can also be viewed as a well-intentioned and welcome response to the United States' passage of the Civil Rights Act the previous year, in the context of the increasingly open discrimination occurring in British cities. Nonetheless, both Labour's tightening of immigration restriction and passage of the Race Relations Act were setbacks to mid-century liberalism and the idealism of the New Commonwealth.

These developments have their mirror in organized black politics, beginning in 1964 with the establishment of the Campaign Against Racial Discrimination (CARD), the first such group in Britain focused squarely on intervening in national British politics, in Parliament, in order to effect change. (Earlier organizations like the Standing Conference of West Indian Organizations and the Indian Workers Associations, were more devoted to local politics, welfare, and pressure group work.) CARD dissolved in

---

5   Ian R. G. Spencer, *British Immigration Policy since 1939: The Making of Multi-Racial Britain* (London and New York: Routledge, 1997), 136.

1967, soon to be replaced by more militant black radicalism, notably in the Black Power movement, and the growth of underground, community-based activity.[6]

However, throughout the 1950s and early 1960s, both white liberal observers and West Indian community representatives consistently rejected the desirability of legislating against racial discrimination. There were, certainly, practical grounds for such a stance, in particular the difficulty of enforcing such a law. More importantly, though, many felt that punitive legislation would interfere with or even reverse the progress of informal, education-based initiatives in their quest for harmonious racial integration; anti-discrimination laws could exacerbate tensions by suggesting that the white majority was racist and in need of discipline, or by conferring on black citizens a special status as a group in need of government aid. This was not only wishful thinking; Paul Rich, for one, has suggested that "widespread liberal optimism in the 1950s was based on the fact that racial attitudes in Britain then were far less fixed than they were to become in the 1960s and 1970s."[7]

Considered in the context of prior opposition to anti-discrimination legislation, then, the Race Relations Act marks out the Labour government's pessimism regarding the potential of organically occurring integration. It was, in part, an admission that the race situation had actually deteriorated since the end of the war, that white prejudice was not simply the preserve of an ignorant minority, and that it could not simply be educated away.

Such a loss of faith was mirrored in the changing professional—and political—strategies of West Indians in London, whether they were artists, activists, or both. Unlike Harold Moody's League of Coloured Peoples, or the myriad interracial societies of the 1950s that sprang up in British cities in response to migration, new political groups founded after the passage of the Commonwealth Immigrants Act demonstrated "a growing opposition to alliances with whites"[8] and emphasized black independence and cultural distinction over connections to the white community that could facilitate integration. West Indian artists, including several of those discussed in this study, became increasingly alienated from the British mainstream and turned their focus to Afrocentric or colonial organizations that catered

---

6   Kalbir Shukra, *The Changing Pattern of Black Politics in Britain* (London: Pluto Press, 1998). See also Anne-Marie Angelo, "The Black Panthers in London, 1967–1972: A Diasporic Struggle Navigates the Black Atlantic," *Radical History Review* 103 (Winter 2009), 17–35; R. E. R. Bunce, "Obi B. Eguna, C. L. R. James and the Birth of Black Power in Britain: Black Radicalism in Britain, 1967–72," *Twentieth Century British History* 22, no. 3 (2011), 391–414.

7   Paul B. Rich, *Race and Empire in British Politics* (Cambridge: Cambridge University Press, 1990), 181.

8   Ibid., 199.

largely to Britain's growing black audience. Pearl Connor evoked this transition period when she explained in an interview:

> I'd never had the idea of just black consciousness but Caribbean ...
> And that time [mid-60s] was a time when we were all in a, what shall
> I call it, in a flux. We were just moving around in a sort of whirlpool
> of activity, I think, and building up impetus to strike into, to move
> into the century into which we were coming as independent people.
> And also trying to make a mark as Caribbean people here. Which
> wasn't so easy when the Caribbean Service went out and a lot of the
> people who mattered to us were no longer there. Because there was a
> whole lot of British—say directors and so—who were devoted to the
> Caribbean as well.[9]

For instance, much of Ronald Moody's work, by the 1960s, was exhibited at shows organized by the Commonwealth Institute or curated around the theme of black art in general (a trend that continues to this day). Cy Grant, as we have seen, became increasingly aware of how his early career had been limited by his color, and he began to educate himself in the works of black intellectuals like Aimé Césaire. In 1974 he turned his attention to creating a space in London for the cultivation of young black artists, the Drum Arts Centre. In 1968 Lloyd Reckord returned to Jamaica, where he founded the National Theatre Trust. These are individual examples, but there are two groups in particular, dating from the mid-1960s, that vividly illustrate the shift in the approaches of Caribbean artists toward their cultural work in London: the Negro Theatre Workshop, established in 1965, and the Caribbean Artists' Movement (CAM), in 1966.

The Negro Theatre Workshop was a direct reaction to the lack of opportunities for professional Caribbean and Commonwealth actors in London, which were wanting in both quantity and quality. It was clear by this time that producers would cast black actors for only a very limited range of roles. One BBC staffer wrote:

> Although Negro Theatre Workshop is not by nature a religious body one
> of its aims has been to bring within the compass of the negro some of the
> great universal themes which, because of social barriers, have hitherto
> been denied him. It is seldom possible, for instance, for a coloured man
> in London to break through the theatrical tradition which would cast
> him as a hot-dog seller, a shoe-shine boy or a bus conductor.[10]

---

9   Transcript, Pearl Connor interviewed by Anne Walmsley, February 25, 1987, 20,
    CAM 6/14, George Padmore Institute, London.
10 Memo, Christian Simpson to Asst. Head of Religious Broadcasting (Television),
    February 7, 1966, T24/73/1, Meeting Point—TX 1/4/66–31/5/66, WAC.

This situation had become dire enough that Pearl Connor, Carmen Munroe, Ram John Holder, and others, instead of scraping for mainstream work, decided to establish an independent theater group that would stage its own plays in and around London—material by Caribbean and African writers, to be sure, but also plays that British producers would have considered to be outside their remit; they staged, for example, all of Ibsen's plays at town halls throughout the city. Another major production by the Workshop was "a jazz version of the St Luke Passion" called *The Dark Disciples*. Here was another, Christian, subject that mainstream producers would have cast with exclusively white actors in Britain at the time, but *The Dark Disciples* (1966) had an all-black cast and incorporated elements of Caribbean, African, and African-American music and dance. In addition, the production took advantage of new venues devoted explicitly to the black arts; it traveled to Senegal for the 1966 First World Festival of Negro Arts, and in London, the newly established Africa Centre "had an empty hall we were able to use very cheaply."[11]

However, the Negro Theatre Workshop received perhaps its greatest British exposure when *The Dark Disciples* was produced for BBC Television as part of the religious drama series *Meeting Point*, and its promotion was very much of a piece with the Corporation's commitment to uplift its viewers, in this case about race relations. The liberal commitment to integrate and educate was still alive in George Lamming's publicity blurb:

> This group of players who originate from different parts of the Commonwealth have shown, in a very short time, the role which drama can play in educating ordinary citizens in the art of living. ... The Negro Theatre Workshop regard[s] the issue of race in contemporary Britain as a major social responsibility for its members. They are a non-racial group whose ambition is to help achieve a similar freedom of encounter between all citizens throughout the nation.[12]

While the BBC continued to boast that its "white producers, technicians and helpers can work amicably (behind the scenes) with coloured artistes and that racial consciousness is forgotten in the endeavour to 'get the show on,'"[13] London's West Indian and Commonwealth artists were busy setting up shop for themselves.

Unlike the Negro Theatre Workshop, which focused on drama and had very specific professional aims, the CAM was designed to encompass all

11 Pearl Connor interview in Pines, *Black and White in Colour*, 41.
12 George Lamming, "The Dark Disciples: Meeting Point," March 2, 1966, T24/73/1, Meeting Point—TX 1/4/66–31/5/66, WAC.
13 Memo, Christian Simpson to Asst. Head of Religious Broadcasting (Television), February 7, 1966, T24/73/1, Meeting Point—TX 1/4/66–31/5/66, WAC.

artistic disciplines, and to facilitate discussion and creative cooperation—it was not designed to create particular business opportunities. Instead, it brought together Caribbean artists working in various fields in London, sometimes in isolation; this was particularly true for the writers, fine artists, and all those outside of the performing arts. CAM thrived for only a few years, but during that time it organized five symposia, two conferences, three art exhibitions, and issued a regular series of newsletters. As Veerle Poupeye has noted, "CAM helped to articulate the debates on race and multi-culturalism that dominate black British art today"[14]—debates about the existence and content of a Caribbean aesthetic (the subject of the introductory meeting), the place of the West Indian artist (and black culture more generally) in British culture, and the extent to which European standards ought to influence members' own work. Trinidadian intellectual Gordon Rohlehr encapsulated CAM's impact when he said:

> often when we speak about there being an absence of tradition, it is really an absence of dialogue, and absence of people … coming together and being made to discuss what they have been doing on some common forum. And I think CAM provided that forum, which is why it created that ferment in a remarkably short time.[15]

Pearl Connor inadvertently echoed Rohlehr's sentiment when she remarked of the 1950s: "We had no history in this country. No history of performance in that way apart from one or two individuals. You had Edric, you had sculptors like Ronald Moody … you had people here but they were all individuals, they were all doing their own thing." Over time, however, these individuals went from being principally committed to West Indian issues, like political independence, to becoming attached to a slowly germinating black or Caribbean community in Britain:

> [T]he longer you stayed, the more you found you were learning and you were getting into a groove which you hadn't even anticipated. A new sort of grouping was being formed. A new set of alliances and so on. … And although we went back and forth to the Caribbean and had a dream of staying eventually, our work got us more and more involved in England.[16]

The establishment of CAM thus heralded the coming of age of the West Indian cultural community that grew up in the postwar period.

---

14 Poupeye, *Caribbean Art*, 140.
15 Transcript, Gordon Rohlehr interviewed by Anne Walmsley in Tunapuna, Trinidad, July 28, 1986, CAM 6/61, George Padmore Institute, London.
16 Transcript, Pearl Connor interviewed by Anne Walmsley, February 25, 1987, 4, CAM 6/14, George Padmore Institute, London.

Lloyd Reckord, who had been working in Britain on and off since 1951, remembered

> being exhilarated that all these artists of the Caribbean ... had come together at last, and that we were really thinking and working along the same lines. And it was such a relief, so exciting, you know, we'd all left our various little bedsitters all over London ... to pool our thoughts, if not resources.[17]

Along with the "exhilaration" and "relief" that came with organizing along Caribbean lines, there was political and aesthetic debate within the CAM that again reveals an historic shift in these artists' attitude toward their work in Britain. As mentioned in Chapter 6, the Movement's November 1967 symposium on West Indian theater exposed a rift between the first postwar generation of actors and writers—including Lloyd Reckord and Pearl Connor—who had more experience working in the London mainstream, and newer arrivals who were more Afrocentric in their aesthetic and professional approach. Ram John Holder, for one, made this change explicit when he commented that "everybody knows the work that Pearl and these stalwarts like her have been doing for years and so on. Now the time has come, for us to move into themes, that relate to us, that relate to our problems." Another attendee, activist Courtney Tulloch, concurred, stating that the West Indian dramatist ought to be

> thinking in terms of developing his own culture, and developing that culture among his own people. Previously, we had bright people who either write novels for black and white people to read, or write plays for black and white people to act in, or go on the West End as black stars in Uncle Tom parts—a lot of black actors you find in television playing nice little niggers. And so where it's at, right now, is for black people to begin, at least[, to] be conscious of their own culture.[18]

Connor, herself one of the "stalwarts," smartly chastened the symposium's rashest insurgents when she cautioned: "we must have a critical faculty about ourselves. We can't just be submerged in self-love, we can't all become narcissised. I love myself and I'm sure you do. But when it comes to the theatre, for our own peoples' [sic] sake, we must give them a standard."[19] Hers was a perspective seasoned by two decades of work within the British

---

17 Transcript, Lloyd Reckord interviewed by Anne Walmsley in Kingston, Jamaica, March 12, 1986, 4, CAM 6/60, George Padmore Institute, London.

18 Transcript, Caribbean Artists' Movement symposium on West Indian Theatre, November 10, 1967, CAM 5/5/1, George Padmore Institute, London, 7–8.

19 Ibid., 25.

cultural establishment. Still, Pearl Connor was eloquently countered by member Marina Maxwell, whose thoughts, as much as anything else, indicated the turn in what would come to be called Black British cultural politics:

> I'm for interest in craftsmanship, I'm for interest in technique, yes, but there is so much and so far that you can go, without destroying your own particular beat, your own particular rhythm. ... When you talk about theatre, you talk about writing nice little plays and putting them on. What about steel band? They didn't ask you anything, they produced their pan. What about calypso and carnival? They ain' ask you nothing, no intellectual came there and told them what to do. They did it. And this is the sort of material we have to be working with, I think.[20]

The heated symposium brings to mind Stuart Hall's question, "Can we ever recognize [Europe's] irreversible influence, whilst resisting its imperializing eye?" The enigma has thus far proved impossible to resolve. It requires the most complex of cultural strategies.[21] Holder and Tulloch did not give sufficient credit to the work of Pearl Connor, Lloyd Reckord, and many others who are the subjects of this study, whose cultural strategies to work with British collaborators and institutions were indeed more complex than they have been given credit for. They were not simply the "first" to arrive after the war ended, indiscriminately sacrificing their political commitment and West Indian pride in order to get to the next paycheck, and acting as placeholders until a more enlightened generation of artists came along to forge a truly "black British" identity and politics beginning in the late 1960s. They set themselves a much more ambitious task: to bring their colonial history and culture into the national mainstream, and to validate their own presence in London by redefining what it meant to be British.

---

20 Ibid., 37.
21 Hall, "Cultural Identity and Diaspora," 233–34.

Bibliography

Manuscript Collections

BBC Written Archives Centre, Caversham, Reading:
Audience Research Files
Copyright Files
Policy Files
Radio Artist Files
Radio Scripts
Scriptwriter Files
Talks Files
Television Artist Files
Television Scripts

British Film Institute, London:
Aileen and Michael Balcon Collection
Film Information Folders
Janet Green Collection
Rank Viewers' Reports
Unpublished Film Scripts

George Padmore Institute, London:
Anne Walmsley Caribbean Artists' Movement Collection

Hyman Kreitman Research Centre, Tate Museum, London:
Aubrey Williams Collection
Ronald Moody Collection

Institute of Race Relations Periodicals Collection, London:
Magnet News
West Indian Gazette and Afro-Asian Caribbean News
West Indies Observer

London Metropolitan Archives:
London Council of Social Service Files

National Sound Archive, British Library, London:
African Writers' Club online recordings
"History of Black British Jazz" lecture series
Stephen Bourne Interview Collection

National Theatre Museum Archive, London:
Blackgrounds Oral History Project Collection
Royal Court Theatre Collection

National Archives, Kew, London:
Colonial Office Files (CO)
Home Office Files (HO)
Ministry of Labour Files (LAB)

Published Works

Aldgate, Anthony. *Censorship and the Permissive Society: British Cinema and Theatre 1955–1965.* Oxford: Clarendon Press, 1995.

Alleyne, Brian W. *Radicals against Race: Black Activism and Cultural Politics.* Oxford and New York: Berg, 2002.

Angelo, Anne-Marie. "The Black Panthers in London, 1967–1972: A Diasporic Struggle Navigates the Black Atlantic." *Radical History Review* 103 (Winter 2009): 17–35.

Araeen, Rasheed. *Making Myself Visible.* London: Kala Press, 1984.

——. *The Other Story: Afro-Asian Artists in Post-War Britain.* London: Arts Council, 1989.

——. "A New Beginning: Beyond Postcolonial Cultural Theory and Identity Politics." *Third Text* 50 (Spring 2000): 3–20.

Archer-Straw, Petrine. *Negrophilia: Avant-Garde Paris and Black Culture.* New York and London: Thames and Hudson, 2000.

Athill, Diana. *Somewhere towards the End: A Memoir.* New York and London: W. W. Norton and Co., 2008.

——. "Prologue." In Yvonne Brewster, ed., *For the Reckord: A Collection of Three Plays by Barry Reckord.* London: Oberon Books, 2010, 9–10.

Auguiste, Reece and the Black Audio Film Collective. "Black Independents and Third Cinema: The British Context." In Jim Pines and Paul Willemen, eds, *Questions of Third Cinema.* London: British Film Institute, 1989, 212–17.

Bailkin, Jordanna. *The Afterlife of Empire.* Berkeley: University of California Press, 2012.

Baker, Houston A. Jr. Manthia Diawara, and Ruth H. Lindeborg, eds. *Black British Cultural Studies: A Reader.* Chicago: University of Chicago Press, 1996.

Baker, Roy Ward. *The Director's Cut.* London: Reynolds and Hearn Ltd., 2000.

Banton, Michael. *The Coloured Quarter: Negro Emigrants to an English City.* London: Cape, 1955.

Beauchamp-Byrd Mora J. and M. Franklin Sirmans, eds. *Transforming the Crown: African, Asian and Caribbean Artists in Britain 1966–1996.* New York: Franklin H. Williams Caribbean Cultural Center/African Diaspora Institute, 1997.

Bidnall, Amanda M. "West Indian Interventions at the Heart of the Cultural Establishment: Edric Connor, Pearl Connor, and the BBC," *Twentieth Century British History* 24, no. 1 (2013): 84–109.

Billington, Michael. *State of the Nation: British Theatre since 1945*. London: Faber and Faber, 2007.

Birbalsingh, Frank. *Passion and Exile: Essays in Caribbean Literature*. London: Hansib Publishing Limited, 1988.

Björgo, Tore and Rob Witte, eds. *Racist Violence in Europe*. Houndmills: The Macmillan Press, 1993.

Born, Richard A. *From Blast to Pop: Aspects of Modern British Art, 1915–1965*. Chicago: The David and Alfred Smart Museum of Art and The University of Chicago, 1997.

Bourne, Stephen. *Black in the British Frame: The Black Experience in British Film and Television*. London: Continuum, 2001.

——. "Secrets and Lies: Black Histories and British Historical Films." In Claire Monk and Amy Sargeant, eds, *British Historical Cinema: The History, Heritage and Costume Film*. London and New York: Routledge, 2002, 47–65.

Bowling, Benjamin. "The Emergence of Violent Racism as a Public Issue in Britain, 1945–81." In Panikos Panayi, ed., *Racial Violence in Britain in the Nineteenth and Twentieth Centuries*. Revised edition. Leicester: Leicester University Press, 1996, 185–220.

Boyd, Kelly. "Moving Pictures? Cinema and Society in Britain." *Journal of British Studies* 34, no. 1 (January 1995): 130–35.

Braithwaite, Lloyd. *Colonial West Indian Students in Britain*. Mona and Kingston: University of the West Indies Press, 2001.

Brandt, George W., ed. *British Television Drama*. Cambridge: Cambridge University Press, 1981.

Brereton, Bridget. *Race Relations in Colonial Trinidad, 1870–1900*. Cambridge: Cambridge University Press, 1979.

Briggs, Asa. *The BBC: The First Fifty Years*. London: Oxford University Press, 1985.

——. *The History of Broadcasting in the United Kingdom, Volume V: Competition*. London: Oxford University Press, 1995.

British Council of Churches. *Your Neighbour from the West Indies*. London: Wm. Carling and Co., 1955.

Bryan, Beverley, Stella Dadzie, and Suzanne Scafe. *The Heart of the Race: Black Women's Lives in Britain*. London: Virago Press, 1985.

Bull, John. "The Establishment of Mainstream Theatre, 1946–1979." In Baz Kershaw, ed. *The Cambridge History of British Theatre, Volume 3: Since 1895*. Cambridge: Cambridge University Press, 2004, 326–48.

Bunce, R. E. R. "Obi B. Eguna, C. L. R. James and the Birth of Black Power in Britain: Black Radicalism in Britain, 1967–72." *Twentieth Century British History* 22, no. 3 (2011): 391–414.

Burkett, Jodi. *Constructing Post-Imperial Britain: Britishness, "Race" and the Radical Left in the 1960s*. Houndmills: Palgrave Macmillan, 2013.

Burton, Alan and Tim O'Sullivan. *The Cinema of Basil Dearden and Michael Relph*. Edinburgh: Edinburgh University Press, 2009.

Burton, Antoinette. "Who Needs the Nation? Interrogating 'British' History." *Journal of Historical Sociology* 10, no. 3 (September 1997): 227–48.

Byron, Margaret. *Post-War Caribbean Migration to Britain: The Unfinished Cycle*. Aldershot: Avebury, 1994.

———. "Migration, Work and Gender: The Case of Post-War Labour Migration from the Caribbean to Britain." In Mary Chamberlain, ed., *Caribbean Migration: Globalised Identities*. London and New York: Routledge, 1998, 226–41.

Castronovo, David. *Blokes: The Bad Boys of British Literature*. New York: Continuum, 2009.

Calvocoressi, Peter. *The British Experience 1945–75*. London: The Bodley Head, 1978.

Chambers, Colin. *The Story of Unity Theatre*. London: Lawrence and Wishart, 1989.

Chambers, Eddie. *Black Artists in British Art: A History since the 1950s*. London and New York: I. B. Tauris, 2014.

Chambers, Iain. *Urban Rhythms: Pop Music and Popular Culture*. Houndmills: Macmillan, 1985.

Cohen, Abner. "A Polyethnic London Carnival as a Contested Cultural Performance." *Ethnic and Racial Studies* 5, no. 1 (January 1982): 23–44.

Colley, Linda. *Britons: Forging the Nation 1707–1837*. New Haven: Yale University Press, 1992.

Collier, Graham. *Cleo and John: A Biography of the Dankworths*. London: Quartet Books, 1976.

Collins, Marcus. "Pride and Prejudice: West Indian Men in Mid-Twentieth-Century Britain." *Journal of British Studies* 40 (July 2001): 391–418.

Conekin, Becky, Frank Mort, and Chris Waters, eds. *Moments of Modernity: Reconstructing Britain 1945–1964*. London and New York: Rivers Oram Press, 1999.

Connor, Edric. *Horizons: The Life and Times of Edric Connor*. Kingston and Miami: Ian Randle Publishers, 2007.

Constantine, Learie. *Colour Bar*. London: Stanley Paul and Co., 1954.

Cook, Pam and Mieke Bernink, eds. *The Cinema Book*. Second edition. London: BFI Publishing, 1999.

Corrie, Joe. *Colour Bar: A Play in One Act*. London: Samuel French Limited, 1954.

Cowley, John. "West Indian Gramophone Recordings in Britain, 1927–1950." In Rainer Lotz and Ian Pegg, eds, *Under the Imperial Carpet: Essays in Black History, 1780–1950*. Crawley: Rabbit Press, 1986, 245–58.

———. "London is the Place: Caribbean Music in the Context of Empire 1900–60." In Paul Oliver, ed., *Black Music in Britain: Essays on the Afro-Asian Contribution to Popular Music*. Buckingham and Pennsylvania: Open University Press, 1990, 58–76.

Crisell, Andrew. *An Introductory History of British Broadcasting*. Second edition. London: Routledge, 2002.

Cross, Malcolm and Hans Entzinger. "Caribbean Minorities in Britain and the Netherlands: Comparative Questions." In Malcolm Cross and Hans Entzinger, eds., *Lost Illusions: Caribbean Minorities in Britain and the Netherlands*. London: Routledge, 1988, 1–33.

Dabydeen, David and Nana Wilson-Tagoe. *A Reader's Guide to West Indian and Black British Literature*. Kingston-upon-Thames: Rutherford Press, 1987.

Darwin, John. *Britain and Decolonization: The Retreat from Empire in the Post-War World*. London: Macmillan, 1988, 146–54.

Davis, Helen. *Understanding Stuart Hall*. London: Sage, 2004.

Davison, R. B. *West Indian Migrants: Social and Economic facts of Migration from the West Indies*. Oxford: Oxford University Press, 1962.

Dawson, Ashley. *Mongrel Nation: Diasporic Culture and the Making of Postcolonial Britain*. Ann Arbor: University of Michigan Press, 2007.

Deslandes, Paul R. "'The Foreign Element': Newcomers and the Rhetoric of Race, Nation, and Empire in 'Oxbridge' Undergraduate Culture, 1850–1920," *Journal of British Studies* 37 (January 1998): 54–90.

Douglas, Roy. *Liquidation of Empire: The Decline of the British Empire.* Houndmills: Palgrave Macmillan, 2002.

Durgnat, Raymond. *A Mirror for England: British Movies from Austerity to Affluence.* New York and Washington: Praeger Publishers, 1971.

——. "Two 'Social Problem' Films: *Sapphire* and *Victim.*" In Alan Burton, Tim O'Sullivan, and Paul Wells, eds, *Liberal Directions: Basil Dearden and Postwar British Film Culture.* Trowbridge: Flicks Books, 1997, 59–88.

Eldridge, Michael. "The Rise and Fall of Black Britain." *Transition* 74 (1997): 32–43.

——. "There Goes the Transnational Neighborhood: Calypso Buys a Bungalow." In Annie J. Randall, ed., *Music, Power, Politics.* New York and London: Routledge, 2005, 173–93.

Elsom, John. *Post-War British Theatre.* 1976; London: Routledge and Kegan Paul, 1979.

Emery, Mary Lou. *Modernism, the Visual, and Caribbean Literature.* Cambridge: Cambridge University Press, 2007.

English, James F. "Winning the Culture Game: Prizes, Awards, and the Rules of Art." *New Literary History* 33 (2002): 109–35.

Esslin, Martin. *Brief Chronicles: Essays on Modern Theatre.* London: Temple Smith, 1970.

Ethnic Communities Oral History Project, *The Motherland Calls: African Caribbean Experiences.* Hammersmith and Fulham Community History Series, No. 4/ECOHP, 1989.

Fanon, Frantz. *The Wretched of the Earth.* 1961; New York: Grove Press, 1966.

——. *Black Skin, White Masks.* 1952; New York: Grove Press, 1967.

Findlater, Richard, ed. *At the Royal Court: 25 Years of the English Stage Company.* Ambergate: Amber Lane Press Limited, 1981.

Foner, Nancy. *Jamaica Farewell: Jamaican Migrants in London.* Berkeley and Los Angeles: University of California Press, 1978.

Forster, E. M. *Howards End.* London: Edward Arnold, 1910.

Fryer, Peter. *Staying Power: The History of Black People in Britain.* London and Sydney: Pluto Press, 1984.

Gale, Matthew, and Chris Stephens. *Barbara Hepworth: Works in the Tate Gallery Collection and the Barbara Hepworth Museum St Ives.* London: Tate Gallery Publishing, 1999.

Gallagher, John. "The Decline, Revival and Fall of the British Empire." In John Gallagher, ed., *The Decline, Revival and Fall of the British Empire: The Ford Lectures and Other Essays.* Cambridge: Cambridge University Press, 1982, 73–153.

Gallup, George H., ed. *The Gallup International Public Opinion Polls: Great Britain, 1937–1975.* New York: Random House, 1976.

Garlake, Margaret. *New Art New World: British Art in Postwar Society.* New Haven and London: Yale University Press, 1998.

Gates, Henry Louis, Jr. "Black London." *New Yorker,* April 28–May 5, 1997, 194–205.

Geraghty, Christine. *British Cinema in the Fifties: Gender, Genre and the 'New Look'.* London and New York: Routledge, 2000.

Gilroy, Paul. *"There Ain't No Black in the Union Jack": The Cultural Politics of Race and Nation.* Chicago: University of Chicago Press, 1987.

——. *The Black Atlantic: Modernity and Double-Consciousness.* London and New York: Verso, 1993.

Glass, Ruth. *London's Newcomers: The West Indian Migrants. University College, London, Centre for Urban Studies, Report No. 1.* Cambridge: Harvard University Press, 1961.

Goldie, Grace Wyndham. *Facing the Nation.* London: Bodley Head, 1977.

Gorman, Daniel. *Imperial Citizenship: Empire and the Question of Belonging.* Manchester: Manchester University Press, 2006.

Greet, Michele. "Inventing Wifredo Lam: The Parisian Avant-Garde's Primitivist Fixation." *Invisible Culture,* no. 5 (2003). Available at http://www.rochester.edu/in_visible_culture/Issue_5/Michele_Greet/MicheleGreet.html.

Griffith, Glyne. "Deconstructing Nationalisms: Henry Swanzy, *Caribbean Voices,* and the Development of West Indian Literature." *Small Axe* 10 (September 2001): 1–20.

——. "'This is London Calling the West Indies': The BBC's *Caribbean Voices.*" In Bill Schwarz. ed., *West Indian Intellectuals in Britain.* Manchester and New York: Manchester University Press, 2003, 196–208.

Hall, Catherine. "Histories, Empires, and the Post-Colonial Moment." In Iain Chambers and Lidia Curti, eds, *The Post-Colonial Question: Common Skies, Divided Horizons.* London and New York: Routledge, 1996, 65–77.

——. *Civilising Subjects: Metropole and Colony in the English Imagination 1830–1867.* Chicago and London: University of Chicago Press, 2002.

Hall, Stuart. "Cultural Identity and Diaspora." In Jonathan Rutherford, ed., *Identity: Community, Culture, Difference.* London: Lawrence & Wishart, 1990, 222–37.

——. "The Formation of a Diasporic Intellectual: An Interview with Stuart Hall by Kuan-Hsing Chen." In David Morley and Kuan-Hsing Chen, ed., *Stuart Hall: Critical Dialogues in Cultural Studies.* London and New York: Routledge, 1996, 484–503.

——. "Black Diaspora Artists in Britain: Three 'Moments' in Post-War History." *History Workshop Journal* 61 (2006): 1–24.

Hall, Stuart, Chas Critcher, Tony Jefferson, John Clarke, and Brian Roberts. *Policing the Crisis: Mugging, the State, and Law and Order.* London: Macmillan, 1978.

Hallifax, Michael. *Let Me Set the Scene: Twenty Years at the Heart of British Theatre 1956 to 1976.* Hanover: Smith and Kraus, 2004.

Hammond Perry, Kennetta. "Black Britain and the Politics of Race in the 20th Century." *History Compass* 12, no. 8 (2014): 651–63.

Hansen, Randall. *Citizenship and Immigration in Post-War Britain: The Institutional Origins of a Multicultural Nation.* London: Oxford University Press, 2000.

Harris, Roxy. "Black British, Brown British and British Cultural Studies." In Claire Alexander, ed., *Stuart Hall and "Race."* London: Routledge, 2011, 483–512.

Heinlein, Frank. *British Government Policy and Decolonisation 1945–1963: Scrutinising the Official Mind.* London: Frank Cass, 2002.

Hernton, Calvin. "Minorities in England: A Report." In Ishmael Reed, ed. *MultiAmerica: Essays on Cultural Wars and Cultural Peace.* New York: Viking Press, 1997, 31–42.

Hill, Donald R. *Calypso Calaloo: Early Carnival Music in Trinidad.* Gainesville: University Press of Florida, 1993.

Hill, Errol. "The Calypso." In Michael Anthony and Andrew Carr, eds, *David Frost Introduces Trinidad and Tobago.* London: Deutsch, 1975, 73–83.

Hill, John. "Working-Class Realism and Sexual Reaction: Some Theses on the British 'New Wave.'" In James Curran and Vincent Porter, eds, *British Cinema History.* London: Weidenfeld and Nicholson, 1983, 301–11.

——. *Sex, Class and Realism: British Cinema 1956–1963.* London: BFI Publishing, 1986.

Hinchcliffe, Arnold P. *British Theatre 1950–70.* Oxford: Basil Blackwell, 1974.

Hiro, Dilip. *Black British White British: A History of Race Relations in Britain.* Revised edition. London: Grafton Books, 1991.

Howe, Stephen. *Anti-Colonialism in British Politics: The Left and the End of Empire, 1939-1964.* Oxford: Oxford University Press, 1993.

——. "Internal Decolonization? British Politics since Thatcher as Post-Colonial Trauma." *Twentieth Century British History* 14, no. 3 (2003): 286–304.

Huggan, Graham. "The Postcolonial Exotic: Salman Rushdie and the Booker of Bookers." *Transition* 64 (1994): 22–29.

"Interview with Michael Relph." In Alan Burton, Tim O'Sullivan, and Paul Wells, eds, *Liberal Directions: Basil Dearden and Postwar British Film Culture.* Trowbridge: Flicks Books, 1997, 241–48.

Jain, Jasbir and Supriya Agarwal, eds. *Shifting Homelands, Travelling Identities: Writers of the Caribbean Diaspora.* Kingston: Ian Randle, 2009.

James, C. L. R. *Beyond a Boundary.* 1963; London: Hutchinson and Co., 1969.

James, Winston. "Black Experience in Twentieth-Century Britain." In Philip D. Morgan and Sean Hawkins, eds, *Black Experience and the Empire.* Oxford: Oxford University Press, 2004, 347–86.

James, Winston and Clive Harris, eds. *Inside Babylon: The Caribbean Diaspora in Britain.* London: Verso, 1993.

Jarrett-Macauley, Delia. *The Life of Una Marson, 1905-65.* Manchester: Manchester University Press, 1998.

Jellicoe, Ann. *'The Knack' and 'The Sport of My Mad Mother.'* New York: Delta, 1964.

Johnson, Howard. "The British Caribbean from Demobilization to Constitutional Decolonization." In Judith M. Brown and Wm. Roger Louis, eds, *The Oxford History of the British Empire: The Twentieth Century.* Oxford: Oxford University Press, 1999, 597–622.

Jones, Claudia. "The Caribbean Community in Britain." In Buzz Johnson, *"I Think of My Mother": Notes on the Life and Times of Claudia Jones.* London: Karia Press, 1985, 137–54.

Joseph, Margaret Paul. *Caliban in Exile: The Outsider in Caribbean Fiction.* Westport: Greenwood Press, 1992.

Kalliney, Peter J. *Commonwealth of Letters: British Literary Culture and the Emergence of Postcolonial Aesthetics.* Oxford: Oxford University Press, 2013.

Keen, Melanie and Elizabeth Ward. *Recordings: A Select Bibliography of Contemporary African, Afro-Caribbean and Asian British Art.* London: Institute of International Visual Arts and Chelsea College of Art and Design, 1996.

Khan, Naseem. *The Arts that Britain Ignores: The Arts of Ethnic Minorities in Britain.* London: Arts Council of Great Britain, Gulbenkian Foundation, and the Community Relations Commission, 1976.

Korte, Barbara and Claudia Sternberg. *Bidding for the Mainstream? Black and Asian British Film since the 1990s.* Amsterdam and New York: Rodopi, 2004.

Kumar, Krishan. *The Making of English National Identity.* Cambridge: Cambridge University Press, 2003.

Kushner, Tony. *We Europeans? Mass-Observation, 'Race' and British Identity in the Twentieth Century.* Aldershot: Ashgate Publishing, 2004.

Lacey, Stephen. *British Realist Theatre: The New Wave in its Context 1956-1965.* London and New York: Routledge, 1995.

Lamming, George. *In the Castle of My Skin.* 1953; New York: Macmillan, 1970.

——. "Journey to an Expectation," in Lamming, *The Pleasures of Exile*. Ann Arbor: University of Michigan Press, 1992, 211–29.

Landy, Marcia. *British Genres: Cinema and Society, 1930–1960*. Princeton: Princeton University Press, 1991.

Little, Kenneth. *Negroes in Britain: A Study of Racial Relations in English Society*. London: Kegan Paul, 1947.

——. *Race and Society*. 1958; Paris: UNESCO, 1965.

Little, Ruth and Emily McLaughlin. *The Royal Court Theatre Inside Out*. London: Oberon Books, 2007.

Mackenzie, John M. *Propaganda and Empire: The Manipulation of British Public Opinion 1880–1960*. Manchester: Manchester University Press, 1984.

——, ed. *Imperialism and Popular Culture*. Manchester: Manchester University Press, 1986.

MacKillop, Ian and Neil Sinyard, eds. *British Cinema of the 1950s: A Celebration*. Manchester and New York: Manchester University Press, 2003.

Macmurraugh-Kavanagh, Madeleine. "The BBC and the Birth of *The Wednesday Play*, 1962–66: Institutional Containment versus 'Agitational Contemporaneity.'" In Janet Thumim, ed., *Small Screens, Big Ideas: Television in the 1950s*. London and New York: I. B. Tauris, 2002, 149–64.

Mansell, Gerard. *Let Truth Be Told: 50 Years of BBC External Broadcasting*. London: Weidenfeld and Nicolson, 1982.

Marwick, Arthur. *British Society since 1945*. London: Penguin, 1982.

——. "The 1960s: Was There a 'Cultural Revolution'?" *Contemporary Record* 2, no. 3 (Autumn 1988): 18–20.

Matera, Marc. *Black London: The Imperial Metropolis and Decolonization in the Twentieth Century*. Oakland: University of California Press, 2015.

McFarlane, Brian, ed. *The Encyclopedia of British Film*. Revised edition. London: Methuen, 2005.

McIntyre, David W. "The Unofficial Commonwealth Relations Conferences, 1933–59: Precursors of the Tri-sector Commonwealth." *Journal of Imperial and Commonwealth History* 36 (December 2008): 591–614.

Miall, Leonard. *Inside the BBC: British Broadcasting Characters*. London: Weidenfeld and Nicolson, 1994.

Mirza, Heidi Safia, ed. *Black British Feminism: A Reader*. London: Routledge, 1997.

Modood, Tariq, Richard Berthoud, et al. *Ethnic Minorities in Britain: Diversity and Disadvantage*. London: Policy Studies Institute, 1997.

Moody, Cynthia. "Ronald Moody: A Man True to his Vision." *Third Text: Third World Perspectives on Art and Culture* 8–9 (1989): 5–24.

Moody, Harold A. *The Colour Bar*. London: New Mildmay Press, 1944.

Moore, Henry. "Primitive Art." In Jack Flam with Miriam Deutch, eds, *Primitivism and Twentieth-Century Art: A Documentary History*. Berkeley: University of California Press, 2003, 268–69.

Naipaul, V. S. *The Middle Passage: Impressions of Five Societies—British, French and Dutch—in the West Indies and South America*. London: Andre Deutsch, 1962.

——. *The Return of Eva Perón with The Killings in Trinidad*. London: André Deutsch, 1980.

——. "Acceptance Speech of the First David Cohen British Literature Prize." *Wasafiri* 21 (Spring 1995): 7–8.

Newton, Darrell. *Paving the Empire Road.* Manchester: Manchester University Press, 2011.

Newton, Francis. *The Jazz Scene.* 1959; New York: Da Capo Press, 1975.

Notting Dale Urban Studies Centre, ed. *"Sorry No Vacancies": Life Stories of Senior Citizens from the Caribbean.* London: Notting Dale Urban Studies Centre, 1992.

Nurse, Keith. "Globalization and Trinidad Carnival: Diaspora, Hybridity and Identity in Global Culture." *Cultural Studies* 13, no. 4 (1999): 661–90.

Osborne, John. *Look Back in Anger and Other Plays.* London: Faber and Faber, 1993.

Owusu, Kwesi. *The Struggle for Black Arts in Britain: What Can we Consider Better than Freedom.* London: Comedia, 1986.

——, ed. *Storms of the Heart: An Anthology of Black Arts & Culture.* London: Camden Press, 1988.

Panayi, Panikos, ed. *Racial Violence in Britain in the Nineteenth and Twentieth Centuries.* Revised edition. London: Leicester University Press, 1996.

Pastor, Robert. "The Impact of U. S. Immigration Policy on Caribbean Emigration: Does it Matter?" In Barry B. Levine, ed., *The Caribbean Exodus.* New York: Praeger Publishers, 1987, 243–59.

Patterson, Sheila. *Dark Strangers: A Sociological Study of the Absorption of a Recent West Indian Migrant Group in Brixton, South London.* London: Tavistock, 1963.

Paul, Kathleen. *Whitewashing Britain: Race and Empire in the Postwar Era.* Ithaca: Cornell University Press, 1997.

Paulu, Burton. *British Broadcasting in Transition.* Minneapolis: University of Minnesota Press, 1961.

Phillips, Trevor and Mike Phillips. *Windrush: The Irresistible Rise of Multi-Racial Britain.* London: HarperCollins, 1999.

Pines, Jim, ed. *Black and White in Colour: Black People in British Television since 1936.* London: British Film Institute, 1992.

——. "The Cultural Context of Black British Cinema." In Houston A. Baker, Jr., Manthia Diawara, and Ruth H. Lindeborg, eds, *Black British Cultural Studies: A Reader.* Chicago: University of Chicago Press, 1996, 183–93.

Pirker, Eva Ulrike. *Narrative Projections of a Black British History.* London: Routledge, 2011.

Porter, Bernard. *The Absent-Minded Imperialists: Empire, Society, and Culture in Britain.* Oxford: Oxford University Press, 2004.

Political and Economic Planning Group. *Colonial Students in Britain.* London: PEP, June 1955.

Poupeye, Veerle. *Caribbean Art.* London: Thames & Hudson, 1998.

——. "Jamaican Art and the Changing National Imaginary: From the Affirmative to the Critical." In Deborah Cullen and Elvis Fuentes, eds, *Caribbean Art at the Crossroads of the World.* New York: El Museo de Barrio and Yale University Press, 2012, 183–200.

Procter, James, ed. *Writing Black Britain 1948-1998: An Interdisciplinary Anthology.* Manchester and New York: Manchester University Press, 2000.

Quevedo, Raymond. *Atilla's Kaiso: A Short History of the Trinidad Calypso.* St. Augustine, Trinidad and Tobago: University of the West Indies, Department of Extra Mural Studies, 1983.

Rabey, David Ian. "John Osborne: Just Like a Man." In Rabey, *English Drama since 1940.* London: Pearson Education Limited, 2003, 32–36.

Ramchand, Kenneth. *The West Indian Novel and its Background*. 1940; Kingston: Ian Randle, 2004.

Rebellato, Dan. *1956 and All That: The Making of Modern British Drama*. London: Routledge, 1999.

Reckord, Barry. "Skyvers." In Michael Billington, ed., *New English Dramatists, Vol. 9*. London: Penguin Books, 1966, 75–135.

Rees, Roland, ed. *Fringe First: Pioneers of Fringe Theatre on Record*. London: Oberon Books, 1992.

Regis, Louis. *The Political Calypso: True Opposition in Trinidad and Tobago*. Kingston: University of the West Indies Press, 1999.

Rhodes, Colin. *Primitivism and Modern Art*. London: Thames and Hudson, 1994.

Rich, Paul B. *Race and Empire in British Politics*. Cambridge: Cambridge University Press, 1990.

Richards, Jeffrey. "Basil Dearden at Ealing." In Alan Burton, Tim O'Sullivan, and Paul Wells, eds, *Liberal Directions: Basil Dearden and Postwar British Film Culture*. Trowbridge: Flicks Books, 1997, 14–35.

Richardson, Bonham C. "Caribbean Migrations, 1838–1985." In Franklin W. Knight and Colin A. Palmer, eds, *The Modern Caribbean*. Chapel Hill and London: University of North Carolina Press, 1989, 203–28.

Richardson, Tony. *Long Distance Runner: A Memoir*. London and Boston: Faber and Faber, 1993.

Richmond, Anthony H. *White and Coloured: The Behaviour of British People towards Coloured Immigrants*. London: Jonathan Cape, 1959.

——. *The Colour Problem: A Study of Racial Relations*. Revised edition. Harmondsworth: Penguin Books, 1961. First ed. 1955.

Roberts, Philip. *The Royal Court Theatre and the Modern Stage*. Cambridge: Cambridge University Press, 1999.

Rohlehr, Gordon. *Calypso and Society in Pre-Independence Trinidad*. Port of Spain: by the author, 1990.

——. "Images of Men and Women in the 1930s Calypsoes: The Sociology of Food Acquisition in a Context of Survivalism." In Patricia Mohammed and Catherine Shepherd, eds, *Gender in Caribbean Development*. Kingston: Canoe Press University of the West Indies, 1999, 223–89.

Rose, Sonya O. "Who Are We Now? Writing the Post-War 'Nation', 1948–2001." In Catherine Hall and Keith McLelland, eds, *Race, Nation and Empire: Making Histories, 1750 to the Present*. Manchester: Manchester University Press, 154–74.

Ruck, S. K., Manley, Douglas, Ivo de Souza, Albert Hyndman, eds. *The West Indian Comes to England: A Report Prepared for the Trustees of the London Parochial Charities by the Family Welfare Association*. London: Routledge and Kegan Paul, 1960.

Rush, Anne Spry. "Imperial Identity in Colonial Minds: Harold Moody and the League of Coloured Peoples, 1931–50." *Twentieth Century British History* 13 (2002): 356–83.

——. *Bonds of Empire: West Indians and Britishness from Victoria to Decolonization*. Oxford: Oxford University Press, 2011.

Salkey, Andrew, ed. *Caribbean Essays: An Anthology*. London: Evans Brothers Limited, 1973.

Sandhu, Sukhdev. *London Calling: How Black and Asian Writers Imagined a City*. London: HarperCollins, 2003.

Sands-O'Connor, Karen. *Soon Come Home to this Island: West Indians in British Children's Literature*. New York and London: Routledge, 2008.

Scannell, Paddy and David Cardiff. *A Social History of British Broadcasting, Volume One 1922–1939: Serving the Nation*. Oxford: Basil Blackwell, 1991.

Schaffer, Gavin. *Racial Science and British Society, 1930–62*. Houndmills: Palgrave Macmillan, 2008.

Schwarz, Bill. "'The only white man in there': The Re-Racialisation of Britain, 1956–68." *Race and* Class 38 (1996): 65–78.

——. "Unspeakable Histories: Diasporic Lives in Old England." In Peter Osborne and Stella Sandford, eds, *Philosophies of Race and Ethnicity*. London: Continuum, 2002, 81–96.

——. "'Claudia Jones and the *West Indian Gazette*': Reflections of the Emergence of Post-Colonial Britain." *Twentieth Century British History* 14, no. 3 (2003): 264–85.

——, ed. *West Indian Intellectuals in Britain*. Manchester and New York: Manchester University Press, 2003.

——. *Memories of Empire, Vol. 1: The White Man's World*. Oxford: Oxford University Press, 2011.

Seeley, J. R. *The Expansion of England*. London: Macmillan, 1883.

Selvon, Sam. *Ways of Sunlight*. 1957; New York: Longman, 1987.

——. *The Lonely Londoners*. 1956; London: Longman, 1989.

Sendall, Bernard. *Independent Television in Britain, Volume 1: Origin and Foundation, 1946–62*. London and Basingstoke: Macmillan, 1982.

Sewell, Tony. *Keep on Moving: The Windrush Legacy*. London: Voice Enterprises Ltd., 1998.

Shellard, Dominic. *British Theatre since the War*. New Haven: Yale University Press, 1999.

Sherwood, Marika, with Donald Hinds, Colin Prescod, and the 1996 Claudia Jones Symposium. *Claudia Jones: A Life in Exile*. London: Lawrence & Wishart, 1999.

Shubik, Irene. *Play for Today: The Evolution of Television Drama*. London: Davis Poynter, 1975.

Shukra, Kalbir. *The Changing Pattern of Black Politics in Britain*. London: Pluto Press, 1998.

Sims, Lowery Stokes. *Wilfredo Lam and the International Avant-Garde, 1923–1982*. Austin: University of Texas Press, 2002.

Sivanandan, A. *A Different Hunger: Writings on Racism and Resistance*. London: Pluto Press, 1982.

Spencer, Ian R. G. *British Immigration Policy since 1939: The Making of Multi-Racial Britain*. London and New York: Routledge, 1997.

Stansky, Peter and William Abrahams. *London's Burning: Life, Death and Art in the Second World War*. London: Constable, 1994.

Steedman, Carolyn. *Landscape for a Good Woman: A Story of Two Lives*. London: Virago, 1986.

Stevenson, John. "Experience of Life." In John Finch, ed., *Granada Television: The First Generation*. Manchester: Manchester University Press, 2003, 126–28.

Sutherland, John. *Offensive Literature: Decensorship in Britain 1960–1982*. London: Junction Books, 1982.

Tarr, Carrie. "*Sapphire, Darling* and the Boundaries of Permitted Pleasure." *Screen* 26, no. 1 (1986): 50–65.

Taylor, John Russell. *The Angry Theatre: New British Drama*. New York: Hill and Wang, 1962. Published in Great Britain under the title *Anger and After*.

Taylor, Patrick. *The Narrative of Liberation: Perspectives on Afro-Caribbean Literature, Popular Culture, and Politics.* Ithaca and London: Cornell University Press, 1989.

Thomas-Hope, Elizabeth. "Caribbean Diaspora, The Inheritance of Slavery: Migration from the Commonwealth Caribbean." In Colin Brock, ed., *The Caribbean in Europe: Aspects of the West Indian Experience in Britain, France and the Netherlands.* London: Frank Cass, 1986, 15–35.

——. "Globalization and the Development of a Caribbean Migration Culture." In Philip W. Scher, ed., *Perspectives on the Caribbean: A Reader in Culture, History, and Representation.* Chichester: Blackwell, 2010, 247–55.

Thompson, Andrew. *The Empire Strikes Back? The Impact of Imperialism on Britain from the Mid-Nineteenth Century.* Harlow: Pearson Education Ltd., 2005.

Tschudin, Marcus. *A Writer's Theatre: George Devine and the English Stage Company at the Royal Court 1956–1965.* Bern and Frankfurt: Herbert Lang and Company Limited, 1972.

Vaughan, David. *Negro Victory: The Life Story of Dr. Harold Moody.* London: Independent Press Limited, 1950.

Wainwright, Leon. "Francis Newton Souza and Aubrey Williams: Entwined Art Histories at the End of Empire." In Simon Faulkner and Anandi Ramamurthy, eds, *Visual Culture and Decolonisation in Britain.* Aldershot: Ashgate Publishing Limited, 2006, 101–126.

——. *Timed Out: Art and the Transnational Caribbean.* Manchester and New York: Manchester University Press, 2011.

——. "Varieties of Belatedness and Provincialism: Decolonization and British Pop." *Art History* 35 (April 2012): 442–61.

Walmsley, Anne. *The Caribbean Artists Movement: A Literary and Cultural History.* London: New Beacon Books, 1992.

Wambu, Onyekachi, ed. *Empire Windrush: Fifty Years of Writing about Black Britain.* London: Victor Gollancz, 1998.

Wandor, Micheline. *Look Back in Gender: Sexuality and the Family in Post-War British Drama.* London: Methuen, 1987.

Warner, Keith Q. *The Trinidad Calypso: A Study of the Calypso as Oral Literature.* London: Heinemann, 1983.

——. "Ethnicity and the Contemporary Calypso." In Kevin A. Yelvington, ed., *Trinidad Ethnicity.* London: Macmillan Caribbean, 1993, 275–91.

Warrington, Don. "Meetings with Barry Reckord." In Yvonne Brewster, ed., *For the Reckord: A Collection of Three Plays by Barry Reckord.* London: Oberon Books, 2010, 245–48.

Waters, Chris. "'Dark Strangers' in Our Midst: Discourses of Race and Nation in Britain, 1947–1963." *The Journal of British Studies* 36, no. 2 (April 1997): 207–38.

Webster, Wendy. *Imagining Home: Gender, 'Race' and National Identity, 1945–64.* London: UCL Press, 1998.

——. *Englishness and Empire 1939–65.* Oxford: Oxford University Press, 2005.

Wesker, Arnold. *The Wesker Trilogy.* New York: Random House, 1960.

Western, John. *A Passage to England: Barbadian Londoners Speak of Home.* Minneapolis: University of Minnesota Press, 1992.

Wilkinson, Alan. "Moore: A Modernist's 'Primitivism.'" In Dorothy M. Kosinski, ed., *Henry Moore, Sculpting the 20th Century.* New Haven: Yale University Press, 2001, 32–41.

Williams, Jack. *Entertaining the Nation: A Social History of British Television.* Phoenix Mill: Sutton Publishing, 2004.

Williams, Tony. *Structures of Desire: British Cinema, 1939–1955.* New York: State University of New York Press, 2000.

Wilmer, Val. *Mama Said There'd Be Days Like This: My Life in the Jazz World.* London: The Women's Press, 1989.

Wilson, Kathleen. *The Island Race: Englishness, Empire and Gender in the Eighteenth Century.* London: Routledge, 2003.

Wynn, Neil A. "'Race War': Black American GIs and West Indians in Britain during the Second World War." *Immigrants & Minorities* 24, no. 3 (2006): 338–39.

Young, Lola. *Fear of the Dark: 'Race', Gender and Sexuality in the Cinema.* London: Routledge, 1996.

Index

269